MYSTICAL THEOLOGY

St. Teresa in Ecstasy (Detail)
—Gian Lorenzo Bernini

MYSTICAL THEOLOGY

A LAYMAN'S GUIDE

The Collected Works of

DOM SAVINIEN LOUISMET, OSB

Vol. 1

The Mystical Knowledge of God
The Mystical Life
Mysticism True and False
Divine Contemplation for All

MEDIATRIX PRESS
MMXXII

ISBN: 978-1-957066-22-6

The Mystical Knowledge of God; The Mystical Life; Mysticism True and False; Divine Contemplation for All were originally published by Kennedy and Sons, 1917, 1919, 1921, and 1923 respectively.

Cover art:
The Conversion of Mary Magdalene
–Paolo Veronese

Mediatrix Press
607 E 6th Ave.
Post Falls, ID 83854
www.mediatrixpress.com

Approbations:

The Mystical Life of God

Nihil Obstat:
F. Thomas Bergh, OSB
Censor Deputatus
Imprimatur:
✠Edm. Can. Surmont.
Vic. Gen.
Westmonasterii die 6 Novembris 1916

The Mystical Life

Nihil Obstat:
H. S. Bowden
Censor deputatus
Impramatur:
✠EDM. CAN. SURMONT
Vic. Gen.
Westmonasterìi, die 29 *Octobris,* 1917.

Mysticism True and False

Nihil Obstat:
F. THOMAS BERGH, O. S. B.
Censor deputatus
Imprimatur:
✠EDM. CAN. SURMONT
Westmonasterii die 19, 1918.

Divine Contemplation for All

Nihil Obstat:
F. THOMAS BERGH, O.S.B.
Censor deputatus
Imprimatur:
✠EDM. CAN. SURMONT
Vic. gen.
Westmonasterii, die 28 Martii, 1920

TABLE OF CONTENTS

St. Luke Contemplates the Cross
—Zurbaran

BOOK I

THE MYSTICAL KNOWLEDGE OF GOD

AN ESSAY IN THE ART OF KNOWING AND LOVING THE DIVINE MAJESTY

TO MARY IMMACULATE MOTHER OF BEAUTIFUL LOVE THIS LITTLE TREATISE IS HUMBLY & LOVINGLY DEDICATED

PREFACE

THE present work is a treatise on the experimental knowledge of God, such as it is possible for every Christian to acquire, if he will but do what is needful thereto. The reader must not expect to find in these few pages the whole doctrine of the "mystic life, nor even of mental prayer, as such; still less must he look for an exposition of the extraordinary and miraculous dealings of God with a few favored souls. I may attempt these higher themes later on, God willing; but in the present work my aim is purely and simply to show that every Christian can obtain a most beautiful kind of knowledge of God, and enlarge it, by the practice of love. It is the substance of a series of sermons, preached by me from time to time at Buck fast, reduced to a body of doctrine for the more convenient use of myself, and those under my spiritual guidance. I have been persuaded to give it to the public at large, in the hope that it may do good.

In the pulpit it was natural to speak "tanquam potestatem habens," as one having a divine mandate to fulfil. In these pages I have not much departed from the same homiletic or hortatory style, judging it to suit the purpose of the work. We cannot improve upon the Fathers of the Church, from, let us say, Dyonisius the Areopagite, down to St. Francis of Sales: in my opinion a grievous mistake has been made in giving to works of piety too didactic a form.

No one need be frightened by the bulk of this treatise; eight short chapters conclude it all. It could be read at one sitting, though in order to benefit from it, it would be more profitable to have it, and read it again and again. Its very conciseness will make this a light task.

In Part I, I endeavor to set before the reader the reality and the true nature of the mystical knowledge of God. In Part II, I treat of the enlargement of the same. Even this second part, if attentively considered, will be seen to be nothing more than a further illustration, and a deeper one, of what is meant by this precious, experimental knowledge of God.

The substance of this work appeared first in the Catholic Review of July and October, 1915.

PART I
THE NATURE OF MYSTICAL KNOWLEDGE

"Our good Lord showed me that it is full great pleasure to Him, that a silly soul come to Him naked, plainly and homely."

—*Juliana of Norwich.*

CHAPTER I

ON THE KNOWLEDGE OF GOD IN GENERAL

KNOWLEDGE, a rational, intelligent knowledge of things, is a mark of man's nobility. Beasts have some kind of knowledge, imperfect and limited, unreasoning, and purely material. Man knows himself by his intellect, as also his fellow-men, the world around him, the sciences, the arts, history; he may even know the "invisible," that which is not apprehended by the senses; and he may know God Himself, and this last knowledge is the greatest, the most useful, the most necessary of all. It is, in fact, of such fundamental importance that Holy Writ tells us *they are rain in whom there is not the knowledge of God* (Wisdom 13:1). They are vain—i.e., useless, unprofitable alike to themselves and world; they are good for nothing, when not positively harmful.

In Heaven we shall know God perfectly. We shall see Him even as He is and face to face, He himself being the Light that will enlighten us; we shall know even as we are known. It is not so now; we see Him but imperfectly and dimly as through a veil, yet, from the very nature of its object, even this imperfect knowledge of God is the most excellent and the most necessary *of* all. Alas! it is a knowledge which is rare—few there are that seek it, few desire or realize its inestimable worth. Men make great efforts to learn of things new and strange and curious, but for the things of God they seem to have no care. It is as though men thought God was of no interest, nor the knowledge of Him worth troubling about. How blind, how foolish, are they, for is it not self-evident, on the contrary, that God is the most interesting object of knowledge of all —the most enthralling, the most absorbing?

There are three ways of gaining a certain knowledge of God whilst we are yet on earth: the first is by natural reason; the second, by faith; the third, by love.

The first kind of knowledge of God is called philosophical.

From the consideration of himself and of the universe it is possible for a man, even without the help of supernatural grace, to arrive at the certainty of the existence of God and at the unity and infinite perfection of God—i.e., man is able, by the light of reason, alone and unaided, to assure himself that there is a Supreme Being, that there is but One, that He is full of the most magnificent perfections, a pure Spirit, supremely good, and wise, and happy; free, intelligent, and personal, distinct from and independent of the universe, first cause of all things, holding absolute dominion over all; and that we men, as free agents and His creatures, are responsible to Him for all we do.

Let us suppose, for instance, that a man had never heard of God—a man of clear intellect, and one blinded by no passions. By applying his mind to the consideration of himself and the world around him, such a man could arrive at this knowledge of God.

The pagan philosophers of old had this speculative rational knowledge of God, and if they had followed it up they would have attained His sacred Love, for it is of faith that God never denies His grace to those who seek Him. Those pagans, therefore, as St. Paul (Rom. 1:20) says, are inexcusable, who, leading evil lives, lost their souls, for they knew God, but, failing to give Him due honor, they were debarred from His grace.

Yet more inexcusable are those men of our own time who refuse to acknowledge the very existence of God. What the pagans could find without the light of Christianity, they surely can find now, if they are willing to seek it.

Likewise inexcusable are those who acknowledge the existence of God, and yet refuse to give Him the homage they know to be His due.

The second kind of knowledge of God is by way of faith. It is ministered to us by divine revelation contained in Holy Scripture, and in the divine Tradition of the Catholic Church. These are summarized for us in the Creed and in the Catechism, and are propounded at greater length in the works of the Fathers and orthodox theologians.

Take, for example, a child who has never seen his father because his father has gone to a distant country. The father writes to his dear son letters full of tender and delicate affection, and little by little informs the son of many things about himself that will interest him. The child in this way, though he has never seen the father, becomes possessed of much knowledge concerning him. In what way? By faith: by believing what his father writes to him. Now, God has done as much for us. Separated in a way from us by the conditions of our present life, God is living in a far-away country we call Heaven, and He has written letters to us, and sent us messengers and messages.

The prophets of old were the messengers of God to mankind. Occasionally He sent His very Angels, and in the fullness of time He sent His own Son, clothed in our humanity. The burden of the message, of which all these were the bearers, has been consigned to Holy Writ, or handed down by divine tradition. Thus the one and the other are nothing else than letters from God to man, teaching him of things which he could not have found out by the natural powers of "unassisted reason.

We learn about God Himself, first of all, that, though He is One in Essence, He is a Trinity of Persons – Father, Son, and Holy Spirit. We shall see, later on, that this knowledge gives us an insight into the very life of God.

Then we are made to know explicitly His great works *ad extra,* viz., that He created the visible and invisible world out of nothing. That He made all things for His own glory, and rules them infallibly to this end by His Providence. That He made the Angels and then man to His own image and likeness. That He tried the Angels, of whom one-third were found wanting—and became devils. That He tried man, and that in this trial the whole race fell in Adam (Mary alone being preserved), whence it follows that every man that enters into the world does so with the stain of sin and all the consequences of sin upon his soul.

We are taught that, nevertheless, God so loved mankind as to give His only Son for its ransom; and how the wonderful love of the Son was manifested in the Incarnation. That fallen man was redeemed by the Cross. That men of goodwill are sanctified by the Sacraments of the Church. And, finally, that the elect will be glorified in Heaven by the beatific vision, and the reprobate will be damned to the fire of hell, separated from God for all eternity.

Now, all these things could not have come to our knowledge by the light of natural reason alone. It was necessary that they should be revealed to us—they have been so revealed, and it is by faith in this revelation that we come to a higher and a greater knowledge of God. How magnificent, how fatherly, how very near to us does God appear in the light of revelation! Let us be thankful for the knowledge it has given us, let us try to appreciate it to the full!

But this is not the end—there is yet a higher knowledge within our grasp. This is the mystical knowledge of God, the peculiar knowledge we gain by love—by active, conscious and constant love of Him. This is a personal, experimental knowledge of God, which every Christian can obtain by the help of grace, and God does not deny His grace to those that seek it. He desires to impart the grace of this knowledge to each one of us if we will but let Him.

CHAPTER II

ON THE MYSTICAL KNOWLEDGE OF GOD BY LOVE

WE have seen that there are three ways of gaining a certain knowledge of God while we are yet on earth. The first is by natural reason, the second by faith, the third by love; and we have seen what is meant by the first two kinds of knowledge of God. Many go no further than this. Through their own negligence and carelessness they never come to the third kind of knowledge of God, by the way of fervent love. This is a thousand pities, for they deprive themselves of a great good, and at the same time refuse to God a satisfaction He has every right to expect. It is this third kind of knowledge of God I will now proceed to describe, so that those who have it not may be awakened to the necessity and desirability of acquiring it.

The first and most important thing about the way of the knowledge of God by love is that it is experimental. Experimental knowledge is that attained by seeing, hearing, touching, or in any way soever coming into contact with, or being united to, the object of which we seek to learn, whereby we make certain proof of this object and of its attributes. If a person had never tasted honey, but had been told that it was sweet, and had read a great deal upon the subject of honey, he would have a certain knowledge of it, but not an experimental one. But let him taste the honey, actually put it in his mouth, and let it melt there, and feel the sensation of delight it gives him, then only will he know how sweet it was; he will have proved its sweetness and acquired an experimental knowledge of it. Knowledge of God by the way of love is of the same order. *Taste and see that the Lord is sweet* (Ps. 33:9).

Let us take another example of experimental knowledge to illustrate our point — that of the poor Samaritan woman we read about in the Gospel of St. John, with whom Our Lord engaged in conversation at the well of Jacob. She was so struck by what He told her that she ran into the city, as one beside herself, crying out: "Come and see a man who has told me all I have done. Come and see if He is not the Messiah." No doubt the good people marveled at first at the woman's description of Our Lord. How gentle He was and how saintly He appeared; how His words had pierced her heart and strangely moved her.... Then they came to Our Lord and "saw Him, and spoke to Him and heard Him. They begged Him to come down to their city, and He did so, showing Himself to them all, the great Teacher, the great Healer, the great Consoler. He stayed with them two days, and many believed in Him because of His Word, and they said to the woman: "We now believe, not for thy saying, for we ourselves have heard Him, and know that this is indeed the Saviour of the world." Note these words: "We ourselves have heard Him." Here we have experimental knowledge. Such is the knowledge of God by love.

Yet another illustration of experimental knowledge. A little child is at his mother's breast, in her arms. Does he know his own mother? Assuredly he knows her. How does he know her? Experimentally. His knowledge is not a rational knowledge, he has not the use of reason; neither is it knowledge by faith or hearsay. If one were to tell the child this was his mother he would not understand, but he finds himself in her arms, pressed fondly to her bosom, and he knows. He feels himself loved, and instinctively, in his feeble way, he returns love for love and caress for caress. If he is taken away from her he cries and holds out tiny hands, for he has no peace until he finds himself once more in the arms of her who is all the world to him. Who will say the child knows not his mother? He could not speak learnedly about her, nor describe her, but he knows that she is sweet; he has proved it for himself, and he would not change her for the whole world. Now, this again is experimental knowledge—the sort of knowledge of God which the fervent soul gains by the way of love.

The loving soul finds herself in the arms and on the warm breast, if I may so speak, of this more than mother, the good God, and she loves to be there. She takes her sole delight in God, and the more she does so the more God presses her to His heart, and secretly manifests Himself to her, letting her taste and see how sweet He is. That soul may be very illiterate, may not be able to discourse very learnedly about God, may be very deficient in philosophical and theological acumen; but who can say that she does not know God? She has the very best knowledge of Him, the knowledge He Himself gives her personally and immediately. She has been able to make proof of God, and she has found Him very sweet indeed.

Yes, to the soul of good will, who allows God to have His own way, God gives Himself to be known thus by experimental knowledge. He communicates immediately to such a soul the sense of His own sweetness. He is in her mouth as a lump of honey, slowly dissolving into unutterable sweetness. He is in the midst of that soul, even as He was in the Samaritan village all affability, and kindness, and consolation, allowing Himself to be approached and touched and familiarly spoken to. He takes the soul, even as the mother takes her child, lovingly into the arms of His affection and feeds her at the breasts of His infinite tenderness.

Now that we know that the knowledge of God by the way of love is experimental, it is easy for us to tell whether we possess it or not. Do you experience at times in the secret of your heart the delightful sweetness of spiritual consolation? Then have no sort of doubt, it is God making Himself known to you. Do you at times feel Him very near indeed, His presence in the midst of your soul, and at such times is-He not like a loving friend come unto his own, one in whose presence you are very much at ease? And does He not then bring with Him a joy that is not of this world? Then have no sort of doubt, it is God giving you to taste and see how sweet He is. Do you experience from time to time the feeling of perfect peace and security, even in the midst of dryness and internal trials, as of one leaning on the very breast of God? And do you, in this reliance on God, find joy even in the midst of tribulations? Then you have indeed that experimental knowledge of God which comes only by love.

If, on the contrary, we know for certain that God exists, because everybody says so, and our reason tells us it must be so, and if by the same process and the teaching of Holy Writ and the Church we come by the knowledge of His goodness, but without any personal inward experience of it, then our knowledge is only by way of reason or faith, but not by the way of love. It is not yet all that God would have it to be. God has not yet been able to make Himself known to us, for we are not such as He would have us be, He cannot yet let us taste and see how sweet He is.

But the fault is our own; we have not loved. Let us begin to love God as He would be loved. Let us now love Him with our whole heart and soul and above all things; not the world or some idol or ourselves instead of Him, but only God Himself. Then he will come to us and manifest Himself and let us taste and see how sweet He is.

CHAPTER III

THE TESTIMONY OF GOD CONCERNING THIS KNOWLEDGE

FROM what has been said it may be inferred that knowledge of God by reason or by faith is an indirect knowledge, from a distance and from without, whilst knowledge of God by love is knowledge at once close, immediate, and from within. It is an infusion of divine light and sweetness and strength, direct from God into the soul, without passing through the channel of outward sight or symbol, such as the Sacred Scriptures, or the Sacraments, or the ministrations of men. Knowledge by reason and faith is good, but the mystical knowledge of God is better, giving more honor to God and bringing more profit to the soul.

The question may be raised: Is such a knowledge of God really given to men on earth? Does God really give Himself to be known by an intimate secret contact with the loving soul? Or is it all imagination on the part of the mystic, or, as scientists have it, auto-suggestion? Is there no illusion in it?

The answer is easy. We have, on the one hand, the testimony of God in Holy Scripture, repeated, emphatic, and explicit; and, on the other, that of all true lovers of God, the canonized Saints, the Doctors of the Church, and the mystics. They one and all affirm that such knowledge is attainable and obtainable by men on earth, even by every man, as we shall see later.

What. is the testimony of God concerning it? Apart from the many beautiful passages of the Old Testament, the Moral Books, the Prophets, and the Canticle of Canticles, let us confine ourselves to what Our Lord says. He is God Himself, the Master of the Mystical Life. He tells us that He does impart such knowledge, and also the conditions necessary for its reception.

Our Lord says (Matt. 5:8): *Blessed are the pure in heart, for they shall see God.* All the commentators are agreed that the meaning of this passage is not only that the pure in heart may count upon the vision of God in the future life in Heaven, but that they shall, in a manner, see God, even during their pilgrimage upon earth. In what way? Thus: they shall have a perception of God, personal, experimental, of a kind that is denied those that are not pure. And to him who does not understand this mystical higher knowledge of God, and who is inclined to be skeptical, I would say, "Friend, is your heart pure? Are you clean in thought and speech, and deed and affection? If not, there is the difficulty. You cannot hope to understand until you are pure in heart." *Animalis homo non percipit ea quae Spiritus Dei sunt* (Cor. 2:14), the poor sinner, the slave of lusts, cannot have any perception of these things. Therefore, let those who desire not only to understand, but to taste and see how sweet the Lord is, become pure in heart. They will then begin to attain to this higher or mystical knowledge of God.

Our Lord says again (Jn. 14:21): *If a man loveth Me, I will manifest Myself to him.* Here it is evident that He speaks of that special manifestation of Himself that comes to a man not by reasoning but by love. It is here no longer question of that official revelation which he has made to all men through the Church, but of a personal favor done to the soul, of that near and immediate contact by which He gives His faithful servant to taste of His sweetness. The words bear no other interpretation: "I will manifest Myself to him"—i.e., I will show Myself to him in a direct and intimate manner, and this cannot but be very sweet. It is obvious that God should reserve for those who love Him a knowledge of Himself more intimate and precious and delightful than that which is vouchsafed to the sinner. Even the most perverse sinner may have a purely speculative knowledge of God, such as is supplied by study of philosophy and theology.

In another place (Luke 10:21), Our Lord says: *I give Thee thanks, O Father, Lord of heaven and earth, because Thou hast hidden these things from the wise and prudent and hast revealed them to little ones.* Here He informs us that there are things which God is pleased to reveal to little ones— i.e., to all those who by humility become little in their own estimation, whilst He keeps that very particular knowledge back from those who are proud of their learning or natural powers. Now, what are the things thus revealed? What is that knowledge of God which is denied to the philosopher and even to the learned theologian, if he be not a little child in humility? It cannot be any other than the higher knowledge, the immediate, personal, experimental knowledge of God, God giving Himself to be tasted by the loving, humble, child-like soul.

Many more quotations from the Gospel and the Apocalypse could be cited, all as forceful and explicit as those we have used, to show that the experimental knowledge of God is no pious fiction, no invention of over-zealous, illusioned devotees.

Amen, I say to you, whosoever shall not receive the Kingdom of God as a little child shall not enter therein (Mark 10:15). How does the little child receive the Gospel from the lips of its mother, or the good Sisters or the Priest? With the utmost simplicity and the greatest confidence. He does not reason about it, or find fault with it, or take this and reject that. No. If we were to go to our children's class at Catechism, we should see how the child receives the truths told to him. There would be no modernism there. Is this folly on the part of the child? Far from it. With the grace of his baptism still fresh upon him, and his natural innocence helping, he will give a rational, earnest and honest assent to all that is told him. The child draws his conclusions strictly. He would be astonished if he were told not to love God, or only to love Him a little. A child is uncompromising in his reception of the Kingdom of God. There was a time when we were such ourselves, but, alas! Many years ago. We were once little children, and received the Kingdom of God in simplicity, and we desired to love our Master with our whole heart.

We have grown indeed, but in worldly wisdom, and the unquestioning and undivided love we vowed to God when we were little has been scattered to the winds. We found it would cost us a great effort, and a lifelong one, to love God as we should, do, so we compromised the matter. We no longer receive and retain the Kingdom of God, the Gospel teaching "as a little child," and so we cannot penetrate therein. This Kingdom of God on earth, which is the mystical life, the knowledge of God by love, the enjoyment of Him and the marvellous sanctification of the soul consequent thereto, are denied us, because the conditions necessary to their acquirement are lacking in us. *Amen, I say to you, whosoever shall not receive the Kingdom of God as a little child shall not enter therein.*

The First Commandment is, *Thou shalt love the Lord thy God.* Jesus did not say, "Thou shalt understand the Lord thy God, or thou shalt be learned about Him," only, "Thou shalt love." And He tells us how to do this. *With thy whole heart, with thy whole soul, with thy whole mind, with thy whole strength.* Thus only may we hope to gain the mystical knowledge of God, to taste and see how sweet the Lord is. The invitation, or rather command, is not to a few, not to a select class or to His Apostles only, but to all men. All are invited, but how few, how very few, come to the feast!

We have seen that this special experimental knowledge of God, with its wonderful sweetness, is given to souls of good will. We know also the conditions necessary for attaining it. They are purity of heart, humility, and holy simplicity, virtues attendant on the true love of God.

Beyond this there is no greater or higher knowledge, excepting that vouchsafed the blessed in heaven, in the beatific vision.

CHAPTER IV

NO POSSIBILITY OF DELUSION IN THE MYSTICAL KNOWLEDGE OF GOD BY LOVE

WHEN we say that God makes Himself known in a special manner to the loving soul, that He manifests Himself to the mystic, people are apt to imagine this to mean that God shows Himself to the mystic in visions and revelations. Or, again, they confuse this inward secret manifestation which God makes to the soul with the well-known phenomenon of sensible or sentimental devotion. Now we must well understand that the experimental knowledge of God by love is neither a kind of miraculous apparition nor the suspicious sweetness of sensible devotion, and it is subject to no possible delusion.

Sensible fervor may come almost to anyone, saint or sinner, and from a variety of causes—even such as have hardly anything to do with the love of God. It may come occasionally to a tepid or negligent Christian upon witnessing some unusual display of religious pomp and ceremony, or on hearing a fine voice, or music beautifully rendered. This is but a shallow, passing impression on the surface of the soul, or, rather, in the region of the senses and imagination. Nevertheless, it is a grace of God in its way, and the Christian will do well to heed it, and make it the starting point of a more fervent life. If he fail to do so, there is a danger that this brief period of sensible fervor be followed by a depressing sense of loneliness and desolation, and a temptation to abandon the whole enterprise of the spiritual life. From this it is plain that a fit of sensible fervor is not a manifestation of God Himself, made by Him directly into the soul. Therefore this must not be taken for the mystical knowledge of God, which, as we have said, is just such a manifestation of God, by God, directly into the soul. Nor does it consist in visions, revelations, and ecstasies such as certain saints have been favored with; nor, again, some miraculous and definite setting before the eyes of the mystic of some form or image of the Divine essence.

In this matter of visions and revelations, delusions are easy. Visions may come from God or they may not. We read in Holy Scripture that the devil has power to change himself, seemingly, into an angel of light, and to work upon the senses and imagination and thus deceive even the saints.

Saint Simeon Stylites, after he had been many years on his column, was visited by a cherub driving a fiery chariot, who told him that God had need of him in paradise. Simeon was about to mount the fiery chariot, but before doing so he was inspired to make the sign of the Cross. Upon this the whole thing fell to earth with a crash. It had been nothing but a snare of the evil spirit.

Hundreds of examples might be cited to show that visions and revelations, seemingly the most trustworthy, may be nothing but the work of the spirit of darkness and most dangerous delusions. This is why all spiritual writers warn us that visions, ecstasies, and revelations may never be desired or prayed for, and that when they come unbidden they must be received with the greatest diffidence and must not be reckoned on for our spiritual guidance without the advice of a most prudent and spiritually enlightened director.

Now, the mystical or higher knowledge of God does not consist in these things. Far from being a kind of vision, all the saints are agreed that it is a blind apprehension or blind perception of God. Such is their doctrine, particularly that expounded by St. John of the Cross, who is no small authority on the subject.

What is meant by a blind perception? We will take, for example, a blind man. He gropes his way about in a perpetual darkness, but does he not hear if spoken to? Does he not feel if objects or persons close at hand come into contact with him? Does he not taste the sweetness of food and drink when given to him? And does he not rejoice at the beneficent warmth of the sun in summer, or of a fire in winter, though he be never so blind? His, then, is what we may call a blind perception. This is precisely what takes place in a spiritual way in the mystical knowledge of God; this is the sort of apprehension of God which the loving soul experiences. Though he does not see God's countenance—for that is given to the blessed in Heaven alone—the mystic nevertheless hears His loving voice in the secret of his heart; he feels the warm embrace of God around him; from time to time he tastes inwardly the sweetness of his consolations; and at all times, even in darkness and tribulation, he feels the strength of God's mighty arm supporting him.

Now, there can be no illusion in this, precisely because it is a blind apprehension of God, and the senses and the imagination have no part in it. It takes place in the most secret part of the soul, where the evil one can have no access to work his wiles. If it were a vision it might be an hallucination of the brain, the work of the prince of darkness; but here there is no image, no representation of any figure or form, no speech heard of the ear. The author of the "Imitation of Christ" is emphatic in insisting that God makes Himself heard to the faithful soul without noise of words (Book 1, ch. 3; Book 3, ch. 2). There is no delusion, nor possibility of delusion, in the mystical knowledge of God.

Is the mystic always able accurately to account for his new knowledge of God? No, he is not always conscious of it. He certainly could not put it into words, and he does not care to do so; he does not care to speak of it. He keeps his secret, or rather the secret of the King, well. He loves: that is enough for him.

This blind perception of God, nor God known to the mystic by a blind perception, is what spiritual writers call "the Divine Cloud" or the "Dark Night," "la Grande Tenèbre," because of the total absence of all images or figures and the failure of creatures to help therein. The naked soul is alone with God. The universe of things visible and invisible is banished, and ultimately the consciousness, even of self, becomes, for the time being, obliterated.

Thus, at times of mental prayer, the soul, not seeing its God, and yet having lost sight of creatures, is engulfed in a very great darkness. This darkness is God Himself, the very substance of God. A palpable darkness, but not in the earthly sense of the expression. A luminous darkness, dazzling to the eyes of the soul, as the light of day is darkness dazzling to the eyes of the bat or the owl. A wholesome, warm, delectable, desirable darkness, brighter infinitely than the brightest day of creatures, be it even that of the intellect as such. And there can be no illusion in it, no going astray or losing oneself in it, except in the blessed sense indicated by our Lord. *He that shall lose his soul shall find it* (Matt, 10:39).

We shall have more to say of this darkness as we proceed. Suffice it to say now that he who begins fervently to love just steps into the Divine Cloud, and he who makes progress in fervent love goes deeper into it; and he who is perfect in fervent love goes deepest into it. On the contrary, he who has not yet begun fervently to love God has not begun truly to know Him: he has not come to the edge of the Divine Cloud. This is, alas! how matters stand with many souls. It is late in the day. *Novissima hora est* (1 Jo. 2:18). Let us begin at once. Let us love God without any fear whatever of the consequences. Let us love God and never fear that such a love will be to us a snare and a delusion. *The Lord is my light and my salvation, whom shall I fear?* (Ps. 36:1).

PART II
OF ENLARGING OUR MYSTICAL KNOWLEDGE OF GOD

"That you may be able to comprehend with all the saints what is the breadth and length and height and depth, that you may be filled with the fulness of God."
Eph. 3:18, 19.

CHAPTER V

WHAT IT REALLY MEANS

DO the saints during their pilgrimage on earth, or even those in heaven who see God face to face, comprehend the breadth and length and height and depth of God? Do they receive the fulness of Him in themselves? In a way they do, or else the Apostle would not pray that it be granted to his beloved Ephesians; and yet when we consider that God is a Spirit, and therefore has no dimensions, no breadth and length, no height and depth—that being infinite He cannot be held within the limits of any created capacity—we are warned to look for a spiritual, mysterious meaning to these words. For this reason let us consider what is really meant by enlarging our mystical knowledge of God.

Human language is a poor instrument when used to express the mysteries of God. It is wholly inadequate, clumsy, and treacherous; but as it is all we have, we must perforce make use of it, being careful to do so cautiously, and to qualify, if need be, the meaning of our words.

Here, for instance, we speak of enlarging our knowledge of God. Now, there is no such thing as enlarging our knowledge of God. Why then do we use the expression at all? For want of a better one. It conveys our meaning, and yet at the same time it perverts and betrays it. It brings with it a notion that does not fit the nature of God and of God's knowledge. Yet we have no better word for our meaning, and it must serve.

The mystic's knowledge of God is not enlarged as knowledge of other things is enlarged. If, for instance, we speak of enlarging our knowledge of English, we mean more words, more rules of grammar, more construction and analysis of phrase and sentence. Of history, more names of great men, dates of great events, of battles, revolutions, and treaties of peace, etc. Of astronomy, more stars and constellations. To extend one's knowledge in these matters means a multiplicity of notions, an extension in surface, a reaching out to more things. Not so an increase in the knowledge of God. This does not gain in surface, nor does it make for multiplicity of notions, but, on the contrary, for simplicity and unity.

This seems subtle and difficult to understand, but it is a most beautiful truth. To enlarge one's knowledge of God, more especially the mystical knowledge of God, does not mean to know more things about God, but to know the one thing, God, more. This is done in a manner void of images and creatures, by a simple, intense, and disengaged apprehension of God, Who is absolutely, infinitely pure and simple, of Him Who has said: *I am Who am.* (Exod. 3:14).

St. Denys, the Areopagite, who is considered the greatest authority on mystical theology, speaks of the double process by which the human mind seeks to form a true notion of God—namely, the affirmative process and the negative process. By the former we consider all the things of the universe in their beauty and goodness, and we say: "God is this, but in an infinite degree." Thus God is life, light, beauty, power, but in an infinite degree. By the latter we deny that God is anything we can see, or comprehend or conceive. This latter, St. Denys maintains, brings us nearer to the truth, for it leaves us only with a simple apprehension of God, and is more worthy of His infinite majesty. It is here—that is to say, at the acknowledgment, conscious or unconscious, of God's incomprehensibility— that the soul enters into what St. Denys calls the Divine Cloud or Darkness, for now, indeed, the human mind is dazzled by the brightness of the splendor of God's truth, and is enveloped in darkness. Blessed is this darkness, and it were far better here to grope in blind and loving faith than to bask in the brightest light of human reasoning.

The same doctrine is set forth by St. Thomas in Tract LX. He represents to us the loving soul thirsting after God, drinking at all the fountains of created knowledge, and saying to each one that she drinks from: "No, ah, no! You are not that which I am seeking for. You cannot refresh me! The light of the sun and of the stars, and the beauty of nature: no, you are not my God! The greatness and the power of the elements: no, you are not my God! The loveliness of man, woman or child: you are not my God!" The saint goes on through all the things that, in the order of creation, might satisfy the soul, but is obliged to confess that nothing, either here below or in heaven above, can bring happiness or give a true idea of what God is, save only God Himself.

But the soul that is in ignorance, the worldly soul, what does she say? To gold and silver and the things of earth, she says: "You are my gods. I love you. You reign supreme in all my thoughts. I delight in you. Surely you will give me happiness." Like the Hebrews of old at the foot of Mount Sinai before the golden calf. *These are thy gods, O Israel!* (Exod. 32:4). So does the sinner say to the creatures of flesh and blood, formed of the slime of the earth, things of a day, that will rot on the morrow: "These are my gods! Would that I might enjoy them here, on this earth, for ever!" It is thus, alas! that the devil interposes himself in God's place, and is worshiped as God. Did he not say to our Divine Lord Himself: *All these* (the pleasures and honors of this world) *will I give thee, if, falling down, thou wilt adore me* (Mat. 4:9).

Comparatively few there are who answer with Our Lord, "The Lord thy God shalt thou adore, and Him only shalt thou serve." To the false gods of the world which can never satisfy, how many there are who sacrifice all: talent, honor, health, time, fortune, body and soul, and even the souls of others dependent on them. Does not treason such as this, if unrepented, throw a lurid light on the reality of hell fire?

But to return to the consideration of the knowledge of God, and of enlarging it by an increase in depth and intensity of the perception of God.

When St. Paul prays that we may be able to comprehend, with the saints, what is the breadth and length, and height and depth, and that we may be filled with the fulness of God, he means two things: the illumination of the mind in regard to Divine mysteries, especially the mystery of the Divine Essence, and a greater fulness of the effects of the presence of God in the secret part of the soul. Indeed, at each new act of Divine contemplation one's notion of God becomes more simple, more ineffable, nearer to the mode of perception of the pure spirits—that is to say, of the angels and souls that are separate from their bodies.

The spiritual experiences of a soul wholly abandoned to God succeed each other with an astounding variety and number.

In the life of St. Angela of Foligno, what strikes one particularly is how each manifestation of God is so marvellous to her that it throws in the shade or blots out entirely all those that preceded it. The saint is at a loss to express her admiration of this effect of God's love. Something similar to this takes place in the mystic soul. It is as though God presented one aspect of His Divine Goodness to her and then withdrew it, saying, "Not this, it is not this," and then another aspect, and withdrew it also, saying again, "Nay, not this, it is not this."

At every fresh mystical experience the perception of God becomes clearer, more evident, more sweet, more penetrating, and yet less and less demonstrable, just because it is so intimate! It works its way through unknown paths into the depths of inner consciousness, and nothing is able to shake the assurance of the soul that God is there, and that she touches Him, and is being acted upon by Him in a way that is altogether different from that previous to her entrance into the mystic life. Now, this is the way the mystical knowledge of God can be said to enlarge.

In reality, what takes place is this: God is working that precious material, the mystic soul, which has become plastic and passive in His hands. He is scooping it out, pressing it from inside, and, as it were, extending its walls and boundaries.

First, He empties it of self and all things else, and makes it absolutely clean, and then He makes it larger and larger, and takes possession of it, filling it with His own fulness. By each fresh spiritual experience, the soul grows more and more capable of tasting how sweet her Lord is. By each Divine touch she is made more pure, more refined, more akin to God, more able to enjoy Him. At the same time she becomes more trustful, familiar, and childlike in her dealings with her Beloved. The soul has now become more dead to self and the world, and more responsive to the least touch of the Holy Spirit.

That is what is really meant by enlarging one's mystical knowledge of God.

CHAPTER VI

HOW WE FAIL TO ENLARGE OUR MYSTICAL KNOWLEDGE

"I will arise and go to my Father." —Luke 15:18.

HOW does it happen that the mystical knowledge that comes by love remains, for the greater part of Christians, but rudimentary and undeveloped? How is it that we have so little of that "intimate, conscious, constant union with God" which is the outcome of true lore, and which constitutes the mystic life? Whose fault is it? God's or our own? Has God perchance failed to make advances to us and to show us the way? I answer emphatically, No! The good God has made loving advances to us, for there is not one of us who has not tasted, at some time or other, that God is sweet. It may have been when we made our first Communion, either on the day itself or after. At other times, again and again, God has allured us by making us feel the joy of being near Him, and conversing with Him heart to heart. Who has not had such spiritual experiences, and, after all, when we look back upon our past life, are they not the happiest? Even Napoleon I., at the height of his glory, confessed to his astonished generals that the happiest memory of all his eventful life was that of the day of his first Communion.

In reality, then, we have all had a taste and a beginning of the higher knowledge of God, the mystical, experimental knowledge, communicated directly into the soul by God Himself. A taste and a beginning, but nothing more. Why is this?

Because we have not kept up the loving intercourse with God to which we were invited. We are to blame; the fault is ours.

If we wish to know a person intimately, we are not satisfied with merely becoming acquainted with that person; we seek to keep up our intercourse with him. Having met a man for the first time and had a little conversation with him, and taken stock of him, we are said to have struck up an acquaintance. Should we meet the man the next day, we should recognize him immediately and be recognized by him, and quite naturally resume our intercourse. No more preliminaries would be needed, no fresh introductions necessary. But if, after having met a man once, and spoken with him, for some reason or other we do not wish to meet him again, if he should avoid us and we him, if, for instance, when passing in the street, we turn away from one another, and have nothing to do with one another, then our first acquaintance cannot be said to develop. The memory of it will fade away into the distant past.

Later, perhaps, if the man is mentioned to us, we may remember him, but the memory will bring with it nothing but displeasure, as though this person had injured us, or is it that we feel we were not all we might have been to him?

But if, after our first meeting, we try to meet him again, and again, and again, and each time converse as long as we can and as familiarly as we can, and do all in our power to cultivate his friendship and to please him; and if, on his part, he lays himself open to be known and loved by us, and shows himself to us without restraint, or disguise; if he opens his heart to us, and has no secret from us, then indeed our acquaintance can be said to have developed into a very real friendship. And should the man be good, the more we see of him the more we shall like him, and the more he sees we appreciate him, so much the more will he love us in return. Thus mutual affection will increase and grow in tenderness and strength, and its effect for good will influence our whole life.

If this be the case with poor human love and friendship, what may we not hope of the Divine? The more we endeavor to come near to God, speaking with Him in the secret of our heart, the more He will make Himself known to us, and, on the other hand, the more appreciative we are of His Divine goodness and the more we strive to cultivate His Friendship, so much the more will He love us in return. Then will He unfold to us the treasures of His Heart. Then shall we be permitted to feel the marvellous charms of His sacred Humanity, and the infinite sweetness of His Divinity. As that great lover of God, St. Augustine, says:" God makes Himself to be our honey, and makes us to be His honey." His honey, his delight! And has not God Himself said: *My delights are to he with the children of men?* (Prov. 8:31). In the Canticle of Canticles, the Heavenly Bridegroom speaks these words to the loving soul: *I am come into my garden, O my sister and spouse, . . . I have eaten the honeycomb with my honey. I have drunk my wine with my milk: eat, O friends, and drink and be inebriated, my dearly beloved. (Cant, v. 1.).* The honey is the soul in which he takes His delight, the honeycomb is the body in which that soul is lodged, as honey in the comb; for the body itself, the flesh and the senses, become affected by the love of God, and, so to say, consumed thereby. The wine which Jesus drinks with the milk typifies the burning charity and sinlessness of the loving soul; and He calls upon His Divine Father and the Holy Spirit, and the blessed Angels and Saints to partake of His joy, as is seen by the words: "Eat, O friends, and drink and be inebriated, O my beloved."

This is the interpretation given by St. Bernard and other Fathers of this passage in the most mystical book of Holy Writ, and from it we may gather to what honor the soul is raised, which follows up her first acquaintance with God and Our Lord Jesus Christ.

We know now why it is that our mystical knowledge of God has remained undeveloped and has borne no fruit. Through no fault on the part of God was it arrested in its beginnings. Loving intercourse by means of mental prayer has not been kept up. We may be in a state of grace, receive the Sacraments and say customary prayers; we have not opened to Him the floodgates of our soul, nor allowed all our affections to flow forth impetuously unto Him, to receive in return the inflowing of His loving tenderness: no wonder we remain in dryness and far from God!

Let us go a step further and ask: Why did we not keep up and develop our first acquaintance with God, by love? Now, it is not always out of indifference or levity that a soul of good-will is arrested on its way to God. Sometimes it is through a lamentable mistake, because what concerns the mystical life is not known or understood. Hence it happens that after the first visitings of God to the soul, the reaction which inevitably follows, plunging the soul into dryness and darkness, surprises her, and causes her to be tempted to abandon the whole enterprise of the spiritual life. She is inclined to think she has made a mistake in aiming so high, and is not called to the ways of the life of love. This season of spiritual darkness, after all, is as natural and as much in order in the spiritual life as day and night, summer and winter, in the physical life of the world. Therefore, should there be someone at hand to tell this soul of goodwill that all is well, and there is no mistake, and that she has only to persevere strenuously in her enterprise: God in his own good time will show her the light again, and revisit her with His consolation.

But again it happens, and this, alas! more often, that the soul has indeed rejoiced at the sweetness of her first meeting with God in the secret of her heart, but that she is not disposed to make the necessary efforts required to keep up this loving intercourse. Mercenary, selfish, ungenerous soul, who would turn her back on God the moment He ceases to pour out upon her His sweetness and consolation. Such a soul as this loves God only for what she can get from Him and so long as He gives her gifts, and not a minute longer. What God gives she loves, but not God for Himself. A very, very low standard of the spiritual life this, and perhaps, if we look well into it, we shall find it to be our own. Small wonder, then, if we go no further than the rudimentary stage in the mystical knowledge of God.

What then is to be done? Change completely our way of acting. Seek out God, and call upon Him, and strive to be ever mindful of His presence. Let us as often as we can enter into the secret chamber of our heart and speak with Him and listen to Him; let us enter resolutely upon the way of love. There need be no fear that the good God will hold aloof from us. A man whom we had so neglected after he had made advances to us, desiring to live with us on terms of friendship, might behave thus. He might reproach us, saying: "What, you come to me after all you have done?" He might thrust the past upon us and turn his back upon us. A man, yes, but the good God, never! Though we have neglected Him in the past, we need not now mistrust Him. We may go back to Him, and we shall find that sooner or later He will welcome us, and lavish on us His treasures. The story of the Prodigal Son does not only apply to great sinners, but also to tepid and negligent Christians, who have turned away from the loving embraces of their Heavenly Father in the mystical life, and squandered a fortune of time, and grace, and opportunities of becoming saints. They have eaten the husks of the swine, which are their vain desires and self-love, and they are spiritually starving and in rags. Let them say with the prodigal: "I will arise, and I will go to my Father, never to leave Him again, never more to stop my loving intercourse with Him."

CHAPTER VII

HOW IT MAY BE DONE

"The path of the just, as a shining light, goeth forwards and increaseth to perfect day."—Prov. 4:18.

THE first way in which we can gain a greater mystical knowledge of God is, of course, by direct intercourse with Him in the secret of our heart. This is done by keeping up the loving intercourse with Him as long as possible, as long as our necessary occupations will allow, as long as our fervor lasts and we feel drawn to it. It is not wise at times of spiritual fervor to turn away from God to talk to creatures; to say, "My half-hour of meditation is over, I will now stop this loving intercourse with God." No; if possible, if there is nothing to hinder, it ought to be kept up, even as we go to and fro on our different duties in the day, as long as God is pleased to draw us to Him and give us to taste and see how sweet He is. No measure of time, neither day nor night, ought to restrain us from the loving embrace of God. Nothing, therefore, except the Will of God Himself, made manifest by the call of duty, obedience, or charity, should stay the outflowing of the soul in love and the inflowing of the love of God into the soul. He that is being entertained at the table of the King, will he turn away to revel with menials and mendicants? He who finds a great treasure of golden coins and precious stones and has but to gather them in, will he waste his time in picking up pebbles and brass buttons? Will the thirsty man who has found a fountain of pure fresh water, turn aside to drink out of a puddle a few drops of stagnant, poisoned water?

And when at last this loving, direct discourse with the Beloved comes to an end, as it will do from time to time in our present condition, let us be eager, let us try to renew it, watching and being ready to seize upon the first occasion, the first motion of grace.

But even when we are quite willing and eager to keep up the loving discourse with God in the secret of our heart, there are times when, try as we may, we are unable to come into touch with the Beloved. We know He is there, in our heart (He is always there), we try to speak with Him, but we fail to get any response. A season of spiritual dryness has set in and this may last a very long time. The good God does not show us His loving countenance, nor let us hear His voice, as of yore, nor does He fill us with the sweetness which so delighted us. What are we to do?

We must love Him as much in dryness as in refreshment, and humbly bless Him. Let us say with holy Job: *The Lord gave, and the Lord hath taken away . . . blessed be the name of the Lord* (Job 1:21), and then bravely pursue our efforts at advancing in the knowledge of God. For this purpose we may turn to the Holy Scriptures.

As one deprived of the loved presence of a friend reads and re-reads his letters, and dwells fondly upon passages he had not noticed at first or had lost sight of, and thus enlarges his knowledge of the absent friend, so, *by patience, and the consolation of the Scriptures* (Rom. 15:4), by piously and thoughtfully reading and re-reading the Gospels and the other parts of the Bible, we shall enlarge our mystical knowledge of God.

But we must read, not for the sake of mere human learning, nor out of curiosity, but for love alone. Such reading ought to be undertaken at all times and by all, no matter in what sphere of life they may be called to labor. If we read the Scriptures with the eager desire of gaining some golden particles of the mystical knowledge of God, we shall assuredly find therein treasures and untold wealth. For, there, God has portrayed Himself in human language, making use of our modes of thought and expression: for love, He has here accommodated Himself to our small capacity, as a fond parent stoops down to a little babe and stammers and babbles with it in a childish way.

Our previous experience in the mystic life, our loving intercourse with God, will throw an intense light upon texts of

Holy Writ which otherwise would have failed to arrest our attention. The very words of God will now enlighten us as to His dealings with our soul, and enable us to understand His ways.

Thus we may enlarge our mystical knowledge of God, at times when we are unable to do so by direct intercourse.

There is yet another way.

We want to know more about God? Let us go to the creatures of the earth whom He has fashioned, and who can speak of Him. Let us seek Him in Creation; let us contemplate Him lovingly in the magnificence of the universe: the sun by day, the stars by night, the earth and the sea, all life and motion, light, joy, beauty, all these are his witnesses! *The Heavens show forth the glory of God, and the firmament declares the work of His hands* (Ps. 19:1). The birds sing of his loving kindness. The tiniest flower of the field, more gorgeously arrayed than Solomon in all his glory, tells of the tender providence of the Father in Heaven. The very stones have a voice and proclaim Him, and, in listening and being attentive to these voices, our knowledge and our love of the good God will grow in depth and intensity. A saint used to stroke the flowers gently with his staff, and say: "Ah, hold your peace, you chide me, you cry out the excess of the love of God!" Then there are those who can speak of Him in our own language, and tell us about Him, because they have known Him: I mean His intimate friends, the saints. In times of dryness, let us read what the saints have written about God, and let us also read the lives of the saints. Let us, in preference to all others, choose those writers whose names are prefixed by Holy Church with the letter S. or B., "Saint" or "Blessed." They are the graduates of the spiritual life; they have their sheepskins, so to speak, their parchments, their degrees; they have been proved and found worthy. They speak with the truth, simplicity, and authority to which mere scholarship could never attain, because they have experienced the life of which they write.

St. John, in his first Epistle, says: *That which was from the beginning, which we have heard, which we have* seen *with our eyes, which we have looked upon and our hands have handled, of the word of life .... we declare unto you* (1 Jo. 1:1-3). These same words the saints and holy writers may justly use in a sense but slightly different. And studying their lives we see how in all things, without ceasing, they applied themselves to God—how their souls were poured out in conversation with Him, and how He met them in a loving embrace. And in this way again we become conversant in the ways of God, and understand His divine operations.

CHAPTER VIII

"THE LAST WORD ABOUT IT ALL"

ST. THOMAS AQUINAS in his youth was insistently asking of his teachers the one question: "What is God? What is He in Himself? In His true self?" To this question human reason ever seeks to give some sort of answer, but after a good deal of stammering, it is obliged to confess: "I do not know. I have not seen God in Himself, but only His reflection dimly mirrored in His works. I cannot conceive what He is in Himself, much less express Him in words of human speech." Even the assertions of reason, that God is the first Cause, the Creator of heaven and earth, or that He is a pure Spirit, do not tell us what manner of being He is. The devil, for that matter, is a pure spirit.

We turn to Faith, Christian Faith, and we ask her to tell us what God is in Himself, and Faith has an answer ready: "God is the Blessed Trinity, Father, Son, and Holy Spirit, Three Persons in One Divine Essence"; and Faith is sure that hers is the right answer, for God Himself has dictated it. But, for all that, Faith does not comprehend what she professes. This is a mystery, the very greatest of mysteries. Faith does but repeat the words she has learnt, with the docility of a child repeating a lesson, but she is like the child who often does not fully understand what he repeats. So that even Faith cannot give a satisfying answer to our question, "What is God?"

Now, love will try his turn. He, of all others, is eager to know what God is. He pushes rapidly beyond all the things of this world, visible and invisible, for he knows they cannot tell him. He hears and hearkens to the answer of Faith, but he is not satisfied. He pushes forward, boldly and blindly, for he cannot see his object, but he will find his answer; it will offer itself to him. When God sees a soul in quest of Him, He meets her, ah, more than half-way. *Seek and you shall find.* Love meets his object. He grapples with it in the darkness of this mortal life, and he forces its secret out: "Tell me, what art Thou?" The answer comes straight from God Himself, not by words of human speech, but by a burning impression of His own Divine substance upon the substance of the soul, wherein He gives her to know what He is. *God is Charity.*

The answer has been given. The soul, like Jacob wrestling with the angel, has been bold enough to ask: "By what name art Thou called?" And she has received an answer sharper than a two-edged sword. The poor, loving soul is wounded by the Divine touch. From now she feels she will never be able to go through life with the same assured step as before. She will halt and reel as one in pain or as a drunken person, and in truth she is both drunken and in pain— drunken with the delight, the perfume, the substantial joy of knowing God to be charity; and groaning and in pain at the weight of the mighty revelation. The stricken soul can say but one thing: God is Charity, *Deus charitas est!* and the world thinks this person must be mad. Have not all the saints, one after another, passed in the eyes of the world for madmen, and their Master before them?

But, you may say, we know this. We have in 1 John, 4:16, God is Charity. Macaulay would say the merest schoolboy knows this. Where is the difference between our knowledge and that of the mystic? The difference is this. "God is Charity" is an article of abstract faith for the mere theologian; for the mystic, it is a living fact. A living fact, glowing and resplendent as the sun in heaven. A fact which he feels in himself, in his own soul and body, with as much personal, experimental knowledge as we have of the sun above our heads on a midsummer day.

Yes, we may read in Holy Writ the words, "God is Charity," and repeat them, and give a learned demonstration of them, and all the while they may be to us nothing more than the statement of a truth which makes no impression on us. This is a light, a light of a kind, subdued and cold, as that of the distant stars. But these same words that leave the philosopher or the theologian cold and loveless, negligent and mayhap in mortal sin, will set the true servant of God all aglow and on fire.

A frigid observer, himself perishing of cold, might be able to analyze and describe accurately how it is that the property of fire is to burn. The charcoal in the fire cannot describe anything, yet it does better, it burns. It shows the process in its very self, even causing to flame up and burn what comes into contact with it. So it is with the mystic. He may be unable to put his perception of God into words, define it, or reason it out. But he apprehends so vividly that God is love, by actual contact, that he is himself set all on fire with love. This knowledge seems, as it were, to transform the mystic into the very substance of the love of God.

The greatest proof of the reality and non-delusion of the knowledge of God by love is that it calls out, in the mystic soul, love in its highest degree. The whole conduct of the saint or mystic (for we must remember that the true mystic is a saint) proclaims the truth that God is love, just as the conduct of the charcoal thrown into the flames proclaims the fact that fire is a burning and consuming element. The hatred of the loving soul for self, her indifference to all the world, excepting in direct reference to the love of God, her turning away from creatures and her complete abandonment to God, her loving attention to the presence of God and joy in the thought of Him, show forth that she has indeed a vivid, vital apprehension of God under this His most enthralling aspect—Charity.

All this takes place in the mystic, the saint, the true servant of God, whether he be literate or illiterate. Whatever his natural endowments or limitations, the mystic is made to feel by immediate contact that God is love, all love, nothing but love, love in three Divine Persons. He is made to realize experimentally that this infinite ocean of love is pressing all around his heart to break into it and make it divinely happy. For him God is a burning sun of love, in the warm light of which the whole world of angels and men, and all inferior creatures, animate and inanimate, are basking, whether they know it or not, as the small gnats and atoms dancing in the rays of the sun.

He knows that God is substantial love, the only love worthy of the heart of man or angel, the only one capable of filling the great yawning void of his heart and its immense desire and capacity for loving and being loved.

All this, whether the mystic be literate or illiterate.

But if he be a learned man, inclined—or, rather, moved by the Holy Spirit—to write on the subject, then the world is the gainer. Then shall we have such works as the "Confessions and Soliloquies" of St. Augustine, St. Bernard's "Sermons on the Canticles," "The Third Book of the Imitation of Christ," "The Living Flame of Love" of St. John of the Cross, "The Treatise on the Love of God," by St. Francis of Sales, to name but a few. The mystic of learning and genius is made to see, and is able to show as no one else, the love of God, in all the pages of Holy Writ, in all the mysteries of religion, in all the events of history, in all the circumstances of his own life and that of others, precisely because the very love that God is in Himself is burning bright in the very center of his soul, illuminating it and all things else for him.

Here, then, is our question answered. This is the last word about God—final in time and eternity: God is Love. If we say: "God is Good, God is Life, God is Light"; if we say: "God is the Creator of heaven and earth, He is our Father in heaven, He gave us His only Son, He pours out His Holy Spirit upon all flesh," we mean only God is Love. And when we shall have come to the Beatific Vision in heaven we shall perceive that to be the ineffable Trinity, to be the Father, Son, and Holy Spirit, is a law of the substantial love of God. Then at last we shall indeed be set on fire with the love of God, and that for all eternity.

EPILOGUE

AS my readers who have had the patience to follow me to the end have no doubt realized, my aim in this booklet has been wholly practical: to fire souls with the love of God and with longing for that special knowledge of God which comes through love alone.

However awkwardly I may have acquitted myself of the task, I hope I shall not be considered presumptuous if . I make my own, on behalf of my readers, the beautiful prayer of St. Paul for his beloved Ephesians, Eph. 2:18.

"I bow my knees to the Father of our Lord Jesus Christ, of Whom all paternity on earth and in heaven is named, that He would grant you according to the riches of His glory, to be strengthened by His Spirit with might unto the inward man; that Christ may dwell by faith in your hearts; that being rooted and founded in charity, you may be able to comprehend, with all the saints, what is the breadth, and length, and height, and depth, to know also the charity of Christ which surpassed) all knowledge; that you may be filled unto all the fulness of God."

And finally, dear reader, before we part company, shall we not add also with the same apostle: "Now to Him Who is able to do all things more abundantly than we desire or understand, according to the power that works in us, to Him be glory in the Church, and in Christ Jesus unto all generations, world without end. Amen."

St. Dominic Embraces the Cross
—Bl. Fra Angelico

BOOK II

THE MYSTICAL LIFE

LOVE AND THE CHILD

Why do you so clasp me, And draw me to your knee?
Forsooth, you do but chafe me.
I pray you, let me be:
I will but be loved now and then: "When it liketh me!
So I heard a young child,
A thwart child, a young child, Rebellious against love's arms,
Make its peevish cry.
To the tender God I turn: Pardon, Love most High!
For I think those arms were even thine And that child even I.

FRANCIS THOMPSON.

PREFACE

THE subject of Mysticism, whatever one may understand by the word itself, is now amazingly popular. Its literature is immense, and is varied bewilderingly, confusion becoming almost day by day greater. So much so, that for anyone wishing to contribute his own share to the general discussion, it is necessary, at the very outset, to define his position.

The Mysticism I speak of in the following pages is Catholic Mysticism. Not any sort of Catholic or would-be-Catholic Mysticism: but Catholic Traditional Mysticism.

Two questions will arise at once in the minds of some readers: Is there a Catholic Traditional Mysticism? and if so, in what does it differ from any other mysticism? For, with many people, the conviction prevails, and is strongly rooted, that Mysticism is a relatively modern discovery, and was quite unknown to the mediæval Doctors, let alone the Fathers of the Church and the Christians of the first centuries.

Well, there is indeed a Catholic Traditional Mysticism, and it is purely and simply the mysticism of our holy Mother the Church, who is the Bride of Christ and the teacher and infallible oracle of truth. And although all the chapters of the present volume, nay, all the other volumes that may follow are, or will be, written for the very purpose of giving a complete sketch of this Catholic Traditional Mysticism; yet it behooves us to present here in a few words, a preliminary description of What we mean thereby.

By Catholic Traditional Mysticism I mean the mysticism with which the Epistles of St. Paul and St. John, and the other Canonical Epistles, and all the other Scriptures of both the Old and the New Testaments, but more particularly the divine Gospels, are overflowing. It is the mysticism of the everlasting Sacrifice of the Lamb on the Cross and on our altars, and of the whole sacred Liturgy around it: the Mysticism of the Missal, of the Ritual, of the Pontifical, of the Ceremonial of Bishops, of the

Breviary, of the Martyrology, of the *Catechismus Concilii Tridentini*, as well as of the Penny Catechism.

Catholic Traditional Mysticism is the Mysticism of the Apostles, of the first Christians, of the Holy Martyrs and Confessors of all ages, whatever their profession, who have glorified God and sanctified themselves in this world. It is the Mysticism of all men of good will: Catholic not only in name, or because it is sanctioned by the authority of the Catholic Church but Catholic also in that it embraces all things and all persons that are Christ's. *All things are yours,* says St. Paul, *and you are Christ's, and Christ is God's* (1 Cor. 3:22-23).

Again, what is to be understood by Mysticism in itself? Is it a body of doctrine? or a set of rules for our moral conduct? or (to use the barbarous jargon of the day) a set of extraordinary psychic phenomena? or is it a special revelation given to some favored souls over and above the official revelation contained in the *depositum fidei*? Nothing of the kind.

Mysticism is an experience.

Mysticism is a soul-experience.

Mysticism—Catholic Traditional Mysticism —the only Mysticism which deserves the name, the Mysticism which is in question in these pages, is simply and solely the special soul-experience of a human being, as yet a wayfarer on earth, actually tasting and seeing that God is sweet, *O taste and see that God is sweet,* exclaimed the Psalmist (Ps. 33:9), and St. Peter thus exhorts the Christians of his days: *As new-born infants, desire the rational milk without guile, that thereby you may grow unto salvation;* adding: *If yet you have tasted that the Lord is sweet* (1 Pet. 2:2-3)..

It is true that from the beginning of Christianity up till within very recent times, no mention was ever made in Catholic literature of a special class of men called "mystics" in the modern acceptation of the word; but from century to century we hear now and again of "Mystical Theology."

This term, introduced into the Christian vocabulary by the pseudo-Areopagite, is taken up at distant intervals, by pious writers until at last, it is fitly enshrined in the immortal treatise on the Love of God, by St. Francis of Sales (Book V, ch. 2, and Book VI, ch. 1); and throughout, Mystical Theology is invariably taken, purely and simply, as meaning the soul experience I have mentioned.

If such a universal writer as St. Thomas Aquinas does not speak of mystics as a peculiar class, is it not because for him, as for the Areopagite, all Christians are *de jure* mystics? And if he does not know of that vague, undetermined, and Proteus-like thing, which in modern language is called Mysticism, is it not because for him such a thing did not exist? And if he never mentions a separate body of Mystical doctrine, is it not because for him there is no Mystical doctrine distinct from the common deposit of faith? As, for Mystical Theology considered as a soul-experience, there can be found no better scientific exponent of it than the Angel of the School himself. We shall have more than one occasion to point this out as we proceed.

We must never lose sight of the fact that the smallest prayer, the smallest act of religion, if performed in the right spirit, is a Mystical act; the act namely of a human soul, reaching out to God unseen. In this act there is the united co-operation of the loving God and of the loving soul. In the act of prayer the Christian is not alone, is not left to himself, God is with him, since it is of faith that without the supernatural help of the prevenient grace of God, no one can so much as pronounce devoutly the name of Jesus. *No man can say, the Lord Jesus, but by the Holy Spirit* (1 Cor. 12:3). Could anything more mystical, more secret and interior, more transcending and potent be imagined, than what takes place when a pilgrim of the earth, man, woman, or little child prays? Thus, all the acts of religion, whatever form they take, if only they are done in the proper spirit, are acts of Mysticism, of the purest and highest Mysticism. I wonder what a contemporary means by talking of the "Mystical element" in religion, as though the whole of religion was not mystical, absolutely and purely mystical.

As for the distinction between what is called "Speculative Mysticism" and "Practical Mysticism," we may neglect it altogether, Real Mysticism is all practical. There is no other speculative Mysticism than the scientific presentment of Divine Revelation in Dogmatic and Moral Theology, and there is no reason for calling it by any other name than the consecrated one of Dogmatic and Moral Theology. For, if Speculative Mysticism means anything different from the doctrine of Divine Revelation, then it must be rejected.

Modern writers have a great deal to say about what they call "the Mystical faculty." Truth to tell, there are two Mystical faculties; and they are no other than the intellect and the free-will of the Christian, informed by faith, hope and charity and the infused moral virtues, and strengthened moreover by the Seven Gifts of the Holy Spirit. These are the mystical faculties: there are no others.

Genius, coupled with a reverent turn of mind, in the arts of romance, music, poetry, painting, commands our admiration, but I would not assign genius or its successful exercise to any extra-faculty. All these proceed from the intellect and free-will, helped on by a vivid imagination and by a skill of hand which is the fruit of hard work and well disciplined sensibility. Unless the element of sincere, supernatural religion be added to these, nothing mystical is there; only a proof of what we might call modifying slightly a celebrated sentence of Tertullian, "testimonium animæ naturaliter mysticæ;" *i.e*„ the evidence that the human soul has a natural disposition to mysticism. The Saints are the great artists. Their masterpiece, their great work of art, is their own beautiful, pure life, the active share they take in the secret of their own heart, in the sanctity and the joy of God.

The experiences in mystical life, for one who abandons himself perfectly to the action of God, and faithfully co-operates with it, are as numerous and as varied as the experiences of physical life. They may not be more particularly noticed than these. For the most part, unless something special happens to call one's attention to them, physical experiences take place unnoticed and unperceived, flowing in a stream which bears one steadily onward. So is it with the spiritual experiences of the mystic: they embrace his whole life and permeate even its minutest details, bearing him swiftly towards the eternal goal.

They begin in the early morning as soon as he awakens from sleep and gives his heart to God, and they go on without intermittence, the whole day long: hardly can they be said to cease at night. *I sleep,* says the bride of the Canticle, *and my heart watches* (Cant, 5:2). Yes, the life of the mystic is one steady flow of spiritual experiences of which some are intensely delightful, others less so, some painful and even terrible, or simply trying to patience. But all are touched with the light of God, all tend to enable the mystic to die more and more to self, and to live to God, aflame with His love.

The genuine Christian life, lived in its fulness, according to each one's vocation and state, is the true Higher Life. Therein the loving soul meets the loving God. Therein man transcends the whole created order of things visible and invisible, to such an extent as even to meet God, to grapple with Him in the dark, and to wrest from Him, if not His name, which is ineffable, certainly, at any rate, His blessing.

There are two kinds of mystics: the dumb ones and the eloquent ones; eloquent, these last, with tongue or the pen, or with both. *My heart hath uttered a good word,* sings the Psalmist; *my tongue* is *the pen of a scrivener that writes swiftly* (Ps. 44:2). These are the only true "mystical writers." The appellation must not be given indiscriminately to all who take upon themselves the task of informing the world at large what they understand by Mysticism. Oh, no! Otherwise a deist, like the philosopher Boutroux, would have to be considered a mystical writer, and many others even less deserving of the title. Thus, to preclude the possibility of hopeless confusion and misunderstanding, we shall reserve the name of "mystical writers" for those only who speak of the soul-experience of Mystical Theology, and who are qualified to do so because they have themselves enjoyed it and are familiar with its manifestations. Such are, for instance, beside the authors already quoted in previous paragraphs, St. Gertrude, Ruysbroeck, Blessed Suso, St. Catherine of Siena, St. Angela of Foligno, St. Teresa.

From the writings of such as these there goes forth a virtue entirely lacking in the writings of other men, be they ever so talented. These give us glimpses, as it were, of Mystical Theology, make us understand its meaning and long for its enjoyment; they even dispose the soul for it and give her a foretaste of its ineffable delights. These are the only authentic "mystical writers." The others are unmystical even when, perchance, they do write about genuine Mysticism, which is seldom the case. Even then their writings have a blighting influence, because they lack the unction of the Holy Spirit, and are the outcome of mere human effort and mere external study of the subject matter of Mysticism; too philosophical, too much of the brain and appealing only to the brain, too dry-as-dust. But, I repeat, it is seldom indeed that they confine themselves to genuine Mysticism and do not stray into blind alleys leading nowhere, or into by-paths that lose themselves in a tangled wilderness of metaphysical nonsense. These writers have done an enormous amount of mischief. It has been said that in paganism everything was God except God Himself; it may be said that in our days everything is called Mysticism except Mysticism itself.

Is it not high time that a halt should be called upon this road to destruction? Such loose and indiscriminate use of the word Mysticism, even among Catholic writers, is in my opinion responsible, not only for much of the present confusion of thought on the subject, but, as an inevitable consequence (though it may not be apparent at first sight), for much of the present slackness in the pursuit of Christian perfection. *Save me, O Lord,* exclaims David, *for there is now no saint;* and the reason he assigns is this: *truths are decayed from among the children of men. They have spoken vain things every one to his neighbor.* (Ps. 11:2-3.)

When I had collected the greater part of my material for this work and made up my mind as to its definitive plan, it was my good fortune to meet with the late Bishop Hedley, of Newport. I mentioned to him my intention of publishing something on Mysticism. The first reply of the great man was not encouraging. He dryly remarked: "There is too much already written on the subject." This thunderbolt from such a quarter came very near to shattering my strongest purpose.

All I could stammer at first in reply was: "Yes, indeed, there has been too much written on the subject." Alas! who knew this better, forced as I had been to face the inconceivable mass of modern bibliography about Mysticism: books of all sizes and articles of Reviews hailing from all the quarters of the world, and from the four winds of human speculation? "But," I added, "if you will kindly listen to me, you will see that I aim at nothing less than putting a stop to the flow of writings which are to no purpose. My ambition is to turn men's minds and wills to *practicing* mystical life instead of writing so much about it."

Then the venerable prelate became interested, and when he had heard me to the end, he turned to me with a very benevolent and smiling face, and said with an emphasis which precluded all idea of mere compliment: "Ah! now I understand. Well, it is a noble and arduous undertaking; but, write your book, and when completed, send it to me: I promise you I will do my best to make it known and read." Here was no small encouragement. I treasured in my heart those kind words of a Bishop, who, more forcibly than any one I had ever met, put me in mind of the ancient Fathers of the Church. Alas! death has robbed me of the prospect of his assistance, unless he grant it me from on high.

I have also had encouragement, recently, in the exceedingly favorable reception given by the Catholic Press and the general public, to my small treatise on the *Mystical Knowledge of God.* In spite of the hard times we are now traversing and of the somewhat high price of the book; in spite of my being hitherto practically unknown to the reading public, a first edition of 2,000 copies has been sold in a few months; the second edition bids fair to go as quickly, and there is already a demand for the translation into several European languages. I rejoice at this success the more that, in my intention, this small treatise is a sort of proem or prelude to my *Outlines of Catholic Traditional Mysticism.*

Just as in *The Mystical Knowledge of God,* I aim in this new book at being eminently practical and doing as much good to the largest number as possible. I am writing not only for the learned, but also for the simple and the ignorant, and I have confidence that both the learned and the ignorant will find something to help them in these pages.

Certainly this is no academic presentment of the subject of Mysticism. No attempt has been made at rhetorical or oratorical display. Hyperbolical expressions have been wholly discarded. Everything in these pages may be and must be taken quite literally. Nay, startling as some statements may appear to the uninitiated, these must be considered as a weak presentment—a very weak one indeed—of the splendid marvellous realities. We have to bear in mind that human language is a poor instrument, wholly inadequate when used for the purpose of expressing divine mysteries.

The object of this work being mainly to state the traditional notion of the mystical life, to formulate it accurately, to set it in its proper light and let it speak for itself, the reader will understand why I have refrained from controversy. It has seemed to me that in the harmoniousness of the development of this doctrine, in its very balance and its comprehensive unity, there is a sort of persuasiveness not to be resisted.

And although, I truly believe, there is not in this work one single proposition which I could not vindicate with the united testimony of an imposing array of the best authorities ancient and modern on the subject, yet I have refrained as a rule from multiplying quotations, for fear of swelling my volume to unwieldy dimensions.

I submit all I have written and may write hereafter to the judgement of our Holy Mother the Church, ready to retract anything that would not meet with her approval. I am ready also to defer to the better judgement of any of my brethren, especially those of the holy priesthood, who might point out any mistake to me; for I hold that after sin, there is no greater misfortune than that of falling, however involuntarily, into the slightest dogmatic error.

The present juncture, with the horrible world war still raging, may not appear a very fitting time for the publication of such a work as this, when men's minds and attention are forcibly turned towards what is taking place on the various battle-fronts. And yet, who knows? Are there not many, sorely-tried and fainthearted, in need of comfort greater than that which mere human views of things can afford? O that these pages of mine might help my brethren all over the world to turn to our Heavenly Father, *the Father of Our Lord Jesus Christy the Father of mercies and the God of all comfort, Who comforts us in all our tribulations!* (2 Cor. 1:3).

The substance of this work appeared first in the American Catholic *Quarterly Review* of July and October, 1915, and January, 1916.

In this Second Edition the Scriptural references have been carefully revised. The version made use of is that of Canon Oakeley, published by Virtue Co., London, without date, towards the end of last century.

CHAPTER I

DESCRIPTION OF THE MYSTICAL LIFE

MYSTICAL life is life with God.

In the words of Bishop Waffelaert of Bruges, in his short treatise *La Mystique et la Perfection Chrétienne,* mystical life is "a life of intimate, sustained, conscious union with God."

It is the life of a loving soul with the loving God.

A wholly supernatural life, spiritual (not sensual), interior, secret, hidden from the eyes of men: hence its name Mystical, which means something hidden.

A certain confusion has arisen in comparatively recent times, as to the meaning of the Mystical life. There is the school of the wider definition, which by mystical life understands purely and simply, that life of active, conscious union of the soul with God, in the secret of the heart, as here described. Then there is the school of the narrow definition which, by Mystical life, understands one of extraordinary miraculous favors from God to the soul, such as visions, revelations, raptures, the gift of prophecy and of miracles, etc. This latter meaning is quite wrong. The wider meaning is the traditional one, the only one current for more than fifteen centuries; in fact, up to the times of St. John of the Cross and St. Francis of Sales, and really the only legitimate and rational one.

The Psalmist says: *It is good for me to adhere to God* (Ps. 62:28). Mystical life is that: actually and perseveringly adhering or clinging to God: turning to Him constantly, assiduously; finding delight in Him, making this the one supreme and sole business on earth: the *unum necessarium.*

Now, is it a one-sided affair, an affair in which man alone is concerned and does all the work by himself? No. Two are actively engaged in the mystical life, namely: the loving soul and the loving God, and God even more than the soul; for it is God who begins by exciting the soul to seek Him, and who raises her above her natural weakness, sustaining her throughout, and who rewards her puny efforts with the magnificent gift of His divine Self; whilst, on her own part, the loving soul answers with alacrity the call of God, faithfully cooperates with the lights and motions of His grace, and yields herself wholly to His divine embrace.

Mystical life, then, we may as well call, at once, life with a partner *(une vie à deux),* as is the married life; with this difference that, in human espousals, the partner is another human being, whilst in mystical life, the partner (wonderful as this may sound) is God. And with this further difference, that human union is principally a consortium according to the flesh. *They two shall be in one flesh* (Mk. 10:8), whilst mystical life is a union of spirits: *God is a Spirit* (Jo. 4:24), and *He that clings to God is one spirit"* (1 Cor. 6:17.) The flesh enters into the compact only to be made one with the spirit, to be first crushed by mortification, and then raised above itself; made, in a way, spiritual.

To the mystic, God is all in all, and other things do not count, except in relation to God. The mystic lives in the conscious presence of God, in the willed and loved company of God, in secret intercourse with God, in the enjoyment of God. There is a constant exchange of love between that soul and God, as between the bride and the spouse, as set forth in the Canticle of Canticles. Only all this, of course, is purely spiritual, and is all hidden in the secret of the loving heart, jealously shielded from the profane gaze of creatures, for *it is good to hide the secret op a King* (Tob. 12:7.)

Mystical life, when it comes after a life of tepidity, inaugurates a new order of relations between God and man; new and very special relations, more intimate, more loving, more sweet, more delicate and tender, both on the part of God and on the part of man. This order of relations was predicted in Osee 2:19, 20: *I will espouse thee to me forever: and I will espouse thee to me in justice and judgement, and in mercy and in commiseration. And I will espouse thee to me in faith; and thou shalt know that I am the Lord.* It was not so before, nor is it thus with the non-mystic. It is indeed for the soul a new state of life, but it is the right one, the one that should have prevailed from the beginning, the one that should always prevail.

Mystical life is simply the holy life God has planned for us as a temporary substitute for the bliss of heaven, and a prelude to it; a life in which all the resources brought by sanctifying grace are fully worked out; where the Sacraments are made to yield all their fruits, and the presence of the Holy Spirit in the soul, with His seven gifts, is given all its efficacy.

Mystical life is the normal Christian life, the full Christian life, Christian life as it should be lived by all, and everywhere, and under all circumstances; whilst the Christian life as it is lived, alas! by the immense majority of people, is simply abnormal and monstrous, shorn of its bearings upon all the details of life, and deprived of its efficacy and of most of its precious fruits.

Mystical life is a human life made supernatural and wholly divine in all its manifestations, even the most lowly and material ones, such as eating, sleeping, recreation, material work. *Whether you eat or drink, or whatsoever else you do, do all things for the glory of God* (1 Cor. 10:31). The mystic becomes *deform,* not only in the substance of his soul as is the case with every man in a state of grace, but also in all his activities. In him, the divine ideal, nay God Himself, has impregnated and transformed everything. *I live,* says St. Paul, *now not I, but Christ lives in me* (Galat. 9:20). God lives in the mystic, throws out and projects his divine life in him and the mystic in his turn lives in God. *Your life,* says St. Paul, *is hidden with Christ in God* (Col. 3:3).

From the very start, the mystic, in order to find God, is led to retire into himself, which act is called *introversion*; and once he has there found Him Whom his soul loveth (for *lo the Kingdom of God is within you,* Luke 17:21), the mystic with great delight loses himself in God, and would fain never quit Him to live with the outer world of creatures. Even when compelled to have converse with the world and to attend to exterior occupations, the better part of him is away from it all, secretly clinging to God and loving Him and enjoying Him.

The mystic, without neglecting any of his external duties, simply lives with God, simply lives upon God, feasts upon God, finds in God his all in all.

To him God is (as He is indeed) the great reality, the only being worthy of perpetually engrossing his attention and winning and retaining for evermore the affections of his heart.

He joys in the thought of the presence of God, of His goodness, of His sanctity, of His divine life and infinite bliss and infinite loveliness. He is never tired of speaking to God of his love, and of laying himself open as far as possible to the divine influences.

And God on His part is not backward with His servant: He lays hands on all the faculties of the mystic and makes His Divine presence felt in him. He floods his mind with wonderful illuminations, and his will with marvellous infusions of strength; and at times (though not at all times), God fills the heart of His servant with ineffable sweetness; whilst at other times He tries him with dryness of spirit and the withdrawal of heavenly consolation. But this never discourages the faithful servant. He knows God is always there, invisibly holding him, and steering his soul safely through the dense fog and the breakers, as does a skillful pilot the ship which a diffident captain has surrendered into his hands.

Now it is this wonderful life with God as a partner which we call the mystical life.

Shall we say that it is a very extraordinary sort of life? If by extraordinary, we mean that it is seldom met with: yes, alas! it is so. But if we mean an impracticable, a well-nigh impossible life, one meant only for a very few chosen souls, we are in error. No; mystical life is neither impracticable nor well nigh impossible, nor is it only for a few. It is simply the very perfection of Christian life, to which we are called, and we shall be severely punished in Purgatory if we have not attained it. Mystical life appears to us extraordinary and well-nigh impossible only because we are *of little faith* (Mat. 6:30), and have allowed our charity to grow cold.

Mystical life is the right kind of life: any other is wrong.

CHAPTER II

WHO ARE MYSTICS AND WHO ARE NOT

EVIDENTLY non-mystics are first of all those who are in the state of mortal sin. Far from living with God, these Eve with His enemy the devil. They have given themselves over to him, they belong to him: he is with them and in them. Yes, in them; they are his dwelling. Read St. Luke, 11:24-26. A terrible state of affairs indeed.

Non-mystics also are all those tepid and negligent Christians, who, though not habitually in a state of sin, and therefore not living with the devil, cannot however be said to Eve with God, but rather with self and the world of creatures. Though in the state of grace, they do not do the actions of grace, but those of a purely natural life. The Holy Spirit in them is not allowed to have his own way: they hold Him, so to say, bound hand and foot, and gagged; they offer Him that indignity! They have not faith enough to believe that God can make them happy; they prefer to try creatures; and though these invariably fail them, they are content to renew the experiment again and again. There is therefore no intimate intercourse between them and God: they never have anything to say to Him from their heart; they take no notice of His presence. They treat Him as a stranger. *Behold,* says Our Lord, *I stand at the door and knock* (Apoc. 3:20), but they turn a deaf ear to Him, and withal they are perfectly satisfied with themselves. A very sad condition this, and how dangerous! Read what our Lord says of it in the Apocalypse, 3:14-20.

Non-mystics also, but quite innocently, are very young children who, though baptized, and therefore in a state of grace, and fit for the immediate possession of heaven should they die, are nevertheless incapable of union with God by active love, which requires discernment by the understanding, and the full play of our queen-faculty, the will.

Many believe themselves to be on the mystical way and qualified to write and speak about it, who have no true experience of it and do not so much as suspect what it really is. On the other hand, many lead the mystical life unawares and sometimes are very far advanced in it without suspecting that God is doing very great things in them, or realizing that theirs is the mystical life. I have found such in all walks of life, notably among the poor and little children and among illiterate persons, and even among the savage tribes of North America.

There are also false mystics, tools of the devil, who would mislead even the true children of God, if these were not on their guard. Their errors generally run into formal heresies and they are easily known by their contempt of the teaching and authority of the Church. Such were the Gnostics of early Christianity, many sects of the Middle Ages; in modern times Molinos, Madame Guyon, and others, and the Modernists of our own days.

There are those who would make the mystical life to consist chiefly in extraordinary graces, such as visions, voices, revelations. If truly humble they will certainly be led to seek none of these things, much less to endeavor to induce them; while if vain and foolish, they may covet the glory of them, and not being able to lay hands on the true gifts of God, they may take to themselves a worthless counterfeit, work themselves into self-induced ecstasies, and self-suggested revelations, and in any case, lay themselves open to the crafty deceptions of the Evil One. Bishops and priests, as well as Religious Superiors, have to be on their guard against pious impostors, hallucinated, self-deluded souls, and to suppress any tendency to a visionary spirit that may manifest itself. For it is such as these, that have brought the very name of Mysticism into ill repute; with how little reason may be perceived when we consider its true nature as already set forth.

The true mystic does not desire visions, revelations or extraordinary states of either body or soul; and if these are vouchsafed to him, he fears them and he would rather wish for their withdrawal, knowing they do not constitute Sanctity and are never entirely without danger. He wishes to pass unnoticed. He is most simple and unaffected, most humble and obedient. Outwardly he does just the same things as other men in his profession and surroundings do.

His glory is within. *All the glory of the King's daughter is within* (Ps. 44:14).

There are, in the wide range of Christian life, privileged situations, where it is more easy and at the same time more imperative to lead the mystical life, by reason of the sacredness of the functions to be exercised and of the abundance of graces received in them. Such are the clerical state, the Religious state, also the state of virginity or widowhood in the world, when persons resolve to give themselves wholly to God, though unable for some reason to enter religion. This notwithstanding, it remains absolutely true that mystical life, even in its fullness and perfection, is without need of a special vocation; it is FOR ALL MEN, of whatever age, profession, or condition of life, as is abundantly proved by the history of the Church and the annals of sanctity.

In order to begin to live the mystical life, only two things are required: first, the state of grace, secondly, a little love or goodwill. Goodwill enough to seek after God, to pay attention to God, to listen to Him, to talk lovingly to Him. Nothing more is required: neither science, nor any sort of talent, nor even acquired virtues. The sinner, fresh from a life of sin, can begin at once and indeed should do so; as David when he repented of his great crime and gave vent to his feelings in the seven penitential Psalms; as Magdalen when she dared to cover, with the kisses of her polluted lips, the feet of the Most Holy One, bathing them with her tears and drying them with her disheveled hair; as the famous penitents of all ages.

Even the good thief on his cross by the side of the dying Saviour lived one or two hours of the intensest and most genuine mystical life. In fact, there, on Calvary, we find all classes of mystics represented in the whole reach of the mystical life, thus: First the Most Holy One, the pattern of all mystics, Jesus crucified; next. His Immaculate Virgin Mother, ADDOLORATA, the Mystical Rose; then St. John, the virgin Apostle, the Beloved, the spoiled child, so to say, of Divine love; close to him, Magdalen, the woman that was a sinner, to whom much had been forgiven because she had loved much; and finally the good thief, a convert of the very last hour from a life of the blackest crimes, who was nevertheless made sensible of the divinity of Christ and turned into the first public herald of it; and who was that very day to step from his gibbet of infamy into paradise.

CHAPTER III

THE LAW OF PROGRESS IN THE MYSTICAL LIFE

THE doctrine of this chapter is set forth against negligent and tepid souls who do not care to make any progress, against Quietists who aim at establishing themselves in a state where there would be no striving after better things, and against those Protestants who contend that faith alone is necessary without any good works, and finally against some souls of good will who allow themselves to remain stationary either through faint-heartedness or out of a false conception of the nature and exigencies of mystical life.

In the first chapter of these *Outlines* I have been at some pains to describe the mystic life in its fulness and perfection. But one cannot expect to arrive at that perfection at the outset, any more than one can reach the top of a mountain at a single stride, or grow from childhood to the full stature of a man in a day, or reap a crop at the same instant that one does the planting or the sowing; any more than one expects to see a birdling fly before it has grown wings, or a babe at the breast do a man's work.

It is true, as Theologians assure us, that by one single act of theirs, in co-operation with the grace of God, the blessed Angels were at once saved and consummated in sanctity, so that one moment saw them *on the way,* and the next arrived *at the goal.* But things do not proceed in the same way with us men. Our nature, inferior to that of the pure spirits, has a mode of action less perfect, so that our trial is lengthened into a period of time.

Moreover, our present conditions for striving after the perfection of sanctity are not those which existed for Adam and Eve, who were innocent. We are now in the condition of probation under sin, that is with the consequences of original sin on each individual soul and body, and in the midst of a world of sin, in the midst of hosts of enemies visible and invisible; all of which tend to make our progress more difficult, and would make it impossible, were it not that "*where sin abounded, grace* doth more abound." (Rom. 5:20).

It is therefore only by an immense multitude of successive, varied and more or less difficult acts that we shall develop in ourselves our latent aptitude for sanctity, which the grace of God, through the Sacraments, has deposited in us; that we shall grow to the full stature of the perfect man in Christ Jesus, and that we shall yield the fruits God has a right to expect of us: in a word, that we shall come to the perfection of the mystical life. Nay, even should we be happy enough to attain to that very perfection (as I shall describe it in the next chapter), it will rest with us to increase it indefinitely, until the very moment of death. For, what is marvellous in our spiritual growth is that, whereas we cannot add one cubit, no, not even half an inch, to our bodily stature, there is no limit to the cubits we may add to the stature of our soul. This process of the transformation of our natural man, or of the old Adam in us into the new man which is Christ, slow and gradual and painful as it is, is a most marvellous thing, a sight for God and His Angels.

Now, this is at least one advantage of our present condition, one that might almost make the Angels and Saints of God in glory jealous of us, this, namely, that we can do and suffer every day and every hour something more for the love of God, gain more merits, enlarge our capacity of loving God, grow in sanctity, ascend higher and higher on the ladder of perfection.

Not only may we do so, but we should do so, we must do so; and if we fail so to do we are guilty, and we shall have to answer for it. Every day ought to find us further removed from our wonted vices and imperfections than the day before. Every successive hour spent in the service of God, every fresh act of piety such as the celebration of the Divine sacrifice or assistance at it, or Holy Communion, or Confession, or prayer; every Pater or Ave or ejaculatory prayer ought, not only to make us so much the richer in merits, but also, at the same time, so much the more skilled in the art of serving God and our brethren, in the art of overcoming self and vanquishing the devil, especially in the art of prayer and contemplation.

John Ruskin, the great art critic, says that a true painter never makes a fresh picture but that it is better than the one he painted before; because each time he sets to his work and gives his whole heart and soul to it, he becomes more master of his tools and materials and of his own faculties. Only the negligent or abject-minded man, who looks upon his noble art but as a means of making money, will content himself with multiplying pictures without any change for the better, without gaining skill in the art; nay, he will even deteriorate and grow incapable. It is much the same in the spiritual life with those half-hearted Christians who are content to go through the same exercises of piety a thousand times mechanically, without stirring themselves to a greater love of God. Not only do they not advance, but they will surely deteriorate and perhaps even come at last to give it all up as they find no consolation whatever in these exercises.

We have so-called . pious people who say numerous prayers and receive the Sacraments often enough to turn them into seraphs, but who yet advance not a step on the way to perfection. They are satisfied with the fruit to be gained *ex opere operato,* and do not bestir themselves to produce the fruit *ex opere operantis* which should never be separated from the former: that is to say, they receive the good things of God, but turn them to no account, just as some men eat hearty meals but do no work.

That we are not at liberty so to act, but that we ought ever to progress, to grow in sanctity, to climb up the ladder of virtues and to become more united to God, is shown by innumerable passages of Holy Scripture in both Testaments. Our Lord tells us: *Be you therefore perfect as also your heavenly Father is perfect,* thereby opening out before us an infinite course, the goal of which we can never say we have reached. Hence the Glossa quoted by St. Thomas II IIæ q. 24 *a. 7,* says: "Let none of the faithful, however much he may have progressed, say: That is enough." In saying this he would step out of the road before reaching the end. Hence St. Paul (Phil, 3:13,14), *Brethren, I do not count myself to have apprehended, but one thing I do, forgetting the things that are behind, and stretching forth myself to those that are before, I pursue towards the mark, for the prize of the supernal vocation of God in Christ Jesus.* And Prov. 4:18, says: *The path of the just as a shining light goes forwards and increases even to perfect day.* And Psalm 88:8, *They shall go from virtue to virtue.* Our Lord again commands us (Luke 19:13), *Trade till I come,* and in the parable of the talents He shows us the reward and the meed of praise bestowed on those good servants who doubled what they had, whilst he that wrapped his talent in a napkin is rebuked and punished.

Hence also the Council of Trent (Sess. VI, c. 10) speaks thus of increasing our justification, after we have once received it: "Therefore, such as have thus been justified and made friends of God and servants of the faith, are renewed day by day as they go, according to the Apostle, from virtue to virtue; that is to say, by mortifying the members of their flesh and turning them into weapons of justice, unto sanctification, through the observance of the Commandments of God and of the Church, in the very justice they have received through the grace of Christ; their faith being united with good works, they grow and become more justified, as it is written: *He that is just let him be justified still* (Apoc. 22:11). And again: *Be not afraid to be justified even to death* (Eccli. 18:22). And again: *Do you see that a man is justified by works and not by faith only* (Jas. 2:24). Now, it is this increase of sanctity which the Church prays for in these words: "Give us, Lord, an increase of faith, hope and charity."

God does not always permit the mystic to see his progress, as this might endanger his humility; but there is an infallible sign by which one may know at least that one is indeed progressing; this, namely, that the sincere and earnest desire to make progress exists.

We may stir ourselves up to that holy desire by observing how worldlings are never satisfied with what they are or with what they have: they always want more, and work themselves to death for it. What they do for temporal riches, honor and pleasure, shall we be less eager to do for eternal bliss and glory?

Therefore whatever others may think of us, or do or not do

for themselves, let us be up and doing, and never relax and never stop till we hear the words of the divine Master: *Well done, thou good and faithful servant, enter thou into the joy of thy Lord!* (Mat. 25:23).

CHAPTER IV

THE THREE STAGES OF THE MYSTICAL LIFE

IN the foregoing chapter we have ascertained that progress in the mystical life must be gradual, steady and unlimited. We ought not to linger on the road, nor halt, nor turn back; neither should we lose precious time loitering in the bye-paths that lead nowhere, nor cover the same ground over and over by moving in a circle. We must march briskly, not crawl, straight ahead, on and on, ever higher and higher.

Spiritual writers use various comparisons to make us understand at the same time the process of the mystical life and its oneness of design, and the stages of it with their necessary consecutiveness.

St. John Climachus compares it to a ladder, St. John of the Cross to a mountain, St. Teresa to a fortress with various mansions, others to a road with relays; St. Benedict, in his Rule, names twelve degrees of humility, Bl. Angela of Foligno describes eighteen steps by which God brought her to the grace of a thorough conversion. Philip of the Most Holy Trinity, Carmelite, in his THEOLOGIA MYSTICA, distinguishes five successive stages of the spiritual life, to wit: I st, that of the sensible delights of grace immediately following conversion or vocation; 2nd, that of the purification of the senses; 3rd, that of the enlightenment of the understanding; 4th, that of the purifying of the intellect; 5th, that of the perfect union with God.

Truth to tell, there are well nigh innumerable degrees and diversities of graces, and probably no two souls on the way are found to be exactly on the same level, just as no two angels and no two saints in heaven have the same degree of glory. Without therefore entering upon a more detailed account of these many degrees, it will be enough for our purpose to set down at some length the division of the spiritual life into the three classical stages, namely:

1. That of Beginners.
2. That of the Advanced.
3. That of the Perfect.

The treatment of these three stages will cover the whole subject of the degrees of the spiritual life, just as a description of the three periods of childhood, youth and manhood, that of man; or as an account of the foundations, wall-structure and roof, that of a house; and will enable us to understand the essential workings of the mystical life.

The first stage, that of the Beginners, is the initiatory one, and is called *The Way of Purity.* Quite a proper appellation, whether the beginner be an innocent child, a virgin soul, since then its main feature is indeed the absence of the contamination of sin; or again, whether the beginner be just coming out of a bad life, because then the main characteristic of this stage for him will be the struggle against sin and vice, in order to secure this wonderful prize of purity.

The second stage or middle one, that of the Advanced, is called *The Way of Enlightenment,* and its main characteristic is ordinarily the acquisition and practice of virtues. To understand this we must bear in mind that the soul of man is the mirror of the Godhead. Sin had previously laid, on that mirror, a thick coating of unutterable filth, and even after that has been done away with by a good Confession, the soul emits the smoke of yet unruly passions, which prevents the beams that issue from the countenance of God from being reflected therein. But as soon as the passions have been repressed, then the countenance of God will shine freely upon the soul and make it luminous, enlightening it splendidly. If now by the prism of analysis we isolate the rays of divine light which the soul reflects, they will be found to be so many virtues, namely, the theological virtues of Faith, Hope and Charity, the infused moral virtues, and the gifts of the Holy Spirit.

The third stage, that of the Perfect, is called *The Way of Union,* and its main characteristic is always a very high degree of mental prayer, practically uninterrupted.

Though such be indeed the main characteristics, respectively, of the three ways: fight against sin, heroic practice of virtues, and mental prayer at its highest, nevertheless we must note also that these three elements are all found together, in each of the three degrees, though in varying proportions. There is the purification and the enlightenment and the divine contemplation proper to beginners; and there is the purification, practice of virtues and mental prayer proper to the advanced; and finally, there is also, for the perfect, still further purification, and still greater flights of virtues, as well as contemplation at its highest. The spiritual man grows all together: not one part of him after another, as who should say the lower limbs first, then after a while the trunk, and only ultimately the head. No, every part of him is there from the beginning, proportionately small, of course, and every part grows harmoniously with the others, just as the hands and feet and brain and heart of a child will grow with the rest of his body.

It is failure to grasp that harmonious, all-round development of the spiritual man, that has caused modern writers to introduce such unnatural distinctions and separations in things that God meant to go together from the very beginning and all along. Let it be understood, once for all, that even a beginner is to be allowed divine contemplation and not to be exclusively confined to the dreary occupation of fighting his dominant fault. There is a very apposite remark of Father Buckler, O.P., in his book on *Spiritual Perfection:* "No small consolation comes to souls anxious to advance when they understand that the work of their perfection lies in the development of their love." In *Sancta Sophia,* the venerable Father Baker has one chapter to show how the exercise of love causes illumination. Hence I conclude that souls are to be urged to begin that exercise of love as early as possible.

How will one know that one has succeeded in purifying oneself and is fit for the second stage of the spiritual life? Abbot Cisneros, in his *Exercises of the Spiritual Life,* answers: "When one has obtained these three gifts: 1st, against sloth, alacrity;

2nd, against concupiscence, self-control; 3rd, against ill-will, kindliness. Then may the soul, without delay, climb the higher way of enlightenment."

And how shall we know that we can place ourselves in the group of the *Advanced*? Cardinal Bona, in his *Manuductio ad cœlum* (c. 19), answers: "When you have such a mastery over yourself as to possess your soul in unity, when things of this world displease you, and you love solitude, and you are athirst after perfection, and you despise the opinions and judgments of men."

Finally, one may know that one has reached the last stage when one has the gift of the Presence of God and of the Beatitudes and of the Fruits of the Holy Spirit. Divine union is an interior state in which the soul of man is completely surrendered to the action of the Holy Spirit. In all his willed and deliberate acts, that man is in permanent collaboration with God; nay more, he leaves the initiative to God to such an extent that, beyond the plain call of duty and charity, he will not move himself as of himself to anything, but rather will wait to be moved to it by the Holy Spirit; and when the Holy Spirit does not move him to anything in particular, that man is satisfied to remain peacefully in his union with God.

An amazing fact is that a comparatively enormous number of persons remain beginners all their lives. Very few, even among Religious and clerics and secular persons making a profession of piety, very few indeed are those who really go beyond the threshold of the mystical life and who answer the loving, pressing invitation of God: *Friend, go up higher* (Luke, 14:10).

And it is not all due to indifference or want of generosity, but in many cases simply to ignorance, or want of proper spiritual direction, or to the altogether wrong idea that mystical life in its fulness and perfection is not made for people like them, and that it requires a very special vocation.

Now, this is a great pity. For it is certain that it requires at least as much effort to keep oneself in the first stage, without falling back into downright tepidity, as it would to go up higher: as though a man were to try to keep a boat stationary in midstream by force of oars. He would have all the exertion, if not more, of those who pass him and go up stream, without their exhilaration and advantages. Oh! when shall we understand that a traveler, after the first days of fatigue, climbs the mountain-side with greater alacrity than he previously walked on low, swampy ground? Mounting up, the air becomes keener and purer, and his buoyancy of spirit proportionately greater. And if the objects he leaves below dwindle into insignificance and he can expect to have but few or no companions in these high solitudes, yet his heart is cheered at the ever widening circle of the horizon and the magnificent prospect of land and sky, and at the felt majestic presence of God. Thus it is also and much more in the progressive stages of the mystical life.

Show, O Lord, Thy ways to me, and teach me Thy paths (Ps. 24:4).

CHAPTER V

DIVISION OF THE MYSTICAL LIFE

MYSTICAL life is divided into two parts: 1st, Divine Contemplation, and 2nd, Saintly action.

Action, and contemplation of some sort, are the two elements which are found in the life of every adult human being, be his life either purely natural or supernatural, be it tepid or fervent: with this difference however, that in the case of the mystic, God is the all in all of his life, whilst in the case of the others, God does hardly enter therein, but self or creatures are almost its all in all.

When one is occupied with God, when God is the direct, immediate object of one's loving attention, that is Divine Contemplation. In its widest sense, Divine Contemplation comprises a great variety of acts: spiritual reading on the divine essence and perfections, or on the mysteries of Our Lord; meditation on the same, vocal prayer, certain pious exercises (such, for instance, as the Way of the Cross), celebration of the Holy Sacrifice or participation therein, and finally mental prayer proper.

Saintly Action in contradistinction to Divine Contemplation is, when for the love of God one is busy about something which is not God, and yet so as not to lose one's union with God. In our present condition We cannot be all the time occupied with God alone, for two reasons: first, because our natural frailty makes us incapable of such an uninterrupted and exclusive attention to God; second, because certain duties to ourselves and our neighbor claim a part of our attention, for the very honor and service of God. This action, of course, does not necessarily imply bustle and noise and much moving about.

This first great division of the mystical life into its two parts is set forth in the words of our Saviour: *The Lord Thy God thou shalt adore, and Him only shalt thou serve* (Mat. 4:10), ADORATION standing for Divine Contemplation, and SERVICE for Saintly Action.

These two elements are always found in every saintly life upon earth, though, of course, in varying proportion in different persons, and even in the same person at different periods of his progress onwards. As a rule, beginners are more active than contemplative. Certain natures are very little gifted with an aptitude for contemplation, whilst others, on the contrary, very little for action. But it remains true that every mystic's life is full of these two elements, Divine Contemplation and Saintly Action, as (to use a homely simile) a fresh egg is full of white and yelk. And as in an egg, there is no place for anything else, so in the mystic's life there is no place for sinful or even purely natural affections. All is supernatural.

Though Divine Contemplation and Saintly Action are always blended together, still now one, and now the other, gains the ascendancy. The two phases alternate continually, succeeding each other with a greater stress now upon contemplation, now upon action, according to the dispositions of the moment and the demands laid upon one by circumstances.

In thus passing from Divine Contemplation to Saintly Action and *vice versâ,* one finds the relief that our frail nature craves for. In the sweetness of prayer and contemplation, one finds repose from the worries of active life, and, on the other hand, the wholesome distractions of saintly activity help one to bear the heavy weight of divine contemplation.

Again, though contemplation and action are, of necessity, found in the daily life of every mystic on earth, still in some lives one of the two elements so markedly predominates over the other, as to give the life of the mystic its peculiar coloring. Thus the life of some mystics is almost all taken up with the direct occupation with God: they are accordingly called Contemplatives. Such were the Fathers of the Desert, the holy Hermits and Recluses of the Middle Ages: such are nowadays Carmelite nuns, Carthusian monks, and most of the enclosed religious Orders. Others, on the contrary, give a markedly predominant share to Saintly activity, in the works of mercy—spiritual and corporal. Such are nearly all Christians in the world, and many in religious institutes, as Sisters of Charity, the Teaching Orders, the Hospitallers, etc. Besides this Contemplative and that Active form of life, there is a third kind, the Apostolic one, which is the proper form of life of all apostolic men, either secular or regular, of Bishops, Priests in the world, Missionaries, Superiors of whatever kind of religious communities of both sexes. All these persons, on account of their exalted position and sacred character and the special nature of their occupations, have to carry to their maximum of intensity and in their most excellent form, and in almost equal measure, both at one and the same time, Divine Contemplation and Saintly Action.

How are people to be guided in their choice of one or the other of these three modes of the mystical life? By the holy will of God in their regard. Now that is made manifest by one or the other or all of the following signs: 1st, one's own natural inclination and special aptitudes; 2nd, the exigencies of circumstances; 3rd, the advice or even command of those in authority over one.

We must be careful when speaking of Action and Contemplation to give to our words but a relative and conventional value. For, indeed, adoration is action also. The sublimest act of adoration, namely, the Holy Sacrifice of the Mass, is an action full of movement. And contemplation, though it seems repose, is action also; nay, it is action at its highest, it is action at white heat, so to say. All this notwithstanding, it is proper for us to retain the two consecrated terms, being careful to assign to each no other meaning, than is agreed upon by all the writers of spirituality.

This may also help one to understand what theologians mean, when they contend that, in heaven, there will be no more action but only contemplation. It might seem at first a rather dreary outlook, but it only means that in heaven there will be no more defects of our own to correct, since we shall be constituted in a state of perfect charity; nor will there be any distress of our neighbor for us to alleviate by our exertions, as all these being also established in perfect charity, will be happy. Thus will be suppressed the two forms of saintly action, of which we shall presently speak, and we may rejoice that they will be no longer necessary in heaven. And as for there being in heaven only contemplation, it means that God will, at last, be manifestly all in all to the blessed; that He will be the unfailing object of their enjoyment, both in Himself directly, and indirectly in the other Blessed, whether taken individually or collectively. They will have so perfectly become forms of God, filled with God, reflecting God, that their loving one another, their conversations, songs, flights through space, solemn processions, explorations of all the depth and width and height of the material universe and of the wonderful world of spirits, all these will be but so many manifestations of the divine joy, overflowing in all the channels of their created natures.

When the Blessed will be contemplating God in Himself it will be *Contemplatio Matutina* (as theologians call it); when enjoying Him in their own selves and in His other works it will be *Contemplatio Vespertina*: thus there will always be Divine Contemplation, and withal a good deal of action and motion on the part of the Blessed. They will pass from the direct contemplation of the Divine Essence in itself to the indirect contemplation of it in its works and *vice versa* with ever renewed eagerness and never satiated appetite, and with a full expansion of all the faculties of body and soul; those only of the purely vegetative life being abolished, as their provisional functions, in the great scheme of things created will then be at an end. It is what the Apostle signifies in the words: *The meat for the belly and the belly for the meats: but God shall destroy both it and them* (1 Cor. 6:13); It does not mean that any part of the body will be wanting to its integrity in the resurrection of the Blessed, but that its lower functions will be no more, it having entered upon the glorious life of the spirit. On the other hand, all the other enjoyments, either of body or mind, of senses, memory, imagination, intellect, will, bodily motion, the artistic faculty etc., all these will be carried to their highest powers and fullest exercise. In this sense there will be action, intense action, of each one of the Blessed personally, and of all of them in groups and in their universality—action of so grand a description that for us it is at present absolutely unimaginable.

This much, to help us understand the relative and restricted meaning of these two terms of mystical theology: Action, Contemplation.

CHAPTER VI

SUB-DIVISION OF THE MYSTICAL LIFE AND CO-ORDINATION OF ITS PARTS

SAINTLY Action is sub-divided into two parts, namely: Interior Action and Exterior Action.

That saintly action which takes place within the soul and has for its object self, the regulation of the affections, the implanting of virtue, and the eradication of vice, is called Interior Action. On the other hand, that saintly action which has for its object the world of creatures outside —principally our neighbor, towards whom we exercise ourselves in the duties of justice and charity—is called Exterior Action.

This gives us, in last analysis, the division of the mystical life into three parts:

1st. Divine Contemplation in its broadest sense.

2nd. Internal Saintly Action or Ascetics proper.

3rd. External Saintly Action or Good Works —Divine Contemplation coming first, Saintly Action second and subordinate; and that Saintly Action, which has our own selves for its object, passing before that which has for its object things or persons outside us. So that our saintly interior action appears as the immediate fruit of our divine contemplation, and furthermore, our saintly external action is shown to be the offspring, so to say, of these two united, viz., divine contemplation and saintly interior action. When self has been renounced by saintly interior action and the soul has been filled with God by divine contemplation, it will inevitably overflow in deeds of charity and kindness to all.

It is necessary to insist on the union and consecutiveness and subordination of the parts of mystical life. In our opinion, much of the conspicuous failure of modern piety is due to ignorance or wilful disregard of this doctrine. A complaint is raised sometimes that active life is destructive of piety, or again, that contemplation disqualifies one for apostolic work; as though these two, Divine Contemplation and Saintly Action, were antagonistic. Far from this being the case, one cannot exist without the other; neither may be sacrificed for the sake of the other, or both perish: only, each must be given its proper comparative degree of precedence or subordination. One must be careful not to neglect prayer and the care of one's own interior under pretext of the exigencies of active life. Is it not remarkable that the Rule of St. Benedict, which has formed some of the greatest workers, whether in the fields of erudition, apostolic zeal or the material arts of civilization, gives no distinct directions as to external work. It is wholly taken up with the care of forming the man of prayer and ascetic habits, and nothing more, and yet it has proved enough —for the Benedictine Monk thus formed has found himself perfectly fitted for every work of zeal.

The order of the ten Commandments of God confirms this co-ordination of the parts of mystical life. The first three Commandments set forth our duty to God, or Divine Contemplation in its widest meaning. The last seven Commandments, though they only mention our neighbor, have for their very first effect (and that is self evident) to impose and to produce order in our own heart by interior action, before it can take effect in our dealings with our brethren by external action. For Our Lord says: *Out of the abundance of the heart the mouth speaks* (Mat. 12:34), and again: *From the heart proceed evil thoughts, murders, adulteries, fornications, thefts, false testimonies, blasphemies* (Mat. 15:19).

It is not difficult to discover again this same co-ordination of the parts of mystical life inculcated in the first three petitions of the Our Father: First, *Hallowed be Thy Name,* which is done by Divine worship, both public and private, or Divine Contemplation. Next, *Thy kingdom come,* which is procured by obedience to the laws of God, which obedience has first to be established in the heart by Interior Action. Finally: *Thy will be done on earth as it is in heaven,* which can be realized only by our taking in hand the interests of God in the whole world by Saintly

External Action. Here we see how wide is the range of saintly external action. Besides his immediate duties to those around him, the mystic is deeply concerned in the welfare of his neighbor and actively employs himself on his behalf. He does not ask to answer it in the negative, *Am I my brother's keeper?* (Gen. 4:9). Every form of distress of body or soul forcibly appeals to him, and he lays himself out to relieve it in the measure of his power. The more united he is to God by Divine Contemplation and dead to self by previous Saintly Action, the more efficaciously will he also do this.

Our duty to God takes precedence over that which we owe to ourselves or to others, because it is the very reason of our duty to ourselves and our neighbor. And it is good for us that Contemplation should thus hold the first place, for we do more and we gain more for ourselves and others when we are with God, when we attend to God, than in any other way. We are enabled to perform our duty to ourselves and our neighbor only through the help of the grace of God, which is obtained by prayer and the Sacraments; that is, by direct intercourse with God, which is an act of divine contemplation.

Even irrespective of our manifold relations to Him, God claims our loving attention first, and more than either ourselves or the whole universe of things, precisely on account of His transcendental excellence. Loving attention to God, or Divine Contemplation of some sort, ought, according to St. Thomas, to be the first use man makes of his reason, when he begins to know himself, and to discern good from evil. By Divine command, loving attention to God ought to fill and sanctify the first day of each week. A Christian need not be told that it ought also to be the very first act in the morning of each day.

Loving attention to God, according to Holy Writ, should be our ever recurring care, our constant and supreme occupation, the most engrossing one, the one about which we should be most solicitous. And so it is to the mystic. In the words of the sacred liturgy, he confesses that "Vere dignum et justum est, æquum et salutare, nos tibi, semper et ubique, gratias agere." It is truly just and right and good and wholesome for us always and everywhere to give thanks to God. The non-mystics, truth to tell, do not feel thus keenly about it, but they are all wrong.

This doctrine of the supremacy and primacy of Divine Contemplation holds good (within certain limits) for sinners freshly converted as well as for saints. It would be a fatal mistake to say: Let them first put some kind of order in their interior dispositions before they be permitted or induced to apply themselves to any sort of contemplation; when *that* is done, then, and *only then,* may they turn to God. No! no! let them, first of all things, turn to God that they may be enabled, through love of Him and by His grace, to put their interior dispositions in order. Besides, this right ordering of the interior man is a work of time; it cannot be accomplished all at once, whilst on the other hand the precept of communion with God is pressing urgently and constantly, and may not be postponed. *We ought always to pray and not to faint* (Luke 18:1). Moreover, God is the Master of His own ways and bestows His gifts as He pleases without following any set rule known to human wisdom; now, if He sees fit to give graces of prayer to a beginner (as observation proves that He often does), it is not for us to say Him nay.

This doctrine of the primacy or precedence of Divine Contemplation holds good even for young children. When Our Lord said *Suffer the little children and forbid them not to come to Me* (Mat. 19:14). He gave us to understand that He wishes them to draw near Him by a contemplation proportionate to the development of their faculties. See how the magnificent act of Pius X, convoking all the little ones to communion and even to daily communion, confirms this view!

Writers who tell us that sinners and children are incapable of Divine Contemplation, have in mind the acme and perfection of Divine Contemplation, which certainly is acquired but very late in spiritual life. But notwithstanding this, it remains true that *acts, occasional acts,* of Divine Contemplation, are called for, long before one reaches perfection, nay, at the very outset of Christian life. Of this distinction between the acts and the habit of Divine Contemplation we shall have more to say later. Let what has been said in this chapter suffice, for the present, to place beyond the possibility of a doubt the fact that in the mystical life there must come first, God, by Divine Contemplation; next to God, ourselves, by Internal Saintly Action; and last, our relations to persons and things outside, by External Saintly Action.

CHAPTER VII

THE CO-WORKERS IN THE MYSTICAL LIFE: THE MYSTIC AND THE BLESSED TRINITY

We are God's coadjutors (1 Cor. 3:19).

MYSTICAL Life is an experimental perception, dim, but intensely real, of the Blessed Trinity.

The Most Holy Trinity is the mystery of mysteries; in fact, the One, Great, Living Mystery; and yet, in itself, the simplest of all: it is God, and when this has been said, what more can be added?

But, to his intellectual creatures, and especially to us men, the Blessed Trinity is rather an immense cluster of mysteries, one gleam from a single star of which is of absolutely dazzling effulgence to the purblind eyes of man in his present condition. No matter! the mystic enjoys basking in this warm light which he does not see, even as a blind man in the glowing warmth of the sun.

To the unspiritual, the mystery of the most Holy Trinity is simply a matter of faith, and appears only in the light of a speculative truth, having no real bearing upon the inner life of the soul. But in reality the life of every Christian, even if he does not advert to the fact, is all interwoven, so to say, with the very life of God, with the three Divine Persons. The Christian is assumed into the very life of God, and the life of God is actually lived in a special manner in the Christian himself.

Now, the mystic is he who, moved by the grace of God, adverts to these wondrous facts, is made conscious of them, and finds his delight therein. Let us try to understand this.

God, we know by the united testimony of reason and revelation, is His own dwelling place. He is to Himself an inexhaustible fountain of purest bliss, ever flowing within Himself. He is His own life; deep, hidden, never going out of itself for its nourishment; naturally unapproachable, and naturally incommunicable to the creature. God is to Himself all in all. He is that, or He would not be the Absolute Good, He would not be God.

What are the acts of His divine life? What are, so to say, its pulsations? They are these two, to know and to love; but to know and to love what? Evidently His own divine Self. Now, faith tells us that in the very act of God contemplating Himself, there is formed in God an image of Him, living, substantial, perfectly like its original, a second Person, inducing between the two the relation of Father and Son. Further, we are informed that in the act of mutual complacency which cannot fail to spring up between these first two infinitely loveable persons, there is formed in God a Third Person, His Spirit, the substantial love of the Father and of the Son, the Holy Spirit: which completes the circle of the Divine Life and makes it perfect.

If God made a world of angels and men together with this splendid material universe, it is not that they add the tiniest drop to His full measure of bliss in Himself, but simply that He has willed angels and men to share in that bliss which is all His own, to drink with Him eternally and be inebriated, in that limitless Ocean of Absolute Good that is Himself; and by a wonderful privilege, not at all due to the creature, to be made partakers of His own Divine Life. As the three Divine Persons of the Godhead are infinitely involved in the existence of one another, so it seems they have willed that we be also involved in them and they in us. The whole economy of the supernatural order is planned and worked out to this end.

The first step towards carrying out such a design, was for God to make angels and men naturally to His own image and likeness; for thus only could He love us, no object without likeness to Him being worthy of God's complacency. Thus, what God loves in us is what He has put there of His own Divine Self: His image and likeness, our natural capacity to know Him and to love Him, and besides, in the supernatural order, the manifold wondrous gifts of His grace. And in proportion as we allow God to make us, through grace, more and more like Him, and know

Him and love Him more and more, in that same proportion does He also love us and communicate to us more and more His own sanctity and bliss.

Thus, even in our present condition of trial under sin (we being a fallen race) we may begin by faith to know God as He is, that is to say, as one God in Three Divine Persons, and to love Him, though alas! so inadequately; pending the time soon to come, when, if we have been faithful, we shall see Him face to face and love Him at last perfectly, sharing His essential bliss in Himself, without let or hindrance. We may, even now, through prayer and the Sacraments, be brought, under the veil of faith, into intimate relations with each one of the Divine Persons.

The grateful, lively recognition of all these things by the Christian, makes him a mystic. Oh! with what rapture does he then pay distinct and special attention to each of the three Divine Persons: to the Father Who so loved him as to give him His only Son, to the Son Who so loved him as to make Himself his Brother and Redeemer, to the Holy Spirit Who so loves him as to constitute Himself his perpetual Guest, his actual and everlasting possession? Yes, says the mystic, to build me up into the greater likeness of God now, and later on to admit me to His glory, it takes no less than the Three Divine Persons, and moreover my willing co-operation.

Thus consciously to co-operate with God, to work with the Three Divine Persons: to become sensible of God's building one up on, or rather into, His own Divine Essence, is mystical life. Through the operations of Grace God lives in a special manner within us. These operations are the vivid pulsations of His own Divine Life; and through holy contemplation, the mystic becomes an enamored witness of so unspeakable a mystery.

People talk sometimes of the exercise of the presence of God; to a true mystic there is no exercise there. To remember God and live with Him does not cost him an effort. To him, the Most Holy Trinity is the great fact before which all else pales into insignificance. To him, the Blessed Trinity is the great reality, which he meets constantly, which produces and fills and sustains and lights up and beautifies everything, and overflows everywhere infinitely. The mystic sees the whole world as a tiny thing in one ray of the glory of the triune God.

The most Holy Trinity is the Promised Land of mystical life. In this regard, there happens spiritually to the mystic all that happened to the Hebrews when they went out of Egypt. The passage of the Red Sea is a good general confession, which drowns, in the waves of the Blood of Jesus Christ, all the proud army of Pharaoh, chariots and horsemen, vices and mortal sins: all buried, never to rise again! Then one enters into the desert, that is, the world begins to appear quite empty and barren, and life in it no better than an aimless roaming about. Soon, however, one receives the Law of Love on two tables, though still experiencing the mutinies of the flesh—for, whilst the spirit is with God on the Mountain of contemplation, the inferior part murmurs and rebels and has to be sternly rebuked— the ways of Purity and of Illumination. Finally, after a more or less protracted roaming about and moving from camp to camp, one passes the Jordan miraculously and takes possession of the Promised Land of the conscious, felt, relished presence of God: this happens when, through an inestimable special grace of God, one is moved definitely to bid an adieu to all things created, that one may live to God alone.

Then not only does the mystic live to God, but he dwells in God; the Blessed Trinity becomes his dwelling place. To the vivid, conscious faith of that man, the Divine Essence unseen becomes the very place of his abode during the rest of his earthly life.

Now, the Blessed Trinity, in which the mystic thus lives consciously, proves to him sometimes a very Paradise of Delights: that is when he is given to taste how sweet God is; then again, at other times, the Blessed Trinity becomes to him a very Purgatory, that is when the scorching rays of the intolerable sanctity and justice of God are made to shine full upon him, to burn away the rust of his sins and imperfections. Be this as it may, that man does not dwell in himself, nor in the creatures of this world, he dwells in God, the most Holy Trinity, to Whom be glory for ever!

CHAPTER VIII

HOW GOD THE FATHER MAKES HIMSELF THE PRIME-MOVER OF THE MYSTICAL LIFE

NOW we must proceed to consider separately and in detail the special, distinct and active relations which each of the Divine Persons deigns to assume towards the child of grace, the Christian: bearing in mind that mystical life consists in the lively apprehension by the Christian of these relations between God and him, together with an active correspondence on his part to the several distinct operations of the Divine Persons. As we go on, the marvel of our supernatural union with God will at almost every step appear more and more startling.

In this chapter I want to show what special active function God the Father deigns to appropriate to Himself in regard to the Christian, and how the mystic is made to realize it plainly by a sort of inward experimental feeling. It is all summed up in the words of St. John: *Behold what manner of charity the Father hath bestowed upon us, that we should be named, and should be the Sons of God* (1 John 3:1), and in these other words of St. Paul: *For the Spirit Himself giveth testimony to our spirit that we are the sons of God* (Rom. 8:16).

To the unspiritual, God the Father is almost a stranger, seen, as it were, at an immense distance, too far away altogether for much notice; Our Lord seems, of course, a good deal nearer, and perhaps the only Divine Person to Whom he has somehow a direct, immediate relation; whilst the Holy Spirit is really nowhere perceived. How grossly erroneous such a view is will soon appear.

First of all, let us observe that God the Father who is the principle of all *in divinis* (inside the Divine Essence) is thereby also necessarily the principle of all *extra divina* (outside the Divine Essence), whence it follows that He is therefore also the very first principle of our mystical life, the very Prime-Mover of it. Consequently, as one trained in the logic of the Schoolmen will readily admit, God the Father is absolutely the very first object the mystic ought to keep in view, and the one he ought to strain every nerve to attain to, and the one he will certainly attain to in the end. Therefore God the Father, Who is the Prime-Mover, and because He is the prime mover, is also the Last End of our mystical life.

I go to the Father (Jo. 14:12) said Our Lord, speaking of the consummation of his earthly life. "I go to the Father," may the mystic truly say, speaking of the whole process and final consummation of his spiritual life. *Be you therefore perfect as also your heavenly Father is perfect,* Our Lord tells us, as if to say: Understand that the whole gist and purpose of the supernatural order is to bring you to the Father: to make you first, as far as your created capacity admits of, good like Him, holy like Him, nay, even rich like Him in the possession of His Son and His Holy Spirit; pending the time when He will crown all His gifts by giving Himself also to you, making you thereby even happy like Him. There you have the perfect circle, the whole evolution of mystical life.

So the Christian, or more strictly, the mystic, is a man who goes to the Father.

But how does he go to the Father, and how does the Father meet him and receive him?

Even as a son!

The mystic goes to the Father even as a son, because God the Father has made him a son, and treats him as such, and will ultimately receive him in heaven as a son. This we must now try to express more fully.

When a man is baptized, what happens?

That man, who a few hours or days, or perhaps years previously, was born of an earthly father and mother, into a fallen race, the great human family, with an ancestral curse or blight upon his soul, with his purely natural faculties not even whole and unimpaired, to a life of many miseries to be followed by death, in this lower natural world—that man is, by virtue of the Sacrament and the operation of the Holy Spirit *(ex aqua et Spiritu sancto,* John 3:5), born again, begotten of God *(ex Deo nati sunt* (John 1:13). He has been cleansed from original sin and, if he be an adult, of all his personal ones; he is now grafted upon the true vine, the natural Son of God, Our Lord Jesus Christ *(Ego vitis, vos palmites* (John 15:5); he is given a share of the divine nature *(divina consortes natura,* 2 Pet. 1:4) filled with the Holy Spirit, assumed into the great family of the Saints *(cives sanctorum et domestici Dei, super addicati super fundamentum Apostolorum et Prophetarum* Eph. 2:19, 20); he is marked in the very substance of his soul with an indelible character of supernatural resemblance, endowed with the new faculties of Faith, Hope and Charity which illumine the darkness of his natural intellect and strengthen the weakness of his natural will; enriched with the infusion of all moral virtues, further enriched through the seven Gifts of the Holy Spirit with a perennial well of special graces springing up in his very soul to refresh it and make it fruitful unto life everlasting *(Fiet in eo fons aqua salientis in vitam aternam* (John 4:14); all these things, in view of his ultimately being granted the essential Beatific Vision, though by strict right it is the exclusive privilege of God alone.

Here is a something altogether new, a new being: he who was before a natural man is now supernaturally changed into a very son of God.

His sonship of God is not as was his sonship from his earthly parents, *in perfectam similitudinem natura,* making him of the same nature: that is impossible, from the fact of his being a creature, and therefore finite, and therefore incapable of the full communication of the Divine likeness. Nor is he made a son of God as the Divine Word, by a natural, substantial and necessary process; no, his sonship is by way of adoption, accidental and gratuitous *(voluntarie genuit nos,* Jas. 1:18), and therefore infinitely inferior to the sonship of the Divine Word. Yet, even when these limitations have been duly affirmed, our state appears all magnificent and a true participation of the sonship of the second Person of the Blessed Trinity. St. Augustine (in Ps. 26, Enarr. 2,2) distinctly says that we are "divinely associated to the mystery of the eternal generation." God the Father, eternal and natural Father of Our Lord Jesus Christ, adopts also the Christian as his own very son, makes him also heir to His Kingdom, really and truly co-heir with His natural, Divine Son, even as though that man had been born of His own Divine Substance, and had had the same natural rights as His Son consubstantial with Him.

Once the child is born, he must grow and wax strong and become a man, and do man's work. For this purpose he must be fed, which care naturally devolves upon the parent. We know in what a tender, touching way that is done in nature, whilst the child is yet little; the mother giving the breast to her little one and letting him draw his nourishment from her own substance. Then as he grows and waxes strong, he is weaned from the breast, and other nourishment proper to his age is given him: bread and meat from the inexhaustible store of kindly nature, so that in time he may be relied upon to do a man's work.

In the order of grace, it is God the Father Who takes upon Himself to attend to the feeding of the Christian, according to the stage of iris spiritual growth. He says (in Is. 66:12), *You shall be carried at the breasts and upon the knees they shall caress you.* And (in Ps. 80:11): *I am the Lord Thy God, Who brought thee out of the land op Egypt, open thy mouth wide and I will fill it.* The mystic, that fledgling of Divine love, does open his mouth wide, shows himself insatiable of God, crying incessantly for more food, and the Heavenly Father, as a loving Pelican, fills him constantly with more and more from his Divine life and substance.

For we must observe here that, though the Christian, when made son of God, is not born of the Divine Substance (this being the exclusive privilege of the Only natural Son, the Word of God) he is nevertheless fed with the Divine Substance.

We are commanded to pray thus: *Our Father . . . give us this day our super substantial bread.* (Mat. 6:11) The Christian calls for a kind of food which God the Father is to draw from His own Divine substance, for a bread made from the kneading together of these two elements: His own Divine Word, and His own Substantial Love; and in answer to the prayer, God the Father, by a marvellous secret operation, begets his Divine Son in that man, and through His Divine Son, produces in that man, by a special presence of love, His Holy Spirit also.[1] That man will therefore be able to do the work of a Christian, and show himself a worthy son of God the Father.

It is now plain that the whole supernatural life consists in receiving from the Father and in duly giving back to the Father. Receiving what? His Divine Son and His Holy Spirit. And giving back to Him what? A son, another Jesus, our very self made one with the Son, and actuated by the Holy Spirit. *For, whosoever are led by the Spirit of God, they are the sons of God* (Rom. 8:14). *That you may be the children of your Father who is in heaven,* says Our Lord, when He enjoins upon us the most heroic acts of charity in the love of our enemies; acts which cannot be performed by man except with the powerful help of the gifts of the Holy Spirit.

Now, perhaps, we begin to perceive something of what passes between the mystic and God the Father. Marvellous to relate, the Heavenly Father, on His part, brings into the life lived in common with the child of His love, the Christian, all that is His own, namely His very Self, Who is the Well-Spring of the Godhead, and His Divine Son, and His Holy Spirit; keeping nothing back; only it is all under the veil of faith, as man, in his present condition, would be unable to bear to see the splendor of God thus investing him. And the mystic on his part brings into this life, lived in common with the Heavenly Father, his whole self. It is little enough; and who is more keenly alive to that fact than the mystic himself? But it is all he has. His whole self, body and soul and faculties high and low: the whole tree, root and branch, with all its actual production of fruits, and possibilities and promises for the future. God the Father, natural Father of the second Person of the Blessed Trinity, constitutes Himself by an act of His Will, Father also of the Christian, impressing on the substance of his soul a special sign of supernatural resemblance,

---

[1] It is not a question here, as is obvious, of the Holy Eucharist; we shall come to that in due course; but it may be as well to note here that each of the three Divine Persons has His own way of contributing to the growth of the child of grace. I am in this chapter stating the way of God the Father.

actively begetting him to the Divine Life; and the Christian, on his part, when he is a mystic, actually, actively, consciously and constantly takes God the Father for his own Father, and endeavors to reproduce and to prolong in his whole life and in all his acts the very Sonship of the Divine Word, to Whom he is so lovingly associated.

For, there is this remarkable thing about it all, that whereas the son of a man cannot increase his sonship, any more than he could have chosen his earthly father, the child of grace, on the contrary, can always and freely choose God for his Father, and it is in his power at every moment effectually to increase his sonship.

Now, the mystic does this, all the time, more and more, and with what delight! But is it really the mystic who does it? Is it not rather God the Father Who operates in him the *velle et perficere* of his sonship? Truth to tell, it is both together, God and the mystic, by their joint action.

And whereas, through natural generation man receives from his parents only a life like theirs, but not their own; a life numerically distinct from theirs, separate and independent: the Christian through his supernatural generation receives a life which is not distinct, nor separated from, nor independent of, the Divine life as it is lived in the heavenly Father; it is identical with the Divine life, numerically one with it; it is that self-same Divine life, as much as the narrow limits of man's being and the play of his free will, allow it to make irruption into him.

During his earthly pilgrimage, then, the mystic endeavors to reproduce in himself as much as possible to so limited a being the sanctity, goodness, love and all perfection of the Heavenly Father, even as does the Divine Word in Him, even as did in His earthly life the Word made Man, Our Lord Jesus Christ. So his delight, his very food, is to do his Father's will. As a loving, dutiful son, he works diligently at the part of his Father's vineyard assigned to him by his state of life, and by the providential course of events. *I must be about the things that are my Father's,* he constantly says to himself, and to those around him, and, for that matter, to the whole world. On the other hand, day by day, God the Father transforms the mystic gradually into the likeness of His Divine Son; more and more He takes possession, by the agency of the Holy Spirit, of all the faculties of that man, to make him perform wonderful acts of edification in the Church, and produce as a branch of the true Vine, fruits worthy of eternal life; and ever *He will purge it forth that it may bring more fruit* (John 15:2).

Such, feebly described, are the mutual relations of God the Father and the mystic.

One last thing to note in this matter is that God the Father, though so loving and generous in His dealing with the mystic, does not as yet give Himself to him as an object of direct, immediate enjoyment. He gives us His divine Son and His Holy Spirit to be enjoyed by us now, under the veil of faith, but He reserves for us the enjoyment of Himself, as the supreme gift in the land of the Blessed. It was no doubt in allusion to this fact that St. Aloysius Gonzaga, in his last illness, wrote, with characteristic insight: "It cannot be long before I go to receive the embraces of the Eternal Father, in whose bosom I hope to find secure and everlasting rest."

CHAPTER IX

THE BEATIFIC VISION THE END OF THE WHOLE SUPERNATURAL ORDER

Si filii, et hœredes.
And if sons, heirs also (Rom. 8:17)

AS the souls of the just, before Christ, were received into Abraham's bosom and dwelt there in the serenity of peace, joyfully looking forward to the coming of Our Lord and their own transference to heaven; so also, in much the same manner, the mystic lives consciously with the Son of God and the Holy Spirit and all the children of God, known and unknown, visible and invisible, in the bosom of the Father, *of whom are all things, and we unto Him* (1 Cor. 8:6). The mystic dwells there contentedly, lovingly and consciously, though still in the darkness of his present condition, awaiting the coming of the Bridegroom, and the lifting up of the veil, and the grand revelation of the Father. *"Lord, show us the Father, and it is enough for us,"* said St. Philip, with more pregnant truth than he was aware.

Now we know that the whole Christian life is ordained to one end, the enjoyment of the Beatific Vision by predestined man. Everything in the economy of Providence is for the furthering of that sublime design of God. The whole supernatural order of grace is for the purpose of making man both worthy and capable of the Beatific Vision. It will therefore enable us the better to understand those means of grace of which we shall later speak at length—Prayer, the Sacraments and all the details of mystical life, as well as the great works of God *ad extra,* Creation, the Missions of the Son and the Holy Spirit, Redemption by the Cross, the mystery of Holy Church—if we take here and now a proper view of the end itself of all, which is none other than the Beatific Vision.

What, then, is the Beatific Vision? In what does it precisely consist? What does it mean, and what does it imply? Let us proceed slowly, cautiously, gradually, and weigh every word in such a difficult, and at the same time, entrancing subject.

The Beatific Vision is the vision of God. But what sort of vision? The vision of God even as He is; the vision of God even as God Himself enjoys it; the vision of God as He granted it to His blessed Angels immediately after their trial. The vision, the vivid perception, the real taking in of the Absolute Good, that is to say, of all beauty, sanctity, loveliness and other infinite perfections as they are in God. *I will show thee all good,* says He to Moses (Exod. 33:19).

It is called Beatific, because God being the Absolute Good, the effect of such a vision is to make absolutely happy, as well as unfailingly good, whosoever enjoys it.

Beatific Vision is the popular appellation.... Now, if we attend chiefly to the manner of it, we should describe it as a sort of direct, immediate vision of God, without any go-between, without anything intervening, whether as an obstacle or as a help. Nothing can help one to see God as He is in Himself. Beatific Vision is not in the soul by way of representation or image as are the things of this world in our senses and imagination and in our intellect; there can be no image of the Infinite. It is a direct intuition of God, hence its other name, "Intuitive Vision."

But it would certainly be more satisfactory to a philosophical mind to call it by a name describing its very nature rather than its manner or its effect: this would be the "Essential Vision," because this expression really tells in what it consists, namely in the perception of God by means of His very essence; or, in other words, in the union of the very essence of God with him who perceives it. Thus we see that the Beatific Vision will be a more intimate and lively process than our vision of the natural world, of scenery, of a person, or of any material object before our eyes; because such a vision of natural objects is made only through an image of these being formed in us, and not through an immediate union of them with us, whilst on the contrary, the Beatific Vision is caused through nothing else but an immediate union of the Divine Essence with the beholder of it. The Beatific Vision, then, will not be a dead thing, merely spectacular and outside us, as the Universe is, and with the distant, unsympathetic coldness of nature; it will be a grand, living, personal fact, throbbing in us as our human heart, taking hold of our whole being, inside and out, knitting itself with every fibre of our soul and body and making us one with God.

It is obvious that God alone has a natural right and aptitude to the Beatific Vision. It is identical with Himself. It is all His own; His property, His personal good, His naturally unalienable and unapproachable privilege, His fenced round and sealed Kingdom of bliss and glory. Neither man, nor highest angel, nor yet any other more exalted being that God might create, could lay claim to the Beatific Vision or be naturally capable of it. The Beatific Vision, as it is in God, as it is experienced by God, is one and the same thing with God Himself, one and the same thing with His very life, with His Divine operations *ad intra,* and the Trinity of His Persons. To speak in a human way, it is consequent upon, or rather concurrently with, the vision or perception of His infinite goodness that God utters His Word: a true, living, perfect, infinite expression of His very self; establishing between Him Who utters His Word and the Word which is uttered, the relations of Father and Son. And as both the Father and the Son have mutually the intuition of their infinite loveliness, they love each other with such a perfect, infinite, essential and substantial love, that it constitutes a Third Person in God, namely, the Holy Spirit; thus completing the cycle of the Divine life, and the fulness of the Beatific Vision as it is in God.

Now, what a stupendous condescension on the part of God to have called His intelligent creatures, the angel first and then man, to share with Him the delights of the Beatific Vision! But, what a tremendous effort (again to speak in a human way) it must have required to raise the creature to a level with God Himself, especially in the case of man after the original fall! None can see God but God Himself; then man must be somehow made God, that is to say, must be raised to a Divine state, constituted into a Divine manner of being; the Divine essence must be infused into him, and so penetrate his whole personality as to make of him in a way a wholly Divine being; he must have the very life of God in him; then he will be capable of the Beatific Vision and have a right to it. A man in the state of grace, a new born infant just baptized, is capable of the Beatific Vision; in the words of St. John: *He hath eternal life abiding in him* (1 John 3:15); that is to say, the very life of God. Thus it will be seen that "supernatural" does not only mean something above the level of created or creatable beings, but SOMETHING ON A LEVEL with God.

The effort has been made on the part of God in the connected works of Creation, Incarnation, Redemption, the institution of the Church and the application through the seven Sacraments of the merits of Jesus Christ to all men of good will. Now, this mighty effort on the part of God calls for a corresponding strenuous effort on the part of man to co-operate with God; and that is made when a man lives the Christian life in its utmost fulness, that is the mystical life as we are trying to describe it here. Christian life, then, is a sort of deification of man, is the making of man into God; and mystical life is, on the part of man, his really acting his God-like part.

Mystical life, by the attention rendered to God present everywhere, and in one's very self, and by the intense, if dim, perception of one's active relations with each of the Three Divine Persons through the efficacy of the Sacraments, and by the laying of oneself more and more open to all the divine influences, and by a contemplation assiduous, keen and pure, of the Divine perfections and the tasting, under the veil of faith, of the Divine sweetness—mystical life, we say, is an apprenticeship to the Beatific Vision. Nothing short of that. Mystical life is a most fitting preparation of man for the Beatific Vision; a training and a raising up of all the faculties to the coming glory, a fusing of all his being into the Being of God; a foreshadowing of the Beatific Vision and a prelude to it.

With the Beatific Vision in prospect, the mystics of all ages and professions have found nothing too arduous, no apostolate too exacting, no martyrdom too cruel, no self-restraint too protracted, no desert or solitude too horrible, no humiliation too great, no service too low or repulsive. In all hardships and tribulations they go about repeating with the Apostle: *I reckon that the sufferings of this present time are not worthy to be compared with the glory to come that shall be revealed in us* (Rom. 8:18).

The mystic bears in mind that the degrees of his Beatific Vision will be according to the degree of charity he has achieved whilst on earth; he considers that time is given him for no other purpose than to work up to his own rank in the grand hierarchy of perfect charity and Divine happiness; and therefore he is very careful not to lose a single moment of time, not to let pass a single opportunity of enlarging his capacity of seeing and loving and enjoying God for evermore. Indeed, the measure of our state of grace when we die will be the measure of our *Lumen Gloriæ* or Light of Glory throughout the blessed Eternity.

Other words of St. Paul in the same Epistle to the Romans are to the point here. He says: *"For the expectation of the creature waits for the revelation of the sons of God"* (Rom. 8:19). It seems as if the whole creation had been taken into the confidence of God and informed of what He had planned for man and was actually in a fever of expectation to see it accomplished. And why, if not because the whole material universe finds its perfection in man, and is raised in him to a share of the glory of supernatural life. Hence, the whole creation will, in a way, be thrilled with joy when man shall be admitted to the Beatific Vision, even as it is said that *the stars with cheerfulness have shined forth to Him that made them* (Baruc. 3:35). It is clear that all this material universe which is without rational knowledge or free-will has been made distinctly with a view to the bringing about of the Beatific Vision in man. It helps him in his ascent to the Beatific Vision. Itself is destined, through him, in some way, to be assumed ultimately into the glory of the Beatific Vision on the day of the General Resurrection and Last Judgement, when sea and land will give up their dead, and then will take place the grand, public, solemn "*revelation of the sons of God*" and a new heaven and a new earth will be inaugurated, Then, indeed, we shall understand the full meaning of the words: *And if sons, heirs also.*

CHAPTER X

THAT THE DIVINE WORD IS THE BRIDEGROOM

ONE of the most magnificent and explicit prophecies of the wonders of Christian life is set forth in Osee, 2:18-20 in these stupendous words: *And in that day I mill espouse thee to me for ever, and I will espouse thee to me in justice and judgement, and in mercy and in commiserations. And I will espouse thee to me in faith, and thou shalt know that I am the Lord.*

But *the thoughts of mortal men are timid* (Wisdom 9:14), and this timidity of the thoughts of men appears especially in regard to this subject of the wedding of the Creator with his rational creature. Men dare not believe in this, the grandest reality of spiritual life. They would fain say to the writer or preacher who proclaims it: "Hold! How dare you say such a thing?" They are of opinion that the comparison of two human lovers in that most amazing relation of Holy Matrimony, as a symbol of our union with God, goes beyond the actual truth and beyond the real thoughts of God, whilst on the contrary, if anything, it falls immeasurably short of expressing the strength and intimacy and tenderness of the mutual relation which God wishes to establish between Himself and the soul.

The *Canticle of Canticles* bears out this truth most vividly, but it does not tell us any more than the above passage of Osee, which of the three Divine Persons it is who speaks in the character of Bridegroom. It needed the fulness of the revelation of the New Testament to make us know that the Bridegroom is the second Person of the Most Holy Trinity; that is, the Word of God. Now, indeed, with the light of the Gospel thrown upon the Canticle of Canticles and kindred passages in the Old Testament, how well even their most mysterious expressions are seen to fit the two natures in Jesus Christ, the events of his life and of his sacred Passion, his Eucharistic Sacrifice and Sacrament, and all his personal dealings with us in the secret mystical life!

Thus, St. John the Baptist calls Him *the Bridegroom* (John 3:29), and compares his own mission of Precursor to that of a *paranumphos,* that friend of the bridegroom whose duty it was to watch at the door of the bridal chamber. Our Lord calls Himself the Bridegroom. To the disciples of John who were finding fault with His own disciples because they did not perform as many fasts as themselves or the Pharisees, He answers: *Can the children of the Bridegroom mourn as long as the Bridegroom is with them? But the days will come when the Bridegroom shall be taken away from them, and then they shall fast* (Matt. 9:15). Again in Matt, 24:44) he says: *Wherefore be you also ready, because what hour you know not, the Son of man will come.* And in chap, 25:1 , *Then shall the kingdom of heaven be like to ten virgins who, taking their lamps, went out to meet the Bridegroom.* In the Apocalypse, where so many marvellous, mysterious things are revealed to us about the Lamb, He is given, not expressly but by the most natural of implications, His title of Bridegroom (Apoc. 21 and 22). It is a page of surpassing beauty. *And I, John, saw the holy city, the new Jerusalem, coming down from God out of heaven, prepared as a bride adorned for her husband. . . . And there came one of the seven angels, and spoke with me, saying: Come, and I will show thee the bride, the wife of the Lamb. . . . And the Lord God of the spirits of the prophets, sent his angel to show his servants the things that must be done shortly, and* (he said): *Behold I come quickly. And the spirit and the bride say, Come; and he that heareth, let him say Come. ... He that giveth testimony of these things saith: Surely I come quickly; Amen! Come, Lord Jesus!*

Truth to tell, the Second Person of the Blessed Trinity sustains towards the Christian what may seem at first sight a bewildering multiplicity of relations. The Word of God has made Himself our blood relation, our true brother, by assuming our human nature. He has made Himself our pattern and our teacher in His life and Gospel doctrine, and our Saviour by dying on the Cross. Then, through Baptism, He has made the Christian His living member, in His mystical body, the Church, of which He is the Head. Furthermore, He makes Himself our very food in Holy Communion, whilst, in the other Sacraments, He anoints and consecrates and sanctifies the Christian's body and soul with His Holy Spirit and the virtue of His own merits, for most special and accurately determined spiritual purposes. In Confirmation, the Son of God makes us His soldiers, and therefore constitutes Himself our captain. In the Sacrament of Penance He heals our wounds, pouring into them His very Blood as a healing remedy. In Holy Orders He communicates His own Priestly office and character to some of the brethren. In Matrimony He makes the human husband and wife to be the very image of Himself in His loving relation to the Church. Finally in Extreme Unction and Holy Viaticum He constitutes Himself the helper and the conqueror of the soul in its supreme struggle at the hour of death.

Now, we must understand that all these personal favors, lavished upon us by the Son of God, are nothing else than His espousing of us unto himself for time and eternity. All the other titles and offices which the Word of God made Man assumes in relation to us, are finally resolved into the one great title, our Heavenly Bridegroom. He is our King, our Shepherd, our Way, our good Samaritan, our Light, our Resurrection and Life; New Adam, Lord, the Lamb that was slain, the Lion of the tribe of Judah, the Conqueror that came to conquer, the Vine, the Wine-presser, our Propitiation, our Advocate, our Reconciliation, our Peace, our Joy, our Reward, the Corner Stone and very Foundation of all the order of things natural and supernatural; the Alpha and Omega of the world's history, as well as of every individual soul's history; our Companion on the way, in the pilgrimage of life; the Morning Star, the Living Bread, the Sun, the Fountain, a Giant, a Friend, a Witness, High Priest, Altar and Victim, Bishop of our souls, Father of the world to come, Pontiff of the future bliss; Judge of the Living and the Dead; the eternal Reward of the good, and the eternal Torment of the wicked; He is all this, and yet it is all comprised in this one, exclusive relation of Himself with us, namely, that He is our Heavenly

Bridegroom.

His most precious Humanity in all its mysteries from His Incarnation to His death on the Cross, and from that to His last coming for Judgement; and in all its states, especially that of His Eucharistic Presence; His whole sacred Humanity, I say, is in a manner the Sacrament, the sign, the sensible token and the very means of our bridal union; but it is truly the Godhead of the Word, the eternal, infinite, glorious Son of God, Who is the Bridegroom; whilst man, without distinction of sex, for here *caro non prodest quidquam: the flesh profits nothing* (John 6:64), man who by himself is a weak and barren nature in regard to things heavenly, man is the bride of that divine marriage, which is not of the flesh but of the spirit; man is the bride of that formidable Lover, the eternal Son of God! A very, disproportionate union indeed, but one wherein an ineffable love fills the gap and levels the highest to the lowest, and raises our nothingness to a share in His very sanctity and beauty and capacity for reciprocal love and eternal, divine life.

Our relation of sons to the heavenly Father, full of divine sweetness as it is, is not unmixed with awe: we cannot allow ourselves to forget the infinite distance that separates our puny selves from the overwhelming majesty and sanctity of God. But with God the Son made Man, our relations are entirely made up of sweetness, if only we look at them in their true light. There is, or there ought to be, no feeling of awe between brother and brother, still less between the members of the body and their head, still less, if possible, between the bride and her bridegroom. There ought to be between them only feelings of the most strong and tender and delicate mutual love. But in order to enter fully into such feelings, one must needs be very watchful over one's sacred relations with the Son of God; one must needs be a mystic.

The Bridegroom is the Word of God: need we, then, insist on this particular and proper aspect of our marriage with Him, namely, that it is wholly spiritual and of the spirit? Whatever, therefore, is boldly borrowed in the Canticle of Canticles and other parts of Holy Writ from the demonstrations of love as between a human bride and her human spouse, is to be interpreted wholly in a spiritual sense. He has already espoused to Himself the higher rational creatures, the blessed Angels, and He is now bent upon espousing all men of good will. And it is the office of mystical life to make us attentive to that espousing of our soul by the Son of God, and to excite us to render, even now, whilst yet on earth, love for love, to this our Heavenly Bridegroom.

The wedding is begun on earth, to be consummated in heaven. It is during the present life that the two lovers, the Son of God and the Christian, plight their faith to one another, and the Bridegroom begins even now to take and to give kisses of love in the passing visits of Holy Communion. Holy Communion is not only the feeding of the child of God, the Christian; it is especially an act of his wedded life with Christ. It is on the part of the Son of God a taking possession of the body and soul of his little bride and a giving to her of her marital rights over Himself *They two will be in one flesh* has been said of the husband and wife according to nature: at Holy Communion we are made one with Christ, so marvelously, so far beyond what poor human marriage can ever dream of! The Divine Bridegroom has placed his infinite power at the service of his love, so that we can say with absolute truth the words of the Canticle of Canticles: *My Beloved, to me and I to Him, who feeds among the lilies* (Cant, 11:16). It is true the little bride cannot as yet see the face of her Beloved, nor feel his embrace all the time, though he is all the time near her in the Blessed Sacrament; she cannot at present see the Son of God in his majesty and loveliness and call him "Husband" before all the Angels and Saints and the Heavenly Father; these things are not for our present condition of mortality: they are the privilege of the coming eternity. Patience! patience! *Till the day breaks and the shadows retire* (Cant, 2:17).

In the meanwhile, if we cannot enjoy our heavenly Bridegroom to the full extent of our desire, we must at least be eager to embrace Him as often and as lovingly as we can in Holy Communion, under the veil of faith and of the sacred species; and we must employ the time of our exile in making ourselves more and more worthy of Him. Does not a king's bride try to adorn herself for him who will soon come and claim her for his wedded wife before all his court? Now, that is precisely the work of the mystic life, thus to adorn the soul, to enlarge her capacity of loving God more and more, to exercise her beforehand in the good manners of the court of heaven, where she is so soon to appear as the bride and wedded wife of the King.

I Jesus, have sent my angel, to testify to you these things in the churches. I am the root and stock of David, the bright and morning star. And the Spirit and the Bride say: Come. And he that heareth, let him say: Come. And he that thirsts, let him come: and he that will, let him take the water of life, gratis (Apoc. 22:16-17).

CHAPTER XI

THE PART SUSTAINED BY THE SACRED HUMANITY IN OUR MYSTICAL LIFE

THE mystic may be considered under two aspects: that of a mere individual, and that of the member of a society. All we have said up to this, refers to man considered as an individual. Now, we cannot continue to view him only as such. We cannot go on looking solely at the relations of each of the Divine Persons with the mystic as an individual. The Christian is not isolated any more in his spiritual than in his physical life. He is a member of a society of which Jesus Christ is the Head; he is one particular stone out of a structure of which Jesus Christ is the very foundation; he is a branch of a tree of which Jesus Christ is the stem. And through Jesus Christ to Whom he is united, the Christian finds himself united also to all those who cling to Jesus Christ. *So we being many, are one body in Christ, and each one members one of another* (Rom. 12:5).

For, not only has the Son of God assumed to Himself, when He came into our world, a human body, which is His own, and which, together with His human Soul, constitutes the Sacred Humanity; but He is moreover, assuming another body, a collective, a mystical one, of which all Christians are members; another body which clings to the physical body of Christ, which is made one with it, and thereby made one also with the Divine Person of the Son of God. In other words: the mystery of the Incarnation, after having taken place in the Sacred Humanity of Our Lord, is, by the very virtue of the Flesh and Blood of Jesus, extended, in a way, to all Christians.

A Christian is, together with all his brethren, an offshoot of the Incarnation, a branch of the mighty tree which has sprung from the open side of Jesus dead on the Cross, he is one of the multitudinous grains of wheat which owe their origin to the death and burial of the Saviour: *Amen I say to you, unless the grain of wheat fall into the ground and die, itself remaineth alone; but if it die, it brings forth much fruit.* (John 12:24-25)

This important truth gives us a deeper insight into the mysteries of the mystical life. The Bridegroom of the Christian soul, as we have seen in the foregoing chapter, is the Word of God, the Son of God, the second Person of the Blessed Trinity. Therefore, the Sacred Humanity of Our Lord, as distinct from His Divine nature, is not the Bridegroom; nay, it is the very first Bride which the Word of God espoused, and it is from this marriage of the Word of God with the Sacred Humanity which was consummated by the mystery of the Incarnation that we are born. *Ex Deo nati sunt,* says St. John (1:13).

This is to be understood not only of the redeemed, that is to say, of mere men, but also of the blessed Angels who needed no redemption, and also of the Queen of Angels and men, the Blessed Virgin, who was to be the very Mother of Jesus according to the flesh only after the course of many centuries, but who in the great plan of God, and by the foreseen merits of her Divine Son, was the true *primogenita,* the first fruit of the Divine Marriage. *The Lord possessed me in the beginning of His ways. ... I was set up from eternity. ... Before the hills I was brought forth* (Prov. 8:22, 23, 25).

The Bull of Pius IX, proclaiming the dogma of the Immaculate Conception, applies these words of Holy Writ to Mary, and asserts that not only was she redeemed *excellentiori modo*[2] before the fall of Adam and Eve, but that she was conceived in the mind of God, and born to an unapproachable height of sanctity, before even the dawn of creation, before the creation and probation of the Nine Choirs of Angels.

We come here upon mysteries which baffle ordinary speech and the narrow concepts of the human mind, as they transcend the common sequence of things purely natural. We must bear in mind that the great Operator of these mysteries is God, the absolute Lord of all, who is infinitely above time, space and all

---

[2] In a more excellent mode, —Editor.

conditions of created beings. From this transcendental point of view, we shall have no difficulty in realizing that, in the plan of God, though not in the order of execution: first, the Sacred Humanity is the first Bride of the Son of God; secondly, the Blessed Virgin Man', the first fruit of the Divine marriage, is the second bride of the Son of God; thirdly, only after Holy Mary, and in strict subordination both to the Sacred Humanity and to Mary, all the blessed Angelic natures are also the brides of the Son of God. Fourthly, all the members of the human race, from Adam down to the last man created, all men, as they come in their millions, generation after generation, may become brides of the Son of God; all are desired, nay, commanded, so to become.

The Christian, of either sex, becomes the Eve of this new Adam, the Son of God made Man: first formed out of His side when He was in the deep sleep of death on the Cross, the fruit of His merits.

Bone of His bone and flesh of His flesh (Gen. 2"22), presented to Him by His Father as a bride, for the love of whom He left His house of glory, and whom He will cherish with the most tender and delicate affection.

The case of the blessed Angels is somewhat different from that of man, in that they needed no redemption. It is true that when St. John tells us that *gratia . . . per Jesum Christum facta est* (John 1:17), we must understand that the whole order of grace, as well for Angels as for men, is founded on Our Lord Jesus Christ; on His Sacred Humanity; that is to say, on the anticipated merits of the Incarnate Son of God. The first grace of the Angels, that of their creation in a supernatural state of knowledge and love of God, was absolutely gratuitous, so far as the Angels themselves were concerned, but it was not quite so on the part of God, as the giver of that grace. With God, the first grace of the Angels was paid for. By whom? By the Son of God. With what? With the anticipated merits of His Incarnation. With the same coin was also bought and paid for the grace of final perseverance for all the Angels, so that they could all have attained to glory if they had wished to. At this point they were called upon, each one individually, to do their own part in accepting the grace that was offered them, and in co-operating with it. It was left to them to do this or not; they were free, so as to have the merit or the full responsibility of their own act with all its momentous consequences.

The greater part of the Angels chose to adhere to God, to make themselves one with the Son of God, by appropriating to themselves the supernatural merits of His Incarnation, and thereby deserving to become His wedded brides for ever. The others freely chose to keep aloof from the loving advances of God. They refused the grace of final perseverance and even put off the first grace with which they had been invested. They were not pleased with the supernatural order as it was revealed to them. They were so much in love with their natural excellence and priority, that they preferred to forego the supernatural gifts of grace and glory rather than lose their first rank, and acknowledge the Sovereignty of the Sacred Humanity of Our Lord, and the superiority of His blessed Mother and some of the greatest Saints. Thus, through pride, they became the first renegades from the love of God, banishing themselves from His Kingdom and plunging themselves headlong into eternal ruin.

Thus it appears that all who are or ever shall be raised to the supernatural state of grace or glory, be they angels or be they men, owe this to the Sacred Humanity of Our Lord. The blessed Angels are not only the servants of the Incarnation, but its debtors as well: they owe everything to it, they are linked to this mystery from the very beginning of their existence; nay, from all eternity, in the mind of God, they are involved in its scheme.

One more very remarkable consequence of the mystery of this union is that, as the Blessed Angels are united among themselves, and to the Son of God, and to the Blessed Trinity, through the Sacred Humanity of Our Lord, so also are we on earth already united to the blessed Angels and made one Church with them, through the same Sacred Humanity of Our Lord Jesus Christ.

St. Thomas assigns to the Sacred Humanity of Our Lord its proper place, function and dignity when he calls it "Instrumentum conjunctum Divinitatis," something not in itself the principal, but subordinate to a higher thing; an instrument, merely an instrument, but such an instrument as has been made one with Him who is using it; an instrument as personally united to the Son of God, as my hand or my arm is united to the rest of my physical being, or as my body is united to my soul and is its instrument for the purposes of physical life. An instrument which has the virtue of uniting all the members of the mystical body of Christ, wherever they be and of whatsoever nature, and of uniting them to the Word of God and to the most Holy Trinity. Thus are we made partakers of the Divine Sonship and of the Divine life either of grace here below, or of glory in heaven.

Thus, therefore, there is a wonderful element intervening in the spiritual marriage of the intellectual creature with the Son of God, there is His Sacred Humanity. Whether Angels or men, all have to be incorporated into Him. His flesh and His blood, which He took from the Blessed Virgin Mary's womb, together with His Human Soul, these are the "cords of Adam" with which, centuries before His advent on earth, He predicted that He would draw us and bind us to Himself. *In funiculis Adam traham eos, in vinculis charitatis* (Osee. 11:4). And the blessed Angels as well as men are caught up in those created meshes of uncreated love.

The mystic revels in the contemplation of these mysteries. He is filled with unspeakable joy at seeing himself an integral part of that marvellous world of grace and glory, and already in full communion with all its denizens, through Our Lord Jesus Christ, to Whom be glory for ever!

CHAPTER XII

HOW JESUS CRUCIFIED DRAWS ALL THINGS TO HIMSELF

Agnus in crucis levatur
Immolandus stipite,
Mite corpus perforatur,
Sanguis, unda profluit,
Terra, mundus, astra, pontus
Quo lavantur flumine.[3]

—*Pange Lingua*
Claudian Mamertus.

THIS most important section on the mystery of the Cross in relation to mystical life, for the sake of clearness, may be divided into three parts. In the first I strive to show the action of Jesus Crucified upon the world at large. In the second part I try to show the direct action of Jesus Crucified upon each individual soul. In the third part I call attention to some important conclusions which follow from this doctrine.

In the two preceding chapters we have been at pains to show that the special function assumed by the Second Person of the Blessed Trinity towards the mystic is that of Bridegroom, and that He unites us to His Divinity through His Humanity. Now, the last touch to this entrancing doctrine will be given, when we

---

[3] As a lamb upon the altar of the Cross,
for us is slain.
Lo with gall his thirst He quenches!
See the thorns upon His brow!
Nails his tender flesh are rending!
See His side is opened now!
Whence to cleanse the whole creation,
Streams of blood and water flow.

are made to perceive that it is in His Passion and Death, and not otherwise, that Our Lord consummates this union of ourselves with Him for ever.

In other words, we have to realize that our Bridegroom is the Second Person of the most Holy Trinity, not simply as such, nor simply as Jesus, that is to say, as the Word made Flesh, but as JESUS CRUCIFIED. Our Bridegroom is the Lamb of God that has been slain for our sins. He is eternally the Victim and the Priest of His own sacrifice, and He comes into our life for no other purpose than to make of each of us an oblation of sweet odor to the Father with Himself, and He makes of all the Christians together "*a holy nation*" of which He is the High Priest for evermore (1 Pet. 2:9).

It has pleased God to build the whole structure of the supernatural order upon the mystery of the Cross, upon that *Verbum crucis* of which St. Paul, the great exponent of this doctrine, speaks in his first Epistle to the Corinthians (1:18), just as it has pleased God to build the whole edifice of the natural order in direct reference to the Sacred Humanity of Our Lord. Starting from the lowest forms of created existence and life, each successive species or series of species in concentric circles is a distinct step towards the final realization of *The Son of Man.* In just the same way, Jesus Crucified is the center of absolutely all the works of God *ad extra.* The sacred Blood of Jesus tinges everything—men, the whole material universe, and even the angelic natures. Several, remarkable passages of Holy Scriptures bear us out in this assertion.

In Ezechiel (c.. 47) we see the prophet, in a vision, led by an angel to the gate of the Temple of Jerusalem, *and behold waters issued out from under the threshold. . . coming down to the right side of the temple, to the south part of the Altar, and* (the angel) *measured a thousand cubits, and he brought me through the waters up to the ankles. And again he measured a thousand, and he brought me through the waters up to the knees. And he measured a thousand and he brought me through the waters up to the loins. And he measured a thousand and it was a torrent which I could not pass over: for the waters were risen so as to make a deep torrent which could not be passed over. . . And behold on the banks of the torrent were very many trees on both sides, and he said to me: These waters that issue forth towards the hillocks of sand to the east and go down to the plains of the desert, shall go into the sea and shall go out, and the waters shall be healed. And every living creature that creeps whithersoever the torrent shall come, shall live; and there shall be fishes in abundance after these waters shall come thither, and they shall be healed, and all things shall live to which the torrent shall come. And the fishermen shall stand over these waters.. . From Engaddi even to Engallim there shall be drying of nets. . . But on the shore thereof and in the fenny places they shall not be healed, because they shall be turned into salt-pits. And by the torrent on the banks thereof, on both sides shall grow all trees that bear fruit; their leaf shall not fall off and their fruit shall not fail; every month shall they bring forth first fruits, because the fruits thereof shall be for food, and the leaves thereof for medicine.* We know by the interpretation of Holy Church, that the spiritual meaning of this prophecy is about the far reaching and all embracing effects of the death of Our Lord on the Cross. The temple is the Body of Christ stretched on the Cross, at once a Temple, an Altar and a Victim of sacrifice. The torrent represents the flood of grace that issued forth from the pierced side of our Lord, together with the water and Blood, and which grows wider and deeper as century succeeds century. The sea is the broad expanse of all nature. The fishermen are the members of the Ecclesiastical Hierarchy. The fishes and creeping things are the souls of the just and sinners that will be saved. Engaddi and Engallim represent the whole earth from sunrise to sunset, or again the whole order of centuries to the very end of time. Those that are not healed but turned into salt-pits, barren of all vegetation and life, are the reprobates who would not avail themselves of this plentiful redemption. Finally, the trees whose leaf shall not fall off and which every month shall yield choice fruit, are a symbol of the glory and bliss in store for us in heaven: thus showing that all the order of grace and glory is a direct, immediate outcome of the mystery of the Cross.

Striking as the above prophecy is, it is not more pregnant

with meaning than the brief statement of Our Lord Himself: "*And I, if I be lifted up from the earth, will draw all things to Myself*" (John 12:32). I will draw all things to Myself, that is, I will gather together and link to Myself on the Cross all the threads of past, present and future events. I will make of My immolation on the Cross the great central fact of all times, far exceeding the requirements for the mere redemption of fallen mankind, embracing in the mighty scheme the angels, not only the blessed ones, but also the fallen and the reprobate souls, reaching out even from eternity unto eternity. Indeed, what other meaning are we to attribute to words like these of St. Paul: *It hath well pleased* (the Father) . . . *through him ... to reconcile all things unto Himself y making peace through the Blood of His Cross, both as to the things that are on earth, and the things that are in heaven* (Col. 1:19, 20); or again: "*God, indeed, was in Christ, reconciling the world to Himself*(2 Cor. 5:19). He does not say "the world of men" only, but simply the world, the whole world, the lower one and as well that of the angels, "of the things that are in heaven." Why did the world, the whole world, need to be reconciled? Because sin had made it hateful to God.

In the light of such passages, in their almost blinding refulgence, one may be justified in assuming that, had it not been for the foreknown atonement of the Son of God by His death on the Cross, God would not have created the world, with the perspective of sin as a corollary to the necessary gift of free will in the intellectual creature. God could not permit His work to be permanently marred by sin; rather than that He would never have made the world. But now the act of obedience of His Divine Son unto death and unto the death of the Cross atoned superabundantly, first for the disobedience of the fallen angels and their perpetual state of rebellion as well as that of the reprobate souls that were to come afterwards, then for the original sin of Adam and Eve, finally for all the actual sins of men until the very end of the world. At the same time, Our Lord unites to His supreme act of obedience by His death on the Cross all the virtuous acts of His elect, both men and angels, either *in via* or *in patria,* those performed before as well as those performed after the time of His earthly life, making them all a victim of sweet odor to God with Himself, or rather, as St. Paul would express it, *in Himself,* for ever. In such a way does Our Lord fulfil His own prophecy: *And I, if I be lifted up from the earth, will draw all things to myself* (John 12:32).

Not to swell this chapter to undue proportions, I will content myself with referring the reader to the celebrated passage of St. Paul (Coloss, 1:12-20), and again (Philipp, 11:5-11), and kindred passages, and especially to the whole epistle to the Hebrews, all of which go to show that the mystery of the Cross reaches out infinitely beyond the mere redemption of men. I cannot, however, in this connection refrain from quoting a page of the Apocalypse which is of surpassing beauty and of transparent significance: In Chapter five St. John is favored with a vision of God seated on His throne in Heaven and holding in His right hand a book written within and without, sealed with seven seals, and a strong angel cries out with a loud voice: Who is worthy to open the book and to loose the seals thereof? And as no man was able to open the book nor even to look on it, John wept bitterly. Then, one of the ancients said to him: *Weep not, behold the lion of the tribe of Judah, the root of David hath prevailed to open the book and to loose the seven seals thereof.* He proceeds then in these words: "*And I saw, and behold in the midst of the throne and of the four living creatures, and in the midst of the ancients a* LAMB STANDING AS IT WERE SLAIN, *and he came and took the book out of the right hand of him that sat on the throne; and when he had opened the book the four living creatures and the four and twenty ancients fell down before the Lamb, having every one of them harps and golden vials full of odours, which are the prayers of the saints, and they sang a new canticle, saying: Thou art worthy, O Lord, to take the book and to open the seals thereof, because thou were slain and hast redeemed us to God in thy blood out of every tribe, and tongue, and people, and nation, and hast made us to our God a kingdom and priests, and we shall reign on the earth. And I saw and I heard the voice of many angels round about the throne . . . thousands of thousands, saying with a loud voice: Worthy is the Lamb that was slain to receive power, and divinity, and wisdom, and strength, and honor, and glory, and benediction. And every creature which is in heaven and on the earth and render the earth, and such as are in the sea, and all that are therein, I heard all saying: To him that sits upon the throne, and to the Lamb, benediction, and honor, and glory, and power for ever and ever; and the four living creatures said: "Amen! And the four and twenty ancients fell down on their faces, and adored him that lives for ever and ever."*

It would be difficult, in my humble opinion, more emphatically to give us to understand that all the mysteries of the works of God *ad extra,* gravitate around the central one of the Cross; and that, though the occasion of it was merely the fall of man and his redemption, yet, at the same time, the death of the Lamb of God consummates, and gives the final reason of, all God's dealings with men and angels and the material universe in time and eternity.

CHAPTER XIII

HOW JESUS CRUCIFIED ACTS UPON EACH INDIVIDUAL SOUL

Verbum crucis iis qui salvi fiunt Dei virtus est. The word of the cross ... to them who are saved . .. is the power of God (1 Cor. 1:18).

TWO distinct actions of Our Lord are to be considered in the economy of Redemption:

First, the paying, by Our Lord, into the hands of God the Father, for all men *in globo,* nay, for all the world of angels and men, as well of the reprobate as of those that shall ever be saved. This we have seen in the preceding chapter.

Secondly, the personal application, by Our Lord Himself, of His plentiful Redemption, separately and individually, to each soul of good will, in particular. It is this which we are now to consider.

How does Our Lord find the means of coming to each one of us individually, to act upon each one of us individually, to unite each one of us, individually, to Himself, as the Lamb of God that was slain on the Cross? In other words, how are we made one with Jesus Crucified? How is such a thing made possible?

The difficulty lies in the fact of Our Lord Jesus Christ being Man. How can that Man, Jesus Christ, *homo Christus Jesus,* Who is now in heaven, be able at the same time, to act upon all men and upon each man individually, in a direct, personal, immediate manner? Furthermore, how can He place us in actual, vivid contact with His sufferings and death on the Cross, which took place so many hundred years ago? Theologians answer that it is the hypostatic presence of the Godhead in the Body and Soul of Christ, which elevates the powers of Christ's humanity, natural and supernatural, to the point of being able to act upon all men and upon every one of them individually, in a direct, personal, immediate manner. It is not a figure of rhetoric to speak of our union with Christ, of a soul's dwelling in His wounds. It is the enunciation of an actual fact.

But (it may be objected) Jesus is not suffering and dying at this present moment, how can we be united with Him crucified? Is not this a sort of pious, hyperbolical expression? No, not in the least; it is the expression of as great a reality as any that can be thought of. Here again, Theologians come to our help, and inform us that the divine personality of Our Lord lifts His Sacred Humanity out of the narrow limitations, not only of space, but of time as well. Jesus, when He was dying on the Cross, because He is a Divine Person, to Whom there is no distinction of past, present or future, to Whom all is an eternal present, was able, even as man, to seize and act upon everything and everyone, distinctly, separately and for his own sake, either before or after the actual taking place of His immolation, at any distance of time, and in any possible number because no created number of persons or things can exhaust the possibilities of a Divine Person. Thus it is that every individual man can really, through faith and the Sacraments, put himself in touch directly and personally with his Saviour dying on the Cross, and receive straight from His wounded side the water and Blood of his redemption.

This doctrine of an actual, immediate contact with Jesus Crucified because Jesus is a Divine Person, may well appear difficult to understand, subtle and metaphysical, for, truth to tell, so it is indeed. Not even all the genius of an Angelic Doctor could make it less difficult for the human mind to grasp. Few Christians have been able to express it satisfactorily, but, this notwithstanding, they all have a sort of instinctive or intuitive perception of it. Not only the great canonized Saints or learned Doctors of Theology, but many a humble follower of Christ, in the most lowly walks and conditions of life, finds it no difficulty to live and die with his Saviour Crucified, as though He were still on the Cross. The *Christo confixus sum cruci: With Christ I am nailed* to *the cross* (Gal. 2:19) of St. Paul has a startling reality and actualness for them as well. They are by their faith and through the efficacy of the Sacraments made contemporaries of the

Passion of Christ and actual sharers in it. These, one will perhaps say, are mystics. Very true; but then our contention is that every Christian is called upon thus to be a mystic, and finds precisely in the treasure of his faith and of the Sacraments the means of being so.

Our Lord has found a way of bringing home to us this great truth of our union with Him crucified; I mean the Holy Sacrifice of the Mass with the Sacrament of the Holy Eucharist, whereby he who so wills may actually eat the flesh of the Lamb of God Who was slain on the Cross, and drink the blood of our Redemption. *The Lord Jesus, the night in which He was betrayed, took bread and, giving thanks, broke and said: Take ye and eat; this is My Body, which shall be delivered for you: do this for the commemoration of Me. In like manner also the chalice, after He had supped, saying: This chalice is the New Testament in My Blood; this do ye, as often as you shall drink* it, *for the commemoration of Me. For, as often as you shall eat this bread and drink the chalice you shall show the death of the Lord until He come* (1 Cor. 11:23-26).

Now, is not this marvellous? There is made at Holy Communion a personal application of the Body of Christ crucified to the mouth of the individual communicant, even we may say, as of the mother's breast to the mouth of her babe. Nay, this comparison of the mother with her infant does not cover our whole meaning; for with us there takes place, moreover, a transfusion of the whole Body and Blood of the Lamb of God into the communicant, through his open mouth, whilst the mother gives but a few drops of her milk. See there Jesus coming to you and acting upon you as the Victim of the Sacrifice of the Cross. If you eat His Flesh and drink His Blood you shall have life "*in Him*"; you will thus be in direct, immediate and lively contact with the mystery of your Redemption. He comes to you in Holy Communion both as Bridegroom and as Lamb of God, to embrace your soul, and He desires you thus to welcome Him and embrace Him.

The Royal Prophet seems to have had a glimpse of these ineffable divine realities, when in Ps. 2:12, of the Hebrew text, he thus speaks: *Kiss the son, lest at any time the Lord be angry, and you perish from the just way.* These words have a close proximity of meaning with those of Our Lord Himself, Who said: *Unless you eat the flesh of the Son of Man and drink His blood, you shall not have life in you* (John 6:54).

The Holy Eucharist is one of the seven Sacraments and the greatest of them, since it is Our Lord's very Person; but it would be a mistake to think that the other Sacraments, in their manifold graces, have any other object in view than that of making us one with Jesus Crucified. Grace, under all its forms, has for its primary object to make the Christian conformable to Jesus Crucified, and one with Him, to make of him *a new creature* in Jesus Crucified. Such is, as proclaimed emphatically by St. Paul, the primary object of all the economy of grace through the sacramental system. *Know you not,* he says to the Romans, *that all we who are baptized in Christ Jesus, are baptized in His death? Our old man is crucified with Him, that the body of sin may be destroyed* (Rom. 6:3, 6), and to the Ephesians: *Now, in Christ Jesus, you who sometime were afar off, are made near by the blood of Christ* (Eph. 2:13). And St. Peter: *Being partakers of the sufferings of Christy that when His glory shall be revealed, you may also be glad with exceeding joy* (1 Pet. 4:13). *He loved me,* says again St. Paul, *and delivered Himself for me* (Gal. 2:20); and every Christian can say the same with as much fulness, and exclusiveness, and actuality of meaning.

It is true, therefore, that through the Sacraments the mystery of Jesus and Him Crucified, enters into the very making of the Christian, and is the whole pervading element, as all the great Doctors of the Middle Ages, St. Anselm, Hugo of St. Victor, the Master of Sentences, St. Bonaventure, St. Thomas, and Duns Scotus have been at pains to show very explicitly and luminously. And these were but the echoes of all the Fathers of the Church who had gone before.

CHAPTER XIV

IMPORTANT CONSEQUENCES OF THIS DOCTRINE OF THE VERBUM CRUCIS

VERY important consequences follow from this doctrine. The history of the Church and the lives of the Saints show that, from time to time there have appeared chosen souls which have received from Our Lord a public mission of special atonement and of vivid representation of His Passion, by miraculous infliction of sufferings and miraculous exterior phenomena, such as the sacred stigmata, wonderful sheddings of blood, etc. To such only does the narrow school of theologians of which we spoke in Chapter I reserve the name of mystics. Now it seems to me, in view of all that we have just stated, that these theologians err grievously.

The true mystical life of the saints does not consist in these exterior phenomena, which may even not come from God, which are at best but extraordinary manifestations of a life of union with our Lord, lying far deeper, where the eye of man cannot fathom. *All the glory of the King's daughter is within* (Ps. 44:14). Mystical life is precisely that hidden, deep, secret intercourse between the holy soul and her Beloved in the sanctuary of the soul, where the Sacraments do their work, where there is no room for deception. Mystics are those who lead this interior life, whether they be favored or not with miraculous manifestations.

The contention of the narrow school of mystics is very mischievous. First it has a tendency to make us lose sight of the fact that all Christians without exception, in all walks of life and in all situations, and in all the details of their daily lives and sufferings, are expected to identify themselves with *Jesus Christ and Him Crucified* (1 Cor. 2:2), and that they are able so to do by faith and the use of their Sacraments. Then it has also a tendency to persuade some silly persons that they are not in actual union with Jesus Crucified unless they do something extraordinary, or unless something miraculous happens to them; which persuasion, as will be readily understood, opens wide the door to all sorts of extravagant desires and spiritual delusions, some of which have come under my own personal observation more than once.

There is yet another consequence to draw from our doctrine of the "VERBUM CRUCIS." It is that, in his turn, the non-mystic, the tepid and negligent Christian also errs grievously, when he looks upon the death of Our Lord, simply as an event which took place nineteen centuries ago, and in which he had no part, except to be somehow benefitted by it; a mighty event, to be sure, but still, for all that, nothing more than a fact of ancient history, with which his personal connection is very remote indeed.

In the eyes of the fervent Christian, on the contrary, in the eyes of the mystic, the death of Our Lord is a never ending reality and actuality, a sacrifice which began on Calvary, which has not ceased, but goes on through time and space, on earth on our Altars, and at the same time on the Altar of Heaven, gathering everything unto itself; and the mystic feels himself caught up in it, and a part of it, now and for ever.

Again, for the non-mystic, perpetual union in life and death with Jesus Crucified is considered as a sort of luxury of the Christian life, a pious excess to which all are not called, whilst in the eyes of the mystic, union and identification with Jesus and Him Crucified is simply the essential condition of being a Christian at all.

A last remark which may help us to realize the mighty scope of the "Verbum crucis" is this. Sinners themselves, in the very act of sinning fall (alas! to their own misfortune), under the spell of the mystery of the Cross as of an event actually taking place, and in which they have a distinct, personal undeniable share: *Crucifying again to themselves the Son of God, and making a mockery of Him* (Heb. 6:6). *Wherefore, whosoever shall eat this bread or drink the chalice of the Lord unworthily, shall be guilty of the body and of the blood of the Lord* (1 Cor. 11:27). *A man making void the law of Moses, dies without any mercy, under two or three witnesses: how much more do you think he deserves worse punishments, who hath trodden underfoot the Son of God and hath esteemed the blood of the Testament unclean, by which he was sanctified?* (Heb. 10:28-29).

Let us conclude this very important chapter with the affirmation of St. Paul: *Verbum crucis his qui salvi fiunt est virtus Dei, i.e.:* the word of the cross . . . to them who are saved is the power of God (1 Cor. 1, 18); that is to say, whosoever shall be saved shall be saved through the virtue of God which is hidden in the mystery of the Cross. In other words, the second Person of the Blessed Trinity, our Heavenly Bridegroom, acts upon us for the ends of the mystical life, through His Sacred Humanity, immolated on the Cross, and He does it through the instrumentality of the Sacraments. The virtue by which we are saved is that of the Son of God; the joint instrument ("instrumentum conjunctum")[4] through which we are saved, is His Sacred Humanity; and He makes use also of separate instruments, as the hand of the workman makes use of tools; these are the Sacraments. And the result is the making of the mystic into the likeness of Jesus and of Him crucified: to Whom be glory and love for evermore!

[4] Summa Theologica, III q. 13. a 2.

CHAPTER XV

THAT THE HOLY SPIRIT IS THE "FIRST GIFT" OF GOD TO THE SOUL

Si scires donum Dei. If thou didst know the gift of God (John 4:10).

IN this chapter we proceed to state the distinctive part played by the Third Person in our mystical life. As a matter of fact, the Holy Spirit is the one of the three Divine Persons with Whom we have most to do in our present condition.

From the moment of our Baptism, provided we commit no mortal sin, the Holy Spirit is in us all the time, day and night, without so much as a single moment's interruption of His presence. He it is by whose operation we are to be changed into a Divine being: so that the whole secret of the spiritual life consists in allowing the Holy Spirit to do in us and with us what He wills. He is, moreover, the Divine Person Whom we may and ought to enjoy most during our pilgrim state, whilst we enjoy the other two Persons only through Him.

God the Father, Who is the Prime-mover of our mystical life, as we have seen in Chapter VIII, acts upon us not directly and by Himself, but through His Divine Son Whom He sent on earth for this very purpose. In His turn, Our Lord, the Son of God made man, acts upon us in two ways: first by Himself; secondly, by His Holy Spirit. He acts upon us, directly, by Himself, through the instrumentality of His Sacred Humanity, under the veil of the Sacraments, as we have seen in the two preceding chapters; and He acts upon us also, and indeed much more, indirectly, through His Holy Spirit. In fact, this is even the very first way, in order of time, in which God the Father and God the Son, do act upon any one they want to draw to the Divine union: they act upon him by the agency of the Holy Spirit, they first of all give him their Holy Spirit. This is what makes St. Thomas say that the Holy Spirit is the first gift, "Primum Donum."

God first loved us, and then created us.

God first loved the world, and then He gave it His only Son.

God first sent out His Holy Spirit upon the turbid elements of what was to be the world, and then He sent out His Word, His *Fiat,* to organize it into the beautiful Cosmos.

In the first explicit revelation of the Most Holy Trinity, when the Angel Gabriel announced unto Mary that she would be the Mother of the Redeemer, the Holy Spirit is first mentioned: His being infused into Mary is the first Divine fact, paving the way, so to say, for the coming of the Son of God. He was the first gift to Mary.

And so it is likewise, not only in the mystery of the Incarnation proper, but also in the extension of the Incarnation, that is to say, in the mystery of the Church, and in the mystery of the union with Christ, of every individual soul.

The Holy Spirit is the first gift we receive, perfectly gratuitous, without any previous merit on our part; so really a gift, that He is never to be recalled or taken away from us, but to be ours throughout all time and all eternity.

It is through His indwelling in us that we enter upon the supernatural life, and that we shall do the supernatural acts it calls for. *If we live in the Spirit, let us also walk in the Spirit* (Gal. v., 25). We live in the Spirit when we are in the state of grace; we walk in the Spirit when attending to the demands of the Holy Spirit for the purposes of the mystical life. It is through His operation that we are united to Jesus Christ in His mystical body of the Church. We are first baptized in water and the Holy Spirit, and, then only, are we admitted to the other Sacraments, and especially to the partaking of the Flesh and Blood of the Saviour in Holy Communion.

In the fourth book of Kings (c.. 4) we read of the great miracle of the oil wrought in favor of the poor widow of Sarepta. In the spiritual sense this was a prophecy of the coming of the Holy Spirit into our souls. The poor widow represents Holy Church on earth, widowed of her husband, Our Lord. The vessels are our very bodies and souls; the oil is the outpouring of the Holy Spirit Himself, this *"oil of gladness"* which wells up from the very heart of God the Father and of God the Son, and desires to diffuse itself and fill our vessels to overflowing. Now, this pouring out of the Holy Spirit in us, this extension of the great event of Pentecost, is not done with great noise as of a whirlwind and with visible tongues as it were of fire, but all silently, secretly, and yet as powerfully and efficaciously, if only the Holy Spirit finds clean and empty vessels, quite free from self-love and the disorderly affections of creatures.

Then, indeed, will He fulfil His office of Paraclete or Consoler. The Holy Spirit is the very gladness of God, the very Joy of God, the mutual, eternal, infinite Love of God the Father and of God the Son. How could such a Person, such a Gift, such a Guest not bring gladness to the fervent soul who sets herself to enjoy Him? He teaches the soul "*all things*" she ought to care for: the ways of purity, simplicity, goodwill to all, solid and cheerful piety, the *beautiful ways* of God (Prov. 3:17). And He fills her with deep, secret consolations.

When you experience joy in your Christian life, in the full adhesion of your mind to the truths of faith, and in their contemplation; in prayer and the receiving of the Sacraments; in the practice of the Commandments and of the evangelical Counsels according to your state in life, it is the gladness of the Holy Spirit making itself felt; the very essence of mystical life is being imparted to you. But if, on the contrary, the performance of your Christian or religious duties affords you no joy; if you have no relish for them; if you find them irksome and tedious, it may be that the Holy Spirit has not found the vessel of your heart clean and empty, and His sweetness cannot take effect in you until disorderly affections have been all thrown out and washed away from the heart.

Finally, let us consider for a moment the case of the Christian in mortal sin.

When, after the Holy Spirit has been given to a man He ceases, on account of mortal sin, to be in that man, it is not that

God has withdrawn His Gift, *the gifts of God are without repentance.* What has happened is this: the man has made himself unfit for the further indwelling of the Holy Spirit. When the light of day is streaming through the windows into a room and filling it with brightness and warmth, if you close all the shutters tightly, there will be darkness in that room. Is it that the sun has withdrawn its rays? The sun has withdrawn nothing: its rays are still besieging this room and shedding their kindly light and warmth all around it. As soon as the shutters are thrown open, the light will flood the room again. It is even thus with the Holy Spirit who is sent to illumine and to inflame our souls.

CHAPTER XVI

THE HOLY SPIRIT, THE SECRET DIRECTOR OF THE MYSTIC

Si Spiritu vivimus, Spiritu et ambulemus. If we live in the Spirit, let us also walk in the Spirit (Gal. 5:25).

THE Holy Spirit, this first gift of God, bestowed upon the Christian by the united action of God the Father and of God the Son at the moment of his baptism, constitutes the Dowry of the soul, the Dowry of our divine marriage with the Son of God.

A dowry assigned to a young maiden constitutes her fortune. It enriches her, it may serve to make her more desirable in marriage. It may serve also to set off her beauty, enabling her to deck herself with diamonds and precious pearls, and costly stuffs of marvellous texture; but for all that it remains a dead thing. Not so our Dowry, the Holy Spirit. It does indeed enrich us; it does indeed deck us with costly gifts and sets off the beauty of our soul, or rather gives it its beauty, for without Him we have none; but moreover It is alive, It is a Person, a Divine Person; It acts; It acts divinely. It is God the breath of God, the flame of the life of God, the substantial love of God, an infinite Person. Such is our Dowry. We can well understand that it should make us instinct with Divine life, breathing spiritually the fire of the love of God, crying out to the Father with the feelings of true children, and yearning with unutterable groanings after our heavenly Bridegroom. The Holy Spirit sets the mystic all on fire with the love of God makes him act in the way that will please God prepares his body and soul for the chaste, fiery embrace of Jesus in Holy Communion, and prepares him from afar for the ardently longed for consummation of his nuptials in the Beatific Vision.

All these things the Holy Spirit works out in us by the two operations of the Mystical Life, Divine Contemplation and

Saintly Action, in the manner that we shall describe later on, at greater length in special treatises. Suffice it for the present to note that it is the Holy Spirit who produces in us sanctifying grace, and with it the infused virtues, both Theological and Moral; also actual graces; and finally that magnificent cluster of special graces which are called the Seven Gifts and the Twelve Fruits and the Beatitudes.

It is the Holy Spirit Who produces heroic virtue wherever it is found; the heroic constancy of the martyrs in the midst of the most appalling torments, the heroic self-inflicted expiations of Penitents, the heroic abnegation of true Christians under all circumstances, especially in the discharge of the varied duties of their state of life, whatever this happens to be, or whether conjugal or celibate, in the cloister or in the world.

The Holy Spirit is the secret Director of the mystic.

The whole art of the spiritual life consists in attending to the Holy Spirit within us; in our becoming docile to His lights and responsive to His motions.

The spiritual father must, so to say, take his cue from the Holy Spirit, in his direction of each individual soul. Priests and Superiors of Religious are not to direct those in their care, arbitrarily or at random, or again by uniform inflexible rules, but according as they read the signs of the peculiar dealings of God with each one separately.

Hence it is necessary that he who wants to be directed properly should be very simple and open and sincere, and should give a candid account of his own interior lights and motions. Particularly is this the case where there is a special attraction. I call by this name a steady inspiration or motion of the Holy Spirit to some particular virtue or form of life, which it is therefore very important first to discern; secondly, to follow up faithfully.

We do not, as a rule, pay enough attention to the real presence of the Holy Spirit in us, to that Kingly, Divine Guest, Who silently came to take up His abode in our soul, and anointed our very body as His temple, and Who, if we only let Him, will take in hand the government of our spiritual life.

If we only let Him: that is to say, if we do not take the government of ourselves out of His hands and give it to some of His rivals.

What rivals? Any of the following; first, our own personal, narrow, ungenerous spirit; then the spirit of the old Adam and corrupt nature in us; then the spirit of the world, finally the evil spirits or fallen Angels that tempt us. The proper discernment of these spirits and of their motions in the soul is a most important branch of the spiritual art, as we shall see further on.

How easy, then, ought to be mystical life, when the very Operator of it is in us, at our beck and call, so to say, and is burning to work it out in us! The Holy Spirit at His very first coming into a soul by Baptism infuses into it all virtues. It is a fact that all virtues are in every Christian in the state of grace. They are there, though perhaps unknown, uncared for, ineffectual, inoperative. They are in the infant child dormant, as the seed just dropped by the sower and covered by the sod. They are in *Beginners* only as germs which may or may not develop, according to the nature of the soil and to the care which they may receive; according, at the same time, to the rain and the sunshine of the actual graces which God will not fail to shower upon the soul. They are in the *Advanced* as blooming flowers, giving out great delight to the beholder, and sweet perfumes and good promise of a rich harvest. They are in the *Perfect* as full and matured fruit, delightful to look at and sweet to the taste. All these virtues, the same Spirit works out in us, according as we leave Him free to act within us.

The Holy Spirit, then, is God making Himself an object of ineffable enjoyment to the fervent Christian in the secret of his heart. He is the hidden sweetness of all our supernatural life. He is the link which binds us to Jesus Christ, even as He is the bond of union between the Father and the Son. He is the substantial unction that consecrates us children of God; the divine oil that insinuates itself into all the cogs and wheels of our Supernatural being to make them work readily and smoothly. He is the well-spring of the eternal joy of God the Father and of God the Son, poured out upon and into our very' souls. He is the perfume of sweet odor which makes us verily objects of delight to the Most Holy Trinity.

In the tepid, negligent soul the Holy Spirit is treated with great indignity, not as an honored guest, but rather as a prisoner, He is fettered and gagged, with all the springs of His divine energies in the soul stopped up and obstructed.

CHAPTER XVII

THE PART OF THE CHURCH IN OUR MYSTICAL LIFE

THE Holy Spirit acts upon us for the ends of mystical life, not only internally by His intimate presence in the soul, as we have seen in the foregoing chapter, but also externally, that is, from the outside, by means of an instrument, which is the Church.

It must not be supposed, when we say that the Holy Spirit is the secret Director of the mystic, that we fall into that individualism in Religion which is the bane of Protestantism. Highly personal and strictly private and exclusive as are the mystic's relations with God in the secret of his heart, they cannot be said to savor of individualism, because they in no way withdraw him from his necessary relations with the whole mystical body of Christ, which is the Church; nay, they render him most submissive to her teaching and her government.

The mystic knows that the Church is the chosen organ of that same Holy Spirit Who secretly moves him, and Who can in no way contradict Himself. He knows that if any interior inspiration of his were in contradiction with the teaching of the Church, such an inspiration would thereby stand convicted of emanating not from the Holy Spirit, but from quite another sort of spirit. The Church is set up by Almighty God to act as a check and as a sort of controlling authority upon the mystic. The true mystic's reliance upon interior experience is never such as to make him prefer his own judgment to that of the Church.

It is worthy of remark that the father and founder of the science of Mystical Theology, Dionysius called the Areopagite, is not only the author of the first treatise on the matter, but also of the treatises: *De Cœlesti Hierarchia,* and *De Ecclesiastica Hierarchia* (treatises small in bulk, weighty in matter), thus demonstrating that the more one is a mystic so much the keener is one's perception of the golden links which bind us to the unseen world of grace and glory. He shows that, through the grand Hierarch and Head of the Church, Christ, the mystic lives in a conscious, vital union with the whole Church of the past and of the present, visible and invisible, militant, suffering and triumphant, of men on earth, of separate souls in Purgatory and in Heaven, of the blessed angelical natures, and of the Three Divine Persons. Can a more opulent, magnificent life for a wayfarer be dreamt of?

Holy Church is the Mistress of mystical life.

To her it is given to invite all men thereto by the preaching of the Gospel, and to initiate all men of good will into it by the administration of the Sacraments. The mystic, wherever he finds himself in the world, and upon whatever rung of the social ladder, is well cared and catered for by Holy Church. The whole Hierarchy of the Church and her oral and written teaching, the treasure of her Sacraments and Sacramentals, with the Holy Sacrifice, and the whole order of the liturgical service the year round are for him. He has a father in the person of the Pope, the Vicar of Christ, and another father in the person of his Bishop, and yet another father, nearer to him, in the person of his parish Priest, and he knows that all these diverse spiritual paternities merge themselves into the universal paternity of Jesus Christ, "who," says Abbot Vonier, "is the true inwardness of the Church."[5]

In fulfilment of her office as mistress of the mystical life, the Church has promulgated, from time to time as occasion offered, and as heresy compelled, a long series of illuminating condemnations of false propositions bearing on the subject of the mystical life, and she has put upon the Index a host of dangerous works on the same subject, from the pens of deluded teachers.

At the same time as he sees in the Church the authorized organ of the Holy Spirit, the mystic sees also in her the fulness of Christ, the *Wife of the Lamb* (Apoc. 21:9) in whom He takes His delights, in whom He still lives on earth, and continues His

---

[5] "The Personality of Crist." (c.. 33.)

work of saving souls to the end of time: a revelation of Him, especially in the lives of her saints and in her works of mercy, spiritual and temporal. To the mystic, the Church is the City of God on earth, and he the citizen; she is the kingdom of God on earth, and he a loyal subject; she is the mystical body of which Christ is the Head and he a living member. The mystic is constantly receiving from the Church, and also constantly giving to the Church, as the ripening bunch of grapes is both constantly receiving from the vine, and adding to it.

The part which devolves upon the Church in the formation of the mystic is that of a true mother. The mystic is born of the marriage of the Son of God with Holy Church: he is the child of both parents. Could he ever forget that she is his mother and the Bride of Christ?

It is in this relation of our vital union with the mystical body of Christ, the Church, and of the external action of the Holy Spirit upon us through the Church, that we must view the part played by our guardian angel in our spiritual life.

Our guardian angel is the personal embodiment of the Providence of God towards us individually. He is the guardian both of our natural and of our supernatural life. To him it belongs, from the moment of our conception in the womb to our last breath upon earth, to foresee and turn aside the many dangers that invisibly beset us on all sides, and which might prevent us from attaining the end of our creation. Theologians tell us that for this purpose God communicates to our guardian angel a large share of His own special love for us, together with a marvellous knowledge of the soul he has to guard, and the power to influence it for good, possessed by no other spirit; without, however, lessening either our own liberty or our responsibility. We shall never know till we are in the land of the spirits, how far this action of our guardian angel upon us and upon the external world in our behalf has extended itself; or how many times his intervention has saved us from material harm, due to the relentless working of the laws of nature, so imperfectly known to us, or to the malice of the evil spirits.

This is but one side, the less lofty, of the Guardian Angel's ministration. He is, moreover, in a certain way, a real partner in the great undertaking of our spiritual life. He is linked to his charge, and his charge is linked to him in a bond of spiritual relationship in such a way that, after the present life, they will stand towards one another in heaven and throughout all eternity in a mutual relationship of love quite apart. At present, and for the purposes of mystical life, this close and active relationship of ours with a particular member of the Celestial Hierarchy is intended by Almighty God to be productive of much good to us: it is for us therefore to be alive to this marvellous supernatural fact; for, then, we shall not fail to turn often to our guardian angel, doing him honor, calling him frequently to help us, and being careful not to make opposition to him through ignorance, stupidity, or tepidity.

What an entrancing thought this, that one of the princes of heaven has charge of me; that he is my own, my very own guardian and brother, to whom I am expected to look for help at any time, and who forestalls my needs, and employs himself in a thousand ways in my service. But that is not all. The very fact of this active relationship and ministration of a Guardian Angel to each one of us brings home to us in a vivid manner how closely related we are to the whole world of glory, to the Church Triumphant. And so it is that in Christ the mystic finds no difficulty in fraternizing with all the blessed Angels, and the dear Saints who are already in heaven, giving them the meed of praise and admiration which is their due, asking the help of their intercession, and animating himself by their example to a more fervent service of God; rejoicing in their triumph, their glory, their security, their bliss; in which he sees a sure token of what is soon to be his also. Thus we see that in giving himself to loving intercourse with God alone in the secret of his heart, the mystic is far from isolating himself. He does not keep aloof from his brethren, either those on earth, or those who are in glory; he does not claim an exemption from the control and action of the Church; on the contrary, he is all the more united to her and to his brethren, inasmuch as he is more closely united to God.

CHAPTER XVIII

MAN, HIMSELF, THE REAL MASTER OF THE WORK

THE master of the work, in the mystical life, strange though it may appear at first sight, is not God, but man.

The person really at the head of it all, the one finally responsible, is each individual man.

True, nothing can be done without God. The raising of man above himself to a share of the Divine nature cannot be done but by God Himself; and we have seen in the foregoing chapters how indeed each one of the Three Divine Persons contributes to this work and employs Himself about it. But the fact is that God the Father, God the Son, and God the Holy Spirit are in this work (I say it in all reverence), nothing more than fellow-workers with man. They start the work because it cannot be started by him; and then wait upon his good pleasure to press it forward and bring it to completion. The three Divine Persons are in collaboration with the Christian in his efforts to become a saint, but they leave to him, if not the principal, at least the decisive action, the casting vote, so to say.

If we were to view things with the eyes of a philosopher we could divide all beings roughly into two classes; first, this supernatural being, God, in the Trinity of His Persons and the fulness of His mysteries; secondly, the universality of things created, all and each in their own peculiar nature. But we are not only philosophers, we are also Christians, and we know th at, through grace the angels first, and then man, at the very moment of their creation, have been lifted out of the low plane of nature and transferred into the sphere of the Divine.

To say nothing more of the angel at present; man, natural man, through the instrumentality of grace, is raised above himself and all earthly things, and transformed into a being of quite another kind. He is transfigured into a Divine being. He is made, in Jesus Christ, partaker of the Divine nature. Body and soul, the whole man, is mysteriously, mystically, united to the Sacred Humanity of Jesus, *as the branch to the vine* (John 15), and thus he receives the influx of the Divine life. It is hereby that he is made capable of the indwelling of the Three Divine Persons who, as a matter of fact, *make their abode with him* (John 14:23). Then is he truly a new being "*nova creatura*" very different from the purely natural man, incomparably more exalted, nobler, richer; for he is endowed with new faculties which make him capable of eliciting divine acts—acts namely of faith, hope, charity, and of the infused moral virtues.

Previously, or by virtue of his purely natural state, man was capable of holding his own place among the bodies of this visible universe, subject to the natural laws which govern them. He was capable, moreover, of feeding and growing and multiplying in the same way in common with the members of the vegetable kingdom; and he was also capable, in a higher degree of excellence than the beasts, of attending to the acts of relation with the exterior world, by means of the senses and of the faculty of local motion. Finally, he was capable, by means of his natural intellect, of discovering the universal under the particular, of comparing ideas and of drawing conclusions; and by means of his free will, of shaping his course of action as he pleased in all the details of his private and domestic and social life, within the limits of the purely natural order of things. All this, but nothing more. Even the most noble among the natural faculties of man, I mean, his intellect and his free will, though they place him at the head of the material universe of things, do not lift him up above the plane of nature.

But, with grace intervening, the same man finds himself impregnated through and through with a marvellous new element, the Divine life; and, as a consequence, he becomes capable of eliciting Divine acts. He is lifted above nature and made wholly Divine and transferred to the family of God, to the society of the Three Divine Persons. The very substance of his soul and even of his body, with their faculties high and low, are filled, invisibly to the eye of sense, with the glory of the Divine Essence, informed by it, colored and made resplendent with it. As a colored glass in a cathedral window when a flood of light passes through it; as a sponge in mid ocean filled with salt water; as a roll of cotton-wool dipped in balm; as a piece of iron in a blazing furnace; as a light cloud in the splendor of the setting sun; even so is natural man transfigured and transformed by the grace of God into a new being.

He is raised to the Divine knowledge, to the Divine sanctity and even, in part at least, and alas! with frequent painful eclipses, to the Divine joy. His mind is rendered capable of apprehending somehow the very mysteries of God, and of giving his assent to them. He is informed, by Divine revelation, of truths which no created intellect could ever reach by itself; God making Himself his witness. His will, strengthened by the virtue of the Sacraments, is made capable of producing, with a Divine energy, acts corresponding to the revelation made to his mind. It is rendered capable of approving and loving what has been revealed to us of the perfections and works and life of God, and of adjusting his whole human life to these new data.

Thus, the Christian knows that God is a Trinity of Persons in the most absolute unity of essence, and of substance; and though he cannot wholly grasp this fundamental truth, he gives joyful assent thereto and adores unquestioningly.

He knows that God wills his own sanctification and deification, and he wills it also, and proceeds to do all the acts necessary to this end. He knows what God loves, namely, Himself, and the works of His hands, each in its degree, and he loves also God with his whole heart, and the things He has made, subordinate to Him and each in its proper rank. Thus, man's higher faculties, mind and will, are made to have the same object of their activities as God, namely, God Himself. Through grace, God grants to man the power to see somehow by faith, and to will, and to love, and to have a share in what constitutes the very life of God.

It is from the summit of these two higher faculties of man, his intelligence and his free will, that the grace of God enlightens his lower faculties, trains them, forces them to fall into line with the Divine order, and makes them serve, each in its proper place, the ends of supernatural life.

So we may say that grace consists in this: first, in God's proposing Himself directly as the object of our knowledge and love; secondly, in His rendering our mind and will capable of these supernatural acts; thirdly, in His actually inclining and soliciting us to perform these acts, and thus to attain their supernatural object, Himself, directly, and without any intermediary. These are Divine operations indeed, not only on the part of God, but on the part of man as well; Divine operations, since they have God directly for object; with this difference, that in God they are subjective and immanent, whilst in man they are necessarily objective and transient, inasmuch as God is distinct from the essence of man and outside it.

God enters into that man in order to cause him not only *to be* divinely but also *to act* divinely. God fills the Christian with His own Divine substance and all His gifts in order that under the Divine impulse and motion man should of himself produce Divine fruits, works of edification. Now in proportion as a man lends himself to these Divine operations and follows their motions, in the same proportion does he grow in Divine life and become divinely fruitful; just as, on the contrary, in proportion as he puts obstacles to the Divine motions and refuses to obey them in the same proportion does he make himself guilty or very imperfect, and will have to redress such a great wrong and to atone for it either in this life or hereafter in Purgatory, unless (which may God avert) he happens to be rejected altogether and condemned to hell for having made himself wholly unfit for the supernatural. All this then is man's doing, man's work. He has always the last word in the matter of his sanctification. God has placed him in the hands of his own counsel, a rational being with rights and duties and responsibilities that can never be shifted. Each man decides for himself whether he will or will not accept the Divine advances, the Divine motions and directions, the Divine supernatural help we call grace, and impregnate his whole life with it.

This casting vote remains with every man all through life, from the first moment of his intelligent conscious activity to his very last breath. He can at any time reconsider his verdict, shift his position, retrace his steps for good or for evil. He is *sui juris*, and God Himself will not tamper with his freedom, or touch the spring of his self-determining will. Man is truly the master of the work; man is the maker of his own self for good or evil, for a fervent life or a tepid one, for mystic life or the very reverse; for eternal merit and glory, or for his own damnation. *Perditio tua, Israel, Destruction is thy own, O Israel,* says the Prophet (Osee 13:9). It is for each man to will for himself and every man does it.

The sooner we understand our exclusive partnership with God, and our paramount, personal responsibility in the affair of our own sanctification, the better. We have perhaps, until now, laid the blame for our not making much headway therein upon this person or that, or upon this or that other outward circumstance. We must cease to do so. We must lay the blame at our own door, take the full and exclusive responsibility of our life, such as it is.

CHAPTER XIX

MAN A CREATURE IN THE MAKING

DURING our pilgrimage on earth, in our present condition of trial under sin, the supernatural state is as yet attended with many infirmities. It does not receive its full development and perfection, still less its full manifestation. It is true as says St. John, *we are now the sons of God, and it hath not yet appeared what we shall be* (1 John 3:2).

We have seen that through the grace of Baptism we enter into the sphere of the supernatural, into the family of God, into the blessed society of the Father, and of the Son, and of the Holy Spirit. But the fulness of eternal life that is promised us will begin only after the General Resurrection "*in regeneratione*" when the Son of Man will take His seat on the throne of His Majesty to judge the living and the dead. This will be the grand birthday, not only of the Bride of the Lamb, Holy Church, who will then at last have attained the fulness of her beauty (Apoc. 21), but it will be the birthday, or, we may say, re-birth-day, that is, the regeneration complete and final, of every individual predestinate from among men.

Till then, man remains in an incomplete state: but it is the swift little drama of our life which decides everything.

Till the Day of the Last Judgement man is a future creature, a creature in the making, a beginning of what God intends to do with him, *initium aliquod creatura ejus* (Jas. 1:18). He will be a creature completed, only after the resurrection, when all angels and all men that shall ever be, being assembled together in one place, each man will receive in his body and soul at last reunited, the full meed of glory or shame due to him for his works whilst on earth. Then also will each angel and each man be assigned for all eternity his definitive rank, either in the splendid hierarchy of perfect charity, or in the gloomy hierarchy of confirmed, unreclaimable malice and reprobation.

The purpose of the present life, it will be seen therefore, is to give each man time to make of himself, with the help of God, that exquisite masterpiece, a saint, worthy of the ultimate glory of the heavenly Jerusalem.

Mystical life consists in a man's working thus with God, at his own making, every day of his life.

What a glorious and good thing, then, is mystical life! The more so when we take into consideration what it is God desires man to become, namely, a being so like Himself, so near His own Divine self, so united to His own Divine goodness, that man may at last live in his body and soul the same Divine life with Him, taste the same Divine joy, take part in the same Divine operations; in a word, really be one with God; and this, no longer under the veil of faith and with many restrictions, but in the perfection of charity and the fulness of the Beatific Vision.

We may go through the diverse degrees of life, beginning with the lowest, and at each we shall be obliged to say: "That is not good enough for man," until we come to the very life of God as it is lived in God. The life of a seed dropped in the ground and buried there until it becomes a blade of grass, or a flower, or a shrub, or a majestic tree: not good enough for man. The life of an insect, of a worm, of a butterfly, of a bee; or that of a bird, a beast of the field or the desert: not good enough for man. The conscious, intelligent, free life of a man as we may picture him to ourselves in a purely natural state, or of an angel as God could have created him, in a purely natural state: not good enough for man as God wishes him to become. The life of a Christian, with the light of faith, and the consolation of charity, but (by supposition) without the hope, and eventually the actual granting of the Beatific Vision; or again, the life of a blessed soul enjoying the bliss of heaven all by herself, I mean without the companionship of the body in which she lived and suffered and merited on earth; not yet good enough for man, not yet all that God wishes for him. Finally, the life of a blessed being in soul and body after the resurrection, but without connection or association (if it were possible to conceive such a thing) with all the rest of the inhabitants of the heavenly Jerusalem; and without the sharing in the accumulated bliss, of all and imparting to them his own bliss: not good enough for man!

Nothing is good enough for this child of the loving God, short of the immortal, eternal divine life as it is lived in God with all His blessed ones around Him, short of the very joy that God finds in His own Self and in His Saints. Each one of us is to be made, through charity, into a vessel of purest gold, into which the Divine glory will be poured, and will fill it to the very brim. Nay, the golden vessel of a man's soul and body, after the resurrection, is to be immersed in and wholly swallowed up by the Divine glory, so that it will be encompassed by it on all sides, both from within and from without. Not an unconscious vessel, but an animated one, which will know and taste, and enjoy the glory thus poured out into it, and will actively and vitally unite itself to it, even as on earth it actively and vitally made itself worthy of it by its own exertion. Then will the saint throb and palpitate with all the accumulated life of all the other saints as well as with the very life of God.

The purpose of the present life is to give us the time and opportunity of hammering ourselves into shape. No wonder that St. James cries out to us: *My brethren, count it all joy when you shall jail into diverse temptations, knowing that the trying of your faith works patience, and patience hath a perfect work; that you may be perfect, and entire, deficient in nothing* (Jas. 1:2-4). No wonder that the book of Ecclesiasticus should describe the saint *as a massy vessel of gold, adorned with every precious stone* (Eccle. 1, 10).

The great secret of mystical life is that a Christian should make himself very yielding to the soft and strong pressure of the grace of God within him and thus enlarge his own capacity more and more, that he should try and become, under the mighty hand of God, ever more and more refined and delicately and elaborately chiseled, and should adorn himself with the brightest pearls and most precious stones of virtues and good works. The mystic should always bear in mind that the greater he makes his capacity of loving God whilst on earth, the more has he adorned himself with merit, so much the more will he give glory to His beloved God throughout eternity. Therefore is it that he sets no bounds to his ambition, and refuses to lose one single moment of the precious time of the present life.

CHAPTER XX

ALONE, WITH GOD ALONE

IF we were to try and reckon up the *dramatis persona* of our own spiritual life from childhood to whatever age we have attained, in the little drama of which we are the center and the hero, it would seem at first as though there were a very large number of persons concerned.

There are servants of God, some visible, like those around us living in the flesh, our parents, teachers, friends, superiors; others invisible, such as our guardian angel, and other pure spirits, and even the saints in heaven, whom at critical junctures we ask to intervene in our behalf, and above all, God and Our Lord Jesus Christ. And, on the other hand, there are also the arch-enemy, the devil, and we do not know how many of his satellites or slaves, some in the flesh, others invisible, because pure spirits, though fallen, all eager to tempt us away from the path of duty and to mold our soul, if we let them, to their own image and likeness.

I am the person around whom all these activities center, I am the stake for which all these adverse forms are aiming. But as it is my privilege (as we have seen in the preceding chapter) to decide finally for myself to which I will adhere and bind myself, we are led to conclude, when we look closely into the matter, that in reality each man lives his own spiritual life alone with God alone.

Other men around us, and pure spirits, good and evil, as also inferior creatures and inanimate nature; all may and do bring to bear upon us their varied influences, but they are outside us; they stop at the threshold of the soul, and it is left to each man to admit their influences or reject them, to turn their action upon him either to his spiritual advantage or the reverse, and thereby to associate himself with God or to separate himself from Him.

Alone with God alone. Each man supremely solitary in the awful presence of God.

But how natural in a way and how easy does not mystical life appear in the light of this great primary fact! The mystic is he who takes heed of this wondrous state of affairs, and for whom, most naturally, God is all in all. Mystical life is a sort of "Divina Commedia" in which all is performed by these two actors God and the faithful loving soul. God plays His part and the soul plays her part. God has engaged in this venture everything that is His; and the mystic, on the other hand, keeps nothing back of all that he may call his own. In this play the more one loses the more one is the gainer: *He that finds his life shall lose it, and he that shall lose his life for My sake shall find it* (Mat. 10:39).

To live alone with God alone consciously and willingly, then, is the ideal. To live with God upon a footing of great intimacy is the very essence and perfection and consummation of mystical life. It is a life full of delight and full of pain by turns, because God is pleased to make the loving soul to taste His infinite sweetness; and then again, He scorches her with the flames of His own infinite sanctity; but such a pain is preferable to all the delights of the creatures.

Thus to live with God does not demand an effort of the imaginative faculty. Indeed fancy has nothing to do in the matter. It is simply the sober perception of the grandest reality which could be thought of. God is always with us; though we, on our own part, are not always with Him. God is nearer to me than I am to myself; God is more within me than I am within myself, because God is within me with the fulness of His infinite essence whilst I am within myself as a created, finite being, held within narrow limits, and moreover diminished by sin; a shadow, an evanescent being. Job says: *Remember that my life is but wind* (7:7); and again: *Man born of woman living for a short time is filled with many miseries; who cometh forth like a flower and is destroyed and flees as a shadow, and never continues in the same state* (14:1, 2). But God invites me to unite my puny self to the fulness of His divine being: yes consciously, joyously, by a free choice constantly renewed, with intensity of love to unite myself to Him. The more I do this the more does God repair the crumbling fabric of my nature, building me up upon and into His own Divine essence; building me up into a being wholly supernatural. And then to the natural presence of God in me is superadded His special presence of love which constitutes me in the state of grace and into a degree more or less exalted of supernatural life.

It will be asked: Is it really possible to sustain such a life of active relation with God, constantly, without interruption, and not be consumed by the intensity of it?

Well, it is very true that the poor sheath of the body may be quickly burnt out by the flaming soul. This has happened to some: a glorious, quick consummation! Is not such a crowded short life of sanctity and consuming love, such as that of St. Stanislaus Kostka for example, a thousand times better than a long, listless, colorless life of tepidity? *Being made perfect in a short space, he fulfilled a long time* (Wisd. 4:13). But this is not always the case. There are special graces of strength and endurance meted out to both soul and body, according to the designs of Providence upon each one. St. Teresa lived 67 years: St. Alphonsus Liguori died at the age of 91; St. Anthony, the founder of cœnobitical life in the East, died at the age of 105; and St. Paul, the first Hermit, at the age of 120.

Besides, it is not a question as yet for any of us, so long as we are here below, of living quite the life of the Seraphim in heaven. We walk by faith, in the infirmities of the flesh, surrounded by enemies which we have to fight, and by fellow creatures whom we have to help; which means that, without ever losing hold of God, we have to do a good deal of active, or even mayhap, of apostolic work; now, all this is a providential check on, and tempering of, the consuming intensity of the pure flame of Divine love.

Moreover, to live with God is also to live in spirit with His servants, the blessed angels and the saints of paradise, and actively to keep in touch with them by prayer and loving intercourse: *Our conversation is in heaven* (Philip 3:20), says St. Paul. This also is a beautiful provision, which helps one to bear the awful weight of the felt presence of God. Then, again, after having for the sake of the Beloved, renounced all things created, the mystic is led back by the Holy Spirit in the very midst of them, to lay hold of all the creatures animate and inanimate of this visible universe, to make them come with him and through him, into the divine encounter; and this is yet another solace to the intensity of pure thought and consuming love; because in giving free play within healthy limits to the senses and the imagination, it diverts the activities of the soul into different channels, and thus prevents a sort of dangerous congestion in the higher part of our being.

We must also own that, in our present condition, owing to the consequences of original sin, which have not all been abolished, there will always be a somewhat tardy and imperfect correspondence to the motions of God unto supernatural life. As long as this is not deliberate, nor fully consented to, the loving God looks leniently upon our shortcomings, and makes it His business to redress and correct them. *I am the Vine,* says Our Lord, *you the branches. My Father is the husbandman. Every branch in Me that bears not fruit He will take away, and every one that bears fruit He will purge it, that it may bring forth more fruit* (John 15). Here an important remark finds its place. To live alone with God alone, means a good deal more than to practice the exercise of the presence of God, so much recommended by modern writers of spirituality. To live with God implies a greater intimacy and familiarity. I was always struck, in Shakespeare's *Henry VIII,* with the accusation of Catherine of Aragon against Cardinal Wolsey that he would tell untruth even "in the presence," meaning the presence of the King seated on his throne. Nothing can convey a higher idea of the state and ceremony surrounding the person of the King, and making him the image of God on earth, to such an extent that even the telling of an untruth in his presence, apart from the moral turpitude of it, seemed such an absolute want of manners. "In the presence"one ought to hold oneself in an attitude both interior and exterior of deepest respect ruled by decorum and stately formality. But when one lives constantly with the King in the relation of father, or mother, or wife, or child, or of bosom friend, admitted to his privacy, there are times when ceremonies and etiquette are dispensed with, especially when not under the public eye. It is the time for unconventional intercourse, full of sweetness and tenderness, imparting deep joy to one another. Now, to live with God is to entertain such a sort of intercourse with Him. Except in the acts of the sacred liturgy where everything is necessarily set down by rule and strict ceremonial, he who lives with God goes at all times to Him with perfect directness, simplicity and familiarity. Says Juliana of Norwich in her quaint but expressive language: "God loves a silly soul to be full homely with Him."

It is an art to know how to live with God. One does not get into it all at once, but little by little. One must learn and practice it before one can hope to become proficient in it. But when at last one has become a past master therein, oh! what joy! what security! And what heaps of eternal merits one piles up, the one upon the other: a multi-millionaire's fortune in heaven! And what enlargement of the heart and progress in sublimest charity! and at the same time what unshakable humility! what simplification of one's whole life! What unification of one's whole being! "The one to the One" sang St. Francis of Assisi. "The one to the One!"—a beautiful and significant variation of our motto: "Alone with God alone." Instead of scattering all one's powers at the mercy of passing impressions, one holds them all together and applies them to the single purpose of the life with God.

It will be the object of subsequent volumes now in course of preparation, to sketch out the rules of this noble art in its two divisions of Divine Contemplation and Saintly Action. But before we proceed to their separate treatment we must complete these Preliminaries by casting a glance upon what may be called *the Antithesis of Mystical Life* in its divers degrees. It will help to give us, by contrast, a still more definite and clearer idea of the Mystical life in itself.

The Virgin of the Apocalypse
—Carlo Dolci

BOOK III

MYSTICISM

TRUE AND FALSE

VIRGINI DEIPARAE IMMACULATAE
BUCKFASTRIŒ
PATRONAE PERPETUAE

PREFACE

IT is not without a certain amount of diffidence that I now venture to offer to the public this new work of mine on "Mysticism True and False?"

I fear that its usefulness and its close connection with the preceding volume on "The Mystical Life" may not be apparent to the casual reader. It is, however, a fact that, in my estimation, the twenty chapters on "The Mystical Life" have done but one half of the work of setting the right notion of it in its proper light. A great deal more remains to be accomplished, and that is the object of this new book.

We have, first of all, to differentiate the mystical life from what is non-essential or exceptional to it, namely, the miraculous. Then we have to contrast the genuine mystical life, which is always characterized by fervor, with its opposite or the state of tepidity; its counterfeits or the spurious forms of mysticism both outside the Church and inside it; its absolute negation or contradiction, which is the state of mortal sin wherever found, either in man or angel or separated soul, whether in time or in eternity. Finally, to crown all, we have to turn to the more congenial task of considering into what Mysticism will ultimately resolve itself.

Only when all this has been achieved shall we be able to say that, by God's grace, we have done full justice to the right concept of the Mystical Life. This is what I am attempting in these pages.

I notice with a deep feeling of gratitude that during the last year the circle of my sympathetic readers has greatly widened. My theme evidently appeals to many on its own merit, despite the shortcomings of my treatment of it. Persons of all ranks and conditions of life, and of widely different religious convictions, have hailed my last book with something akin to the feeling of joy at coming suddenly upon a long lost friend. The idea of the mystical life being simply and solely THE LIFE WITH GOD, THROUGH ACTIVE LOVE seems now well on its way: "*Ella est en marche; elle fera son chemin."* It will win; such is my unshaken hope. It may yet encounter contradiction; it has done so from the very outset of my pleading for a return to it. It invites discussion. Men's minds have to be enticed away from the wrong notion which is relatively modem, and brought back to the traditional one. This requires time as well as dispassionate consideration. Already signs of recognition and (if I may use the term) reconciliation, can be discerned. Some persons who, upon the appearance of the first treatise on "The Mystical Knowledge of God," had failed to grasp my meaning or to agree to the idea of its being the legitimate one, now come forward and are kind enough to acknowledge that, at any rate, my second treatise on "The Mystical Life" has cleared the way to a better understanding. Let us hope that this third one on "Mysticism" will overcome the last remnant of their intellectual difficulties.

As I write this Preface, the awful world-war is still raging and the end is not yet in sight. From time to time, here and there, in the periodicals or in the speeches of public men, the pregnant topic of *reconstruction after the war* is touched upon. Every one is adjured to bring to bear upon the problems that will then confront us all the wisdom and good will at his command. By all means let this be done; at the same time let us also realize that no efforts of ours will avail unless we take God into account as well, and no sort of reconstruction of the social edifice will be durable which does not reinstate the Lord Jesus Christ in his place as the "foundation stone" of the whole fabric. Should my book, in however modest a way, contribute to this result, I should feel amply repaid for the hard work it has cost me.

It is with great reluctance that, owing to shortage of paper and the increase in price of everything else, the editors have found themselves obliged to raise the price of this volume. The alternative before them was either to do so or to postpone indefinitely the publication of the book. In view of the close connection of this work with the preceding one, "The Mystical Life," and of the many and pressing demands for it, we have thought it advisable not to wait until the conditions of trade are normal again: for who knows when this will be?

The substance of this work appeared first in the *American Catholic Quarterly Review* of January and April, 1916.

THE ABBEY, BUCKFAST,
ON THE FEAST OF THE BLESSED JOAN OF ARC.
May 30, 1916.

CHAPTER I

THE MIRACULOUS

Vere to es Deus absconditus: Thou, O Lord, art indeed a hidden God (Isa. 44:15).

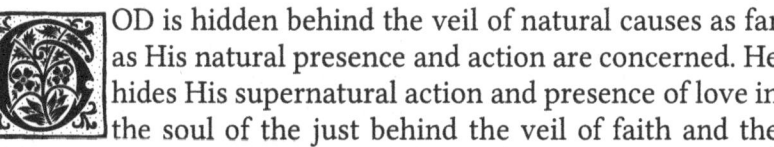

GOD is hidden behind the veil of natural causes as far as His natural presence and action are concerned. He hides His supernatural action and presence of love in the soul of the just behind the veil of faith and the Sacraments. During the thirty-three years of His life on earth, the Son of God was hidden behind the transparent veil of His sacred flesh, taken from the most pure womb of the Virgin Mary; and He is now totally hidden behind the veil of the sacramental species in the Sacrament of His love.

Is then God without the power of showing forth His presence and His action? Is He deprived of the means of lifting or drawing aside from time to time one or the other of these veils which are of His own making? Cannot He, when He so wills, intervene directly in the affairs of this lower world and manifest Himself to men? It would be absurd thus to set bounds to the Infinite power of God, and it would amount to a denial of God, pure and simple. Besides, we have positive evidence of such an intervention of God in human affairs. History, both sacred and profane, that of our own time as well as that of all past centuries, bears witness to the fact that God has a way of His own of showing forth, when He so wills, His presence and His action. God has a sign all His own, and when it appears, men even the most obtuse or the most obdurate, are compelled, unless they deliberately stultify themselves, to exclaim: *Digitus est hic: Here surely is the finger of God* (Exod. 8:19), the mark of God, the sign of God, the unmistakable sign of His presence and of His action.

That sign is *the miraculous.*

What is a miracle? What place does it hold in the economy of religion? What position does it occupy particularly in this department of religion which we call the "Mystical Life?" Is the miraculous the all in all of mystical life as some modem writers would fain have us believe? Or is it but an exception or at least an accidental adjunct to mystical life proper?

It is time that we should at last grapple at close quarters with this question, which is not difficult in itself, but which has been terribly obscured by the rashness of some writers. I propose to do so in this and the next two chapters. I want to show clearly that the miraculous is not an essential element of the mystical life, and that it is a grievous mistake to make the two terms *miraculous* and *mystical* synonymous. In order to do this successfully, I can think of nothing better than of offering first in this chapter a summary of the doctrine of miracle as I have gathered it from the Summa Theologica of St. Thomas. However, in order not to tax the patience of the reader by incessant quotations, I will give here all together, for the use of the diligent student, the references in their proper order: I, quæst. 105 a. 6, 7, 8.—quæst. no a. 4.—in, 3, 4.—114 4.—117, 3 ad prim.—I IIæ, quæst 111, a. 1, 4. —113, 10.—Secunda Secundæ, quæst. 171 – 178.—III, quæst. 13—27—36.—38 a. 2. ad 2.—40. 2 ad 1.—43-45.—76. 8.—84. 3 ad 4.

What, then, is a miracle?

A miracle is an event of the sensible order, which totally exceeds the capacity of created nature, and therefore can have but God alone for its secret cause. It is a marvellous sort of event, calculated forcibly to draw upon itself the attention of men, and excite their admiration. It is a kind of a sign, the special sign of God, which He employs in order to give to men an extraordinary demonstration of something supernatural, as for example, of His divine attributes: infinite power, justice, mercy, love; or of some mystery of religion as the Holy Trinity, the Incarnation, the Redemption, the glory of Christ in Heaven, His real Presence in the Blessed Sacrament; or again, in order to give some glimpse of the Church Triumphant or of the Church Suffering, or of the present or of the future state of the Militant Church, or of the awful secrets of the world of sin and damnation; or, finally, in order to set in its proper light the wonderful sanctity of some servant of God, even during the days of his pilgrimage on earth, or to enable him to accomplish some special mission. This was the case, for instance, with St. Catherine of Siena, when she brought back the Papacy from Avignon to Rome, and with Blessed Joan of Arc, when she delivered France from the yoke of the English, to the greatest benefit of both nations.

From this description of miracle as a marvellous sign of God, totally exceeding the capacity of created nature, and given to men to teach them something supernatural, it will be easy to determine, and useful to point out, what is no miracle.

First, the work of the six days of creation was not a miracle properly speaking, though indeed the immediate work of God and stupendous beyond expression; because it was no exception to the laws of nature, but their very institution, and there was no man as yet to be a witness of the process. Secondly, the immediate creation of souls by Almighty God day by day, generation after generation, throughout all centuries is no miracle, since it evades the direct observation of man and „ is; inviolably linked with the natural laws which rule the propagation of the race. Thirdly, the purely spiritual effects of grace under all its forms, of the Sacraments, of Prayer in all its degrees, of the Holy Sacrifice of the Mass; the justification of the sinner, the internal illumination and invigoration of a soul, the transformation of the fervent Christian into Christ; the wonderful ascent of the same Christian, from virtue to virtue, even to the highest peak of heroic sanctity: all these purely spiritual effects are not miracles, because, in themselves, they are out of the sphere of the direct observation of men. Fourthly, the intervention on the one hand of our guardian angel, on the other of the devils in the affairs of our soul, have nothing of the miraculous as long as they do not take some tangible or visible form. Fifthly, the illusions of the devil, as is obvious, cannot be called miracles. Sixthly, the tricks of clever mountebanks, the frauds of sacrilegious scoundrels, be they ever so inexplicable to the simple minded, are not miracles.

Seventhly, nor are miracles those natural phenomena of rare occurrence, and the cause of which may happen to be unknown, such as an eclipse of the sun or of the moon, the aurora borealis, comets, shooting stars, etc., which have the privilege of exciting intense wonder, especially among the unlearned. Finally, though most of the ecstasy of the great servants of God are genuine miracles, some however, are not, as we shall explain in its proper place, in a subsequent volume.

There are three degrees of the miraculous: the lowest, the higher, and the highest. The lowest degree of a miracle consists "in the manner" in which an event takes place, as for instance, when a sick person is suddenly cured, as is related of St. Peter's mother-in-law (Mat. 8:15), or when a conversion from unbelief and sinfulness to sanctity is made, as that of St. Paul, in an instant, all gradual process being dispensed with. The higher degree is the miracle called "in the person," as for instance, when a dead man is made to live again, or one born blind, to see.

The highest degree of miracle is when "the whole substance" of the event totally exceeds the forces of created agencies, as when the shadow on the sun-dial of Ezechias was made to go back so many degrees (4 Reg. 20:11), or when two bodies are made to occupy the same space, as was the case in the virgin birth of Our Lord, and in His coming out of the tomb without removing the stone, and in His coming into the room the doors remaining closed; as will be the case also with all the predestined, after the resurrection of their bodies, whenever they encounter material obstacles to pass through them with the ease of a ray of light through clearest crystal.

Not all miracles are public. Some are accomplished in secret, so that only he who is the object of miraculous intervention knows the fact, and can give testimony of it. Such miracles have very often happened in the lives of the Saints. Some hidden miracles are Articles of Faith: thus the conception of Our Lord from a virgin, and His virgin birth. But those wrought in confirmation of the true faith are necessarily manifest: such were the many miracles performed by Our Lord during His public apostolate, as also those in favor of the people of God in the Old Testament, and those which the Apostles, the first Christians, the Martyrs and the Saints of all centuries have performed in order to establish or to consolidate the religion of Christ.

Although the gift of miracles is of the kind of graces called "gratis datæ," and therefore must not be confused with the grace "gratum faciens," which is properly sanctifying grace, nevertheless certain dispositions such as a lively faith, either in the performer of the miracle or in him who is the object of it, perseverance in prayer and fasting, chastity, and an heroic spirit of mortification contribute greatly to the operation of miracles, as Our Lord has taken pains to inculcate time and again in His Gospel Except in the blessed Soul of Our Lord, Who had it in its fulness to exercise it for Himself, and to communicate it to men as He willed, the grace of miracles is not an habitual possession but only a passing impression.

To what sort of operation of God is the performance of miracles to be ascribed? Simply to His natural intervention: God suspends the laws of nature by the same power that He established them. The invisible ministrations of the angels are pressed into service for the carrying out of miracles, just as they are pressed into service for the government of this material universe. *Nonne omnes sunt administratorii spiritus? Are they not all ministering spirits, sent to minister far them who shall receive the inheritance of salvation?* (Heb. 1:14).

Almost innumerable are the varieties of miracles that have been wrought out by Almighty God at various times in the sky, on the earth, on the sea, on the persons of men, in beasts and plants and rocks and all the elements, in all departments of this material universe; as was fitting indeed to show forth His absolutely sovereign dominion over all the works of His hands.

Here, now, are some of the most common miracles:

The marvellous command given to some men over brute nature, animate and inanimate. This was very conspicuous in Moses, Elias, Elisaeus, Our Lord, His Apostles and certain privileged Saints. The gifts of tongues, of healing, of casting out devils, of prophecy, of reading the secret thoughts of men and the hidden state of their conscience; seeing God face to face in bodily form, as did Adam, Abraham, Moses; or after the resurrection of Our Lord, seeing Him in some incident of His earthly life and dolorous passion, or in His glory, or in the Blessed Sacrament; also seeing the Saints in glory, or the Holy Souls in Purgatory; or Angels or devils in bodily form and having speech with them;

The constancy of martyrs in the midst of the most horrible torments. Certain extraordinary diseases of the Saints, as for instance, those of St. Lidwine of Schiedam. Living a considerable time without food, or on no other nourishment than the Holy Eucharist. Bearing the Sacred Stigmata or a Crown of Thoms, sometimes visible, sometimes invisible, etc.;

Levitation of the body in the air; its instantaneous transportation at enormous distances, bilocation, whether real or only apparent;

Visions, revelations, locutions either perceptible to the senses or purely intellectual, raptures or the like extraordinary phenomena met with in the lives of the Saints.

The rules for discerning genuine miracles from apparent or spurious ones will find their proper place in a subsequent volume, when we shall have to treat of the "Discernment of the various Spirits," Suffice it to say that the Church is the supreme, infallible judge of the genuineness of miracles, because she has received from Our Lord, together with the Holy Spirit, the fulness of teaching authority and the promise of His own personal assistance: *Behold,* He said to His Apostles, on the day of His Ascension, *I am with you all days even to the consummation of the world* (Mat. 28:20).

CHAPTER II

MIRACLE VERSUS MYSTICISM

IT is difficult to imagine the confusion of mind which has led some modem Catholic writers to make Mysticism synonymous with Miracle.

Compare the two notions: they are simply contradictory of each other. The essence of Mysticism consists in its pure spiritualness and secrecy; on the contrary, that of Miracle in its manifestation, its coming into the order of things perceived by the senses, its striking wonder in the mind of those who witness it.

Mystical life, as we must by this time have realized, is nothing else but the intercourse of a loving soul with the loving God, in the secret of the heart. It is something hidden, secret, hence the name. Now, as long as God is blindly perceived by the loving soul in the secret of her heart, there is no miracle, because it is a purely spiritual fact; but the moment the vision of God takes a definite aspect, or words either intellectual or articulate are spoken and a distinct message delivered to the mystic, or some extraordinary, sensible token of what is passing between God and him is given to the outside world, then we are in the miraculous.

One may be justified in thinking that if all Christians lived the fulness of Christian life; the mystical life, pure and simple and common; lived it to the best of their ability, and to the fullest extent of the grace that would undoubtedly be given them—they would all be favored, at some time or other of their pilgrimage, publicly or in secret, oftener in secret, with some miraculous communication from God. I am inclined to believe that whenever God meets with a truly faithful and generous soul, He cannot restrain Himself, and in the impetuosity of His love, He feels compelled to lift a corner of the veil and allow His servant a glimpse, just a passing glimpse of heavenly things, or to deal out to him now and again one of those entrancing, heavenly delicacies which fill a soul with unutterable, unearthly delights.

The wonder, perhaps, is not so much that this should occur now and again, as we see in the lives of the Saints, but that it should, even with the Saints, be but the exception and not the constant rule. The wonder is that the supernatural presence of the loving God in the loving soul should not betray itself oftener in the body by miraculous effects, and that this marvellous new being, the fervent Christian, this true child of God, this little God should go through life appearing in no way different physically from other men abandoned to sloth and sin and infidelity. But there is good reason for such being the case. A comparison will help us to understand this.

During the earthly life of Our Lord, for obvious reasons, it was not desirable that the glory of His hypostatic union should break forth openly and habitually upon His human countenance, and shine in the eyes of all. It would have interfered with the plan of God as to the way of our redemption, made the Passion of Christ an impossibility, and wrung from men, by a sort of moral violence, the assent they ought to have given Him freely. Still the divine glory was even then, by right, due to His sacred Humanity, and it was, no doubt, in order to teach us this truth that the incident of the Transfiguration took place. Was the Transfiguration a miracle? It was rather the momentary cessation of a long continued miracle. It was by a miracle that the divine glory did not shine all the time around our Saviour, from the moment of His virginal birth to that of His entombment, and the Transfiguration was but a short respite, an interruption for a brief space of time of that life-long miracle.

Now very much in the same way we may assume that, for obvious reasons, it is desirable that during the days of their pilgrimage on earth, the essential glory of the mystical union of the Saints with God should not be allowed to shine continually in the eyes of men, by miraculous phenomena, such as visions, revelations, raptures, the gifts of healing, of prophecy, of command over nature. Otherwise it would gravely interfere with the conditions of our present life of trial, during which we are to walk by faith. It would put an earthly premium upon sanctity, tamper with the purity of our intention, take away the merit of faith, and threaten the solidity of the whole supernatural order. It would so glorify the true Church in the eyes of men as to interfere, by a sort of moral violence, with their free will. Moreover it would have within the Church the grave inconvenience of revealing, not only who are mystics, but also by contrast who are not; of publishing to the world the secret of consciences, since then we should have in our hands a test whereby to perceive who is a Saint, and by implication, also, who is a sinner. Furthermore it would make the lives of the Saints unbearable by reason of the many who would gape at them, follow them everywhere in order to see miracles, crowd around them and importune them. Finally, the gift of constant visions and revelations would render the lives of the Saints unendurable also by reason of the too intense joy and proportionately intense revulsion of sorrow which would be their lot: intensest joy at what they would be made to see and taste of the heavenly mysteries and, immediately after, sadness unspeakable at being compelled to live yet a while in such a world of sin and to mix with men who love not God.

From all this it clearly follows that we must look upon it as one of the laws of the genera] economy of grace, that with the Saints, as well as with the Holy Church and the world at large, miraculous phenomena are the exception and not the rule.

Is it not evident in view of all this, that those modem writers who now talk of mystical states, meaning thereby only extraordinary and miraculous states, make themselves guilty of an intolerable misuse of language? The mystical states are the following: first, that of a beginner, which is called also the Way of Purity; secondly, that of one making progress, or the Illuminative Way; thirdly, that of the Perfect, or the Unitive Way. There are, in reality, no other mystical states but these three, and they are so irrespective of the presence or absence of any miraculous element. If some miraculous phenomena are occasionally superadded, these are something absolutely accidental, distinct from the mystical state as such, and they must not be confused with it.

Some miracles may, indeed, be a manifestation of the mystical life within, but they are not the mystical life itself, nor are they essential to it; they are simply an overgrowth, as it were, an ornament, as ivy on the wall of a beautiful castle, or on the rugged trunk of a giant of the forest. It is not because of some miracles wrought in their favor or performed by themselves that the Saints are mystics, but just the reverse: it is because they are mystics that some miraculous phenomena happen to them occasionally. The Saints are mystics first; and for some of them, at some time of their life, miracles are superadded by Almighty God, according to His Will, for some wise purpose of His own, over and above the common measure of mystical life. Our Lord proclaimed John the Baptist unsurpassed in holiness by the other men (Mat. 11:11), and yet we have the popular testimony of the Jews that he worked no miracle (Jo. 10:41).

In fact, one can very well be a mystic without any miraculous adjunct, as on the other hand, one may happen to be no mystic at all, and yet, for some wise purpose of God, be the subject of miraculous intervention, or even a performer of miracles. Thus the Fathers of the Church are agreed, on the evidence of the Gospel, that Judas, as well as the other Apostles, exercised the gifts of healing and of casting out devils. Thus also, at Lourdes, among the many persons miraculously cured, have been found infants, also adults in the state of actual sin and even downright infidels. Ivy is found on crumbling walls, and though it adorns them and the scenery at large, it is no sign of their solidity.

CHAPTER III

THE TWO CONTRARY DEFINITIONS OF MYSTICISM

AT this point we find ourselves confronted with the two definitions of mysticism: on the one hand the more modem or narrow definition, very much in favor today, both with Catholic and non-Catholic writers, which confines mystical life within the circle of extraordinary, miraculous phenomena; and on the other hand, the wider definition, the truly Catholic traditional one, which places the essence of mystical life in the secret intercourse of a fervent soul with God.

It would be possible to cite a mighty host of witnesses in favor of this contention, that the broad definition of mystical life as simply the life of union with God, is the Catholic, traditional one. Let a few suffice for the moment. The "Theologia Mystica" and other treatises of Dionysius the Areopagite, the "Scala Paradisi" of St. John Climachus, the "De Quantitate Animæ," "Epistola De Videndo Deo," and other works of St. Augustine; the "Conferences of Cassian," the "Holy Rule" of St Benedict; the "Moralia" of St. Gregory the Great; the mystical works of Hugh and Richard of Saint Victor; the treatise of Albertus Magnus, "De Adhærendo Deo"; the Second Part of the "Summa Theologica" of St. Thomas; the "Vitis Mystica," attributed by some to St. Bonaventure; the "Following of Christ,"; the many and marvellous treatises hardly known today of John Gerson on the mystical life; the "Via Compendii ad Deum" of Cardinal Bona; the "Exercises of the Spiritual Life" of Abbot Cisneros, the celebrated Exercises of St. Ignatius Loyola; the "Treatise of the Love of God" of St. Francis of Sales; the deep and luminous treatises of St. John of the Cross; the spiritual works of Blosius; all these, with hundreds of others (every one of which is in its own way a practical introduction to the mystical life), make no mention whatever of miraculous manifestations as an essential part of the mystical life. It is true that a contemporary writer of no small repute informs us that "The Following of Christ is not a mystical book." What next? Perhaps we shall be told soon that the Epistles of St. Paul or even the Four Gospels are not mystical books. The Sermon on the Mountain will not be considered as very mystical: there is no mention in this *Magna Charta* of Christianity, of any miraculous states or miraculous phenomena. We only read there: *Blessed are the poor in spirit ... the clean of heart . . . they that suffer persecution, ... If thy right eye cause thee to offend, pluck it out and cast it from thee .... Let your speech be yea, yea, no, no! . . . Love your enemies . . . that you may be the children of your Father who is in Heaven,* and many such expressions.

There is one Saint in the Middle Ages who towers above all others as a mystic—St. Bernard. Let us single out this well-known and universally appreciated master. Now what is for him the main thing in mystical life? For St. Bernard the only thing that matters, in the long range of spiritual life, is loving union with God, no mention being made of miraculous manifestations of any sort, in favor of the loving soul, the Spouse of Christ. Read his Sermons on the Canticle of Canticles, and all his other sermons and treatises and letters, and you will be convinced that for him mystical life is the loving intercourse of the soul with God in the secret of the heart—simply that and nothing else. Here is a real master of the spiritual craft, and do not fail to note this, one very highly favored with the gift of miracles, and he brings back for us the notion of mystical life to its true and only legitimate meaning.

How mischievous the modern idea of mysticism is will readily appear, when we consider that it has a tendency to make us lose sight of the real value of the most wonderful gifts of God, which are by no means the extraordinary and miraculous ones, but the common ones. The best gifts of God in themselves, if we only knew how to appreciate them, are Baptism, Confirmation, Penance, Holy Communion, the Holy Sacrifice of the Mass, and the Real Presence day and night on our altars. No other gifts of

God, here below, can be compared with these.

It has also a tendency to make weak-minded, superficial Christians desire the extraordinary favors for themselves, not indeed for any spiritual good there is in such gifts, but only for the sake of their exterior *éclat,* and the admiration of men, which these manifestations are apt to win for one. Moreover, it has given occasion not infrequently to bad men to play on the credulity of people and to feign miraculous powers, thus making themselves guilty of sacrilegious imposture.

Let us understand, once and for all, that what is greatest and most admirable in the Saints who have received visions, revelations, raptures, and perhaps stigmata, and who perform miracles, is not these things, but their union with God; yes, just what they have in common with us: their union with Christ through Baptism, their official enrolment in the active militia of Christ through Confirmation; and if they are Priests, the stupendous fact of their sharing in the eternal priesthood of Christ; and whether Priests or laymen, the marvellous privilege of eating the Flesh of Christ and drinking His Blood in Holy Communion. The difference lies in this that the Saints knew how to co-operate with the grace of these Sacraments and make them yield the fruits of sanctity.

The treatises avowedly written " for the guidance of those who are favored with extraordinary and miraculous graces" would seem almost calculated to provoke a smile, for the writers would appear to be pursuing a method exactly opposite to that of the Good Shepherd.

They do not leave on the mountain ninety-nine good sheep in order to run after one single erring one and bring it back to the fold; they seem rather to abandon the many erring ones, the enormous number of tepid, unsatisfactory Christians to their sad and dangerous condition, instead of shepherding them back to the mystical life pure and simple, to that life which is meant for all in common with the Saints; for that life is after all the life of Faith and the Sacraments, of the Theological virtues, of the Seven Gifts, of the Beatitudes, of unmiraculous mental prayer, of unmiraculous contemplation and of Good Works, Thus they labor uselessly in the endeavor to establish the rules of miraculous mystical life for a few souls here and there, who do not need such direction and will never read their book. One feels tempted to tell them: O my friends *Æmulamini charismata meliora. Be zealous for the better gifts* (1 Cor. 12:31).

Need we add that the Saints never desired the extraordinary favors of God? They feared them, for they knew that the way of safety is that in which there is no room for illusion, namely, the common way, the unmiraculous path, where Christians walk by faith under the steady guidance of Holy Mother Church. They knew that private revelations, though they may come from God, may come also from quite another sort of spirits, either from the devil or from one's own hallucinations, and that even when absolutely genuine and coming from God, a private revelation may be unconsciously wrought upon, added to or distorted by the recipient's own bias of mind and imagination. Hence the extreme reserve of the Church in receiving and approving visions and revelations even the most authentic, vouchsafed to the greatest servants of God and related by them in obedience to their confessors or Superiors, or moved thereto by the Holy Spirit, so subtle and so difficult of elimination is the personal element. Hence also the absolutely child-like obedience of the Saints to the direction of their spiritual fathers, even when these ran counter to their revelations, well knowing that obedience is more pleasing to God than sacrifice. The great St. Theresa is an example in point.

Before leaving this question of the respective merits of the two definitions of Mysticism— the one broad and traditional, the other modem and narrow—it may not be amiss to call the attention of the reader, for the last time, to what may be considered as the logical aspect of the case. In his "Doctrine of Development" (c.. 1, section 3) Cardinal Newman lays down several distinctive tests whereby may be made the distinction between true and legitimate development of an idea and what is no development but a downright corruption of it. In a genuine development of an idea there is always to be found:

I. Preservation of type of Idea.
II. Continuity of Principles.
III. Power of Assimilation.
IV. Early Anticipation.
V. Logical Sequence.
VI. Preservative Additions.
VII. Chronic Continuance.

Now, the idea of Mysticism in the Catholic Church, up to the sixteenth century, has been that of a secret intercourse of love between God and the Christian. Can we say that the modem idea is a desirable substitute for this primitive, traditional idea of Mysticism? or that it is a legitimate development of this primitive idea? In the light of the above seven tests, does it not rather appear as a deviation from the traditional idea and a corruption of it? A volume could be written in proof of this, but let it suffice to call the attention of diligent students of philosophy and theology to this line of observation, for it would fully repay their labors to work it out for themselves.

The purpose of this volume is quite different. It is not contentious or controversial, except within the strict limits of absolute necessity. My aim is to state the traditional notion, to formulate it, to show it forth under all its aspects, to set it in its proper light and let it speak for itself. In the very harmoniousness of the development of this doctrine, in its weight and depth and unity and logical sequence, there is, it may be hoped, a sort of persuasiveness that can hardly be resisted.

CHAPTER IV

TEPIDITY IN THE LIGHT OF MYSTICISM

THUS far we have been considering the part played on the one hand by the loving God, on the other hand by the loving soul, in the joint affair of the mystical life. Now, for these preliminaries to be complete, we have to consider also the case of the bad servants, of those, that is, who, in some way or other, will not abandon themselves to the loving advances of God and refuse to work with Him.

There are three different ways or degrees of being a bad servant: first, Tepidity; secondly, False Mysticism; thirdly, Mortal sin. This statement will help us, as shades in a painting, to set forth more clearly and, by contrast, to bring into its proper light, the idea of mystical life. For one thing, they serve at once to show us the essential requirements of a mystic, namely: *orthodox faith* as against false Mysticism; the state *of grace* as against mortal sin, and *fervent love* as against tepidity. No one can be called a mystic to whom any of these three gifts is lacking. Indeed, he that has suffered shipwreck of the faith, through heresy, or who never had the faith and consequently is outside the pale of the Catholic Church, how could he lay claim to the most exquisite familiarity with God? He is not of the family; he is not even yet born to supernatural life. As for the man, even if he be a Christian, who has fallen into mortal sin, he is dead to God: there is an abyss between him and God which must be bridged and passed over before he can again have the intercourse of love with God. The case of the tepid Christian, though not so desperate in itself as the other two, is bad enough, as we shall now see, and is perhaps the most perplexing of all.

What is tepidity?

We may define it as a certain state of the Christian soul, which Our Lord declares most unsatisfactory to Himself: that of being "neither hot nor cold," neither greatly criminal, nor at all fervent.

A Christian in that state provokes the divine nausea. Our Lord says of such a one: "*I know thy works, that thou art neither cold nor hot; I would thou wert cold or hot, but because thou art lukewarm and neither cold nor hot, I will begin to vomit thee out of my mouth*" (Apoc. 3:15,16).

The tepid Christian does as little as he possibly can for God. He has no relish for heavenly things. He grudges all the time given to pious exercises; reduces his Confessions and Communions, Sunday devotions and daily prayers to the strictest minimum, and finds all religious functions tedious and irksome. The fact is his heart is elsewhere. Without perhaps owning it to himself, he secretly worships at the altars of the world. He has tried that compromise, of which Our Lord speaks in the Gospel, of *serving two masters* (Mat. 6:24), and has proved in himself that it will not work: so he takes inwardly and outwardly the attitude of a worldling, and he follows the maxims of the world, and he repeats its shibboleths with conviction.

It can hardly be said of him that he wants to avoid mortal sin: what he wishes to avoid is simply eternal punishment. Mortal sin, as such, has no terror for him, but he fears damnation. His faith avails him at least thus far. Has he still hope? It may at least be said that he has a kind of presumptuous hope of reaching Heaven some time and somehow; but he has certainly no keen desire of gaining it, and if it were possible to loiter indefinitely here below, he would much prefer this. Has he still charity? He may be said to have yet a spark of it, just enough for him to be still in the state of grace; but the spark is quite out of sight, buried under a mountain of ashes and in perpetual danger of going out for good and forever.

Tepidity is a sort of half-way house between Mysticism and its opposite: the diabolical life, which is the life of sin. For the Christian who does not resolutely turn to mystical life, the state of grace itself is but a very precarious possession, and no one must be surprised to see him fall again and again into mortal sin. The tepid one falls thus occasionally, but because he manages somehow to rise again by means of attrition and the Sacrament of Penance, he is not in the least alarmed at his own condition.

The tepid Christian is well satisfied with himself as he is, and is quite determined to remain as he is. In fact this self-complacency in the midst of the grossest and most alarming imperfections, and this firm resolve not to change for the better, are the two characteristic features of tepidity. Our Lord rebukes him in these scathing terms: *Thou sayest: I am rich and made wealthy, and have need of nothing, and thou knowest not that thou art wretched, and miserable, and poor, and blind, and naked. I counsel thee to buy of me gold tried in the fire, that thou may be made rich, and may be clothed in white garments, that the shame of thy nakedness may not appear; and anoint thy eyes with eye-salve, that thou might see* (Apoc. 3:18). But the lukewarm takes no heed. He is quite pleased with himself: he lives in a fool's paradise and persuades himself that all will come out right in the end. He is like the foolish virgins of the parable, up to the moment when the cry goes up in the middle of the night: *Behold the Bridegroom cometh, go ye forth to meet him!* (Matt, 25:6). Then indeed there is sudden trepidation of the lukewarm, and confusion, and looking for assurance to others who are not able to help him. Our Lord's threat in the Gospel is certainly intended for such as he has become, and when this foolish one knocks at the gate of Heaven He will answer: *Amen, I say to you, I know you not* (Matt, 25:12).

Behold I stand at the door and knock, says Our Lord Himself, still speaking to the lukewarm: *If any man shall hear My voice and open to Me the gate, I will come in to him and sup with him and he with Me* (Apoc. 3:20). Here we have in these few words a most touching invitation to the mystical life and the description of it, but the tepid Christian will have none of it. He does not hear, or he does not want to hear, the gentle knocking and the pleading voice of his Saviour and Lover. He will not open to Him.

A homely similitude will serve further to illustrate the negative attitude of the tepid Christian in regard to God. If an empty bottle were dropped into the sea we know that water would rush into it at once and fill it to its utmost capacity. But suppose the empty bottle, instead of being open, is tightly stopped up and sealed, then the whole ocean presses around it in vain: no water will get into it. The whole strength of the mighty ocean is defied and set at naught by that puny thing. The sealed bottle may be caught up in the currents of the sea, or tossed up by the waves, or finally dashed against the rocks and shattered to bits: but so long as it remains whole and sealed up, it will also remain empty. Behold here an image of the tepid Christian soul.

The Christian is immersed body and soul in the infinite ocean of the love of God, in the divine supernatural order. If he be void of self, and of all worldly, inordinate affection, he will be filled to his utmost capacity with the divine element. He then becomes, so to say, a form of God: every mystic is in himself a form of God. (The word is not of my own invention; it is to be found in many spiritual treatises, notably in those of John Ruysbrock and in that of the celebrated Bishop Gay on the Christian Virtues.) But if the Christian is closed against the inrush of God by self-complacency, or filled with inordinate love of created things, no entrance can be made into him.

It seems at times that it would be easier for God to break this human being, the lukewarm Christian, to annihilate him altogether, than to put an end to his obstinacy, and persuade him to lay himself open to the advances of divine love. But God does not annihilate. It is repugnant to His transcendent goodness that the end of his act should be nothingness. He has not created His own image and likeness in order to destroy it. What He has made out of love and for the purpose of sharing His own happiness, will have to stand for ever. The whole ocean, then, of the love of God, is pressing around this puny vessel in order to fill it with sanctity and happiness; but a time must come at last when the very love of God, defied and set at nought, will compel Him to reject the vessel that will not be turned to the purposes of love and cast it away on the shores of eternity, into the waste and desolate land which is called the hell of the damned.

In beautiful contrast with the callousness of the lukewarm stands the anxious sensitiveness of all souls of good will. When they hear the subject of tepidity mentioned they fear that all that is being said applies to them, and this very fear is the best proof that it is not so. A great searching of heart takes place on their part, and they find themselves full of imperfections. Such a one, on being questioned: But, do you love your imperfections? Do you want to keep them? will answer: Ah! no, I have a horror of them; I am constantly fighting against them, but they always manage to return. Be of good cheer, my friend: the very fact that you are fighting your imperfections, with whatever measure of success, makes it plain that you are not a slave of tepidity.

Let us never tire of repeating it, the characteristic feature of the tepid is not that he has imperfections, but that he will not amend them. Even fervent souls may happen to have a good many imperfections. A man may not yet be a saint, not yet have attained to a very high degree of perfection: he may be but a raw recruit, a beginner, just emerging from the slough of an impure life and the bondage of sin; nevertheless, provided he be fervent and zealous, provided he set to work with fervent love, and press on with fervent love, and persevere in fervent love, he will really be a mystic, even in the midst of distressing imperfections.

There are even souls who are eternal beginners, who seem unable somehow to get any further than the threshold of mystical life, and who yet should not be considered as tepid. Where the trouble lies with them may not be easy to determine; sometimes it is the fault of a wrong spiritual direction. But the very fact that they have the courage to keep beginning over and over again shows them to be of good will. Let them keep on; Our Lord will give them at any rate in Heaven a very great reward for their brave fighting.

Not unfrequently it happens also that a truly fervent soul, whilst passing through the ordeal of spiritual darkness and interior desolation, will mistake her state for that of tepidity, suffering thereby a twofold distress. Such a soul ought to be tenderly consoled and encouraged, to be assured that all is well with her, and that, in God's good time she will again see the light of His loving countenance. Meanwhile let her be patient: she is gaining great merits for Heaven. It is in the hottest and driest days of summer that the harvest turns to golden sheaves, and the fruit comes to full maturity.

To sum up all this chapter we may say that as tepidity is the unmistakable sign of the non-mystic, so is fervent love the hallmark of mysticism in all its degrees, from its beginning to its sublimest consummation.

CHAPTER V

PSYCHOLOGY OF THE TEPID CHRISTIAN

THE root of the trouble with the Tepid Christian lies in this: that he is satisfied with simply BEING a Christian, and will not ACT as one. It is the same disorder as that of a man who is satisfied with simply existing and declining to make use of his limbs and of his natural faculties, and refuse to play the man and to act as a reasonable free agent When a man has been raised to the supernatural state he is expected to act up to it. God wants the Christian to think of Him a great deal, and lovingly and tenderly, and to use creatures as a ladder by which to raise himself into the sphere of the supernatural: all this the tepid Christian steadily refuses to do.

It is true that all the human acts of a Christian, which are morally good, are in themselves supernatural and worthy of an eternal reward. They are, so to say, automatically directed heavenwards by the very fact of his being in the state of grace. But this holds good only on condition that he does not introduce into his acts an element positively unchristian, such as an unworthy or perverse intention, either explicit or implicit Now this is precisely the misfortune of the tepid man: that in his acts the Christian element, the implicit, habitual, pure intention is positively eliminated, and the quite explicit intention of simply gratifying self is substituted. This, apart even from any material, sinful disorder which often creeps in, is enough to take away from one's acts all savor of sanctity, all supernatural meritoriousness.

The whole substance of the Christian, body and soul, has been made one with Christ: the tree we may say has been taken bodily out of the sphere of pure nature, and rooted in God. Does it not follow that the fruits of such a tree should now be all supernatural? Is it not a disconcerting phenomenon, a monstrous anomaly, when the tree, root and branch and all, is divine, that the fruits thereof are not also divine? The explanation is not far to seek. We are two entities in one being. The old Adam, though mortified in the Christian, is not yet dead; and when not kept down with the strong hand of the will, helped by the grace of God—when allowed to raise his head again and have his own way, this old Adam becomes the rival of the new man Jesus Christ and supplants Him, and becomes the ruling power and principle of all his acts. Thus his actions will have a bitter earthy taste, and will lose the divine savor. For the old Adam is of the earth earthy, and his natural inclinations are to pride, covetousness, lust, envy, gluttony, anger and sloth.

The Council of Trent (Sess. VI, ch. 5-7), declares that in the work of the justification of an adult person two distinct activities concur and co-operate in order to bring that man to the illumination of faith and the Sacrament of Baptism. By Baptism he has been made a new creature, the adopted child of God, brother of Jesus Christ and His living member, and the living, breathing temple of the Holy Spirit. The two activities are, on the one hand that of God, and on the other that of the party interested; God by His grace, rousing, strengthening, uplifting and upholding man above his natural self, and man by his will consenting and co-operating in all these divine effects. Such a happy concurrence of the two activities ought not to end at Baptism; on the contrary, it is more needed than ever thenceforth; for to live up to the requirements of the Christian state is no easy task. In the midst of a world of sin and invisible, spiritual enemies, such as the evil spirits who are full of cunning and of malice, and with the wounds of the threefold concupiscence in his nature, man, without divine assistance, stands in imminent peril. Not only is the grace of God necessary, but it must be abundant and superabundant, or rather, let us say, it must be taken by man abundantly and superabundantly; for on the part of God, grace is offered to the soul with prodigious prodigality. There are the Sacraments, and the treasure of Holy Scriptures, and all the other means of sanctification found in the Catholic Church, to say nothing of the countless multitude and variety of interior, actual graces showered constantly upon all, good and bad, without any distinction. Truly it is not God Who ever fails man: it is man who betrays both God and his own interests, when, through tepidity, he will not make use of all the love of God and of all the graces at hand.

The two activities, that of God and that of man, should then go hand in hand, working harmoniously all through the life of the Christian in order to bring about this most marvellous result, the sanctity of mystical life. God, on His side, is most desirous to do His part. Man, on the other hand, is free either to co-operate heartily with God, or to haggle and try to drive a hard bargain, yielding himself as little as he possibly can, or even completely refusing his co-operation.

The tepid Christian has everything that God can give him in order to make him a mystic. He has received (to use the words of the Gospel) *one talent* (Matt, 25:24). On the one side of this talent is stamped the grace of the orthodox faith; on the other, the grace of the Sacraments. Now it is required of him that with this he will earn yet another talent. It is required that he will by his own exertion draw out of his orthodox faith the illumination of divine contemplation, and out of the grace of his Sacraments the practice of all Christian virtues, the three Theological ones, and the infused moral ones. The lukewarm Christian is too lazy to do this, or, at any rate, he has not love enough. His first talent he keeps wrapped up, so to say, in a napkin, and put away out of sight; he will not earn the second talent, and so, through his own fault, he fails to become a mystic.

One can sometimes be made a Christian by Almighty God without any actual co-operation of one's own will: this we see in the case of infants when they are baptized; but one can never be made a mystic by Almighty God without one's own co-operation.

Why stand you here all the day idle? asked the householder in the parable, of those whom he wanted to send to his vineyard (Matt. 20:6). It is not said that they were idle after they went there. The tepid Christian is in the vineyard, and it is *there* he is idle. He is in the Church of God, in the state of grace, and he makes nothing of his privileges and opportunities. He neglects the exercise of virtues and divine contemplation through mental prayer. This is enough to deprive the Sacraments, even if he receives them frequently, of the greater part of their efficacy.

The Israelites in the Desert, cared for and marvelously fed by the constant intervention of God, should have been carried beyond themselves with admiration and gratitude; instead of this they repined and grumbled, calling to memory, with loud voices of regret, the flesh pots and onions of Egypt, and they were ever ready to throw themselves into some gross, monstrous infidelity. These Israelites seem to represent an image of the Christian who allows himself to fall into the natural life of the old Adam. He is moving in the midst of a supernatural world, infinitely more marvellous than the Desert of Sinai. He is each day surrounded by divine favors incomparably more prodigious than those of the Israelites; such, for instance, as Holy Mass, Holy Communion; the Real Presence of Our Lord in the Blessed Sacrament, day and night; the presence of love of God within him, with the infused virtues and the seven Gifts of the Holy Spirit, and innumerable actual graces, if he will only attend to them; but all these most precious favors of God make no impression on him. He looks aside and lusts after the worldly pleasures of those who know not God. The Holy Will of God, even when he is the direct object of all its tenderest cares, has no attraction for him.

How different the attitude of the true mystic, whether only a beginner, or already progressing or perfect . With his lips, with his body and soul, with his whole heart, he cries out to God constantly: Lo, *here I am!*, . *Lord, what wilt Thou have me to do? . . . Speak Lord, for Thy servant heareth. Behold! I come, and Thy law is in the midst of my heart ... I am Thy servant, and the son of Thy handmaid. . . . Behold the handmaid of the Lord, be it done to me according to Thy word. . . . Father, not my will, but Thine be done. . . . Thy will be done on earth as it is in Heaven.*

CHAPTER VI

THE FURNACE OF PURGATORY

WE must now turn our attention to the ultimate results of tepidity.

In St. Mark's Gospel (11:12-31) we have the statement that one day, as Jesus came out with His Apostles from Bethania, He was hungry. And when He had seen afar off a fig-tree having leaves, He came to look if perhaps He might find anything on it. He found nothing but leaves, for it was not the time for figs. Then Jesus uttered this solemn imprecation upon the tree: *May no man hereafter eat fruit of thee any more for ever.* And the next day, *when they passed by in the morning, they saw the fig-tree dried up from the roots. And Peter said to Him: Rabbi, behold the fig-tree, which Thou cursed, is withered away.*

The fig-tree with leaves and no fruit represents the lukewarm Christian. He has a certain promising appearance from afar, but no fruit to satisfy the hunger of Our Lord. It is said in the Gospel that it was not the time of fruit, and therefore it seems at first it was a strange act on the part of Our Lord to curse the fig-tree; but in the tree He cursed the Christian who yields no fruit, because with the Christian there is no time when he is not expected to bear fruit. The swift withering away of the tree is a terrible image of the doom of a fruitless soul, abandoned by grace, and called suddenly to its account.

Does Our Lord's action, with its consequence, mean death, physical death? or does it not perhaps mean the death of the soul, that is its being definitely abandoned by Our Lord, and, in consequence, falling into mortal sin and remaining in it, till death supervenes, whenever that may be? Either interpretation may be accepted.

Sometimes the doom does not overtake the sinner quite so suddenly. In St. Luke, 13:6-9, Our Lord utters this parable: *A certain man had a fig-tree planted in his vineyard, and he came seeking fruit on it and found none. And he said to the tiller of the vineyard: Behold, these three years I came seeking fruit on this fig-tree, and find none. Cut it down therefore; why doth it take up the ground? But he answering said to him; Lord, let it alone this year also, until I dig about it and dung it, and if haply it bear fruit; but if not, then, after that, thou shah cut it down.*

Thus we see that if some are lost instantly, some also are granted a respite. The parable does not state whether after the year of grace, the fig-tree, hitherto barren, did produce some fruit and was saved; but let us suppose it was. The dresser of the vineyard, the guardian angel of that tepid soul, intercedes for it, and obtains a respite, and by dint of the most urgent solicitations, he wrings from it at last some poor, paltry fruits of good works. And, on the other hand, the mercy of Our Lord is so unspeakable that He will seize upon the least excuse in order to save even a lukewarm Christian. He will then be saved, *yet so as by fire* (1 Cor. 3:15).

For whom is Purgatory intended if not for the tepid, half-hearted Christian? Who will make a long and terrible stay there if not the lukewarm? He would not burn during life here below with the flames of fervent love, so he will have to be burnt after death with the flames of divine wrath. He has wronged God very much, therefore he owes His divine justice and slighted love very great and prolonged satisfaction.

Apart even from its debt to the divine justice, it would seem that the tepid Christian's soul has to be detained in Purgatory, also for its own sake. The following comparisons will make the meaning plain.

The tepid Christian, whilst on earth, makes no progress. He may be compared to a rose-bud which should fail to open out and become a full-blown flower. The light, the heat, the dew and rain, all the atmospheric influences, so to say, of the love of God, surround him, press on him on every side. But by a sort of inverted miracle, he will not open out under the action of divine Revelation and the grace of the Sacraments. All thorough life he remains as a rosebud, shut up in himself and self-contained, and will not become the full-blown spiritual man. In vain does God call him to an active, holy life, and the joy attendant upon it. He will not drink in the light and heat of the love of God shining full upon him; he will not rejoice the eyes of God and His angels by putting on the vivid, bright colors of deeds of charity; he will exhale no perfume of supernatural goodness, but rather the rank odor of an almost purely natural life. Now, even if such a languid, undeveloped bud of a Christian does not eventually die out altogether on its stem, and have to be thrown away on the heap of rubbish which the fire of hell is to burn for ever; at all events, before it can be transplanted by the divine Gardener into the bowers of paradise, it will have to go through a very violent process of treatment by fire, in the hot-house of Purgatory.

I would again compare the Christian who fails during life to become a mystic, to a silkworm which has entered its chrysalis state but never progresses to that of a butterfly. The worm is our old man of sin, as he is before Baptism: the chrysalis is the infant or adult as he comes out of the Baptismal font wrapped about with the dazzling white cocoon of innocence. He is then a new being, with all the outlines and rudimental beginnings of the splendid supernatural faculties of Faith, Hope and Charity, and the infused moral virtues. All these are as so many lovely wings, which must spread out and take their full development before he can wing his flight into the azure of the Divine Essence, and bask in the warm light of God's love, and alight on His infinite perfections, as on so many bright flowers, full of sweetest honey, out of which he would draw his nourishment. Only he must first of all break through the fetters of spiritual sloth, spread out his wings, that is to say, exercise his faith and hope and charity and other virtues, raise himself above the earth and, through mental prayer, fly on high and go in quest of the divine nectar of the sweetness of God, which he will draw into himself by holy contemplation, AU this the tepid Christian leaves undone, satisfied with remaining a stunted, apathetic, motionless and colorless thing, until God takes it and thrusts it into the dread oven of Purgatory, where the poor soul cannot help but bestir itself at last and become, through most severe treatment by fire, the perfect butterfly of God, worthy of the garden of Paradise.

But are we not carried away here by our imagination? This

may be true, but after all only to a slight extent. It is difficult to express the mysteries of the next world. The truth is that on the one hand the tepid soul which is finally saved, arrives at the end of her life undeveloped, but that the development after death is made instantly, and not progressively, whatever length of time that soul may have to abide in Purgatory.

There are two views concerning the state of a separated soul, which has to undergo the punishment of Purgatory. The first view is that which finds favor with the popular mind; the second, that which is the expression of strict theological truth. The first view is equivalent to what we say of the sun, when we speak of it as rising, and setting and moving, according to the time of the year, round us, through all the signs of the zodiac; the other is equivalent to the bald statement that it is not the sun which moves, but that it is the whole world of planets which moves around the sun. The comparison, of course, must not be pressed: it is brought in here only to illustrate two different attitudes of the human mind respecting an objective, concrete fact of the next world, as revealed to us by the light of faith.

The popular mind about Purgatory is that one ends there by gradually acquiring purity and saintliness, whilst the theological truth is that a man, not a reprobate at the moment of death, becomes a perfect saint the moment after, whatever be his debts to the divine justice, which indeed will have to be paid to the very last farthing.

It is not every one who can grasp this theological truth, and that is why we need not try to make it prevail in the popular mind. But the greatest theologians assure us that the very first effect of the separation of the soul and body of a man who dies in the state of grace, is to constitute that soul in full and absolute moral rectitude. This is due to a certain law of the world of pure spirits into which this soul has now entered. Her very first act in her new condition has all the qualities proper to the acts of pure spirits: it is produced with full intensity and irrevocableness. Now, as this first act is one of adhesion to the Divine Goodness suddenly manifested to the soul, it is an act of perfect charity, which does away at once with all past blemishes of the soul.

Then one will be tempted to ask, why should this soul be detained at all in Purgatory when by her first act she is constituted in perfect sanctity? The answer is that she is so detained in order that she may pay the debts incurred during the days of her vanity. Can we not conceive the case of a personal friend of a King, loving his sovereign perfectly, and still more loved by his sovereign, and yet detained for some time far from him, in order to purge in prison some previous condemnation, so that perfect justice be done? This, then, is how the case stands with the holy souls in Purgatory!

CHAPTER VII

OUT OF THE CHURCH NO MYSTICISM

OUT of the Church there is no Mysticism, just as "Out of the Church there is no salvation."

This may appear at first sight not only an intolerant, but also a preposterous and unjustifiable proposition, and yet, when we look closely into it, we find it to be as sober a scientific statement of the matter in hand as was ever formulated, whether in the abstract sciences or in those of observation.

First of all let us see the meaning of these words: "Out of the Church." They mean out of the one and only Church which God made, out of the Church which Jesus built; out of the Church which is One, and Catholic, and Apostolic, whose visible head is the successor of St Peter, the Pope of Rome; out of the Church of the seven Sacraments and of the true Sacrifice of the Mass. Out of that Church there is no real Mysticism, no mystical life, no salvation.

On the Day of General Judgement all the redeemed will be found to have been, whilst in life, real Catholics at heart, whether they knew it or not, whether other men knew it or only God. They will be found to have been saved by no other agency than the grace of God through faith in Jesus Christ and incorporation, public or secret, in His mystical body the Church, and to have lived the life supernatural, the life of grace: thus, and in no other way, shall they be proclaimed worthy of admission to the eternal Nuptials of the Lamb. None but such shall find an entrance there.

Taken in this sense and with this qualification, that many who are not known to men as children *of the household of the faith* are nevertheless really so in the eyes of God, are really in the Church and not out of it, these propositions: Out of the Church no salvation, and Out of the Church no Mysticism are absolutely incontrovertible and intolerant of any addition or subtraction.

Do we then really contend that only a Catholic can be a mystic? Most assuredly this is the case.

Mysticism is a gift of God. Now, God is the Master of His gifts, and He has laid down His law in regard to that one gift precisely: the intercourse of mutual love between Him and man. It cannot be contested that God is the law-giver of the supernatural order, as much at least as of the natural. There man has not a word to say. Whenever he has attempted to establish the mystical connection outside the conditions laid down by Almighty God, he has conspicuously failed and not unfrequently fallen into monstrous errors.

God has laid down as the supreme law of mystical life that the means or medium of union with Him is FAITH IN CHRIST: before His coming, faith in Him as in the Promised One of God, the Messiah; and after His coming, faith in Him as in the acknowledged Son of God and Redeemer of the world. Man has neither right, nor power to change this ordinance of God to introduce another name whereby he shall be illumined, united to God, and finally saved. For, says St. Peter (Acts 4:12) *there is no other name under heaven given to men whereby we must be saved.*

This is really an axiom and needs no demonstration. The wonder is that it should have to be recalled.

Therefore any man, in the past history of the world, or at the present time, or in the future, laying claim to supernatural authority to teach, and to power to unite to God, outside the Catholic Church, or within the Church outside her sanction, stands convicted of being either deluded or a sacrilegious impostor. Show us the sign of God, we may ask such a man, show us miracles; or, without miracles, show us the sign manual of the Bride of Christ, her approbation.

Thus all pagan, idolatrous worships of one God or many gods, of devils, of nature, of natural objects, or of the dead are disproved and rejected. They are false Mysticism. So are the occult sciences of the past: they could never procure a loving intercourse between man and God. False Mysticism, all the ancient Mysteries, whether austere or licentious, of Koré, of

Eleusis, of Dionysius, of Adonis, of Atys, of Mithra, of the Celtic religions. False the Mysticism of the Greek and Roman philosophers, *who,* says St. Paul, *had known God and not glorified Him as God . . . for professing themselves to be wise, became fools* (Rom. 1:21, 22); as well as that of the Neoplatonists of subsequent epochs. False the Mysticism of the Gnostic heresies of the first centuries, A.D. and of the Middle Ages. Also the Judaic religion after the destruction of the second Temple, since it consists in the rejection of the true Christ, and the vain expectation of one of their own invention. Also the religion of the Qur'an, started by that impostor, Muhammad, and which spread so rapidly, well nigh threatening the extinction of Christianity. False the Mysticism of Pantheism under all its forms, the religion of the Brahmins, of Buddha, Shintoism, Hinduism, Totemism, whether of the Primitives past or present, or of Ancient Egypt: all forms of divination, magic, sorcery.

False the Mysticism of every' Protestant heretical sect as such; and of all emotional forms of religion, without any doctrinal foundation; all the pious extravagances of revivalists, whatever be their names and colors, as, for instance, the so-called Salvation Army of today. Theosophy, Spiritualism, Christian Science, Occultism are on the same level, as also Freemasonry in all its degrees, whether it be British Freemasonry or Continental Freemasonry; for although it is admitted that there is a great difference in the animus of the two kinds, yet they both equally vindicate to themselves a sort of doctrine and sacred rites and spiritual hierarchy not sanctioned, nay, formally disapproved and condemned by the Church. Finally, the farrago of all heresies," branded by Pope Pius X with the name of Modernism, incurs the same censure. It is self-evident that none of these human or diabolical inventions can lead a man to God, and establish between him and his Maker the sweet intercourse of supernatural love.

A man can be very spiritually-minded indeed, really and truly austere and ascetical in his mode of life, as was for instance Plotinus, the founder of Neoplatonism, and yet, for all that, not be supernatural. The faint shadow of Mysticism that is discernible in such a case bears the same relation to true and genuine Mysticism as nature to the supernatural order. It is not the thing itself, it is at an infinite distance from it, and yet it shows already a certain aptitude for it. This aptitude may become the substratum or pedestal for true Mysticism to rest upon, if it be ever given by Almighty God, that is to say, if that man will ever lay himself open to the illuminations of faith and the inrush of the love of God.

The real mystics, known to God alone, that have existed before, the time of Christ outside the people of God, and after the time of Christ outside the public membership of the Catholic Church, are such, not by virtue of their heresy or schism, but in spite of it. By virtue of their genuine faith, either explicit or implicit,5n Jesus Christ the Redeemer, and of their good will, they have been enabled to accomplish the law of God according to their light. The illustrious patriarch of Idumea, in the midst of his most grievous affliction, exclaimed: *I know that my Redeemer live th, and in the last day I shall rise out of the earth, and I shall be clothed again with my skin, and in my flesh I shall see my God. . . . This my hope is laid up in my bosom.*—Job 19:25-27.

We conceive it as very likely that Job stands as the type and representative of a comparatively large number of righteous men, scattered among the Gentiles of all ages before Christ, whose privilege it was, by the grace of God, to have preserved faith in the primitive revelation and led a pure life, and thus to have laid themselves open to the mystical communications of the love of God. Furthermore, this may have been the case, and may be so to this day, and yet in times to come will be so with a number of souls, known to God alone, from among the wild tribes of the American forests or of darkest Africa, where Catholic missionaries more than once have come upon undoubted remains of the primitive religion, standing as majestic and indestructible ruins in the midst of the most cruel and degrading superstitions. As a matter of fact, before they have heard from the lips of the missionary the Gospel message of salvation, these people seem to me to stand, in regard to Our Lord, in the same relation as the Gentiles before His coming, and consequently to be under the same *régime* as to the economy of divine grace.

Marvellous indeed are the ways of God and the inventions of His love for the salvation of men of good will, wherever found, at all times and under all circumstances, be these never so unpromising, in appearance. Theologians assure us that even those heretics, who have not received the Sacrament of Baptism, either because it is not administered in their sect, or because it is administered so wrongly, or so carelessly, as to be vitiated in its form, may happen nevertheless to have the Baptism of desire; that is to say, the grace of Baptism without the Sacrament. The consequent result in such a case is that original sin is blotted out of the soul, and such a soul becomes as truly as other Christians the adopted child of God, the living member of Jesus Christ, a secret member of the Church, and is, of course, enabled to live in the mystical intercourse of love with God,

The Bible—where it is not vitiated and added to by interpolation—as it is the true Word of God, helps a large number of souls of good will whose heresy is but material and not formal, to obtain glimpses of the mystical life, to come very near to it, nay, even to begin to live it: when they read, not in a spirit of contention, but in a spirit of prayerful humility, and for the very purpose of seeking God and finding Him.

It is true, at the same time, that they are at a terrible disadvantage, in that being left to their own private interpretation, they may, as St. Peter warns us (2 Pet. 3:16), wrest the sacred text to their own perdition, and be led into the grossest form of self-delusion. The evolution of Protestantism has but too vividly illustrated this grave peril.

Still another terrible disadvantage of heretics is that they are deprived of the Sacraments of Confirmation, Holy Eucharist, Penance and Extreme Unction, the first three of which are such mighty helps unto mystical life. The Greek schismatics and other Oriental Churches, which have preserved an unbroken succession of duly ordained priests and bishops are, in this regard, much better situated.

From all this it must appear how greatly favored we

Catholics are, being children of the household of the faith, true children of light, and in full participation of all the treasures of grace to be found in the Church. How easy it is for us to be mystics if we only desire it; as indeed it is incumbent on us to do. What confusion if, when we come to judgement, we are found wanting, when some poor savages, some sorely puzzled heretics have succeeded, in the midst of most inauspicious circumstances, in making their way to God, and leading the mystical life. What a horrible judgement, though so palpably just, if the children of the Kingdom have to be ejected, when these strangers from the four winds of Heaven shall come and be seated at table in Paradise, with Abraham, and Isaac, and Jacob and all the Saints.

CHAPTER VIII

FALSE MYSTICISM WITHIN THE CHURCH

I. JANSENISM.

B*EWARE lest any man impose upon you by philosophy and vain fallacy; according to the tradition of men, according to the rudiments of the world, and not according to Christ* (Coloss, 2:8). Such is the warning of the Apostle to the Faithful of his time, at the very outset of Christianity. This same warning assuredly holds good after nineteen hundred years of the Church's life. The manifold and varied experiences through which she had to pass, have proved among other things, that not only is there no salvation for Mysticism outside the Church of God, but even within the Church there is no salvation for Mysticism but in perfect docility to her teaching.

Every form of spurious Mysticism within the Church has proved simply a perversion of the idea of the mutual love that ought to' subsist between God and the fervent soul.

It is always a palpable, gross deviation on some particular point, from the true spirit and express teaching of the Gospel of Christ and a perversion, one way or another, by exaggeration or attenuation, of the Gospel ideal of Christian perfection.

All forms of false Mysticism tend to one or other of the two extremes; either Rigorism or what for want of a better word we will call Laxism. Either they lay upon the man of good will who wants to go to God, burdens which Our Lord does not impose—a yoke which is not His own, light and sweet; or they proclaim the gate to be wide and the way to be broad that leads to life, whereas Our Lord declared these to be narrow and strait. Either they raise gratuitous obstacles between the loving soul and God Who is the object of its love, or they wantonly do away with the necessary safeguards to perfect love, which are purity, piety and justice.

Whether they are aware of it or not, false mystics derive their peculiar principles from some formally heretical doctrine or from one tending to formal heresy. Rigorism links itself to Jansenism, which in its turn has a close affinity to Calvinism. Laxism, on the other hand, not unnaturally links itself to Quietism, which in its turn has affinities with Protestant Antinomianism and Hindu Pantheism.

It is only fair to remark that much spurious Mysticism is not Mysticism at all, but only talk, a mere dissertation upon Mysticism. *My little children,* says St. John, *let us not love in word nor in tongue, but in deed and in truth* (1 Jo. 3:18). True Mysticism is all for practice.

It is not difficult to avoid the snares and pitfalls of spurious Mysticism. We could even contend that it is more difficult to be a false mystic than a true one; because science and erudition and skill of a sort are required thereto. A man has for this to be able to discourse with great subtlety upon God and man, upon grace and nature, upon free-will and delectation, and many other things; and it becomes necessary to force the soul into attitudes which are neither natural nor supernatural.

The plain Gospel is all that one needs in order to enter into the ways of mystical life, and to discern true Mysticism from false. With much more reason even than the Psalmist can the Christian exclaim: Thy *word is a lamp to my feet and a light to my paths* (Ps. 118). The true mystic guards himself as carefully from Rigorism as from Laxism, testing every suspicious doctrine by the plain teaching of the Gospel, and where doubt may still exist, referring the matter to the judgement of Holy Church. It is not necessary even to know that there are such spurious forms of Mysticism: all that is necessary is to keep the Gospel in mind and follow the lead of interior grace; just as it is not necessary to know the heresies in order to avoid them, but simply to keep in mind the lessons of the Catechism.

Here one may perhaps be tempted to ask: But if true Mysticism is so easy, why should there be any false Mysticism at all? We may then put another question: Why should there be any sinners at all? The truth is, there need be no sinners, and there need be no false mystics, but God has placed man in the hands of his own counsel: he is free to do right or wrong, to love truth and embrace it, or to prefer error. This is precisely the root of merit; and it is one of the trials of our present condition that a wrong course of action should offer allurements to us. The love of novelty, the pleasure of having a following, of originating a new school of thought, of posing before the world; the natural restlessness of some minds and the wish to show one's erudition or skill in dispute: all these causes (and there are many others) would suffice to account for the existence of false opinions in matters where the Gospel teaching is as clear as daylight, and where it is of the greatest importance not to swerve from it.

St. Paul says to his disciple Timothy: *The end of the Commandment is charity from a pure heart, and a good conscience, and an unfeigned faith: from which things some going astray are turned aside to vain talk, desiring to be teachers of the law, understanding neither the things they say nor whereof they affirm* (1 Tim. 1:5,6). And again in the same Epistle (6:3, 4): *If any man teach otherwise and consent not to the sound words of Our Lord Jesus Christ, and to that doctrine which is according to piety, he is proud, knowing nothing, but sick about questions and strifes of words, from which arise envies, contentions, blasphemies, etc.* In his second Epistle to the same Timothy, St. Paul says again: *Know this, that in the last days shall come on dangerous times. Men shall be lovers of themselves . . . an appearance indeed of piety, but denying the power thereof. Of these sort are they who creep into houses, and lead captives silly women laden with sins, who are led away with divers desires: always learning and never attaining to the knowledge of the truth* (2 Tim 3:1-7). One might almost fancy in reading these prophetic words that St. Paul had in sight the Abbé de Saint Cyran with his famous Mother Angelica, and the Barnabite Father Lacombe with his no less famous Madame Guyon.

The affectation of embracing the most rigorous opinions in matters of faith or of morals is usually the failing peculiar to men without experience, such as theologians, who spend their whole lives indoors at their studies, or again, men, young and rash, who have not yet come into contact with real life, and the souls of their fellow men. Seldom is Rigorism found among the evangelical workers, priests and missionaries, who have grown grey in the care of souls. Their zeal, matured by experience, is naturally sweetened with charity and mercy, and their opinions in matters of doctrine, in consonance with the Gospel of Christ are those that exalt the mercy of God above His justice. They know how necessary it is to comfort the faint-hearted and encourage the poor sinner in his hard struggle against evil habits, as also the man of good will and the Saint himself, in their many difficulties. They know how easily weak souls fall into discouragement and despair. And they know the yearning tenderness of the heart of Our Lord and of God for all, even for sinners the most wretched and abandoned.

The Jansenists have given us a horrible idea of God, a caricature, representing Him not as the Heavenly Father and Divine Saviour, and Spirit of Joy that He shows Himself in the New Testament, but as a harsh, whimsical, tyrannical master, unloving and unlovable. They made of the Sacrament of Penance such a difficult process that men finally gave it up in despair. They frightened people away from Holy Communion. They cast such a gloom over all the practices of religion, that it is no wonder large sections of Christians practically left the Church and would have nothing to do with it for the rest of their lives.

Could these men have ever read in the Gospel. that God is love, and did they realize that God made us, His reasonable creatures, to His own image and likeness; that is to say, capable with the help of grace of loving Him and of deserving to be loved by Him? Is it possible that they ever read the merciful utterances of Our Lord, the history of His miracles, the parables of the Good Samaritan, of the Prodigal, of the Good Shepherd; and the moving drama of His Sacred Passion? In order to frame their new Gospel, harsh and conducive only to despair, they must have deliberately turned aside from the Gospel of Jesus and from the lessons of divine mercy and tenderness, which breathe forth through all the Epistles of St. Paul and the other Apostles, just as the Pharisees of old turned away from the person of Our Lord.

A spirit of Rigorism persisted long after the main tenets and maxims of Jansenism had been routed. Those of us who have passed the meridian of life may remember having seen in their childhood very saintly priests whose usefulness in the Church of God was marred by their unbending severity. Thanks be to God, this Rigorism has at last been exorcized from our midst, and Pope Pius X has dealt its deathblow in his decrees concerning daily Communion for all classes of Christians, and even for little children. It now requires but very little skill to detect and reject any Jansenistic venom which may yet be lurking in some old books of piety.

Unfortunately this is not the case with that other form of false Mysticism, summed up and represented by Quietism, as we shall presently see.

CHAPTER IX

FALSE MYSTICISM WITHIN THE CHURCH

IL QUIETISM.

THERE is a great resemblance between laxism and tepidity, but there is also a difference, and it is this, that, while tepidity makes no pretense at giving itself a theological status and justification, laxism does.

Laxism is the system of so-called spirituality, which would conciliate piety with the widest concessions to worldliness, sensuality and self-love. It is a conception of Christian liberty growing beyond all reasonable bounds, even to unlimited licentiousness. It will, for instance, take hold of such a maxim as this of St Augustine: "Ama et fac quod vis" — "Love God and do what thou wilt," which, rightly understood, is an affirmation that he who truly loves God can be trusted never to stray away from the faithful observance of His commandments. But people of this stamp twist it and pervert it to quite another meaning, wholly foreign to the mind of the great Saint who formulated it. Thus a frivolous Christian lady will succeed in forming her own conscience, or rather deforming it, to the point of finding it quite the correct thing to be seen in the morning of a great feast day, Christmas or Easter, at Holy Communion, as modest and pious as an angel, and in the evening of the same day, in the ballroom, err *grand décolleté,* taking part in those fashionable dances which, as at present carried on, are revolting to every feeling of delicacy and propriety. The world approves of such doings. Now what is Our Lord's verdict in the Gospel? Vow *have heard that it was said to them of old: Thou shalt not commit adultery; but I say unto you, that whosoever looks upon on a woman to lust after her, has already committed adultery with her in his heart* (Matt. 5:27, 28). But if it be a grievous sin for a Christian man to look on a woman to lust after her, will it be no sin on the part of the Christian woman to expose herself in an improper dress to be gazed at and lusted after? "Ah, but there can be no harm in it," is the excuse; "my intention is not evil?' As well might the incendiary say he does not want to burn the house when he applies the flaming torch thereto. Is it not evident that these public exhibitions of immodesty, offer the greatest possible incentive to both private and public immorality in its worst and most insidious form? It is said that there even are spiritual directors who countenance, excuse, and justify such a course of action. Blind are they, leading the blind. The possible consequence is terrible to contemplate.

Upon the vantage ground of the wrong interpretation of "Ama et fac quod vis," these worldly-minded Christians meet with another class of dogmatists, who have deluged the world of piety with books about the pure love of God, and at the same time have authorized, under the garb of Mysticism, all sorts of licentiousness. Gentle reader, beware of books written "on the pure love of God," except those written by Saints, if such there be; for though there is an infinitude of books from the pens of Saints on the love of God, under one title or another, hardly will a single one be found bearing the suspicious label of "the pure love of God."

Simpleminded persons may be scandalized at this warning; but whoever knows the history of Quietism, will readily understand this caution.

As Jansenism is answerable for the falling away of large numbers of people in Catholic countries, from the public practice of religion, so Quietism, with all its vagaries, is answerable for most of the odium and ridicule that has been thrown upon the very idea of Mysticism, as also for the prejudices which are entertained against it to this very day. Many persons unite in the same reprobation genuine Mysticism and spurious Mysticism. No distinction is made between them. People will put on the index all books on Mysticism, even those written by canonized Saints, which are full of the true spirit of the Gospel. They are afraid of reading such books; they not only will not recommend them, but will even dissuade others from reading them. They prefer to such works pious literature of an inferior quality, written by authors devoid of experience in the ways of God. And thus it is that souls are famished, and that modem piety has descended to such a degree of weakness and inefficiency.

This is as yet but an indirect result of the influence of Quietism. Were we now to detail all the direct injuries it has done to religion; were we to track its baleful influence in all branches of the spiritual life, and to point out how many otherwise good books of piety, especially in the seventeenth century, have been damaged by a single touch of Quietism, it is not one chapter only, but a whole volume and a very large one indeed, which would have to be written in order to do full justice to the subject. It will suffice for my present purpose to state the working principles of Quietism. Besides, we shall have more to say on the subject, in subsequent volumes, when treating at length of Divine Contemplation and Saintly Action.

The capital error of the Quietists is, that they propose to the mystic a state of union with God, absolutely impossible in the present life. They make perfection to consist in uninterrupted contemplation. But words are misleading here. For every right-minded and unbiased person, on hearing the word contemplation, would naturally think of an active application of one's mind to the thought of God. Now that is not at all what the sectaries mean. In the state of quiet in which they pretend to plunge the soul, one must cease to reason, to reflect, nay, even to think on either one's self or on God. One must even cease to perform any of the ordinary acts of faith, hope or charity: the sole function of the spiritual man consists, as they say, in the passive reception of the infused heavenly light which is supposed to accompany this state of inactive contemplation.

Carried to its logical conclusion. Quietism would infallibly lead to Antinomianism. This is the error of those who pretend that to the perfect all things are permitted, as they are incapable of losing their spiritual holiness by any act of theirs, be it ever such a direct violation of the law of God. In this sublime state of contemplation, all external things are held to become indifferent to the soul, because it is absorbed in God. Hence good works, the Sacraments, prayer, are not necessary, nay, they are hardly compatible with the repose of the soul. Hence also, in so complete a self-absorption, the soul is said to become independent of corporeal sense to the point that even obscene and licentious representations, impure movements of the sensitive part, criminal actions of the body, fail to contaminate the contemplating soul, or to make it incur the guilt of sin.

The Spanish priest, Molinos (1640-1696), the father of modem Quietism, does not shrink from giving expression to these monstrous tenets, as may be seen in Denziger's "Enchiridion Symbolorum," by the list of 68 propositions extracted from his works and duly condemned by Pope Innocent XI. Madame Guyon, the French propagandist of Quietism, though she protested that she had not read the works of Molinos when she elaborated her own system of spirituality, and though she professed to be horrified at the logical conclusions which might be worked out of her own principles, fully deserved the strong denunciations and severe measures of which she became the object both from the Church and the State. Fénelon himself, the otherwise saintly Archbishop of Cambrai, can hardly be absolved of rashness and obstinacy throughout all the controversy which raged around his book, entitled "Maxims of the Saints," which culminated in its condemnation by Pope Innocent XII.

Quietism is the very antithesis of Mysticism. Mysticism is, if anything, an active intercourse of the loving soul with the loving God; Quietism, on the contrary, condemns activity as a wicked thing, and is all for passivity. Quietists, in aiming at the simplification of man, do not take into account his complex nature, and the present conditions of our life on earth, so removed from the direct intuition of God. Catholic Mysticism takes man as he is at present, and without trying to bring about an impossible simplification of his nature, it simplifies his life in sanctifying him in body and in soul, through the efficacy of the Sacraments and the practice of all virtues, centering all his affections upon God, through Jesus Christ.

Our deification as described by Catholic Theology, and as brought about by true Mysticism, is not an absorption of out own substance into that of God, for then we should cease to be our own selves; that is to say, we should simply cease to be. God would not, humanly speaking, gain anything thereby, and we would lose all. Nor is our deification a sort of transubstantiation of ourselves into God, as Eckart contended: for this also would be tantamount to a suppression pure and simple of our very existence. The Christian, the true mystic, in his union with God, whether in this life or the next, will always preserve his own identity. He will remain himself for evermore in the individual substance of his own created being, personally distinct from all the rest of the world and from God; a little god by the grace of God, and yet not God. The divine transformation which gradually takes place in him through his vital union with Jesus Christ to be consummated in glory, is a mighty change indeed, but accidental and not essential; a stupendous change in the quality of his substance, and in the habits of his faculties, and in the merits of his acts, but his person remains essentially the same human person for ever, marked with his own individuality, such as he will have formed it for himself. Adam will be Adam for ever. Paul will be Paul for ever: and it is in this preservation of their identity that their happiness will be rooted in eradicably.

Therefore, when St. Teresa tells us that, in her raptures, there were moments when she could not distinguish any more her own being from that of God, we must take it in this wise, that though she at the time was unable to discern the distinction, nevertheless her own being remained quite distinct in itself from that of God.

Quietism has a very pronounced leaning towards the monstrous error of Pantheism, whilst orthodox Mysticism has an invincible horror of it.

CHAPTER X

THE BEST MANUAL OF MYSTICISM

THE Gospel of Our Lord Jesus Christ, the holy Gospel as it has been written by the four Evangelists, Matthew, Mark, Luke, and John, the pure and simple Gospel, is the first, and by far the best, manual of Mysticism, as high above those written by the hands of men as the heavens are above the earth. And the best commentary upon this first manual of Mysticism is, taking them altogether as one book, the Acts of the Apostles, and the Epistles of St. Paul and the other canonical Epistles, and the Apocalypse, Only the commentary is, in places, much more obscure than the text it is made to illustrate, and so it is not everyone who can understand it or profit by it. But every one, even the least cultured and most simpleminded, can understand all that is needful from the Gospel to profit by it, without diving below the surface to its very depths. For it is the characteristic of this marvellous book, that the most sublime genius will never be able to grasp its full meaning, whilst there is not even a child's mind to which it does not bring the plain message of the love of God in all its splendor.

The Old Testament is also a commentary upon the Gospel, but still more obscure and difficult to understand than the Epistles of St. Paul and the rest of the New Testament; because, though it is the preparation and preface of the Gospel and contains it in anticipation as the bud contains the flower, still it presents to us a different character and physiognomy. Hence it is a mistake, under the law of Christ, to go back to the terrors and harshness of the first covenant. This mistake has been made by many a false mystic, and it is one reason among others why the Church has found herself compelled to put some salutary restraint upon the indiscriminate reading of the Scriptures.

The Gospel is a manual of Mysticism at once theoretical and practical, illuminating and moving. All others are borrowed from it, and are but echoes and repetitions, commentaries or explanations of it. All must conform thereto most accurately, under pain of failing to be in any way mystical. Some of these so-called spiritual treatises are weak dilutions of the Gospel: just a few drops of its generous wine, drowned in a sea of meaningless verbiage. Why not have the pure wine? There it is, at your elbow; it is all contained in the New Testament: *Eat friends, and drink, and be inebriated, my dearly beloved* (Cant. Cantic., v. 1.) Christians at the present day, as a rule, do not know their Gospel well enough, and are not conversant with it. It is small wonder that they are so frail and unstable, so easily upset or led astray. He alone who reads the Gospel assiduously can realize how far short he falls from practicing it, and only he who really tries to put it into practice comes at last to understand it.

There are two ways of knowing: the first is by rote, mechanically, without touching the inner consciousness; the second is by a vital process of discovery or rediscovery, as it were, of that which previously made no impression, and a vital process of tasting, enjoying and assimilating it. Thus until by much reading and re-reading, prayer and meditation, one has made this discovery or rediscovery of the Gospel, one can hardly be said to possess the knowledge of it. When the point is arrived at, where it seems we had heretofore not known it, then is the soul flooded with light, and inundated with an inexpressibly entrancing spiritual delight. We must come at last to feel that the Gospel is not a book, a dead letter, but a teacher, a living person, the very one we sought for in our mystical life, God Himself, Our Lord Jesus Christ, the Son of the living God. He it is and not the Evangelist who speaks to us from the Gospel page, straight into our very heart, if we only lay it open before Him. Then our Lord will cease to be a stranger, a distant person, shadowy and unreal: we shall come into touch with Him, we shall live in His company, even as the Apostles did; we shall watch Him lovingly, and He will discover to us His secrets.

Some there are who have never read the holy Gospel, not even once, from end to end. They only know the extracts which are read at the Sunday Masses through the liturgical year, always the same, year after year. This is certainly good as far as it goes, only it does not go far enough: it leaves out too many of the sayings and doings of Our Lord. These persons have not the complete knowledge of Our Lord that they could and should have, and their souls suffer a loss in proportion to their ignorance. The Church does not intend that we should content ourselves with these extracts from the Gospel; she gives them to us as choice morsels and samples of the feast that is in store for us, to tempt our appetite and lead us on to partake of the whole course.

I would therefore suggest that every Christian read one of the many learned and beautiful Lives of Christ, written of late years by eminent Catholic authors, and in which all the events and discourses of Our Lord in the four Gospels are fused into one continuous story. This done, I should suggest that he take up the text itself of the Evangelists and read at least one chapter every day. Let him read and re-read it until he becomes quite familiar with it; and even then, keep on reading and rereading it, for it is the experience of all who have done so that at every fresh perusal new grace is imparted and new light and a new infusion of joy. Of course this is on condition that it is read slowly, thoughtfully and prayerfully. Once a habit has been formed of thus reading the Gospel and tasting the sweetness of it, there is little danger of becoming tired of the exercise. It would be easy to read the whole of the New Testament once a year, as it contains in all but 260 chapters: whilst it would take a little over three years to read the whole Bible, from Genesis to the Apocalypse, at the rate of one chapter a day.

Most pious priests make it a practice of reading their daily chapter of Holy Scripture on their knees, and of devoutly kissing the sacred text. This certainly helps one to enter into a spirit of reverence and love. Still, one could not be blamed for sitting down at ease, whilst reading pen in hand, in order to follow up and note down any light received from the sacred page. The pen, plied industriously, is a marvellous instrument and a revealer of hidden secrets, even of the secrets of God.

If every educated Christian, layman as well as priest, were thus to feed his soul every day with the marrow of spiritual life, as it is in the Gospel, what a change there would soon come upon the world. How much more enlightened piety and sterling virtue and happiness for men, and glory to God there would be. Then indeed we should see Christians worthy of the name, like those of the Middle Ages or better still, of the first centuries of the Church.

It is for us, priests and religious, to bring again into the world such a happy state of things. It is in some measure within our power to achieve this desirable result. But we must begin by being real mystics ourselves before we can think of making others such; and for this purpose we must use the means set forth in this chapter.

Every good priest, ambitious of entering on the ways of true mystical life, and of teaching them to others, should make an analysis and a synthesis of the Gospels, breaking them into their component parts, and industriously reconstructing their whole scheme for himself upon some kind of a plan. The fallowing would be as good as any: first, all that Jesus is; secondly, all that Jesus did; thirdly, the sayings and discourses of Jesus; fourthly, all that Jesus suffered in order to enter into His glory—bringing all the texts of the separate Gospels under one or other of these headings. Or again, one could marshal all the texts under the two headings which form the double characteristic of mystical life: first, its uncompromising austerity; secondly, its unutterable sweetness; for Our Lord has said: *How narrow is the gate and strait is the way which leads to life*; but He has said also: *My yoke is sweet and my burthen light* (Mat. 11:30). In these two sayings of Our Lord we have the whole Gospel in a nutshell; and it would be a labor of love to distribute all His other sayings and all His acts under one or other of these two fundamental principles of spirituality. It may prove still more interesting to the priest, if he uses a plan of his own devising.

Now, I feel quite sure that a person will not go far in this kind of work without being struck with the beauty and loveliness of the Gospel in a way previously unknown to him. He will be led naturally to the loving contemplation of Christ. He will spontaneously set himself with a will to make the Gospel the rule of his every thought and word, and desire and act. He will be drawn sweetly and irresistibly into imitating the apostolic life of his Divine Master. Jesus will thus become to His priest a living reality, and a perpetual presence, and an inspiration beyond words to express. What fruits of sanctity may not be expected from such a one, and what good work will he not do in his Master's vineyard.

A mystic? Yea, and much more than a mystic; for he will be also a father, a teacher and a guide of mystics. All this, thanks to his earnest, unremitting study of the first manual of Mysticism, the Holy Gospel of Our Lord Jesus Christ, to Whom be glory for evermore!

CHAPTER XI

SIN IN THE LIGHT OF MYSTICISM

THE existence of moral evil or sin is a fact which cannot be denied. In whatever light it may be viewed, or however one may try to account for it, one is compelled to admit that there are disordered actions of men, such, for instance, as murder, theft, perjury, adultery, intemperance, ungodliness: all arising from disordered affections such as hatred, envy, lust, sloth, pride. We meet with gross, palpable evidence of this evil everywhere around us, to say nothing of our personal experience of it in our own selves. Moreover, by natural implication and by the testimony of history, we know that it has been so throughout the past ages, going back from century to century to the very dawn of the history of the world. At this point divine revelation unveils before our eyes the fountain-head of this ocean of human misery and guilt, in the original sin of our first-parents—and the same authority furthermore discloses the fact that even the sin of Adam and Eve was not the first link in the long chain, for this sin connects itself, by the temptation of the evil one, with his own sin and that of the other fallen angels, when they raised the cry of rebellion against God in the paradise of their trial.

Sin is essentially a free, deliberate act contrary to right reason. The psalmist asks this question: *Who can understand sins*? (Ps. 18:13). No one can understand sin in itself, because it is a monstrous absurdity, the act of a reasonable creature, and yet an act contrary to right reason. Therefore, on the face of it, it is an act of self-destruction, an obliterating of the likeness of God in one self with one's own hands, a guilty returning to nothingness. Considered in the abstract—even apart from the incidental sufferings it entails on its perpetrator and on its victims, which are very grievous, as we shall see in the next chapter—sin is the greatest evil that can ever happen, for it is the evil of the spirit. It is a falling away from God, a wilful cutting off of communication with the spring of spiritual life, a throwing of oneself headlong into a bottomless abyss, a suicidal act; and, at the same time, an awful lie. Whilst the mystic says with the king-prophet: *It is good for me to adhere to God* (Ps. 72:28), because indeed he has experienced it to be so; the sinner, on the other hand, declares by his acts, if not by words of mouth: "It is good for me to turn away from God; it is good for me to adhere to created things instead of God; it is good for me, by falling back upon myself and things created, to return as far as in me lies into nothingness"; and all the while the event is giving him the lie. It is not good, it is very harmful for him to do these things.

There are two formidable aspects of sin. First, there is the evil done against God, inasmuch as sin is an attack upon Him, an offence to His sanctity and love, an infringement upon His absolute sovereign rights. There is at the same time the evil done to the reasonable creature, in that sin separates him from God, Who is his very life, and precipitates the perpetrator of it into a depth of degradation and misery proportionate to the height of glory and happiness to which God had predestinated him.

The original mistake of the sinner is that, for the gratification of his passion, he practically refers everything to himself To this unworthy end he turns the noble faculties of his body and soul, which were given him as so many instruments for the exclusive service of God. Moreover, he lays guilty hands upon the creatures animate and inanimate of this natural universe, all of which are God's property, and he reduces them to an unjust captivity, making use of them in spite of their groaning for his own nefarious purposes against the will of God, and against God Who created both him and them for a noble end. But the height of injustice and folly is reached when the unfortunate sinner damns himself in this world and in the next by misusing his fellow men, even his own flesh and blood, a wife, children, subordinates, friends, dragging all these along with him into sin.

For this egotist the whole universe of things created is but a vast circumference of which he constitutes himself the center. He refers and subordinates everything to his own self, even God, since he would have Him yield to his puny will. Now God cannot acquiesce in such a monstrous overthrow of his inalienable sovereign rights. The sweetness and harmony of order demands that everything be referred to God and subordinated to Him; the more so that God has in view the procuring of His own glory by means of our own happiness. Could anything be more desirable? The sinner, on the other hand, proposes to himself and to all he can press into service his own glory instead of that of God, his own will instead of that of God, at the cost of his own happiness, both temporal and eternal, and at the cost of the precious souls of those he scandalizes. Could anything be imagined more felonious and idiotic?

Now though he may, through want of faith or through inadvertence, be all unconscious of the fact, the terrible truth is that the center towards which the sinner really gravitates, to which he is attracted, and to which he tends by the sheer weight of his guilt, is the hell of the damned. It is an article of faith that were he to die suddenly, unrepentant, as suddenly would he fall into the pit of hell, just as a stone, held above water, falls and is engulfed in the water, the instant it is released and abandoned, to its natural attraction. The sinner would not be with God, and out of God there is no future place for the reasonable creature, guilty of such a crime, but the eternal prison of hell.

In this regard there is no difference between him who is guilty of but one mortal sin and the man who is guilty of a multitude: they both belong to hell, though they are not in it as yet.

The moment that the sinner by a first mortal sin achieves his severance from God, that very moment his name is blotted out of the book of life and inscribed on the rolls of hell. By right he now belongs to hell as much as the lost souls themselves, though it is yet in his power, with the grace of God if he will accept it, to cancel the terrible indenture.

The difference between sinner and sinner on earth, as also between reprobate and reprobate in hell, lies in the respective amount of guilt each one has incurred, and the special punishment meted out to him in consequence. We might say it lies radically in the degree of rottenness and filthiness to which each one has descended. A man just dead is as dead as one who died yesterday, or a week ago, or a month ago, or six months ago: but he is not yet such an object of horror as these latter, so the sinner who is guilty of but one mortal sin is as absolutely dead to the life of grace as he who is laden with a thousand mortal sins, but this latter is a greater object of the reprobation of God and of His vindictive justice.

This may serve to explain the warning of Our Lord to the sinner in the Apocalypse 3:1-2: *I know... that thou hast the name of being alive, and thou art dead. Be watchful and strengthen the things that remain, which are ready to die.* In the unfortunate Christian who has lost charity by but one mortal sin, there survive usually, first, the theological virtue of hope, then that of faith; formless, both of them, it is true (Latin *informes),* but still able, even as such, to prevent a greater ruin and to become somehow principles of a spiritual resurrection. There survive, moreover, all the acquired moral virtues, and finally, at times, a certain lingering shadow of the spirit of prayer. There may even perchance be found in that soul a certain imitation of charity: a dangerous survival of the former state, because, says St. Francis of Sales ("Love of God," Book IV, c. 10 and 11), it serves but to deceive the wretched sinner, and keep him in illusion as to his real state. *The things that remain which are ready to die,* of which Our Lord speaks, are therefore the formless theological virtues of hope and faith, and the acquired moral virtues. The infused moral virtues which are as the suite and the handmaidens of Charity are struck dead the same moment as their queen.

The theological virtue of hope, rendered formless by mortal sin, may at last perish altogether, by the repetition or multiplication of criminal acts. There will come a moment when the soul will pass almost without transition from the height of presumption to the depths of despair. The yoke of sin grows heavier and heavier, the evil habits, like so many iron chains, become firmly riveted to the soul, and all prospect of deliverance is out of sight. Then the wretched man falls into discouragement, and drifting at the mercy of circumstances, is a ready prey to the most violent and sudden transports of passion, after which he is haunted by temptations of despair or even of suicide.

Christian hope being dead, faith may still survive formless and further weakened by the sad fate of hope: how very ailing, how severely shaken is shown by its occasional fainting fits, so to speak, or, to use another metaphor, by the partial and more or less prolonged eclipses of its light. Still even such a weak and fitful light is better than absolute darkness, and it may help the soul to avoid the worst pitfalls, and even direct its first steps towards a return to God.

The worst state of all is arrived at when faith itself has finally been put out, either by the sinner's committing certain particularly heinous crimes, or a deliberate intention on his part to extinguish its persistent flickering. However, do what he will, the light which he received in Baptism, with the indelible character or sign which marked him as a Christian, is never totally done away with, but from time to time from its dying embers sparks and flames spring up unexpectedly, which are the last appeals of God to a soul obstinately bent upon its own destruction.

To conclude, we may say that in the moral order there are two great centers of attraction, and only two: God, the loving God, and Hell, the Hell of the damned. All reasonable creatures, whether in *via* or *in termino*, converge towards one or other of these centers; attracted to the one by the mysterious force of charity: or to the other by that other force, the antithesis of charity, which is sin, habitual sin; for actual sin becomes habitual if it is not at once repented of and abolished by a good confession or an act of perfect contrition. Those *in termino*, both angels and the souls of the dead, are not only attracted to their center, whichever this happens to be, but they are bound to it for ever. Souls which are yet m *via* have it in their power to wrench themselves from the one and transfer themselves to the other. All, whether m *termino* or m *via*, gravitate towards their center of attraction with a force proportionate to their affection for charity or sin, respectively. The tepid Christian himself, just as the mystic of all degrees or the sinner of all shades, is also actually gravitating towards one of the two spheres of attraction, that of the God of love, or that whose focus is the hell of the damned. Only when, by not being actually in the state of mortal sin, he happens to be gravitating towards God, Who is the natural center of charity, still he keeps himself at such an enormous distance from this center that he cannot be warmed nor illumined by its rays, and, being hardly conscious of the force that draws him, he obeys its attraction but sluggishly. He is so very near to the confines of the sphere whose center of attraction is the hell of the damned, that it is not to be wondered at if he be suddenly whirled out of his former orbit and tossed into this one, to become one of those *wandering stars* of which St. Jude speaks, *to whom the storm of darkness is reserved for ever* (Jud. 1:13). May the loving God preserve us from such a terrible fate.

CHAPTER XII

THE HARD WAYS OF SIN

My people have done two evils: they have forsaken me, the fountain of living water, and have dug to themselves cisterns, broken cisterns that can hold no water (Jerem. 2:3).

THE keynote of mystical life is joy: a joy deep and pure, but hidden from the eyes of men; it does not preclude severe sufferings, both mental and physical; these will ever be the part of the pilgrim sojourning in this land of exile. After their severe flagellations in the presence of the council of their nation, the Apostles *went away rejoicing for that they were accounted worthy to suffer reproach for the name of Jesus* (Acts 5:41). *I am filled with comfort,* says St. Paul, *I exceedingly abound with joy in all our tribulation* (2 Cor. 7:4). The keynote of a sinful life, on the other hand, is sadness; but a secret sadness, which eats its way relentlessly into the very core of the sinner's heart, and though perforce it is concealed from the world, yet in spite of every effort, it will often manifest itself. How could it be otherwise with one who chooses to make himself the enemy of God and of his better self and of his fellow-men?

It is certainly a merciful dispensation by which sin always brings its own chastisement, even in this world—the poor sinner may take heed and escape at least eternal punishment. It is a law of the universe that every disorder brings uneasiness. A broken limb, a dislocated bone will cause an agony of suffering until it is properly set. Now, sin is the greatest of disorders, a moral disorder, causing uneasiness to the spirit even of angel or man; but very often with man it is also at the same time a physical and material disorder, bringing in its own train both material and physical pain.

Let us glance rapidly at some of the sufferings, moral and physical, which are to be found in the trail of sin. First of all there is remorse. This skeleton in the cupboard is not at all a comforting companion for the diseased mind. The sinner tries to forget it, but he never completely succeeds. Then the fear of disclosure; and the confusion when one is discovered and becomes an object of reprobation to all (right-minded persons, and even to the wicked and hypocritical, by whom, perhaps, the temptation and sin were caused. Bitter disappointment, disgust and nausea are also frequently in attendance; for the object which promised to give such rapturous delights has turned out to be a veritable apple of Sodom, alluring in appearance but changing to ashes and sulphur in the mouth. Loss of health, the squandering of fortune, exasperating recriminations, bitter regrets, burning reproaches: all these come as a matter of course. Then the distressing, maddening question which cannot but rise in the mind: How will all this end? It may be silenced for a while, but it rises again, importunate and persistent The wretched sinner wrings his hands, turns his head away and feigns not to hear.

And now if the sinner remains obdurate, refusing to return like the Prodigal to God his heavenly Father, by true repentance and amendment of life, a new series of alarming symptoms will begin to manifest themselves. These are: 1. Deformation of the conscience. Though it is hard to kick against the goad, and with open eyes, yet at this point the sinner tries to persuade himself that black is white and white is black. 2. Spiritual blindness. An infatuation with the object of his passion now takes possession of the sinner, so that he cannot see anything else that matters in the whole world. 3. A weakening of the queen-faculty, the will. Resisting power ceases entirely, and the soul is ready for every sort of abdication. 4. A hardening of the heart. Here sin is loved for its own sake; the sinner refuses to be released from his evil, resolved to pursue his course whithersoever it may lead him. 5. A lowering of the character to untold depths. Probity, sincerity, self-respect, natural affections, consideration for others, regard for public decency: all go by the board. 6. A monstrous perversion of the natural appetites, unbridled licentiousness of the imagination; overpowering, well- nigh irresistible tyranny of the senses, and a thorough disorganization of the whole being, body and soul. 7. Terrible, shameful diseases, leading to the very verge of folly and despair. 8. The horrible fear of stealthily approaching death and of what lies beyond. There is none who fears death like the sinner: his all in all is in and of this world—is it surprising that he should tremble at the very thought of Judgement? Then the probable transmission of the accursed germs of disease and vice to an innocent offspring.

Is this an overdrawn picture? Anyone acquainted with the world will be able to point out scores of cases, no less terrible than this.

Finally, there will be the posthumous effects of sin; that is to say, a whole brood of sins, which, after the sinner's death, may spring up from the scandals he caused during life. These may go on spreading and perpetuating and propagating without limit or end, till the very day of Judgement. Then will all these evils be attributed to the sinner who fathered them, and demand will be made for a revision of his account with the Divine Justice, and for proportionate aggravation of his eternal punishment.

And all along, during his wretched life on earth, to all the self-inflicted chastisement of the sinner, is added the uneasiness arising from the fear of God: not a holy fear like that of the true children of God, who are in dread lest they offend their heavenly Father and incur His displeasure and lose Him; but an abject fear, a fear which makes the sinner shun God and look upon Him as an enemy. Adam, in order to taste freely of the forbidden fruit, put away his habit of the filial, holy fear of God; and on eating of the forbidden fruit was immediately seized with the abject fear of God. He shuns God, he avoids meeting Him as heretofore, he hides from Him in the woods with his guilty consort, and when perforce he must face his offended Creator and Benefactor, he becomes impudent, which is another way of running away from God, He says: *The woman whom Thou gave me to be my companion tempted me* (Gen. 3:12), as much as to say: "She is blameworthy, not I; nay, if we look well into it, Thou my God, Thou Who gave her to me, Thou art the One to blame."

Does not every sinner in a way conduct himself like Adam,

and blame God for his own evil deeds? Look at the typical modem man of the world: he entertains no holy fear of God, and can drink in sin like water. Nevertheless, he has at the same time a horrible dread of God. He cannot bear the thought of Him. The mere mention of His Holy Name is enough to throw that man into a frenzy. For months and years at a time he will not set foot in a church; and when forced to do so by worldly conventionality, to attend a wedding for instance, or the funeral of a friend, or for some civic demonstration, he does so with a shudder, as is plainly shown by his whole attitude. He flies in abject terror from before the face of God; be flies with a flight which very soon may be eternal. And all along he blames God, the loving God, the Holy One, not himself, for his own wickedness, The literature of the day, in all its branches, high and low, refined and coarse, light and learned, is saturated with this sort of blasphemy. But it is not convincing, nor is it reassuring, and the louder the voice which gives expression to these horrors, the more evident becomes the abject fear of God, by which those who cry out are tormented.

Is it fear, even abject fear? Nay, it is something much worse: it is hatred, positive hatred of God of which the habitual sinner becomes at last possessed. Of course, the beginner in the ways of sin does not arrive all at once at such an extremity as this. He comes to it little by little, but he comes in the end to the point of actually hating the good God Who made him, and the loving Saviour Who died for him on the Cross. Because God forbids sin, and punishes it terribly even in this world and threatens an eternal, fearful punishment of it in the next, the sinner is brought step by step to hate with a positive and explicit hatred, the sanctity of God, His justice, His infinite perfections and His very Being. This is indeed one of the hard ways of sin. *We wearied ourselves in the ways of iniquity and destruction, and have walked through hard ways.* Thus speak the reprobates in the Book of Wisdom 5:7.

These, then, are the hard ways of sin. When we tell the silly youth bent upon eating of forbidden fruit, that sin hurts, he will not believe it. He argues with himself that these tales of woe are inventions of priests which at the most can only frighten little children. He persuades himself that he at least will not feel the worse for quaffing a generous draught of the cup of pleasure; that he will know when to stop, and that even if he gets a touch of fever in consequence he will soon be well again. Poor fool! How many such are to be seen, terribly caught indeed, and they are forced at last to cry out that sin does indeed hurt.

When by a very signal mercy of God the sinner is given the grace to desire to retrace his footsteps and return to a saintly life, he is confronted with really appalling difficulties. To mention at present but one, among many, there is literally "the devil to pay." The devil holds him and will not let him go. The devil has bought his soul; the sinner sold it to him, very cheap it is true, and he has been cheated in the bargain, but still the devil has his bond. He has taken his assurances. He holds a mortgage on the brain, another on the willpower, another on the imagination, another on the senses, still another on the nerves of the sinner. Oh! how hard it is to wrench oneself free from the devil's clutches! It must, nevertheless, be done, and that at all costs. It is a question of life and death, and of life and death eternal; and the longer the delay in the great and desperate effort towards the liberty of the children of God, the more the devil rivets his chains and weighs down the soul of the poor sinner with an iron yoke.

CHAPTER XIII

THE PRODIGAL'S RETURN

IT may, at first sight, seem impossible for a poor sinner, after years of slavery to evil habits, to retrace his steps and return to a healthy and saintly state of life. But what is impossible to man is not impossible to God. If a miracle, or even a series of miracles, be needed to help the repentant sinner's good will, miracles will be forthcoming.

I do not mean thereby that the sinner will be spared the hardships of conversion; for these are a part of his expiation and a necessary discipline. It is required that by as many acts of self-indulgence as he descended to his present position on the road of perdition, by at least as many acts of self-restraint and self-renunciation shall he now retrace his steps before he can scale the heights of sanctity.

Do you think that the Prodigal's return home in the state in which he found himself was not fraught with appalling difficulties to his self- love? When the Good Shepherd lifted up the erring sheep from the thorny bush on the mountain crag where it had fallen and all but killed itself, and took it tenderly into His arms. He could not for all His loving care prevent the bruised sheep from feeling the pain of its hurts, nor the tediousness of the journey back to the fold, nor the discomfort of the heat of the day.

The Good Samaritan, it is true, poured oil and vinegar into the wounds of the unfortunate traveler, who had fallen into the hands of highwaymen, been robbed and left half dead on the wayside. He skillfully bandaged the wounds, and with infinite care placed the man on his beast and led him to the nearest inn on the road. But for all that, he could not prevent fever setting in during the night; that was a consequence of the great loss of blood and the terrible nervous shock which the poor man had sustained: neither could he forestall nor shorten the slow progress of recovery.

Although God has forgiven all past transgressions, as soon as a full, sincere and sorrowful confession of them has been made, and although the penitent has, by confession, banished the loathsome presence of sin from his soul, and is resolved with God's grace to begin a new life, nevertheless the consequences of sin still remain. He will have resolutely to grapple with these, nor can he hope to overcome them all at once, but gradually and by dint of patient and unremitting effort. The arch-fiend has been forced to evacuate the country he had invaded, but he leaves it bare and desolate, the fields are burnt, and the houses in ruins. Time and labor will be needed to clear the rubbish, to break up the ground again, to rebuild the houses, and thus bring the country to its former flourishing condition.

It may even happen occasionally, in the beginning of his conversion, that the poor penitent will relapse into sin after a long and protracted struggle. Has he really given full consent to evil? No one can tell—himself less than anyone. Whether quite a mortal sin or not this relapse is horribly painful, yet the poor sinner must rise at once. He remains dazed, sick and disgusted with himself, and very much frightened. Saint Angela of Foligno had such a relapse in the beginning of her conversion.

Thus it is absolutely certain that the sinner wishing to return to God has before him, besides the hardships common to all the servants of God, the prospect of some special sufferings which are the effects of his past sins, and would have been spared him if he had never left the path of virtue. He is therefore in need of a very powerful grace of God; but he is no sooner resolved to correspond to grace than he is, at once, lifted out of the depths of perdition and assumed into the economy of divine life. This is already an immense miracle, the proportions of which we shall be able to appreciate only in paradise.

This is only the beginning. The penitent sinner has now to set out on his Way of the Cross and to climb his Calvary. He does so dragging himself heavily along, groaning under the wright of the awkward cross which he has hewn and carved out for himself, with his own hands; a cross made up of the shame of his past sins, of the falterings of nature and of the tyranny of inveterate evil habits; a heavy cross which occasionally bears him down and seems on the point of crushing him to death. So it proved to be with the illustrious penitent Mary of Egypt, in the first years of her solitary life. Now and again she fell into discouragement; almost but not quite into despair. It is so with every true penitent. At this point we behold a second miracle. Lo, the Lamb of God, the Divine Saviour walks before the weary pilgrim of Calvary, laden with His own still heavier Cross; bleeding, falling, rising again, and beckoning to him to follow. And virtue goes out of the sweet Saviour, so that, though trembling, the poor penitent is able to rise to his feet again and totter on; and now (marvellous to relate!) as he climbs higher and higher up the steep hill, he finds it more alluring than the broad way of his former life of sin, and he begins to love its very hardness.

Humiliations will not be spared him on the way: kicks and cuffs, and sneers and lashes of the tongue, and curses deep and loud from his former associates in sin. No one can leave with impunity the service of the world. How the devils hate the man who turns away from them to follow Jesus to Calvary!

Nor are these the severest trials. To the innocent Jesus Himself, the worst afflictions during His sacred Passion came, not from the hands of men but from those of His Heavenly Father and from His own Hands; that is, from the horror and hatred with which He looked upon the sins of the world which He bore in His own Person. So also the true penitent must suffer. The severest trials come to him from the hands of God, and from his own hands.

Although God has forgiven him, the penitent himself will never until death forgive himself for having offended the Divine Majesty. Many and many a time will he break his heart in silent prayer, and melt into bitter tears at the recollection of his former offences. Thus did St. Peter bewail all through his life the misfortune of having in a moment of weakness denied his Master. Tradition tells us that the tears in coursing incessantly from his eyes had traced deep furrows in his cheeks. The immortal Penitential Psalms bear witness to the deep, long-abiding sorrow of King David after his crime; and they furnish the penitents of all ages with an inspired form, in which to express their bitter regret for having offended God.

Now, in this abiding and persevering sorrow of the penitent sinner lies one of the greatest safeguards against a relapse into sin. There is little danger of doing again what is bewailed so bitterly. Lifelong observation goes to show that the reason why so many Christians lamentably relapse into grievous sin, even soon after good confessions—as good, at any rate, as attrition with holy absolution can make them—is chiefly that they do not cultivate an abiding sorrow for their former offences; or, what comes to the same, they do not cultivate a true love of God for Himself. They have received holy absolution with joy and with a deep sense of relief, but they perform no further penance than the light one imposed by the priest, nor do they feel the necessity of watching and praying against the recurrence of temptation. As soon as for given their sins are by them forgotten. And yet we are warned by the oracle of the Holy Spirit. *Be not without fear about sins forgiven* (Eccli. 5:5). Hence the deplorable weakness of many Christians. What would also seem incredible is that repeated falls do not help them to grasp this principle of spiritual life,—that, though God forgives the sinner, the sinner must never forgive himself: therein lies the surest safeguard for the future.

Wash me yet more from my iniquity (Ps. 50:4) sighs the true penitent with the King-Prophet. God hears his prayer and cleanses him more. For, although our heavenly Father has forgiven the sins of His penitent child, yet He chastises him, makes him suffer, allows him to feel the full weight of their horror and wickedness. This God does, not in anger but in love, not only in order to cleanse the soul more perfectly but in order to make it gain precious merits for heaven, thus redeeming lost time.

Hence it is that after the first transport of joy and sweetness, and fervor of conversion, there usually sets in a period of darkness and dryness and a withdrawal of spiritual consolations. Prayers, meditations, Communions—all seem absolutely devoid of the unction of piety. Sometimes a well-nigh invincible horror of confession will come upon the soul; fearful doubts arise, as to whether the sins of the past have been duly confessed and are really forgiven; for the time being the soul loses sight of the infinite mercy of God and the efficacy which the Sacraments derive from the merits of the Passion of Our Lord. The perplexed penitent, seeking vainly to alleviate his sufferings, desires while at the same time he dreads, to repeat over and over again his general Confession and, though he may do this, it will but serve to involve him in an inextricable maze of explanations and difficulties. The unbearable torment of scrupulosity and doubts against Faith infest the soul; and frightful temptations against purity alternate with the fear of death and the judgement to come.

All this suffering is terrible and yet is it not better to be so tormented and pleasing to God than to be as heretofore a slave of the devil, living on the brink of hell? This soul is happy deep down within herself. She would not exchange her present state for the most joyful moments of her former life. She has become a spectacle to the world and to angels, to the Saints in heaven and to God Himself. We may reverently conjecture the palpitating interest with which they follow each incident, in the beautiful drama of the transformation of a sinner into a Saint, even into another Christ!

The supreme act will be accomplished in the mystical crucifixion and death on the Cross of the poor penitent. He must submit to be stripped of all created affections, and allow his soul to be torn to shreds by the most cruel tortures, and finally to be nailed to the Cross, there to hang by its wounds. Then all the pains of this soul shall be gathered up into one, the greatest of all, the torment of thirst: the thirst for love, for the feeling of loving God and of being loved by Him. Of this cooling draught she shall be refused even one drop, and instead she shall be offered bitter gall and vinegar. She must go through the supreme ordeal of feeling abandoned by men and by God Himself, and cry out with Jesus in His extremity: My *God, my God, why hast Thou forsaken Me?* (Matt. 27:46).

Meanwhile there is more joy in Heaven upon the

transformation of such a sinner into Jesus, and into Jesus Crucified, than upon the perseverance of ninety-nine just, who need not penance. This were enough, if it were possible, to fill even the Saints with envy of this poor penitent.

But the sublimity of his state is wholly hidden from him as yet. Hidden also, quite out of sight is the marvellous crown of jewels of eternal splendor, which all these painful victories over self are gaining for him.

Behold, at last, the moment of triumph is at hand, Jesus says to the dying sinner, his own friend and fellow-sufferer. *This* day *thou shalt be with Me in Paradise* (Luke 23:43). *Consummatum est. It is consummated* (Jn. 19:30). *Come, beloved, for winter is now passed* (Cant, 2:11); sadness is no more; the joyful voice of love is heard in our land; the flowers of eternal glory break forth all over thee: *enter thou into the joy of Thy Lord* (Matt. 25:21).

What a chorus of congratulations then bursts forth upon the ears of the penitent elect, and what hosannahs of praise to God and jubilation are heard in Heaven when such a one makes entrance there.

Sinner, O my brother, it is yet in our power, yours and mine, with God's grace to secure ineffable joy such as this for ourselves, and to give joy to the hosts in Heaven above. We are wretched, yes, but the more wretched we are at present the greater will our achievement be. Shall we not start forth upon the journey?

CHAPTER XIV

THE UNCLEAN SPIRITS

THESE Outlines of the Doctrine of the Mystical Life would not be complete, and we should be guilty of a serious omission, were we not to take into account the fallen angels, their sin, and their action upon the world at large, as well as upon the Church of Christ, and upon each individual soul in particular. This consideration will help towards a true appreciation of Mysticism. It will also serve to bring out in clear perspective the fate of the purest and brightest of God's creatures, when once they have separated themselves from Him, Who is their life; and it will show us at the same time the wisdom and power of God Himself, Who from the evil of sin draws a greater good, namely, that of the sanctification of His elect and the manifestation of the treasures of His charity. Indeed the Church of Christ and every predestinate soul would be far less bright and holy than they now are had they not passed through the severe ordeal of temptation by devils and persecution by the wicked, and we should never have known the excess of the love of God for us had not the sin of our first parents given occasion for the awful mystery of our Redemption by the Cross.

By a wise counsel of God the devil is permitted to have a hand in the making of history. We cannot reckon without him. Nor could we explain without him the superhuman perverseness of some historical personages, such as Cain, Pharaoh, Antiochus, Judas, Nero, Domitian, Arius, Mahomet, Luther, Voltaire, Robespierre, the Antichrist that is to come; nor the superhuman perverseness of associations such as Continental Freemasonry; nor the ugliest features of such great social upheavals as the so-called Reformation of the sixteenth century, the French Revolution at the end of the eighteenth century, and the present world-war, with its atrocities, sacrileges and immoralities on the part of, at least, some of the belligerents. The activity of Satan does much more than merely add a further source of temptation to the weakness of the world and of the flesh; it brings to bear also a combination and an intelligent direction of all the elements of evil. Man, even fallen from innocence and grace, would never have descended to the depths of wickedness he is capable of now had he been left to himself.

The devils are spirits of darkness; they are set out upon the task of casting darkness over the souls of men, to make them fall into errors, dogmatic and moral, and thus achieve their eternal ruin. It is worthy of the infinite wisdom of God to allow them to have their way for a time, whilst turning their malicious intent to His own ends. By their insane efforts the devils only succeed in threshing out the wheat of the divine Husbandman, separating it from the chaff upon the threshing floor of this present world. The wheat is being constantly taken up into Heaven by the blessed angels: only the chaff remains in the hands of the devils to be burnt for ever with them in the flames of hell.

St. John Climachus, that great master and teacher of mystical Theology, in "The Steps of Paradise," shows us the devils, full of cunning and malice, incessantly applying the keenness of their intellects and the unbending strength of their perverted wills, to the one purpose of burning down, by means of the very fire which torments them, the temple of God; that is to say the Church of Jesus Christ, and every individual soul which, when in the state of grace, is also the temple of God. *Brethren,* says St. Paul, *put you on the armor of God, that you may be able to stand against the snares of the devil, For our wrestling is not against flesh and blood, but against principalities and powers, against the rulers of the world of this darkness, against the spirits of wickedness in the high places. Wherefore take unto you the armor of God, that you may be able to resist in the evil day and to stand in all things perfect. Stand therefore having your loins girt about with truth and having on the breastplate of justice: in all things taking the shield of faith wherewith you may be able to extinguish all the fiery darts of the most wicked one* (Eph. 6:11-16).

Our Lord calls the devils *unclean spirits.* It would be impossible to find another name which would characterize them more truly. The idea of uncleanness seems at first sight very repugnant to that of spirituality. The devils are angels, that is to say spirits, unmixed with bodily matter and therefore absolutely free from the passions of lust which are derived therefrom; how then can they be called unclean? Do not the two words, "unclean" and " spirit" involve a contradiction and an anomaly? However, we are prepared somewhat to understand this by what we have read *(supra,* Ch. XI) of sin in the abstract, namely, that it is an absurdity, an anomaly, a guilty return to nothingness and therefore a corruption, making the subject of it unclean.

The devils are justly called unclean, though spirits, because they have embraced the state of sin and live in it for ever. The love of God is the only aroma which can preserve the reasonable creature from corruption. This love they have deliberately and definitely put away. They are moreover justly called unclean, because sin is now their only occupation: hating and blaspheming God, tempting men and tormenting themselves and one another and their victims, the reprobates in hell. These are the only uses to which they put their bright intellect and strong will. Finally, they are justly called unclean because they tempt man to commit the sins of the flesh for which they themselves, as pure spirits, have a horror intense and abiding. Such is their hatred of God that they incite men to this thing which causes in themselves an intolerable nausea: just as if a man of noble birth and education and of refined tastes should hate another man to such an extent that he would do violence to himself and take in his hands the most unclean substance, in order to fling it at the picture of his enemy whose person he was unable to reach. Unclean indeed must they be accounted who are the instigators of all uncleanness.

From various passages of Holy Scripture— more particularly from Ezech. 28:12-15, Isaiah 14:13-15, Luke 10:18, and Apoc. 12:1-9—the Fathers of the Church and Scholastic Theologians have evolved the story of the fall of the Angels in the manner following: they assert that the sin of Lucifer and his followers consisted in their refusing to abide and persevere in the supernatural order in which God had placed them in the first moment of their existence. All the Angels of God, in the beginning, were created in a like state of grace. They were all made angels of light, children of God, dearly loved, highly exalted, and they were all alike destined after due probation to the glory and bliss of the Beatific Vision. They were not only endowed with a most excellent, purely spiritual nature, free from any defect or inclination to evil and sin, but they were moreover raised by grace, above their nature, to an unspeakable height of positive sanctity, and endowed with most admirable supernatural illumination and virtue. It was from such a height that, with open eyes, by their own choice, and without any temptation, they deliberately precipitated themselves.

Lucifer revolted against the precedence given to love over intellect. The splendor of his own natural gifts seems to have so dazzled him that he loathed the supernatural order, wherein magnificence of intellect counted for nothing if not accompanied by humility and love. He was enraged to see in the light of the revelation that was given to all the angels during their probation, this great wonder in Heaven, a future Lucifer or Light-bearer brighter than himself, namely, the Virgin with the Child-God in her arms. He could not bring himself to acknowledge that a woman inferior to him in nature should at some future epoch be made his Queen, and that the seed of that woman should be preferred to himself for the honor of the Hypostatic Union. Thus it was that, when God the Father made known to all the Angels the coming of the First-Begotten in the humility of our flesh, and commanded them all to adore Him (Heb. 1:6), Lucifer raised his great battle-cry, and his rebellion spread to some of the ranks of the angelic hierarchies, and we know the sequel.

So it followed that the devils, though still perfect in the incorruptible nature of pure spirits, are vitiated in their intellect and will in that they do not accept the supernatural order: they protest against it, they unceasingly wage war against it, and God allows them for a while to fight against it with all their might Saint Thomas says: *Daemon non habet cognitionem matutinam, necque vespertinam sed nocturnam* (Ia Quest, 64. I, ad 3). The devil will, on the one hand, never have the knowledge proper to the blessed in the Beatific Vision. On the other hand, by his apostasy he has fallen away from grace and from the divine light that was in him at his creation. He has merely the knowledge that is common to all pure spirits, which is very great indeed, but is only of natural things and does not make for happiness; it is but darkness in regard to the whole supernatural order. In his affections and in his acts the devil is monstrously deformed. From an angel of light he has changed himself into an angel of darkness; from a pure flame of love he has made himself a dragon and a burning brand of inextinguishable malice and hatred. Our quaint mediaeval painters were not, after all, far from the mark, when they pictured the Devil in all sorts of shameful deformations and grotesque attitudes.

CHAPTER XV

"THE WORLD OF THIS DARKNESS"

IN the banding together of the devils with the sinners of the world, is to be found an explanation of that strange phenomenon and that formidable power of evil upon earth called by the Apostle *The World of this Darkness* (Eph. 6:12).

By this expression St. Paul does not mean the material universe of things visible, which God made, and which He solemnly declared in the beginning to be *very good* (Gen. I, 31), nor even that portion of it, the earth on which living men, divided into two opposite camps carry on their deeds of sanctity or of shame. By "the world of this darkness" the Apostle signifies only the whole company of sinners, together with their evil works in every department of human activity. This is the world over which the devil is proclaimed prince. *The prince of this worlds* as Our Lord says (Jo. 12:31). When Christ was tempted in the desert, the Devil *Him up into a high mountain, and showed Him all the kingdoms of the world and the glory of them, and said to Him: All these will I give Thee if, falling down. Thou wilt adore me.* (Mat. 4:8, 9). This is the world against which Our Lord launches His anathemas: *Woe to the world on account of its scandals* (Mat. 18:7). O *Father . . . I pray not for the world but for them whom Thou hast given Me. . . . They are not of the world, as I also am not of the world* (Jo. 17:5-16). To His brethren who did not believe in Him He said: *The world cannot hate you, but Me it hates, because I give testimony of it that the works thereof are evil* (Jo. 7:7). To the Jews who did not receive His teaching, He declared: You *are from beneath, I am from above; you are of this world, I am not of this world* (Jo. 8:23). This is the world which St. John says is *wholly seated in wickedness* (1 Jo. 5:19), and of which he gives us solemn warning: *Love not the world, nor those things which are in the world. If any man love the world, the charity of the Father is not in him: for all that is in the world is the concupiscence of the flesh, and the concupiscence of the eyes, and the pride of life which is not of the Father but is of the world. And the world passes away, and the concupiscence thereof, but he that doth the will of God abides for ever.* (1 Jo. 2:15-17).

So the world is the society of the wicked on earth, under the leadership of the devil. It is social, collective, cumulative, organized ungodliness. It is the City of Evil, *The great city which hath dominion over the kings of the earth* (Apoc. 17:18)—the city of confusion, the Babel of contradiction and strife, the image of hell on earth, where men hate one another and agree together in but one thing, namely, in *fighting with the Lamb* (Apoc. 17:14)—it is *Babylon the Great* (Apoc. 17:5), as opposed to the City of God on earth, the Church Militant, which is made up of the servants of God under the leadership of Christ.

Between these two cities the Church of God on the one hand and the great Babylon of this world on the other, as the genius of St. Augustine has sketched them out in his immortal work, "De Civitate Dei," there is irreconcilable enmity. The boundaries which separate them are not material ones, walls of stone or ditches dug in the earth. Their respective soldier-citizens are intermingled the ones with the others: and though God knows His own, the eyes of men cannot always distinguish in the strife and confusion, which are of God and which are of the devil. The world finds confederates in the very heart of the citadel, even on the steps of the sanctuary. At the same time the Church of God is fearlessly sending forth apostolic men to all the nations of the earth, who cease not continually to snatch victims from the lures of sin and from the very jaws of hell, and she finds her faithful subjects in all classes of society. To the Angel of Pergamus Our Lord said in the Apocalypse: *I know where you dwell, where the seat of Satan is* (Apoc. 2:13). To every servant of God living in a great city where corruption is seething, these words may also fitly be addressed.

As the Church of God on earth has affinities with Heaven, and constant intercommunication with the blessed Angels and Saints and with God Himself, so the world of sin has affinities and constant intercommunication with the hell of the damned and its inhabitants. The Spiritism of today, like that of all past ages, would bear out this contention, were it necessary after the clear, emphatic and abundant testimony of the Scriptures.

The world is, at one and the same time, a lunatic asylum, a convict prison, a home for contagious and incurable diseases, a Barracks of the devil's militia, a den of unspeakable malefactors, a jungle full of wild beasts; it is a low and sordid theater where, from one generation to another, the same ignoble tragi-comedy is enacted by drunken players; it is the shambles of all innocence and purity; an immense whited sepulcher, beautiful without, but full within of dead men's bones, and every sort of filth.

The world is the "Cloaca Maxima" of the sweet universe of God, into which all the festering rottenness of the seven capital sins is continually being shot in overwhelming quantities to be discharged into hell. No wonder its atmosphere is stifling. Its stench almost kills outright the souls of those who venture incautiously into its midst. Men marvel sometimes that young people, whose innocence has been safeguarded beneath the parental roof, or who have been educated by priests or nuns, suddenly fall into sin and give scandal, soon after making their appearance in the world. These scandals must needs appear occasionally (as the Gospel warns us), but they need surprise no one. The education such young people receive at home or in the Convent school, or at the Catholic college may not be to blame in the least. Even if it is all it ought to be it does not because it cannot, prepare these young people for what they have to contend with in the world. That is more than ordinary virtue can withstand.

A comparison may make this plain. Suppose we were to thrust into the main sewers of some great city, let us say, London or Paris, a swarm of bees, some butterflies, some birds—swallows, nightingales, larks or some squirrels—how do you think these lovely denizens of the azure and of the realm of the pure air would fare in so dark and foul a place? How long do you think they would Eve? Not for a single day; perhaps not even for an hour. Only rats and bats could thrive in such an atmosphere. So it is with pure souls thrust into the world, that sewer or "Cloaca

Maxima," which is carrying along on the impure stream of its literature, business and so-called pleasures and honors, the floating corpses of souls in all degrees of putrescence. No wonder the mystic—that child of light and song—having once tasted how sweet God is, will have nothing to do with it.

The question now naturally arises: if the dangers of the world are so appalling, so universal, so manifold, who can hope to save himself therein? It is not everyone who can betake himself into the desert as the hermits of old or seek the seclusion of the Cloister. What will the poor Christian in the world do?

A very pertinent question this, and one which brings into view one of the aspects of mystical life which is least understood, namely, the part played by the Seven Gifts of the Holy Spirit in the general economy of grace.

In becoming a perfect Christian by the Sacrament of Confirmation, a man receives all he needs to enable him to cope with the difficulties of his situation in the midst of a corrupting and corrupted world. He is made a soldier and he is presented with a breastplate, arms and munitions. By the internal unction of the Holy Spirit, he is rendered immune from the poisonous gases as also from all pusillanimity and human respect. The slight blow he receives on the cheek at the hand of the Bishop is not only a symbol of what he ought to be ready to suffer for Christ, but it does actually and permanently confer on him the grace to be thus ready to suffer for the faith, even unto the shedding of his blood or even unto death, like the martyrs of old. All he needs henceforth is to live up to his promotion in the spiritual life, and make good use of the resources at his disposal. Let him bear in mind that he is now no longer a child, but a soldier, and that he must comport himself as such, unsheathe his weapons, inhale and breathe forth the sweet odor of Jesus Christ, be strong in faith and fervent in love; in a word, that he must be a mystic.

In subsequent volumes we shall see at greater length how the Gifts of the Holy Spirit raise a man above himself, above nature, above even the grace of ordinary virtues, theological as well as moral, and they will, if he be attentive and docile to the internal movements of the Holy Spirit, make him a hero, not only on extraordinary occasions such as when he is called upon to confess his faith before tyrants, but even in all the ordinary circumstances of life: a genuine persevering and constant hero, by the purity of intention, the fervor of love and the perfect contempt of the world which he displays in all he does. It is enough for the present purpose in this chapter, if the consideration of *The world of this darkness* has furnished us with a fresh proof of the fact that every Christian ought to be a mystic. By the very perils of his situation in the world a man is called to be a mystic, and he has, in the grace of the Sacrament of Confirmation, the wherewithal to become a mystic, if he will only lend an attentive ear to the inspirations of this grace.

If the further question be asked: why is it that such a high proportion of Christians who have received the Sacrament of Confirmation fail to conquer in their struggle with the world? the answer is simple: it is because, after having received this Sacrament, they think no more about it. They do not suspect the magnificence of the riches they have received, nor do they realize the serious obligation to strive after sanctity, for which every means has been put into their hands, which has thereby been laid upon them. Thus, through their own ignorance or culpable carelessness, the Divine Guest, the Holy Spirit, is bound and fettered in their soul: the omnipotence of Divine Love is reduced to inefficiency, and this great failure is entirely brought about by the lack of good dispositions in the lukewarm Christian.

CHAPTER XVI

THE SIGN OF THE BEAST

THE sure *mark of the beast* (Apoc. 19:20) in fallen angel or sinful man, on earth or in hell, through time and eternity is unmysticism. This word may not be English as yet (the more the pity), but it will have to do duty as there is no other at hand which would render so accurately my meaning.

The exclusion of the grace of God, the actual and habitual state of sin, the being a slave to the concupiscence of the flesh, that of the eyes, the pride of life or to any of the capital sins, all these states of soul have one common characteristic, and can all be ranged under one comprehensive head: unmysticism, meaning thereby the negative attitude towards the supernatural.

There is speculative, philosophical, highly reasoned and dogmatical or pedantic unmysticism; there is impulsive, instinctive, and highly unreasoning unmysticism; there is practical, downright matter-of-fact unmysticism; and there is even religious unmysticism, one might almost say mystical unmysticism. Now, the negative attitude towards the supernatural is, without any guilt on its part, the attitude proper of the beast. Therefore when it is guiltily assumed by the reasonable creature it reduces him to the level of the beast,

Tertullian calls the proud man "animal gloriæ," just as St. Paul calls the sensual man *animalis homo* (1 Cor. 2:14), and indeed is not the slave of pride, as much as the slave of sensual indulgence, one who has no relish for the things of God and who perceives not the things of mystical life?

What after all is the so-called intellectual, the modernist, the dilettante in matters of faith? A beast! "*Animal Gloria*!" He may strut and pose and play the Sir Oracle, yet by his unmysticism he has descended, together with the poor slave of drink and debauchery, to the level of the unreasoning brute. Here is tragedy! Here is irony with a vengeance!

The damned in hell will all be on the same level, in that they have rejected God and His knowledge; they have thus made themselves unreasoning creatures like unto beasts: they are beasts, every one of them, and Lucifer the greatest beast of all, *Bestia* (Apoc. 20:9). This rejection casts him down to depths as great as were the heights of supernatural illumination and sanctity to which, as a pure spirit, and a very prince among the pure spirits, he had been raised by the loving God. Disobedience or the breaking off of proper relations between creature and Creator, was taken by him and all his train for a mark of superiority, but instead it has proved an unmistakable sign of deterioration. Of a truth, only the humility of faith, coupled with the fervor of charity, makes us true men and children of God.

Ultimately the sinner on earth and the reprobate in hell, man or angel, have this in common: God displeases them Who is the sovereign good. They are filled with regret at the thought that God is infinitely holy, just and good, loving and omnipotent, the First Cause, the Last End and the Supreme Lawgiver. They would have a god of their own fashioning or none at all. They put the question to themselves: Why does not God leave us alone? Why does He refer us to Himself? Why does He not allow us to be happy in our own way? Why should we take any account of Him?

Now we declare emphatically that whoever is touched with this blight shows the mark of the beast.

It is his attitude towards the Divine order and plan which is itself a source of torment and vexation to the reprobate. The manifestation of God in nature, the revelation of the Three Divine Persons in Holy Writ, the mystery of the Incarnation of the Son of God, of the Redemption of man by the Cross, of the Church of Christ with its Holy Sacrifice of the Mass and the Seven Sacraments: these things cause him tortures of disquietude. He is enraged at the multitudes of angels that remained immovable in their allegiance to God, and thus attained the glory and bliss of Heaven; that so many men are saved by serving and loving God, that the Virgin Mary is Queen over all; and that the Nuptials of the Lamb will fill the Blessed with everlasting glory. All these facts, so inexpressibly grand and beautiful and good, displease him, and this is why we say he is unreasonable, like unto the brute.

The reprobates, then, are the unloving ones, "les sans-amour," and they are themselves unlovable. Unmysticism, such is their disease, and they themselves have made it incurable. Is not this a frightful state of affairs?

There are two courses open to all men: that which leads to a life with God, in his friendship and active love, by the deliberate acceptance of the whole supernatural order, culminating in the mystical union of the soul with God; or that which leads to a deliberate refusal of the friendship and the love of God and to a wilful withdrawal from the supernatural, which renders the mystical union of the soul with God impossible.

The sin of the rebel angels was a refusal to abide and persevere in the mystical union with God in which they had been created. The sin of Eve in yielding to the temptation of the devil and eating the forbidden fruit was likewise a discarding or rejection of the supernatural order, and by this rash act her mystical union with God was brought to an end. Adam's sin also, in giving preference to the wishes of his guilty wife rather than to the known will of God, was a terrible descent from the high supernatural regions of mystical union with God, to the domain of the purely natural—a descent which he also consummated, freely and with open eyes.

In the same way every actual sin, if analyzed, is found to be a refusal to enter into the supernatural order or a wilful withdrawal from it, whereby all possibility of mystical union of the soul with God is precluded. By sin, therefore, the soul either contravenes the light of reason and refuses the light of faith; or having received the light of faith, she fails to follow it up to the consummation of chanty in the mystical union with God.

We shall find that all false religions, after all, are nothing but a substitution of natural elements for the supernatural ones. What is Paganism but the worship of nature under symbols more or less ingenious or more or less brutish? Heresies, in their attacks against certain revealed truths, are simply so many attempts at putting the human sense in the place of the divine authority. Freemasonry, as has been ascertained from its secret teaching as well as from its consistent public action all over the world, has no other end but to snatch the whole human race from Jesus Christ and subjugate it to the worship of pure reason. Now, the worship of pure reason is not quite the same as the worship of purity. This was startlingly demonstrated during the French Revolution, when "la Déesse Raison" impersonated in "le marbre vivant d'une chair prostituée" to use the words of Lacordaire— was unveiled with sacrilegious pomp and ceremony on the high altar of Notre Dame in Paris. Every sinner, by going against the light of reason and revelation, substitutes for the worship of God the idolatrous worship of the creature, that is to say, of his own self, or some other created object, animate or inanimate: gold or flesh or filth. Like the devil, he desires something more than the mystical union with God, and that something more in the end is found to be infinitely less and horribly degrading.

CHAPTER XVII

THE MYSTICAL ORDER OF THE UNIVERSE

FROM the survey in the preceding chapter of the common characteristic of sin in all its manifestations, we have a right to say that the supernatural order might as well be called the mystical order.

Since the purpose of true religion is no other than to bring man to a perfect union of love with God, in which the mystical life truly consists, we arrive at the remarkable conclusion that the whole question of the supernatural is really one of Mysticism.

The question put first to the angels, and afterwards to Adam, and now to each one of us individually, is this: Do you accept the mystical union of love with God or will you not? Sin is a flat refusal, regardless of consequences, to embrace or sustain this mystical union with God.

Tepidity on the other hand may be said to be, as we have seen, a dangerous benumbing of the mystical faculties, a paralysis verging on the confines of spiritual death. Only the avowed and uncompromising mystic is safe. "Mystici in tuto," we might say, using a phrase of Bossuet in a somewhat different way from him. Only the mystic embraces the supernatural order with all its consequences, in all its bearings upon human life, as summed up in the Commandment: *Thou shalt love the Lord thy God, with thy whole heart, and with thy whole soul, and with thy whole mind* (Matt. 22:37). Now one who so wholly and perfectly loves God, loves himself also wisely, and cannot but love his neighbor in a chaste and generous spirit and in a manner wholly supernatural Only mystics can love thus; that is to say, in such a manner that their union with God is not hampered by their love of any person or thing created.

But we will go a step further and prove that all things whatever are mystical, each in its proper place and degree (the sinner and his sin, of course, excepted). Not only the things of religion, such as Holy Mass, the Sacraments, the Divine Scriptures, persons and things consecrated to God, and the pious acts of Christians in their different states of life are mystical, but the whole material universe also. The firmament bedecked with millions of stars, the earth with its varied productions and inhabitants, the mighty ocean, the laws of nature, the elements, the seasons, the lengthening out of time in days and months and years and centuries; each separate system of things and each creature individually, from the constellation in the remotest depths of space, down to the infinitesimally small, invisible speck of a being, situated seemingly on the very verge of nothingness: all these, and along with them, man, poised as it were, between two immensities, the one of greatness above him, the other of smallness below him; all these may properly be called mystical. They are mystical, not only by their value as demonstrations of God's existence, of His transcendence and infinite perfections, or again by their symbolical and allegorical value which is very great—this all mystics delight in telling us —but moreover in themselves, in their proper substantial reality, as things sanctified in Our Lord Jesus Christ and in a way united to Him. Not only is God naturally and necessarily implied in the existence of all things, He being present in each one by His divine immanence: not only does God maintain and support them by a continual putting forth of His creative energy; but it has pleased Him moreover gratuitously to establish between them and His Divine Incarnate Son a relation of an incomparably higher order, to give them a share now in the sanctifying of souls and the perfecting of the elect, and hereafter to assume them into the realm of His Infinite Glory.

We distinguish for the sake of convenience, the different orders in the scheme of the universe: the order of nature, the order of grace, and the order of glory, but we must not speak of these as if they were separate and independent of one another: in Christ Jesus they are integral parts of one grand order, which, if we must call it by a comprehensive name, I would propose to style "the Mystical Order."

That the order of nature is not isolated from that of grace, and that both are destined to be together transmuted into the order of glory in Christ Jesus is evident as far as man is concerned. The two elements, nature and grace, are as the warp and woof of our present state, necessary one to the other, upholding one another and coming to naught if separated. It takes a man to make a Christian, as it requires a pure spirit to make a Blessed Angel. On the other hand, if the supernatural element be taken from either man or angel, this noble being will be shattered and become respectively a devil or a reprobate. Then both the good Angel and the Christian were from the first predestined to be raised to glory, and not only they but the whole material universe together with them.

We shall be repaid for our trouble if we examine thoroughly this proposition: that the whole material universe, along with men and angels, is involved in the Mystical Order. We have been too much accustomed, in this infidel age of ours, to look upon the whole world of creation with secularized intellects, if we may use the expression, and to think of it all as an order of things in which sinner and saint alike have common right of dominion; whilst the truth is that the whole order of nature should be viewed only in the light of God Who made it, and of the purpose for which He made it, which is the filling in of Christ; and that the sinner, precisely because he has broken with God, has forfeited all right over the things of this world. If he is still allowed for a brief space to use them freely, it is only on sufferance, and to give him time to return to a better frame of mind. *Knowest thou not (O man) that the benignity of God leads you to penance?* (Rom. 2:4).

Everything that is, whether animate or inanimate, is of God, and is in God, and is for God and His Christ and His Saints, and exists for them only.

The material world is a divine parable of the love of God for man. Heaven, earth, sea and hell itself witness with a million voices the secret which is the sole felicity of man: the love of God; but how many refuse to hear? Each single creature is a portion of the great created mirror of God, Nature; and each part reflects in its tiny compass what the whole mirror reveals upon a more magnificent scale. Everything that is, reflects in its own way the Power, the Wisdom, the Goodness, and above all, the Love of Our Heavenly Father. God is love; all love in Himself, in His operations ad extra, in the necessary relation of all things to His divine goodness, and in the gratuitous supernatural relations He has introduced into the world through His Son Jesus Christ. Thus everything that is steeped in the divine essence and love, made part of a grand mystical order, and manifests it in Christ.

Reason alone, unaided by divine revelation, might discern much of this truth, but a brilliant flood of light is poured upon the subject by the mystery of the Incarnation. The Martyrology, on the 25th of December, opens out with this sublime announcement: "Jesus Christus, æternus Deus, æternique Dei Filius, MUNDUM VOLENS ADVENTU SUO PIISSIMO CONSECRARE, de Spiritu Sancto conceptus, nascitur ex Maria Virgine factus homo." The whole universe of things created is consecrated and sanctified in the Sacred Humanity of Our Lord, and in Its turn, the Sacred Humanity consecrates and sanctifies the world by being made from it and part of it and its crowning glory, and also by acting in it, with it, and upon it.

The whole world was already sacramental, leading to God, vibrating with the glory of its Maker and quivering with unspoken aspiration to enter through man into the mystical union of love with God. The whole inferior world was already aflame with the love of God for us and groaning and travailing in its dumb desire to render love for love. It was left to man to make or mar the happiness of the inferior world; and man was betraying its expectations, when lo, there comes down upon it one of the Three Persons of the Blessed Trinity, the Son of God. He takes His stand in the midst of things created, making Himself one of them when at the same time He is the center of the universe of all things visible or invisible. He gathers into His Hands the threads of nature and holds everything fast to His own divine Self, all in love. Shall we now say that the world is not mystical?

We may consider the Universe as a book written by the finger of God, in which He narrates His infinite perfections and sums them all up in this one stupendous word: Love. In this book the readers themselves, angels and men, are some of the most beautiful chapters; yet the last and crowning one of all, the summary and the triumphant conclusion to which the rest lead up, is Jesus Christ. We have already seen in a preceding volume ("The Mystical Life," ch, 12) how the different species of beings in the whole range of inferior nature form as it were, so many steps towards the fulfilment of the Incarnation, Our Lord in His Human nature being the end of all the works of God "ad extra." He is not only the Last Chapter, but the First as well: *The image of the invisible God, the first born of every creature* (Coloss, 1:15). *In the head of the book it is written of me* (Heb. 10:7). *I am Alpha and Omega, the beginning and the end, . . . the first and the last* (Apoc, 1:8, 17). Therefore nothing can escape the mystical grasp of the Son of God made Man. Jesus must be named in all the chapters of the book of creation, for indeed they speak of Him be it in the faintest accents or the most obscure terms. We must spell out His sacred name from every page and read everything in its light, under pain of not understanding what we read. The misfortune of our infidel modem scientists even as it is that of the fallen angels, is precisely that they do not read the Book of God thus, and, as a consequence, their science stands self-condemned. It is not "cognitio matutina" nor "vespertina," it is "nocturna"—it is all darkness. Jesus is not in it, He Who is the very light of the world (Jo. 8:12), the all in all of this world and the next. *The Father loveth the Son and He hath given all things into His hand* (John 3:35). *All things are delivered to Me by My Father* (Matt. 11:27). *He has pul all things in subjection under His feet* (Heb. 2:8).

With fine scorn did the great Bishop of Tulle, Mgr. Berteaud, in his pastoral of 1864, rail at the men of his time who would have ousted God from the world and claimed the nineteenth century for their own. "Is anything their own?" he asks. "Is time theirs? Is the world theirs? Who gave it them?" He goes on to show that God has given all things to His Christ, and that if the present world is still preserved in existence they may thank the Church of Christ which they are persecuting, for its preservation.

For as the Father does everything for the sake of His Christ, so Jesus Christ in His turn orders everything for the sake of His mystical Bride, the Church of the elect. The present world will not endure one moment longer than is necessary for the making of the last of the Saints.

Hear the inspired accents of the Royal Prophet celebrating these mysteries: *Why have the Gentiles raged and the people devised vain things? The kings of the earth stood up, and the princes met together against the Lord and against His Christ (saying): Let us break their bonds asunder, and let us cast away their yoke from us, He that dwells in Heaven shall laugh at them, and the Lord shall deride them. Then shall He speak to them in His anger, and trouble them in His rage; but I am appointed King by Him over Sion, His holy mountain, preaching His commandment. The Lord hath said to Me: Thou art My Son; this day have I begotten Thee. Ask of Me and I will give Thee the Gentiles for Thy inheritance and the utmost parts of the earth for Thy possession. Thou shalt rule them with a rod of iron and shalt break them in pieces like a potter's vessel* (Ps. 2:1-9).

Mysticism therefore, far from being something exceptional, an overgrowth or an outgrowth of religion, is the very breath of it: it is the whole of religion, for it is the great law of all the world in its every department. It is the force of attraction which goes out from the Sacred Humanity of Our Lord Jesus Christ to all things created, consecrating and illuminating them. In violently wrenching themselves, as far as in them lies, from this all pervading and powerful attraction of the mystical order of things, the sinner and the reprobate do but give greater evidence to this law of the universe, as we shall see in the next chapter.

CHAPTER XVIII

"THE SECOND DEATH" IN THE LIGHT OF MYSTICISM

PER ME SI VA NELLA CITTA DOLENTE,
PER ME SI VA NELL' ETERNO DOLORE.
PER ME SI VA TRA LA PERDUTA GENTE,
GIUSTIZIA MOSSE IL MIO ALTO FATTORE:
FECEMI LA DIVINA POTESTATE,
LA SOMMA SAPIENZIA E IL PRIMO AMORE.
DINANZI A ME NON FUR COSE CREATE
SE NON ETERNE, ED IO ETERNO DURO:
LASCIATE OGNI SPERANZA, VOI CH' ENTRATE.[6]

Dante, *L'Inferno*, Cant. III.

God spared not the angels that sinned, but having cast them down into the place of torments, delivered them into the chains of hell, to be tormented, to be reserved unto judgement (2 Pet. 2:4). *The fearful, and unbelieving, and the abominable, and murderers, and fornicators, and sorcerers, and idolaters, and all liars, their portion shall be in the pool burning with fire and brimstone, which is the second death* (Apoc. 21:8). *And His zeal will take armor, and He will arm the creature for the revenge of his enemies* (Wisd. 5:18).

Then shall He say to them also that shall be on His left hand; Depart from Me, ye cursed, into everlasting fire which was prepared for the devil and his angels (Mat. 25:41). *The smoke of their torments shall ascend up for ever and ever* (Apoc. 14:11).

[6] Through me is the way into the sorrowful city; through me the way into the eternal pain; through me the way among hte people lost. Justice moved my High Maker; Divine Power made me, Wisdom Supreme, and Primal Love. Before me were no things created but eternal; and eternal I endure. Abandon all hope, ye who enter here.

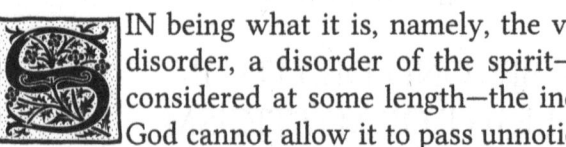

SIN being what it is, namely, the very worst kind of disorder, a disorder of the spirit—as we have now considered at some length—the ineffable sanctity of God cannot allow it to pass unnoticed, to go for ever unrepressed, or at any rate, unpunished. To the immaculate law of love and of the mystical union of the reasonable creature with its Creator, there needs must be attached a chastisement in case of transgression. This must have been sufficiently promulgated, that is to say, announced beforehand, that it might act as a deterrent and a providential safeguard to the would-be evil doer. Then if sin be committed, this sanction must, in God's good time (immediately and with lightning-like rapidity for the rebel angels, with merciful delays in the case of man) be sternly applied, that the balance of right order in the sweet universe of God, be not permanently disturbed.

This chastisement by the very nature of the case can be no other essentially than the irrevocable separation from God, Who is the life of the spirit—the rejection by Him in this life and in the next. *Depart from Me, you that work iniquity* (Mat. 7:23). *Depart from Me, ye cursed, into everlasting fire* (Mat. 25:41).

The sinner on earth makes light enough of being cast away from the grace and the love of God. Mystical union with the Sovereign Good has for him no allurement, nor has actual excommunication from the mystical order, thus far, any terror. Only the formidable prospect of the hell of the damned can make any impression on the wretch. Even that, if he still continue in his sin, may fail at last to rouse him to a sense of his guilt and of his awful danger, even when his sin has already spoiled his life on earth to the extent of making it an anticipated hell.

In *what day soever thou shalt eat of it, thou shalt die the death* (Gen. 2:17). Thus spoke God to Adam, when He notified to him upon what condition he was to hold the tenure of his present happy state and earn the future eternal bliss of Heaven.

The mind of the first man, at once ancestor and representative of the whole human race, was then in all its pristine vigor, fresh from the hands of God and from his first entrancing intercourse with Him, with the light of reason and that of revelation shining full upon him in all their splendor, and there can be no doubt that he caught the full import of these words of God. There can be no doubt, either, though the Scriptures are silent on the subject, that all the Angels, at the time of their probation, were fully informed beforehand of the secrets of eternal life, that is to say, of Heaven and hell as an alternative requital of the goodness or perverseness of their own free acts. Only, in the state of primal innocence, neither the angels first, nor man afterwards, knew experientially what the threat of death could mean. This, however, placed them under no disadvantage whatsoever.

Speculative knowledge coupled with the love of God ought to have been sufficient to save them from committing sin. A man need not go through the process of breaking his own neck before he can make up his mind to enjoy life rather than throw himself down a precipice.

Hell is at the same time a place and a state.

It is the final state of those who have failed in the great business of making themselves fit for divine union and a state of unredeemable wickedness. The first chastisement of sin persevered in to the end of one's life on earth is that it remains what it is. It remains sin, that is to say, a painful and monstrous disorder, and it will be such from henceforth and for evermore. Only the grace of God could have changed the sinner into a penitent and a saint during the days of his probation. He refused grace obstinately and perseveringly, to the very end, until death supervened and made him radically incapable of receiving it any more. The sinner now can change himself no more than a dead carrion carcass can change itself into a living body. By his own act he has become for ever a dead thing, a corrupt and stinking corpse (metaphorically speaking), and an abomination before God and His blessed Angels and Saints.

Of course a monstrous thing like this cannot be allowed to remain for ever in the open to disgrace the fair face of creation. Of necessity it has to be swept out of sight, and cast into the great pit, into the awful great sink of hell, which was excavated by the just wrath of God for the fallen angels on the morning of creation.

Some pious people cherish the fond imagination that if a lost soul were set free from bell and allowed to return to earth for ever so short a time, it would appall the world by the rigor of its penance in its efforts to make its peace with God. This cannot be maintained theologically. In the face of the serene and admirably reasoned out doctrine of St. Thomas (I, II, *quæst.* 84-87) it would appear that such a soul would rather appall the world by its absolute recklessness and obstinacy in sin, and that if, through a singular permission of God, the experiment were repeated not once, but ten times, a hundred, or a thousand times, the lost soul returning to earth would, each time, refuse penance and resume its life of sin ten times, or a hundred, or a thousand times; clearly and openly manifesting that its case is absolutely hopeless, and that there is no alternative but to intern such a maniac where his presence could do no harm. Deep *calls on deep, at the noise of thy flood-gates* (Ps. 41:8). The abysmal wickedness of the reprobate calls for the abysmal punishment of hell. Our Lord, in the Apocalypse 2:24, speaks of "*the depths of Satan.*" There are also the depths of all the other reprobates.

In our extremely superficial way of regarding this dread mystery of eternal damnation we are sometimes inclined to think that God is very severe to the unrepentant sinner, and that hell is perhaps too great a punishment. There is, however, no other way left to God. The sinner refused to be wholesome; he deliberately chose putrescence for his portion: he must therefore be ejected with a curse to endure the penalty of eternal fire. Fruit or meat that has become corrupt is thrown away in disgust but not in anger, and there is no blame attached to its condition, but corrupted angelic natures and putrid human souls are guilty of their own evil.

Hell is thus the destined place where, day by day, generation after generation, century after century, from the beginning of the world till the day of the Last Judgement, all the filth and corruption of spoiled angelic and human natures meet, intermingle, and accumulate: filth and rottenness that is moral, not material, of the spirit not of the flesh. O Lucifer, proud rebellious spirit without love, here is thy kingdom, worthy of thee: thou art the prince over all this immense and deep world of unspeakable filth. And you, sinner, my brother, do you realize that this is the goal to which you are tending and running with all your might, even as a river hastens its course to lose itself in the ocean? Can it be that you wish to dwell in that pool of filth and fire with all those miscreants for all eternity? Then indeed it will be *The second death* (Apoc. 20:14), that death from which there is no possible resurrection!

Hell, then, is at one and the same time a state and a place; even as Heaven itself is a state and a place. The two things in either case cannot be separated. The special state calls for the particular place. Heaven is the place, or rather it is the Kingdom of the glory of God, and at the same time it demands of its inhabitants a state of perfect charity which can never be lost.

If, to suppose an impossibility, a devil or a reprobate were admitted into paradise, he would be in the realm of glory, but because he would not be in the state of charity, the splendor surrounding him would burn him with shame more fiercely that the very flames of hell. Hell itself is a mercy for the damned compared with the suffering that paradise would inflict upon them.

On the other hand, if a Saint, whether from among the blessed angels or Christians, one in whom the love of God was confirmed, were cast into hell, hell itself would not be to him the place of torment which it is to the reprobates; because he would love the very torments inflicted on him, as coming from the hands of the One he loved above all things. In other words: he would not be in the state of soul which makes hell what it is; he would be in the place of damnation, but not in the state of damnation. Now hell is simultaneously the state and the place of damnation.

This may help us in some measure to realize what it will be for the damned to appear at the Last Judgement, naked, unclean, and monstrously deformed as they are, in the midst of the splendor of the blessed Angels and Saints, and to face Our Blessed Lord in all His majesty of God made Man, and of Saviour of the world and of Supreme Judge of the living and the dead. This will prove so unbearable a torment to them that they will cry out to the mountains and the rocks: *Fall upon us and hide us from the face of Him that sits upon the Throne and from the wrath of the Lamb . . . for the great day of their wrath is come, and who shall be able to stand?* (Apoc. 6:16-17).

Hell has its place in the grand Mystical Order of which we spoke in the preceding chapter.

The state of the reprobate is due to the act of sin, and it is true that by sin the reprobate has taken himself, as far as possible, out of the mystical order. The place of the reprobate, however, the hell of the damned, is not of his making. It is due to the direct intervention of God: like all the other works of God, it is good in itself and shows forth His wisdom, His justice, and His sanctity. It forces the reprobate, in spite of himself, to fall back into the harmony of the universe and of the mystical order.

If there were no hell, God would be overcome by the sinner; good would be defeated by evil. There must therefore be a hell. If the fact of free will both of angels and men be granted, and the wilful guilt of angels and men, and their final impenitence, then hell for them is as unavoidable a necessity as Heaven itself for the reward of the faithful mystic, angel or man. Hell is a part of the mystical order of the universe.

There is yet another aspect under which hell appears in the mystical order: that is as a real demonstration of the extent of the love of God. All these reprobates will stand for ever as so many monuments of the unspeakable love of God. God has loved each one of these fallen spirits, each one of these reprobate men, with a personal love most tender and strong and delicate. He has loved them from all eternity, and it was because He loved them that He created them. He made them in love, loving them and yearning to love them for all eternity, and in order that they also might love Him and be happy with the very happiness of God, This is proclaimed by their whole shattered being.

Just as a pitiful and yet majestic ruin, as, for instance, that of the Cathedral of Rheims today, proclaims through its broken arches and noble pillars still standing erect, with its mutilated statues and fragments of moldings, the vastness and magnificence of the building when it stood in its integrity, and the skill and love with which its architect had planned and built and adorned it; so the incorruptible essence of the pure spirits and of the human souls of the reprobates, and the persevering keenness of their intellects and the unbending strength of their wills, and the nobility of their incorruptible bodies after the Resurrection—all will bear witness to the splendid uses to which God in His love had destined them, having made them first in His own image and likeness, and given them in His grace, the means of intensifying this their likeness to God, to an untold degree, until at last they would have been assumed into the very glory of God and made a part of it.

Our forefathers, in the Ages of Faith, understood this great truth that Hell itself is a proof and, in its way, an eternal monument of the love unspeakable with which Divine Goodness pursues his rational creature. They found it no difficulty in reconciling this formidable dogma of an eternal Hell with all we know of the necessary attributes of God. In the famous inscription on the gates of his Inferno Dante reads:

To rear me was the task of power divine,
Supremest wisdom and primeval love.

CHAPTER XIX

THE MARRIAGE OF THE LAMB

T*he Marriage of the Lamb* (Apoc. 19:7), as it will be inaugurated after the Last Judgement, is to be the final stage in the marvellous evolution of mystical life.

Arrived at this point of our task we feel like a mountaineer whose courage flags at the foot of the last and sublimest, but most dizzy and difficult peak. The temptation is strong to abandon the attempt, and good reasons would not be wanting to justify such a course.

The questions shape themselves in our mind: Why should we try to say something on so difficult and inaccessible a subject? Who ever before tried to tell what will follow for the Blessed, upon the Last Judgement? Is it not madness, and presumption to dare such a climb? Is it not like courting disaster?

Again: Why not leave this to the secret teaching of the Holy Spirit in the hearts of the mystics, very few in number, who care to look forward so far into the mysterious future? Does it not baffle description? Does it not set at naught the possibilities of human language? Does it not defy even pure spiritual conceptions of the kind which are accessible to us in our pilgrimage? Fain would we cry out: O my brothers who have followed us thus far, do not press us to go on: a man like you and a worse sinner, we have never gazed upon the divine realities on the other side of the veil. One who was once more favored, even during his pilgrimage days, could only stammer about it: *The eye hath not seen nor the ear heard, neither hath it entered the heart of man what things God hath prepared for them that love Him* (1 Cor. 2:9). Not even now from what they see and experience, could the Blessed in Paradise give a description of the bliss that is to come, after the present order of things has been abolished altogether and superseded by the pure Order of Glory at its highest. Is it not remarkable that the divine Revelation of Holy Scriptures, which tells us so much of what will happen between now and the last sentence of the Divine Judge, does not enter into details as to what will follow the words of Christ: *Come ye, blessed of My Father, possess the kingdom prepared for you from the foundation of the world* (Mat. 25:34). Might we not, then, for the purpose of this chapter, content ourselves with saying:

It is simply ineffable!

And yet, somehow, this would not be satisfactory. It would seem little short of treason not to indicate at least in a few words, the final stage of the wonderful mystical evolution. We have not led our reader so far and so high along the paths of the mystical doctrine, to abandon him before reaching the most desired spot; before, at least, like Moses dying, casting a glance from afar, upon the Promised Land not only of the actual bliss of the Saints in Heaven as it is now, but further at that of the After Judgement Nuptials of the Lamb; just as Moses dying was given a view of the material Promised Land, and in it a further revelation of the Kingdom of Christ, the Catholic Church, of which the first was only the image and prelude and a sort of faint beginning.

When the end of the world in its present condition shall have been accomplished, when the cursed ones shall have been banished for ever to their fiery prison, and the Blessed shall have been assumed into glory, are we to consider that the last stage of the grand evolution has been reached? We may if we like, still we must not call it an end, but rather a beginning. All that has gone before will then appear in its true light of a grand preparation for infinitely more magnificent realities, which are to last for ever. The mysteries of time had to be consummated ere the as yet unrevealed mysteries of eternity could begin. These are all summed up in the entrancing words: *The Marriage feast of the Lamb.*

And I saw, says St. John in the Apocalypse: a *new Heaven and a new earth; for the first Heaven and the first earth had passed away, and the sea is no more. And I, John, saw the Holy City, the New Jerusalem, coming down from God out of Heaven, prepared as a bride adorned far her husband. And I heard a great voice from the throne saying: Behold the tabernacle of God with men, and He will dwell with them, and they shall be His people, and God*

Himself shall be their God. And God shall away all tears from and death shall be no more, nor mourning, nor crying, nor sorrow shall be any more, for the former things are passed away. And He that sat on the Throne said: Behold I make all things new. (Apoc. 21:1-5).

Jesus, the Heavenly Bridegroom, will not be perfected in us until after the General Resurrection and the Last Judgement. Only then will the Church, His mystical Bride, come at last to the fulness of her charms. Only then also will each one of the Blessed be all that God wishes him to be. Till then the mystical body of Christ, and every individual member of it, is still in the making. Till then Christ is not filled in, and the real feast cannot begin. Creation goes on as long as men are to be born. Incarnation has to be extended to every Christian that will be made to the very end of the world. Redemption will have worked out its full and final effect only when death has been overcome in the resurrection of all flesh. And only when all the Blessed shall have received their reward in soul and body, according to their works and the after-effects thereof, will Sanctification shine in its full splendor.

The Church as it is now, even the Triumphant Church of the Angels and Saints, is yet but as a little maid, compared to the perfect Bride God the Father desires her to become for the delight of His Son. *Soror nostra parva,* says the chorus in the mystical love-drama of the Canticle of Canticles—*Soror nostra parva et ubera non habet* (Cant, 8:8). This is equally true respectively of the whole Church and of every individual predestined, whether already in Heaven or yet on earth, whether of angelic or of human nature: each one in regard to the Heavenly Bridegroom, is at present, but as a little maid, dearly loved indeed and very happy in His love, but not yet come to the rounded fulness of her charms which arc to give joy to the Beloved, nor to the fulness of her capacity for the enjoyment of His mystical divine embraces. This twofold perfection will be realized in the Church as the mystical body of Christ, and in each separate Saint, only after the winding up of the affairs of time by the grand assize of the Last Judgement, not only because then each one will receive according to his works, but also because each one will then be assigned his definite place in the eternal hierarchy of perfect charity. This could not have been done before.

The capacity for enjoyment of the Blessed in Heaven, Angels and Saints, immense as it is and immensely gratified, is far from having reached its utmost limit. It is not known to the Blessed themselves; it will come to them as a revelation. Indeed, they may take for themselves the words of St. Paul, addressed to us: *Nondum apparuit quid erimus. It hath not yet appeared what we shall be* (1 Jo. 3:2). Even the Angels of God, each in his own capacity, will receive, after the Last Judgement, an ineffable increase of personal nobility, brightness and joy, resulting from the fulfilment of Jesus Christ in the Church, and from the perfect loveliness of His Bride, for whom they employed themselves so diligently whilst time lasted and she was a pilgrim on earth.

It would be wrong indeed to imagine that the joy of the Blessed, even the essential joy of the Beatific Vision as they now taste it, cannot be increased. It all depends on whether their capacity for knowing God and loving Him is susceptible of an increase. We must remember that God is the Master of the feast yet to come of the eternal Nuptials of the Lamb. God is the Maker both of feast and guests, and He will fit them, the former to the latter by giving the finishing touch of His omnipotent hand to each one of the Blessed on the occasion of the Last Judgement. There is a great difference between the lovely apple blossom in early spring, and the full ripe fruit in russet autumn; the one is but the first fair promise and early token, whilst the other is glorious fulfilment. Thus with the blessed as they are now and as they will be at the end of the world.

The Nuptials of the Lamb will not be barren. This Virginal marriage of the Son of God with His predestined Bride, the Church of the Blessed, will bear a fruit inferior only to that of the mystic marriage of the Virgin Mary with the Holy Spirit, which was Christ Himself. This is the fruit it shall bring forth: THE PERFECT PRAISE OF THE CREATOR.

And this marvellous new birth will be of a begetting proper

to God: eternal—eternal, not only in its endless duration, but in its very mode. Eternally does God the Father say to His Son: *Filius meus es tu, ego hodie genui te;* eternally also and with infinite rapture of joy will the Lamb of God and His Bride, the Church of the predestined say to the Perfect Praise of God: Thou art my child: this day have I begotten thee (Ps. 2:7).

CHAPTER XX

CONCLUSION

WE have now arrived at the end of what we may consider as the Preliminaries of the Doctrine of the Mystical Life.

Before we could begin to treat of the two great functions of the Mystical Life which are Divine Contemplation and Saintly Action, the ground had to be cleared and the right notion of the Mystical Life itself had to be vindicated. This we have now done at some length, more by way of statement and development of the traditional idea of mystical life than by way of controversy, trusting that the splendor of this traditional view will win back to itself many minds which have been led astray by more modem, but narrow and unsatisfactory, definitions. We do not think there is one single chapter in these two volumes presenting some special aspect of the traditional notion, which is not calculated to help to a more thorough and practical understanding of the workings of the Mystical Life.

Our readers ought by now to be quite convinced that the Mystical Life is simply life with God; simply a conscious, sustained, loving attention to God; that is to say, the life of a fervent soul with God, under the veil of faith, in the sanctuary of its own heart; in other words, the intercourse of mutual love between God and the fervent Christian.

Only when thus understood, in the light of the traditional notion of Mysticism, will the religion of Christ and the Catholic Church receive its true import. Only traditional Mysticism does justice to the idea of God and to the idea of man, as these are presented to us in Divine Revelation. The mystic alone does full justice to his Christianity.

"Hominem quæro, I seek a man," said the old cynic Diogenes, groping in full day-light with his lantern. He sought and sought in vain; he could never find a man until he found a true servant of God; and there was none at Athens in his day, though it was the proud boast of that city that she was then the Queen of Intellectualism.

The mystic alone is worthy of the name of man, because he alone grasps the divine purpose of life. The others are simply beasts of burden, or beasts of prey, or beasts of pleasure, or beasts of pride, as we have seen.

The world is in labor of a definite order which will be all mystical, all supernatural, all glorious and divinely blissful. The present world is in labor of the Heavenly Jerusalem, which is to receive all the predestined children of God and to embrace one day, within its precincts, all this material universe. As man is a creature in the making, so is Heaven, and so also, for that matter, is hell. We are called upon to help. This material world of our probation is the workshop. We are pressed into the service of one side or the other, and none but the infant or the idiot, is allowed to remain neutral. If one is not with Jesus one is against Him. He, therefore, who shall not fit himself ultimately for mystical life in Paradise will be a reprobate.

The mystic is really the only man on earth who knows how to enjoy himself and make the best of the present life. The others enjoy death, not life; for what they call life is death. God is life, and the mystic alone is wise enough to enjoy God.

O that all men might become true mystics! O that it might be given us to allure them to this the only true life, more and more, in displaying to their gaze the splendors of Divine Contemplation and the supernatural charms of Saintly Action, as we hope to do, with the help of God, in the volumes yet to be published.

The Vision of St. Thomas Aquinas
—Santo di Tito

BOOK IV

DIVINE CONTEMPLATION FOR ALL

THE SIMPLE ART OF COMMUNING WITH GOD

PREFACE

THE notion of Divine Contemplation is not less in need of being elucidated and brought back to its legitimate, traditional, Catholic meaning than was that of the Mystical Life. It has suffered just as much at the hands of modern writers, by a host of whom it has been misunderstood, distorted, narrowed down and all but made a bug-bear; whilst in its true self Divine Contemplation is the grandest, noblest, sweetest, easiest thing in the world; in some measure, and under some form or other, obligatory on all; and as necessary to the Christian at every stage of his spiritual life as is the act of breathing to the physical well-being of every animal, wherever situated in the scale of life, and at whatever stage of its development.

In this new treatise I take Divine Contemplation in its widest meaning, as understood by St. Thomas in his *Summa Theologica, Secunda Secundæ, quæst.* 179-182, and by St. Francis of Sales in his treatise on *The Love of God, Book vi, ch. vi, last paragraph,* where he says: "In order to attain to contemplation it is usually necessary to hear the divine word, hold spiritual conferences with others like the anchorites of old, read devout books, pray, meditate, sing devout canticles, and entertain good thoughts. Holy contemplation being the end and purpose of all these exercises, they are comprised under the same heading, and such persons as practice these are called contemplatives, as also this sort of occupation is called the contemplative life."

This new treatise will, therefore, deal with Contemplation in all its varieties of form, and at the same time all the preliminaries to contemplation, all the acts which lead up to it or accompany it; in short, all the acts whether of the mind or of the will, whether of the spirit only, or of the body with the spirit, which have God directly for their object; rudimentary contemplation and perfect contemplation, and between these extremes, all the degrees—that is to say the entire gamut—of divine contemplation.

It needs no demonstration—because it has in itself the force of an axiom—that every adult Christian, whatever his age, profession, condition, or natural endowment, should in some degree be a genuine contemplative: that is to say, should, within the limits of his own capacities, natural and supernatural, be a sincere and convinced adept in Divine Contemplation. When we consider his state of grace, and all that state means: namely, his vital union with Christ; the presence in him of the Holy Spirit; the grace of manifold prayer *(spiritum gratiæ et precum)* (Zach. 12:10); the spiritual dower of the infused virtues, moral and theological, and of the seven gifts; and his having at hand all the treasury of the Sacraments, the Sacred Liturgy, the Holy Scriptures, the lives of the Saints and their writings; to say nothing of numberless actual graces showered upon him all day long: in face of all this, we feel justified in holding that a Christian is inexcusable if he be not in some degree a contemplative.

Why then are there so very few contemplatives even among professed Christians?

It is only too true that for some it is a case of downright indifference and tepidity: Christians though they be, at least in name, they simply do not care. *Flens dico!* With the Apostle (Philippians 3:18), I *say it weeping:* God is the least and last of their concerns. But there are also those who do care, who would indeed like to become contemplatives in the measure and in the manner willed for them by their loving God, and, perhaps, some have even made an attempt towards this.

Now what is it that has prevented the latter from succeeding in their attempt at Divine Contemplation?

This: they have met with no encouragement. Or it has been put before them in a wrong way. Perhaps they have been positively dissuaded from Divine Contemplation as from something dangerous. Or, finally, they have been bewildered or disgusted by the works they have read on the subject.

Now it is principally for such persons that I venture to publish this treatise. It may be a great presumption on my part, but it is true that I have no other ambition than to help souls of good will to lay hold of, or to return to, the Catholic traditional notion of Divine Contemplation, and to teach them how to use it to good purpose in their spiritual life.

This doctrine that all men are called to Divine Contemplation is no novelty. It has been the constant and insistent teaching of the Catholic Church for the past nineteen centuries; and it is so to this hour, if only men would receive it as they should and carry it out in their lives.

The first questions and answers in the *Catechism* are: "Who made you? God made me. Why did God make you? God made me to know Him, love Him and serve Him in this world, and to be happy with Him for ever in the next." In these few words we have the whole philosophy of Christian life, its very essence, and also its proper division, all taught in a popular way by our Holy Mother the Church, to the little ones of the flock. We have here, in a nutshell, so to say, and shorn of technicalities, the whole concentrated doctrine of Christ about the mystical life. We are plainly told that this sort of life is lived between God and the individual soul; that it concerns the here and the hereafter; that so far as it concerns the present life our first business in it is "to know and love God"—that is to say, to have direct dealings with Him—and our next is "to serve Him" in acts of justice and charity to our fellow men: the first thing being Divine Contemplation, the other being saintly action, as we have already explained at some length in a previous volume *(Cf. Mystical Life*, ch. v).

Now in this treatise, we are concerned with the first and principal part of the mystical life, namely Divine Contemplation or the knowledge of God united to the love of God. This is the sweet knowledge, the *Sapida Cognitio* of which the Saints speak in their works on the spiritual life. And they do but follow in the footsteps of Our Lord who proclaimed this truth: Now this is eternal life, that they should know Thee *(Father, who art)* the only true God, and Jesus Christ whom Thou hast sent *(John 17:3).*

This view, large and truly Catholic, of Divine Contemplation, at one stroke unceremoniously sweeps away, like a cobweb, the modern mistaken idea that Divine Contemplation is the exclusive privilege of an intellectual aristocracy; as though the little ones of Christ did not count; as though the dealings of God with them, and their dealings with God, were beneath notice and could be ignored; or as though the dear and loving God were beyond the reach of these, the lowliest and humblest of the flock. Too long has this fatal mistake played havoc in the sphere of the spiritual life. It has restrained hundreds of thousands from loving intercourse with God. It has thwarted ever so many well-meant attempts towards union with Him. It is well, therefore, that the wide, generous, traditional doctrine of the Church on this momentous subject should be placed in the clearest possible light, and that this truth should be proclaimed with unfaltering voice, even from the house-tops: DIVINE CONTEMPLATION IS Indeed for the Million.

Therefore, in this new volume, I am going to try to be more and more simple, homely, direct, and unconventional. If, however, there should occur some passages difficult to understand, I would entreat my reader not to be discouraged nor to give up the attempt. These obscure passages should be read and re-read attentively, and if light does not dawn, they should simply be passed over. Later, when one has read the whole book, especially when one has begun to practice it in real earnest, in all likelihood the difficulty will vanish altogether, and what at first appeared obscure will become clear and luminous and helpful.

It will be noted that the present volume bears a number (4). The reason of this is that buyers of my books begin to be uncertain as to the order in which they should be read. A person who wishes to follow out in them the logical sequence of thought, and the natural development of the subject, should read the volumes in their order of production:

The Mystical Knowledge of God.
The Mystical Life.
Mysticism—True and False.
Divine Contemplation for All *(the* present volume).

Other volumes will be produced (please God) in due course of time, and will each bear its proper number, until the series be completed. So will each of the first three as they may have to be reprinted; as for those which are already in circulation, it will be an easy matter for their owners to number them according to the above indication. I would advise them to do so: for, although I have made it a point so to compose each volume that it may stand by itself and be read with pleasure and profit separately and for its own sake, as it treats of one special point of Mysticism, nevertheless the interdependence of the volumes and their cumulative cogency, arising from comparison and logical sequence, is evident and cannot fail to be more and more felt as we proceed.

CHAPTER I

AN ATTEMPT AT DEFINING DIVINE CONTEMPLATION

AT the outset let us lay down this definition: Divine Contemplation is the act of communing with God. The word "communing" requires explanation. To commune is to share something with someone. It implies a twofold action, that of imparting something of one's own and that of receiving something else in return, or, vice versa, that of first receiving from another person and then imparting something in return. Thus, conversation is a sort of communing: in it one imparts one's own views and receives in return communication of another person's views. Any loving intercourse between two persons is a communing, for it is an exchange of marks of mutual affection. Thus mother and child, husband and wife, brother and brother, friend with friend, Jesus in the Holy Eucharist and the fervent communicant, God our Heavenly Father and the priest at Holy Mass.

Let us at once note that in loving intercourse, it is not so much the brain which is called into requisition, as the heart: we shall have more to say later upon this particular point. Now Divine Contemplation is just that kind of intercourse or communing. It requires two persons: the loving God and the loving soul; it is an exchange between them of marks of mutual affection.

Man, owing to his composite nature of spirit and flesh, is able to commune first with himself, his own *self*, and then with nature, that is to say with the world of creatures outside himself, both visible and invisible, particularly with his fellow-men; and finally, even with God, even with each one of the three persons of the Most Holy Trinity, and with the Sacred Humanity of Our Lord as it is enthroned in heaven or hidden in the Holy

Eucharist.

It is because the soul of man is a spirit that man is able to commune with himself. Only a spirit is able to turn, so to say, upon itself and take stock of its own nature, and observe what passes within it, and institute with its very self a sort of conversation about it all. He raises questions and proffers answers, and achieves at times by this inquisitive process, when wisely conducted, startling discoveries, finding within himself depths hitherto unsuspected and well-nigh unfathomable, discerning wants and secret cravings which God alone can satisfy. We have a magnificent monument of that sort of inquiry in page after page of the *Confessions* of St. Augustine.

This sort of communing with self is called introversion. I have already alluded to it in my book on *The Mystical Life* (ch. I). Very useful in itself and for its own sake, introversion is still more so as a preparation for and introduction to communing with God. How could communing with self fail to be useful and interesting? Next to God and Our Lord Jesus Christ, no other person or object ought to be dearer to a man than his own spirit which is within him.

This practice of introversion, when conducted in a prayerful spirit, will enable a man to discover in himself the trysting-place of the loving God. This is the very deepest and most secret part of a man's spiritual being, that wherein lies the divine resemblance, where the sacraments engrave their character, and the voice of conscience makes itself heard. It is the very heart and core of our personality. It is described in the writings of the mystics sometimes as the ground of the soul, sometimes as its apex, *la fine pointe de l'esprit,* says St. Francis of Sales. St. Thomas Aquinas calls it *Synderesis,* and St. Bonaventure *Scintilla*, or the luminous part of the soul, the *funklein* of the German mystics. God alone can enter into that *Sanctum Sanctorum*, or remotest sanctuary, of the human soul; God who made it—and the spirit of the man who is practicing prayerful introversion. The whole world of other creatures is for ever barred out of it, and it is not even in the power of man to lay open this part of himself to anyone: *For, what man knows the things of a man, but the spirit of a man that is in him?* (1 Cor. 2:11). It even seems that it will be so after our death and entrance into the spirit world, and throughout all eternity. This inviolability of each human soul, as well as of each angelic nature, will be one of their deepest satisfactions. I gather this from such texts as, for instance, this one in the Apocalypse, 2:17: *To him that overcomes ... I will give a white stone and in the stone a new name written, which no man knows but he that receives it.* Does not this new name, which no one knows but he to whom it is given, show us God and the individual blessed spirit in the light of two lovers, who in their privacy give one another endearing names which they would consider it profanation to repeat in the hearing of others?

Communing with Nature, when done in the right spirit, is an indirect way of communing with God, since Nature but reflects in faint accents its Maker's omnipotence, infinite wisdom and loveliness. I shall say more on this later on.

Communing with our fellow-men is much more difficult to turn to good account. Conversation between them and me is a pouring out of spirit into spirit; a pouring out which may be of things good, or frivolous, or useless, or most horrible; which may help me in my union with God, or be an obstacle to it, making me incapable and unworthy of it; a pouring out and an imparting which may be met half way, eagerly sought for and seized upon, or which on the contrary should be protested against and vigorously resisted. Therefore, in every attempted communing of my brethren with me, the attitude of my spirit ought to be one of alertness and watchfulness, and of prompt decision as to what line of action I ought to take. The same is true in regard to the written word, whether of the living or of the dead.

This communing of men with one another is accomplished not only by the spoken or written word, but also, and at times much more effectually, by look and gesture, by general deportment, and by self-manifestation of the spirit or of the flesh. It is no trespass on the boundaries of justice or of charity to state, in a general way, that the communings of men among themselves are but too often far from good, because so easily tainted with the evil inclinations of corrupt nature. "Whenever

I have been among men," says the author of *The Imitation of Christ,* "I have come back less a man." But this is not as God would have it to be. The right order is that our communings with one another, as well as our communings with Nature or with self, should be but an indirect way of communing with God. *If any man speak* (let him speak) *as the words of God* (1 Pet. 4:11).

The highest privilege of man is that he should be able, even in his present condition during his pilgrim days on earth, to commune with the loving God, if only he care to: thereby showing himself as far above animality as heaven is above the earth. By communing with God, the darkest life can be illumined; that of the slave, of the convict, of the prisoner of war, of the bedridden sufferer, of the victim of injustice and persecution or even of his own past misdeeds—indeed, the victim of any kind of misfortune. The life of every Christian, whatever his lot, his calling, the pressure of his occupations, ought to be illumined and glorified at least twice a day, morning and night, by communing with God; and if it may be so, much oftener, by the constant use of ejaculatory prayers. As for the life of the priest, or of the religious of either sex, it ought to be very holy and very happy, being one of constant communing with God. At almost every hour of the day, and for some even during the night, they are called upon to cease their communings with self or creatures and to converse with God instead, if only they will enter into the spirit of it and not be satisfied with a mere mechanical performance of their duty of public prayer—to say nothing of the facility they have all day long for private communings with God, in the secret of their heart.

Let this, therefore, stand at the outset as our definition: Divine Contemplation is the act of communing with God, wherever performed, howsoever performed, be the act brief and passing, or long sustained and frequently recurring.

O my brother, you who read this poor attempt of mine at setting before you the right notion of Divine Contemplation, do you really want to understand? Then, leave off reading; put the book aside, and at once begin to practice communing with God. Set out anyhow and anywhere. The loving God is just waiting for you to speak to Him, or—may it not be?—for you to hearken to Him. You cannot possibly miss Him. You may have sometimes wished to commune with an earthly friend of yours and not have found him, or perhaps you were stopped at the door with the cold and significant word: *Not at home!* You may have set out in pursuit of him, and have had the mortification of seeing him try in every way to dodge you, because, perchance, your conversation bores him, or he is afraid you come to ask him for a loan, or some other favor which he is not ready to grant. Now no such affront is to be feared from the loving God. He is always at home to us. He is never so pleased as when we want to have speech with Him and press Him for favors. *My delights*, says Divine Wisdom, *are to be with the children of men* (Prov. 8:31).

CHAPTER II

A FIRST DIVISION OF DIVINE CONTEMPLATION

NOW that we are in possession of a working general definition of Divine Contemplation, we may proceed to give our first division of the same. I promise myself a great advantage therefrom, a decided increase of light on the whole subject.

The first division then is this: (1) Divine Contemplation as it is in God Himself, who is the fountain head of it all; and (2) as it is derived from Him and communicated to His reasonable creatures.

A critic reviewing my book on *The Mystical Life* took exception to my speaking of Divine Contemplation "as it is in God." Well, and is it not in God? Divine Contemplation is the very life of God.

Divine Contemplation is the secret of God's infinite bliss in Himself. It is the very act by which God the Father eternally begets His Divine Son, and the further act, to put it in our own poor human language, by which, in an ecstasy of mutual love, God the Father and God the Son eternally breathe out their Holy Spirit.

This twofold but simultaneous act of Divine Contemplation as we conceive it to take place in God—an act in which God is at the same time the object contemplated and the subject contemplating, the object loved and the subject loving—this act is necessarily blissful, and infinitely so, as its object is the absolute good and is apprehended fully. Therefore, Divine Contemplation is—if we dare use the expression—the primary, essential feast of God, the rich banquet spread before His Divine Majesty, the never-failing source of the torrent of His delights.

Evidently, God could have reserved this rich banquet of Divine Contemplation for Himself alone. No creature can be conceived with any inherent right to, or any natural aptitude for, seeing and enjoying God as he is in Himself—in other words, the Beatific Vision. Now, out of His own infinite goodness, God has willed gratuitously to share His eternal bliss with some created natures. For this purpose He made the universe, a world of things visible and invisible, and in it He placed the Angels first, and then man, raising both of them to the supernatural state. After having created them to His own image and likeness, He made them come by grace into a share of His divine nature, preparatory to assuming them into the realm of His glory, there eternally to see Him face to face, and share His divine operations and His bliss.

God, who is the eternal and blissful object of His own contemplation, unveils the same object to the enraptured gaze of the elect in paradise. These happy children of God are seated at the very banquet of their heavenly Father; they are fed, so to say, with the same viands as Himself; they are inebriated by the same torrent of delights. Says the Psalmist: *They shall be inebriated with the plenty of thy house; and thou shalt make them drink of the torrent of thy pleasure.* (Psalm 35:9). And there is no danger, indeed there is no possibility of their ever losing such happiness, nor any danger of their ever growing weary of it, for it is infinite and inexhaustible, ever new and ever imparting to them new strength to bear the intensity of its delights.

Are we, who live on earth, completely debarred from a share in this divine banquet? Not so. By an inestimable favor, we are at least admitted to gather, if we will, and to eat, the crumbs which fall, so to say, from the table of God and of the Blessed in heaven. We, too, are called upon to practice Divine Contemplation after a manner suited to our present condition of wayfarers, who are yet far from home, and who walk by faith in a state of trial under sin. We are admitted already to share in some measure in the knowledge of God as He is in Himself and to partake of the divine blissful love. All we have to do is to consent to apply our minds to the loveliest of all objects, God as He is revealed to us by faith, and to open our hearts to the sacred effusions of His love.

All men, without exception, are invited to this feast of God, as all men are called unto salvation. The banquet hall is the Catholic Church. All are urged to come into it; not only the rich and well-to-do—I mean the intellectual, the men of high gifts and culture and refinement—but the poor as well, the halt, the maimed, the blind, the mendicant—that is to say, the uneducated, the illiterate, the simple-minded, the little children, the ignorant, and sinners, too, if only they will abandon sin. *Wisdom hath built herself a house, she hath hewn her out seven pillars. She hath slain her victims, mingled her wine and set forth her table. She hath sent her maids to invite to the tower and to the walls of the city: Whosoever is a little one let him come to me. And to the unwise she says: Come, eat my bread and drink the wine which I have mingled for you* (Prov. 9:1-5). *Compelle intrare: Compel them to come in, that my house may be filled,* says the divine host, Our Lord Himself, in the Gospel (Luke 14:23). A sweet violence is offered to everyone to sit at table, and to eat and drink his fill of the good things of God spread before him; that is to say, everyone is pressed to give himself to the exercise of contemplation, lovingly to attend to the mysteries of God and Our Lord Jesus Christ. "The grace of contemplation," says St. Gregory the Great, "is not one which is given to the highest and not to the lowest, but oftentimes both those who are the greatest and those who are the least receive it; oftener those who live in retirement, sometimes even those who are married. There is no rank or state of the faithful from which the grace of contemplation is excluded" *(In Ezech.* l. ii, Hom. 5, number 19).

Two conditions only are required of the guests: first, that they put on and keep on the wedding garment, which is the state of grace; and then, that they bring in with them, to the banquet, a good appetite, that is to say that they be of right good will to *taste and see that the Lord is sweet.* No one is to sit there in the nakedness and confusion of mortal sin; and no one, even wearing the wedding garment of grace, ought to sit there idly, looking bored by the company, disgusted at the bill of fare, and wishing for something different. *He hath filled the hungry with good things and the rich he hath sent empty away* (Luke 1:53). In the banquet of religion, God imparts a certain knowledge of Himself and experience of His sweetness to simple souls, who relish such nourishment. As for the pompous fool who disdains the humble process of prayer, and who looks upon himself as the rich man among his brethren (because, forsooth, he may happen to possess some trumpery erudition, some superficial knowledge of Scripture, or philosophy, or history, or the natural sciences), God sends him away empty; that is to say, God does not make Himself known to him in the secret of his heart by an ineffable communication of divine sweetness. And yet, he is such a fool that he does not perceive that in the midst of plenty he is starving!

If our first parents, and with them the whole human race, had retained the state of primitive innocence, contemplating God and delighting in the act would come as a second nature to us. We should easily discern God's most lovable perfections reflected everywhere on the face of the material universe, and in our own composition of body and soul, and in the society of perfect men and good Angels, and in the deposit of revelation and the whole order of religion such as it would be in this case. It would then have come as easy and natural to man to think of God and live in His presence—though not yet seeing Him face to face—and to love Him, and to delight in His contemplation, as it is pleasing and natural to us to crave for the food and drink needful to our body, and to take them with relish.

Divine Contemplation is the engrossing occupation of the Holy Souls in Purgatory; a most sublime contemplation, but extremely painful. Indeed, it is the keenest and most searching of their torments. They are out of this our region of shadows and in the land of perfect light of the pure spirits; they are, by this very fact, in possession of a marvellous infused knowledge of the universe, and of its laws, and of the laws of their own being, and of God as the Maker of all; they are fully aware of the jarring of some of their own past acts with these laws of God, a jarring which makes them debtors to the Divine Justice; moreover, they have had a glimpse of the infinite loveliness of God as reflected upon the countenance of Christ, whilst He was in the act of judging them immediately after their death; finally, they are no longer occupied with such saintly activities as they had on earth, and which might afford them some distraction and relief: for all these reasons, the Holy Souls cannot turn away their minds from the thought and contemplation of our Lord and of the Divine Essence; nor, indeed, do they wish to. They are pierced through and through with the burning arrow of the love of God. They are pining away with the most ardent desire to see face to face the object of their love and to be with Him forever. They are experiencing a holy hunger and thirst for the banquet of God, of which, perhaps, they made too light whilst they were on earth. They realize at last, as here below no one can, how sweet the Lord is; and now they experience how terrible a thing it is to have been made for the enjoyment of so sweet an object, and, through their own fault, to be deprived of it for a time.

To be definitely, irrevocably, deprived of God, and thereby to suffer untold torments, is of course the very essence of damnation. The crime of the reprobate is precisely that he would not have Divine Contemplation whilst on earth, and thus, and then, he made himself unfit for Divine Contemplation and the bliss that goes with it in heaven. So God had perforce to cast him away for ever into the exterior darkness.

Not that the very devils in hell, together with all the reprobate, do not practice some sort of contemplation. They do: but oh! what a terrible contemplation!—that of their own black heart, that of the accumulated guilt and misery of all their companions. They would not have the contemplation of the loving God, they would not taste how sweet He is; as inevitable consequence they must now taste the horrible bitterness of all else without Him. *Know thou and see how evil and bitter a thing it is for thee to have left the Lord thy God* (Jer. 2:19). And this bitterness they will experience throughout all eternity. The spirit of man, like the nature of the angel, is a mirror that reflects faithfully the things with which it lives.

CHAPTER III

ON NATURAL CONTEMPLATION

CONTEMPLATION as it is given to man to practice on earth, in his present condition of trial, and of trial under sin, must be divided into two species: (1) That which is purely natural, and (2) supernatural, or Christian, contemplation.

Purely natural contemplation is that in which no light of faith, no ray of the Divine Revelation intervenes. The Christian or supernatural species is that in which, whatever be its object—God or anything inferior to God—one never considers it apart from the data of the Divine Revelation, deposited in the hands of the true Church of Christ, the Catholic Church.

The act of contemplation in itself is natural to man and is an integral part of his rational life. Every human being practices it, even the babe in arms after it is a few months old. See what eyes full of wonderment he opens upon the world. There is an element of contemplation at the bottom of every rational enjoyment. By the very fact that man is *animal rationabile*—"an animal endowed with the reasoning faculty," his life is an entanglement of action and contemplation: action corresponding chiefly to the animal element in his composition, and contemplation chiefly to his rational element. Every man, at some time of every day, provided only he enjoys the use of his faculties of sense and intellect, indulges in some sort of contemplation.

This serves at once to show how vain is the excuse put forward by the tepid Christian, that he has no aptitude for contemplation. The aptitude indeed exists within him and is frequently employed by him; only he does not care to apply it to the object which is supremely worthy of its exercise—namely, the Divine Goodness—because, forsooth, he would have to change his own negligent way of living, and this he has quite made up his mind not to do.

St. Thomas (*Secunda Secundæ*, *quæstio* 180, *a* 4, *ad* 3), after Richard of St. Victor, distinguishes six kinds or degrees of contemplation:

The first is attention to material objects.

The second is attention to the order and disposition of these.

The third is when from the consideration of things visible man is led to conceive the idea of things invisible.

The fourth is when the mind turns to the contemplation of things invisible, without the help of images.

The fifth is when, in the light of Divine Revelation, the mind of man rises to the knowledge of truths which are above the capacity of pure reason.

The sixth is when in the same light of Divine Revelation a man comes to the knowledge of truths which not only are above the capacity of human reason, but even seem to go counter to it, such as, for instance, the mystery of the Blessed Trinity.

In this illuminating page of mediæval Theology we run the whole gamut of human contemplation, from its lowest degree to its most sublime. We shall do well not to dismiss it lightly. Observe that in the first four degrees man is shown to be naturally equipped for the work of contemplation, as though this were to be (as indeed it is) his life's great work in time as well as in eternity.

These first four degrees place before our eyes a penetrating analysis of the workings of man's mind within the limits of its natural capacity. They constitute the purely natural process which must necessarily precede any perception of the supernatural, even as the foundation must be laid down before the house can be reared. It is worthy of remark also that these four degrees of human contemplation, as they succeed one another, coincide with the successive stages in a man's life thus:

The first degree of contemplation, or the perception of sensible objects, is the sole contemplation of infants. The beasts, likewise, have this perception of sensible objects: but with them it is not a first degree of contemplation, as there is to be no second degree. Their experience goes no further, and is turned wholly to the purposes of animal life. Hence it will appear that when man does the same—when he turns wholly to the purposes of animal life his perceptions of the world of creatures—without passing further on, he makes himself like unto the unreasoning brute. "God," says the pagan philosopher Epictetus, "has introduced man as a spectator of Himself and His works, and not only as a spectator but as an interpreter of them. It is, therefore, shameful that man should begin and end where irrational creatures do. He is rather to begin there but to end where nature itself has fixed our end, that is, in contemplation and understanding and in a scheme of life conformable to our nature" (*Moral Discourses, vi*—On Providence).

The second degree of contemplation indicated by St. Thomas is the passing from sensitive perceptions to intelligible ones: it is also that of the child growing into the age of discretion and assuming moral responsibility. The third degree is peculiarly that of the adolescent; and the fourth characterizes the workings of the mind of the youth verging on manhood. The other two degrees belong only to the Christian as such, that is to say, to man when, through Baptism, and the other sacraments, he has come to his full growth in Christ Jesus.

The field of natural contemplation extends all the way from the atom, or infinitesimally small particle of matter, even to God as the Primal Cause, through all the various and intricate grades of inanimate matter and of life; but it does not extend beyond the boundaries of Nature, nor does it call for the use of any other tools than the faculties of sense and intellect within their natural compass. For the pagan, ancient or modern, the most Holy Trinity, Jesus the Son of God, His mystic bride the Church of the elect, the grace of the sacraments, the promises of eternal life in glory; all these are as though they were not, just as to a blind beast the light of the sun and the splendid pageant of nature are as though they were not. The natural man simply ignores these mysteries, as he ignores also the fact of original sin, the finality of the present life and its high purpose, reaching out beyond the grave, and the fearful consequences attending his failure to achieve moral goodness. Such is the case also with the modernist, even though he use words filched from the Christian vocabulary, as he has been careful first to deprive them of their original, substantial, dogmatic and historical meaning.

It is impossible now to discern to what extent the pagan philosophers of old have been unconsciously affected in their natural contemplation by, on the one hand, stray remnants of the primitive revelation, and on the other by infiltrations of either Jewish or Christian thought. Nor are we prepared to deny that the Holy Spirit intervened with His prevenient grace in some of their meditations. Heraclitus, Pythagoras, Socrates, Plato, Aristotle, Epictetus, Plotinus, and, outside this classical circle, the barbarian philosophers Confucius, Gautama and others, have said some very wise things; only there seems to have occurred a process of petrification at some point in the natural contemplation which should have led them on to God.

For the whole gist and purpose of natural contemplation, from its start to its finish, is to lead man to the knowledge of God, and consequently to His love, and to the will to give Him pleasure by obeying His laws and praising His perfections. Arrived at this point, a man, even though as yet deprived of the light of the supernatural revelation, is open to the influence of divine grace which is pressing all around him, and if he will but let it have entrance into his heart, he is thereby transformed into a child of God. May it not be that we ought thus to interpret the declaration of Pope Pius IX that "if a man be by the force of circumstances kept in invincible ignorance of the true religion, God will not condemn him:" (*Cf.* Denzinger's *Enchiridion, editio* 11, 1647). It would seem as if the pagan, at the precise moment when he fulfils the whole natural law—that is to say, follows it out to its practical consequences in the worship of God and in the amendment of his life—has his natural contemplation changed into supernatural, and the grace of God infused into him, and he is made through the implied Baptism of desire, into that new creature, a Christian, all unknown to himself and to the world.

It is for not having thus followed out natural lights to their ultimate consequences that those philosophers of antiquity alluded to by St. Paul, were so severely condemned: For the invisible things of him, from the creation of the world are clearly seen, being understood by the things that are made, his eternal power also and divinity, so that they are inexcusable, because that when they knew God, they have not glorified Him as God or given thanks, but became vain in their thoughts, and their foolish heart was darkened (Rom. 1:20-21).

CHAPTER IV

CHRISTIAN CONTEMPLATION

THE field of Christian Contemplation is incomparably vaster than that of natural contemplation. It is none other than the most Holy Trinity as at present made known to us by Divine Revelation—the official external revelation of which the Catholic Church is the guardian—and the internal experimental revelation of Mystical Theology: that is to say, the three Divine Persons with all their ineffable operations within and without *(ad intra et ad extra)* are the primary objects of Christian contemplation: and within these three Divine Persons, and together with them, the Sacred Humanity of Our Blessed Lord Jesus Christ; and ourselves and all things else in Jesus: for, *All things are yours*, says St. Paul ... *and you are Christ's and Christ is God's* (1 Cor. 3:22 and 23).

This immense field opened before the contemplative Christian is admirably outlined and, so to say, mapped out by the Church in the Nicene Creed, which is but a resetting of the Apostles' Creed in more explicit terms. Therein one is taught to view first oneself, and then all things else—whether visible or invisible, terrestrial or heavenly, present or future, ephemeral or eternal—in reference to God, and in the light of the most Holy Trinity. All things are meant to lead a Christian to the knowledge and the love of God not only as the Primal Cause, as He is knowable through the splendors of creation, but also as He is in Himself, that is to say, as a Trinity of Persons in the absolutely transcendent unity and simplicity of the divine essence.

That which the blessed in glory contemplate face to face, and enjoy for ever, in an ineffable ecstasy of love—the very same, we on earth, if we will, do contemplate in the dim light of faith and begin to enjoy in the secret of our hearts.

However, the greatest difference between Christian and purely natural contemplation arises, not from the vastness of its field and the peculiar light under which it is seen, but, above all, from the fact of its being an act of our mystical life, that is to say, of the joint-life with God which every Christian is expected to live in the secret of his heart.

Natural contemplation is mainly a brain process and is all one-sided, being the exclusive act of the contemplator. All the vitality of the act springs from himself. Christian contemplation on the contrary is, as far as man is concerned, mainly a heart process; and, moreover, it is not his own exclusive act. Before and over, and accompanying, the act or acts of the contemplator, there is the vital action of God upon him, to prevent him, to excite him, to draw him, to seize upon him and to bind and knit him to God. All which is expressed with much felicity in innumerable passages of the sacred liturgy, particularly in the well known prayer: *Actiones nostras, quæsumus, Domine, aspirando præveni*—"Prevent, we beseech Thee, O Lord, our actions by Thy holy inspirations, and carry them on by Thy gracious assistance, that every prayer and work of ours may always originate from Thee and through Thee be happily ended."

If every act of the fervent Christian is not a purely human act, but an act of his joint-life with God, and thereby is sure to have a divine element in it, how much more so the act of prayer, the act of Divine Contemplation?

There is, then, in Christian contemplation a new element which is not found in the philosophical or scientific or aesthetical contemplation. The catechism calls it the grace of God. Let us put it plainly: this new element is the presence of God, the intervention of God, the direct action of God, the share of God in the life of the mystic. In Christian contemplation man does not do all, is not left to his own puny resources, nor does he view God at a distance or in the abstract; he actually meets the living God; he meets Him in a vital embrace, giving to Him and receiving from Him, or rather receiving first and then giving. Not only is there a supernatural revelation of God proposed to the mystic, by our holy Mother the Church, and a dogmatic utterance apprehended by him, and the supernatural faculty of faith granted him in order that he may grasp the divine truth and give assent to it; but God Himself comes to meet him, to embrace him, and to pour out the Divine sweetness into his heart. All this, of course, takes place under the seal of faith.

The joy that is felt in Christian contemplation is not only *gaudium de veritate*, the joy of truth in the abstract—such joy as may be tasted by any man who makes a right use of his natural powers—but it is also something of a much higher order, for it is the direct doing of God: the act of God lifting the Christian and folding him to His fatherly heart; it is the touch of His hand, the beating of His heart, God's *hiding of the mystic in the secret of His face* (Psalm xxx, 21), God having secret speech with His servant without any sound of voice.

This new element of the presence and active intervention of God is found in Christian contemplation in all its degrees, even in the very lowest and humblest ones, though, of course, it is more manifest in the highest, rendering them all absolutely supernatural. Christian contemplation in all its degrees, in all its forms, is the meeting of God and man in a loving embrace. It takes two to meet and embrace: here they are, the loving God and the loving soul. Whenever a man is ready, and willing, and sets about the act of meeting his heavenly Father, God is also ready for him; nay, it is God Himself who has been secretly rousing this man, and exciting him and moving him, and sweetly drawing him on, and knitting him to His own divine self.

The whole process of Christian contemplation makes for a closer, more active, more intimate union with God through a gradual simplification of the soul. Here are some of the stages:

1. Discursive orison;
2. Affective orison;
3. Orison of simplicity;
4. Orison of quiet;
5. The experience of Mystical Theology;
6. Semi-passive orison;
7. Passive orison;
8. Ecstatic orison;
9. Miraculous orison;

All of which we shall describe in their proper place.

Now, at each of these successive stages the action of God grows greater, while that of man seems to dwindle because it grows more and more spiritual: and his enjoyment of God grows in proportion, though it becomes more and more secret, more remote from the observation of men, and is jealously guarded from their prying curiosity. *Secretum meum mihi* (Isaiah 24:16): "I keep my own secret," says the mystic: even as the Blessed Virgin Mary kept the secret of the Incarnation locked in her breast until it pleased God to reveal it to St. Joseph.

It is hardly necessary to remark that this new element in Christian contemplation is overlooked by non-Catholic writers on Mysticism. As they never had any experience of the active and preponderant part played by the loving God in the Christian's joint life with Him it is not surprising that they should ignore it completely. What is a legitimate subject of wonder and disgust is to find it overlooked by Catholic writers. There are some who treat of Divine Contemplation as though it were purely man's doing and nothing more. They have introduced into modern piety a sort of contemplation dry and barren, absolutely disconcerting, and more likely to defeat its own professed purpose of uniting one with God, than to bring it about. They seem to say to the loving God who is ready and eager to play His part and act with them: "Nay, nay, Lord: please let me do it by myself. Do not interfere. I am going to spin it all out of my own brain. I only require that You will give me a sitting. Just let me have a good look at Your Divine Majesty. I am the artist, Yours the likeness I want to throw on the canvas of my faculties."

Is this impertinent enough?

And whilst man is fondly imagining that he is contemplating God, he is much more contemplating his own fatuous self, admiring and congratulating himself for being so clever. Of course, he is quickly brought to a dead stop. God will not sit for him. God will not accept contemplation on those terms. God eludes his grasp, his gaze. Then there comes discouragement; the rash and ill-advised Christian gives up the attempt, and will have nothing to do henceforth with Divine Contemplation. The very name of it will rouse his resentment, as though he had been treated unkindly by Our Lord.

Who is to blame here? Surely not the loving God. What is amiss is the method, the "brain process," and those who teach such a method, whoever they may happen to be, and those who follow it! Instead of seeing in Christian Contemplation what there is in it, namely a lively, hearty communing with God, they have made of it an intellectual communing with self. Little wonder that it is found unsatisfactory in the end.

Let us never grow tired of repeating that Christian Contemplation is an act of our joint life with God, an act of our family life with God. By the merits of Our Lord Jesus Christ, and through the efficacy of the sacraments, we have become members of this family. Now, every well-bred child embraces his beloved parents at least twice a day, morning and evening, giving and receiving those delicate tokens of affection which mark him as one of the family and one very dear indeed. The true child of God, the fervent Christian, will do the same with regard to his heavenly Father.

Let us here sketch out the ideal day of a Christian in the world, in regard to Divine Contemplation.

It begins with the fervent morning-offering and prayer, and possibly a quarter of an hour's meditation, and perhaps even holy Mass and Communion.

How cheerfully and bravely does a man face the day's drudgery after such a beginning!

The Angelus at noon and Graces before and after meat give him occasions to look up again to the Father in heaven, and lovingly to speak to Him, to talk with Him, to kiss His bountiful hand. Perhaps he will be able to wedge in, at this point, a flying visit to the Blessed Sacrament, or a decade of the Rosary and a quarter of an hour's spiritual reading.

Perhaps, again, between the evening Angelus and night prayers he will manage to read to himself or to the whole assembled family, a chapter of the beautiful lives of the Saints, from such books as the *Miniature Lives of the Saints* of Father Bowden, or the *Fioretti* of St. Francis of Assisi, or the *Golden Legend* of James of Voragine, or Abbé Grimes' *L'esprit des Saints* (a wonderful collection, a library in itself, seven vols.). The lives of Saints issued in penny pamphlets by the Catholic Truth Societies of England and of Ireland are also most excellent reading.

And all through the day, all through his various occupations, manual or mental, he will know how to breathe in the perfume of the loved presence of God, how to hearken to the secret inspirations of His grace, and how to season all he does with the constant offering of ejaculatory prayers.

Now it should not be difficult to realize such a programme: it is ideally simple, and I have, in divers countries, seen it carried out by Christians living under healthy and sane conditions of life. But, alas! we are obliged to own that the tendency of society is more and more to render impossible even so moderate a demand and such a rational disposition of the day. For one thing, there is no more privacy. Almost everyone now, almost from childhood upwards, is thrown amongst a huge crowd of fellow-students, fellow-workmen, fellow-soldiers or sailors, and can hardly call his soul his own. Then the conditions of work have become so inhumane: men are caught and whirled about at top-speed in a vortex of mechanical drudgery, until they are giddy and incapable of mental freedom, or rational enjoyment, or prayer. Even after work, under such conditions, there is a dangerous depression.

Next to that of the priest and the religious, especially those of contemplative orders, the mode of life the best suited for Christian contemplation is that of the husbandman. Here again one might exclaim with Virgil, though with a higher meaning: *O fortunatos nimium sua si bona norint agricolas:* "Too blissful would the husbandmen be if they only knew how to appreciate their happy lot." Next to theirs come those quite manual professions which can be pursued at home and leave the mind free to be with God a good deal, if only one will turn lovingly to Him.

Can a person be truly called a Christian, in whose daily life, God, and the thought of His presence, and loving converse with Him, hardly find a place?

CHAPTER V

SOME CHARACTERISTICS OF CHRISTIAN CONTEMPLATION

THE end of the Mystical Life, as we have seen at some length in the treatise which bears this title, is to unite us closely to God, to render us deiform, to communicate to us the very life of God, making us sharers in His sanctity and His happiness. The two functions of the mystical life, namely, Divine Contemplation and Saintly Action, contribute each in its own way to bring about these marvellous effects, to make the mystic, and to show him to the world, as truly deiform; but the function which does this more directly and effectually is, for obvious reasons, Divine Contemplation. It deals directly with God, comes into immediate touch with Him, actually feeds upon Him. If you handle gold powder, your hands will shine like gold. If you saturate your hair and your clothes with perfume, you will carry about with you its pleasing odor. The little child at his mother's breast who knows no other food, exhales the wholesome odor of milk. The man who keeps company with well-bred, refined, gentlefolk only, will naturally make their good manners his own. So likewise, if you associate constantly with God, if you live with Him and feed on Him, and handle Him, and saturate your whole being with His divine grace and presence and love, you will become God-like, deiform.

How shall we know that this is being, or has already been, effected? Are there characteristic proofs, authentic marks by which we may discern how the case stands with us? Yes, there are such marks.

In genuine Christian Contemplation the following characteristics are always found:

1. Compunction.
2. Humility.
3. Admiration.
4. Joy.

Sometimes all of them stand out distinctly like the primary colors in the rainbow; sometimes one of them is more conspicuous; at other times they are all blended together, like the primary colors in a ray of white light: but they are always there and always absolutely supernatural. Wherever these four marks are found together, you have authentic testimony that there is indeed genuine Christian Contemplation, that the Holy Spirit has a hand in it, that the loving God is in it, that He is half and more than half of it. Whenever you can prove the absence of any one of these four characteristics, depend upon it, the other three are absent as well, whatever appearances may be. You may have the contemplation of a Christian, perhaps even of a theologian, but you have not Christian contemplation, you have not an exercise of the first function of mystical life; you have but a sham: *æs sonans, cymbalum tinniens:* "sounding brass, a tinkling cymbal" (1 Cor. 13:1), nothing more.

The first two qualities, Compunction and Humility, ought in fact to precede contemplation; they are preparatory dispositions. When contemplation supervenes, they go along with it, and are deepened by it and made an abiding possession of the soul. The other two, Admiration and Joy, are after-effects of contemplation; they grow out of it, and hang on it as most beautiful and sweet fruits upon their native tree: fruits which become the more plentiful and luscious, the more one cultivates Divine Contemplation.

There is this also about these four properties of genuine Christian Contemplation, that the mystic can at all times almost infallibly bring about for himself the contemplative mood, simply by making the acts of these four virtues. Dear reader, if you are sceptical, just try and see.

Compunction, first. This is only saying that we have to begin at the very beginning. As the Pseudo-Areopagite observes, "purification" is the first act of the hierarchy and the first stage of the spiritual life. No well-bred child will present himself to be kissed by his parents with a dirty face. The first care of a man who wants to be admitted to the presence of a king and have speech with him, or even sit at his table, will be to have a thorough cleansing and to put on clothes befitting the occasion. The first gift of the Holy Spirit in order of execution and usefulness is "Fear of the Lord" (Isaiah 11:3).

Compunction bruises and breaks and melts away the stony hardness of our sinful hearts. This process must be gone through before we can hope to feel the touch of divine love and become plastic under its hand. It is clear that compunction is not a brain process: it is mainly of the heart and will, in so far as man is concerned in its production, and then there comes into it the united action of Our Lord and His Holy Spirit. To the tears of true and abiding sorrow of the fervent soul are added the efficacy of the Blood of Jesus Christ and the flames of the love of God kindled by the Holy Spirit present in the heart of the Christian.

The author of the *Following of Christ* says: "I would gladly feel compunction, than know its definition." One of the reasons why a great many Christians fail in the business of the mystical life, and signally in the work of Divine Contemplation, is that they overlook the necessity of compunction. (See what I have said in *Mysticism—True and False,* ch. xiii, about the necessity of an abiding sorrow for our past sins to guard us against relapsing into them.) For it seems that the more one is a sinner the less he realizes his state, or is sensible of its consequences. On the other hand, the more the Saints make progress in the love of God and the spirit of prayer, the greater become their sorrow for past sins, and their self-contempt and self-hatred and self-persecution by way of expiation and of salutary discipline. One morning the holy Curé d'Ars was found all bathed in tears. "What has happened?" asked his companion. Nothing in particular had happened, he answered. "I am only bewailing the sins of my poor life." "Je pleurs mes pauvres péchés."

As we are bent upon this noble enterprise of the mystical life, let us begin at the very beginning of every attempt at divine contemplation: sorrow for sin. Let us lay ourselves open and responsive to the powerful solicitations of divine grace, and break our hearts over the misery of having offended so good and loving a Father. Let us in true sorrow strike our breast, chide ourselves, and exclaim: "Oh! how could you do such a thing? How could you stay so long without repentance? How could you have so little compassion on your merciful Saviour? How could you despise the terrible judgments of God?"—and then turn to the loving Lord and tell Him of our repentance.

The *Confessions* of St. Augustine exhibit a fine illustration of this spirit of compunction which ought to be at the basis of all our attempts to have speech with the Divine Majesty. Now, suppose we try this. Suppose we make it our practice to stir up our sorrow for past sins every time we desire to pray. Let us try, and then see how we get on with our contemplation.

Look at the order of the liturgy of the Mass. Before the priest is permitted to go up to the altar, he and the people present are made humbly and publicly to confess their sinfulness and to crave the intercession of all the Saints in view of the pardon of God. Sometimes the Psalm *Judica me,* and the joyful *Gloria in excelsis* and the solemn profession of the orthodox Faith, the Nicene Creed, are omitted; but the *Confiteor* of the Priest, and then that of the people, never.

CHAPTER VI

HUMILITY OF THE CONTEMPLATIVE

IN the wake of Compunction, issuing from it and begotten of it, comes Humility. But it soon overtakes and long outstrips its father. Thus we reach the most fundamental disposition of the soul for the work of Divine Contemplation.

No one is so humble as the genuine mystic, and no wonder: he lives in the presence of God! Let us try and realize what this means. Does it not stand to reason that the fervent Christian who habitually keeps the gaze of his soul fixed upon the Divine Majesty, and then looks at his own puny self in the overwhelming splendor of the light of the Three Divine Persons, cannot help having an amazing feeling of his own native void and indigence? He soon gets out of sight, sinking himself into depths of self-abjection which only Saints dare fathom, as did St. John of the Cross with the plummet of his "NOTHING."

Those who fear that entering upon the ways of contemplation and mystical life may lead one to become puffed up, show that they know nothing about it. The exercise of the presence of God is much more conducive to solid humility than even the consideration of one's own past sins and wicked life. One cannot really contemplate God and be proud or vain. The more a man perceives the loveliness of God, and tastes how sweet He is, and allows himself to be united to Him, so much the more is he inclined, nay compelled, to think little of himself.

We must insist on this fundamental humility, which is practiced by every mystic independently of all consideration of personal sinfulness. For, indeed, if in order to be humble it were required to have sinned, then Our Lord could not have said: "Learn of Me, because I am humble of heart." And His immaculate sinless Virgin-Mother could not be, as she is in very deed, the humblest of all pure creatures while at the same time she is the most exalted. Nor could the Blessed Angels be humble, in whom not the lightest shadow of sin has ever been found—and yet we know that they are: the Liturgy of the Church, with the Prophets of both Testaments, represents them to us in the attitude of deepest self-annihilation before the Divine Majesty.

In the act of contemplation the fervent Christian holds himself annihilated before God, and with the whole Church, Militant, Suffering and Triumphant, proclaims that He is alone worthy to receive blessing and praise and honor and glory. This utter self-abasement before the Most Holy Trinity is the true exercise of love which Martyrs have practiced in the midst of their torments, and holy Confessors in the midst of all sorts of temptations and contradictions, and which made them capable of enduring or accomplishing so much.

This fundamental humility of the Christian contemplative does not prevent his freely acknowledging, and if need be, recounting and even proclaiming the great things God does in him. Only he takes no credit to himself, but gives all praise to God alone. "He hath done to me great things: holy is his name" exclaims the Blessed Virgin Mary at the moment when she is greeted as the true mother of God. And thus also did St. Teresa, on the order of her confessors, in spite of her own repugnance, give to the whole world the secret of her life of union with God. In our own days, one of her sweetest, most lovable daughters, Sister Thérèse of the Child Jesus, popularly known as "The Little Flower," committed to writing, with the most charming simplicity, the story of her beautiful soul.

Now it is my contention that this second characteristic of genuine Christian Contemplation is never found anywhere else; and also that whenever it is absent from the contemplation even of the Christian man, his contemplation ceases to be Christian: it is spoiled, it is corrupted, it will do no good, even were it the most brilliant piece of theological study.

Such is in particular the misfortune of the wilful heretic. Dionysius the Areopagite says: "If the human intellect, dissatisfied with its allotted portion of the Divine blessing, endeavors to trespass over the limits which God has set; if it applies itself rashly to the contemplation of splendors which are above its comprehension; no doubt the light will not cease to shine, but the soul will neither obtain what was never meant for her, nor even will she, on account of her insane pride, be allowed to preserve what had been freely given her. This is the penalty of her meddling indiscreetly in things above her capacity."

Then he adds: "This notwithstanding, the blessed light keeps perpetually shining upon all: ever present before the minds of men, ever ready to communicate itself with a divine liberality, so that they are free to receive it" (*Eccles. Hierarch.* Ch. ii, p. 3, no. 3).

In Ruysbroeck's *Adornment of the Spiritual Marriage*, there is a beautiful page on the "Humility of the mystic," and the blessings that go with it. He says:

"Now understand this. When the sun sends its beams and its radiance into a deep valley between two high mountains, and, standing in the zenith, can yet shine upon the bottom and ground of the valley, then three things happen: the valley becomes full of light by reflection from the mountains, and it receives more heat and becomes more fruitful than the plain and level country. And so likewise when a good man takes his stand upon his own littleness, in the most lowly part of himself: and confesses and knows that he has nothing, and can do nothing of himself, neither stand still nor go on, and when he sees how often he fails in virtues and good works: then he confesses his poverty and his helplessness, then he makes a valley of humility. And when he is thus humble and needy and knows his own need, he lays his distress, and complains of it, before the bounty and the mercy of God. And so he marks the sublimity of God and his own lowliness; and thus he becomes a deep valley. And Christ is a Sun of righteousness and also of mercy, who stands in the highest part of the firmament, that is on the right hand of the Father, and from thence He shines into the bottom of the humble heart; for Christ is always moved by helplessness, whenever a man complains of it and lays it before Him with humility. Then there arise two mountains, that is two desires; one to serve God and praise Him with reverence, the other to attain noble virtues. Those two mountains are higher than the heavens, for those longings touch God without intermediary, and crave His ungrudging generosity. Then that generosity cannot withhold itself, it must flow forth, for then the soul is made ready to receive and to hold more gifts. Then, this valley, the humble heart, becomes more radiant and enlightened by grace, more ardent in charity, more fruitful in perfect virtues and in good works" *(Adornment of the Spiritual Marriage.* C. VI, Translated by Dom. C. A. Wynshenk).

The fundamental humility of the contemplative soul seems to me also wonderfully brought out in the *Showings* of Mother Juliana of Norwich. In Chapter III she relates: "He showed a little thing, the quantity of a hazel nut, lying in the palm of my hand, as meseemed, and, as it were, round as a ball. I looked thereon with the eye of my understanding, and thought: 'What may this be?' And it was answered generally thus: 'It is all that is made.' I marveled how it could last, for methought it might suddenly have fallen to nought for littleness. ..."

In Chapter VIII she thus comments on this: "Well I know that heaven and earth and all that is made is great, large, fair and good. But the cause why it showeth so little to my sight, is that I saw it in the presence of Him that is the Maker, for to a soul that sees the Maker of all things, all that is made seems full little."

I wonder whether the holy recluse who describes herself as "a simple creature, that could no letter," was aware that in this last sentence she was repeating word for word what one of the mightiest geniuses and most illustrious mystics of the world, St. Gregory the Great, says in his *Dialogues* (II, 45). There, after having described how St. Benedict in one of his visions saw the world under the form of a tiny sphere, lost in a ray of the glory of God, he drops this casual remark: "For indeed, to the man who sees the Creator, all things created appear very small." Videnti Creatorem angusta est omnis creatura.

To conclude this chapter: there is no fear, then, that the true contemplative shall ever wax vain-glorious. And thus, whenever you see a man boastful, self-assertive, noisy in his speech, depend upon it, that man is not addicted to the practice of Divine

Contemplation. An empty wain rattles as it goes along the road; one laden mountain-high with the golden sheaves goes along slowly, silently, majestically. A shallow river makes a loud noise as it rakes the stony bottom; the deep, full river, ominously silent, slides by with irresistible power. And so humility—deep, sincere, solid—is an unmistakable characteristic of genuine Christian contemplation: the deeper that it says not a word, that it makes no demonstration.

CHAPTER VII

ADMIRATION AND JOY

COMPUNCTION and humility together produce their first effect by setting the Christian free from all inordinate love of self or of creatures; and, further, they cleanse the soul, rendering it exceedingly bright; and, still further, they cause it really to receive, and really to reflect, the rays of divine light as they shine full upon it—nay, upon all men, and upon all the world.

So the divine goodness floods the contemplative soul with its splendor and benignant heat; there is immediate contact between the loving God and the loving soul; God allowing Himself, in a manner, to be seen and touched, to be handled and tasted by the spirit of this fervent Christian, in whom there then arises a feeling of admiration, that usually breaks forth into praise and melts away into an overwhelming sense of joy.

Compunction and humility are, indeed, peculiar characteristics of Christian contemplation; seldom if ever are they found anywhere else: although one might be inclined to think that these two new feelings, admiration and joy, are also found in purely natural contemplation. It is true that some kind of admiration and joy is the reward of natural contemplation; but these feelings are of a different description altogether. The Christian's admiration in the act of Divine Contemplation is a joint product of the exercise of his natural reason, theological Faith and the gift of Understanding; while his joy is a joint product of the exercise of his natural affectionateness, the theological virtue of Charity, and the gift of Wisdom. These two feelings then, in their origin, in their motive, in their mode of operation, and in their results, are essentially supernatural.

A man casts his eyes upon the loveliness of nature in its majestic totality or in some of its wondrous details, and he is seized with admiration: if he be a mystic, his admiration will at once rise above what evoked it, and it will ascend straight up to

God the Father as the benign creator of all these marvels, to God the Son as their divine exemplar, to God the Holy Spirit as the sustaining principle of them all. *By the word of the Lord the heavens were established and all the power of them by the spirit of his mouth* (Psalm 32:6). Then he casts the eyes of his soul upon the mysteries of Our Blessed Lord as they are presented to us by the Church in the Gospel-revelation, and he discovers in them (as we shall see at some length in a subsequent volume), a new world full of incomparably greater wonders: and his admiration grows by leaps and bounds. Finally, from the Sacred Humanity of his Saviour, our fervent Christian is led on to the contemplation of the divine personality of the Word, and of the Father who eternally begets Him, and of the Spirit of Love who proceeds from both Father and Son as from one principle, and to the contemplation of their infinite perfections, and there his admiration is unbounded and unutterable.

Some modern writers, of the infidel school of thought, accuse Christianity of having a tendency to render men insensible to the charms of nature. How unjust this indictment is, the lives of our Saints, and almost all the monuments of Catholic art and literature, demonstrate. What has sometimes happened is that the contemplative has, on particular occasions, been so overwhelmed by the spiritual beauty he beheld with the inward eye, that there was left in him no power to enjoy the loveliness of natural scenery. Thus, St. Bernard could travel a whole day on the shores of one of the most beautiful lakes in the world, and not look at it, because he was then rapt in the greater loveliness seen by his spirit united to God in ecstatic prayer. This only shows that there are divers grades of beauty which solicit man's admiration, and that in our present condition our reserve power of actual perception and enjoyment is strictly limited. And so it will happen that, if it be mightily drawn upon by one particular object, none of it can be spared for another. The fountain-head of St. Bernard's rapturous admiration lay deeper than the surface of things: consequently, it was of a finer quality, and incomparably more refreshing and potent than any purely natural feeling; and sprang up even unto eternal life, to the very throne of the Blessed Trinity.

From this admiration of the contemplative flows spontaneously the praise of God: the loving and rapturous praise of Our Father in heaven. This is abundantly illustrated in the whole range of the sacred writings from Genesis to the Apocalypse, in the sacred liturgy, and in so many burning lyrical effusions of the Saints; for instance, to name but one: in the canticle of St. Francis of Assisi to "My brother the Sun." It is also borne out by the daily experiences of fervent souls who live in close union with God and are careful to banish from their heart all that displeases Him. Praise, rapturous, burning praise of the Beloved, not always set in words or sounded in the ear—for when admiration is intense, one is struck speechless; the feeling expresses itself only in the ecstatic attitude of soul and body. And is not this the loudest praise: "*Tibi silentium laus!*" *Silence is thy fitting praise* (Ps. 64:2, in the Hebrew version). Does not the recollected, serene, winsome countenance of the Saints proclaim to the world that *the Divine Wisdom's conversation hath no sadness, nor her company any tediousness but joy* (Wisd. 8:16)—joy unspeakable?

In his contemplation, our mystic emulates the admiration shown by the simple-hearted shepherds of Bethlehem at the angelic message, and at what they found in the grotto of the Nativity; the admiration of the Blessed Virgin Mary and of St. Joseph at the things they heard said of the Divine Child; the admiration of the angelic hosts at witnessing the Lord of glory become an infant of a day, when they made the country-side of Judea resound with their songs of praise. This also enables him to picture to himself the admiration of the same angelic hosts at the mystery of the Holy Mass and of the real presence of Our Lord in the tabernacle. Oh! how the contemplative sees at times, "in his mind's eye," these Blessed Spirits pressing around him after holy communion, adoring their Lord just new born in the poor stable of his own heart, and praising Him there! And if we, too, are dimly conscious of the glory that is visiting and investing us at such a moment, how we should break forth into songs of gladness and praise at the loving condescension of Our Lord!

We have spoken of joy. May we not use a stronger word—more expressive, at any rate—and say "exultation"? So it is styled hundreds of times in the Scriptures. The song of praise of the Blessed God on the lips of the mystic, or in the inmost sanctuary of his heart, is not only a sign of admiration but of exultation as well.

And now, mark. The praise seems to go forth from man to God; in reality it comes from God, passes through the heart and lips of man, and, then, from man, returns to God. The exultation that goes along with it is an overflow from the heart of the loving God, flooding the heart of the pure and fervent Christian. It is the very bliss of God making itself felt in man. It is the Holy Spirit, the substantial gladness of God the Father and of God the Son, manifesting His presence in the soul and body of the wayfarer who is yet so far from home; and filling him already with delight and heavenly consolation.

People of little faith cannot understand this. Seeing the servants of God experience, as they themselves do, so many of the sorrows and hardships of the present life, they find it difficult to reconcile visible facts with assertions concerning the great joy of the spiritual life.

The explanation is simple.

There takes place in the fervent Christian something like the wonderful phenomenon of the bliss of the beatific vision in Our Lord's soul, at the same time as He was plunged in the horrors of His agony in the garden and of all His sacred Passion. It is of faith that Jesus enjoyed the beatific vision in the highest part of His soul, without cessation for a single moment; and it is of faith, also, that He truly suffered all the bitterness of the torments described in the Gospels, and much more, that may be read between the lines of the sober narrative.

Now, in much the same way—if we may liken small things to great, and the servant to his Divine Master—in much the same way, the mystic experiences at once joy and pain. The common sorrows and trials of the present life are not spared him. He has his full share of them; nay, at times, much more than the rest of men: still—deep down in his inmost heart there is the joy of the presence of God, the exultation of the conscious possession of the Holy Spirit.

It is precisely the task of divine contemplation to render the Christian aware of this well-spring of heavenly consolation which he carries about with him; to bring it to the surface; to make it flow freely and water all the garden of his soul, in the measure of the actual dispensation of divine grace.

The devil tries hard to make the Christian who is in trouble from outward circumstances abandon the practice of prayer, and, especially, commit mortal sin. He knows that then, indeed, the poor man will be in sore distress, for he will no longer have the resource of going down into the secret place of his heart, there to seek and to find the consolation of God—and the God of consolation. A mortal sin is like a corpse, thrown by a murderer into that deep well, the conscience of man, poisoning its sweet waters with abomination.

On the other hand, the tepid Christian, through grace—so long as he preserves it—possesses, indeed, in the depths of his soul this well-spring of the presence of the Holy Spirit and of His consolation: but he keeps the mouth of the well obstructed. A heavy stone lies there, which he never takes the trouble of lifting up or rolling aside, so as to draw and drink of the refreshing waters. May not this, perchance, be our case?

CHAPTER VIII

THAT GOD IS ALL FOR MAN'S ENJOYMENT

ARE you surprised, dear reader—or possibly even scandalized—at the heading of this chapter? Yet we have already, at least a score of times, met with this great truth that God is all for man's enjoyment, not in these precise terms, it is true, but in equivalent ones. Our obtuseness of mind, when it is a question of the things of God, is such that the same principle has to be set before our eyes repeatedly, and under several different aspects, before we are able to take it in and give it not only a notional, but a real assent, thus making it a part of our mental equipment and our possession for ever.

Not without some confusion do I remember my own amazement when for the first time, in one of Ruysbroeck's works, I came upon the statement that God, indeed, is alone for man's enjoyment, whilst creatures are only for his use. At first it struck me as a novel doctrine, and truly extravagant. Then, on further consideration, it dawned upon me that, at any rate, it was a most consoling doctrine and entrancingly beautiful. I began to wish it were true. It took me some time to realize that, in making this statement, the great Flemish mystic of the fourteenth century was but the echo of still greater mystics: St. Thomas Aquinas, Peter Lombard, St. Augustine, the Pseudo-Areopagite, St. Gregory the Great, nay, St. Paul, and St. John, and Our Lord Himself.

Let us concentrate our attention upon this astounding proposition: God is all for man's enjoyment. Let us consider it; let us weigh it; let us take it in—or at least, as much of it as we are able, and with our whole mind and heart. We shall not grasp or fathom its full meaning: it is so deep, so wide, so sublime a truth, and we are such shallow vessels; yet even so, what we do grasp of it should serve to bring about a happy change in our outlook upon life.

God is all for man's enjoyment: creatures are only for his use! God the Father, the abysmal fountain of the Godhead; God the Son, the eternal, infinite, resplendent Word; God the Holy Spirit, the substantial love of the Father and of the Son; the Sacred Humanity of Our Lord: all, ALL, for man's enjoyment; whilst created things, animate or inanimate, spiritual or temporal, are but so many means of leading up to God and helping him to take his delight in Him alone, above all things. Says St. Augustine: "This world is for our use, not for our enjoyment. The things that are for our enjoyment are The Father, and the Son, and the Holy Spirit." *(De Doctrina Christiana.)*

Enjoyment is actual possession with pleasure. To enjoy a thing is to take delight in it for its own sake. To be real and full, enjoyment must give satisfaction to the whole man of us, and principally to our spiritual part, to our reason, to our will. Now God alone can do that. This is peremptorily proved every day by the experience of all men, good or bad: the good finding, indeed, perfect delight in God alone; the bad trying to find perfect delight and repose in things created, and failing conspicuously in the attempt.

To judge from the way in which most people order their lives, and carry on their activities, it would seem as though creatures only were for our enjoyment. As for God, He may be feared, or worshiped at a respectful distance, or placated by prayer and sacrifice; but where is the worldling who would ever think of seeking his delight in Him? A good meal, fresh air; the beauty of a landscape, some masterpiece of the arts, the sweets of human love and friendship; elegance of face and figure, and other personal accomplishments; health, honor, success, fortune, luxurious surroundings; in a word, all the good things of this world—these, according to the world's gospel, are the things to be sought after and to be enjoyed. But to consider God as a proper object of enjoyment—who has ever heard of such a proposition!

Even to some professedly pious people, the idea that God is for man's enjoyment may appear simply preposterous. Nevertheless, it remains true that God, and He alone, and the whole of Him—if I may so speak—is for man's enjoyment; and not only at some future date, when we shall have gained heaven and shall see Him face to face, but even now, here on earth, during our days of pilgrimage, in our present condition of trial, and of trial under sin, here whilst we are still walking by faith.

If only we get hold of this great truth, what wonderful light it will throw for us on the whole subject of the Mystical Life, and more particularly on the right notion of Divine Contemplation.

Do you ask: How is it possible to enjoy God now? I would rejoin: Rather, how is it possible *not* to enjoy Him, Who, though unseen, is ever with us, the Supreme Good? We might thus counter with cross-questions to little purpose. But let us look at the facts. Is it not a fact that on the one hand there are those who, on their own showing, do really enjoy God and the things of God: prayer, the sacraments, Mass, holy reading and the exercise of all virtues; whilst, on the other hand, there are those who do not, who shun and loathe the very thought of God and of heavenly things?

More pertinent questions are: How do these contrive to fail to appreciate such a supreme good as is God, and how do those manage to find their delights in Him? Both of them manage the matter in a most obvious and direct and simple manner. They allow love to do it all. It is a question of the will, of the free choice of man, of his affection. Let me try and illustrate this by some examples from Holy Writ.

In the book of Exodus, we have the contrast between the people of Israel and their saintly leader, Moses. On the one hand the people cry out to Moses: *Speak thou to us and we will hear; let not the Lord speak to us, lest we die.* (Ex. 20:19.) And this same people is ready at any moment to forget the Lord and all the wonders He has wrought in their behalf, and to turn to the worship of the golden calf! On the other hand we see the Lord speaking to Moses familiarly, *face to face, as a man is wont to speak to his friend* (Ex. 33:11), and Moses growing very bold, indeed, to the point of daring to ask: Lord, show me Thy Glory! God answers: I will indeed show myself to thee: I will show thee all good; but, in a manner appropriate to thy present condition.

Thou canst not see my face, for man shall not see me and live; but behold, there is a place with me, and thou shalt stand upon the rock, and when my glory shall pass I will set thee in a hole of the rock, and protect thee with my right hand till I pass, and I will take away my hand and thou shalt see my back parts; but my face thou canst not see. (Ex. 33:18-23.)

The Christian contemplative is like Moses: He knows he cannot as yet see God face to face, that being the exclusive privilege of the blessed in heaven; nevertheless he keeps asking of the beloved God: *Show me Thy glory*—that is to say, "Grant me a passing glimpse of Thy infinite perfections; give me a taste of Thy ineffable sweetness. Even without my being able as yet to see Thee, give me, oh! give me, to embrace Thee, and feel Thy arms around me!" The mystic dares thus to press his Lord. The dear God has pity on him. He answers: "O little man, puny creature of a day, in thy present infirmity, indeed *thou canst not see me and live.* But *there is a place with me* where thou canst have a firm footing as upon the solid rock—the sacred Humanity of my beloved Son; from thence thou canst have a glimpse of my infinite majesty and yet not be consumed. I *shall set thee in a hole* of this rock—in the deep wound of the side of thy crucified Saviour; there thou shalt be secure from all danger of spiritual pride and consequent blindness: then shall I pass before thee in the Dark Cloud, and then thou shalt see me, thus, and not otherwise."

So it comes to pass that the mystic, like another Moses, really enjoys the company of God, has speech with his beloved Lord, hears Him speaking to himself as a man to his friend; whilst the immense crowd of negligent, halfhearted, lukewarm Christians cry in abject terror: "No! no! let not God speak to us, lest we miss enjoying the other things; this would indeed be as death to us." They never give a thought to all the marvels God has wrought expressly to make them His own chosen people, nor to all the benefits He has so lavishly bestowed upon each one of them, personally, in order to win their love, and make them cling to Him, and seek their delight in Him. Instead they are ready to turn to the insane worship of any idol!

The Gospel narrative offers us another contrast: the peoples of two cities who came out to meet Jesus, but on very different errands: the Gerasenes and the Samaritans of the town of Sichar.

The Gerasenes came to ask Our Lord to leave their country, because they had lost their herds of swine in consequence of His casting devils out of a madman possessed by a legion of them. Between having Our Lord in their midst or keeping their swine, they did not hesitate: they chose to do without Jesus.

On the other hand we see Our Blessed Lord, at Jacob's well, entering into friendly conversation with a woman of the laboring class, a poor sinful creature. She had had five husbands, and the man with whom she was then living was not her husband—perhaps, even, he was that of another woman. To such an one, because she was not unwilling to listen, Our Lord reveals and explains the deepest truths of salvation and the very secrets of the mystical life. And when in an outburst of irrepressible enthusiasm, the poor sinful woman has become the herald of the Messiah to her own people—men and women of her own condition, no doubt, working people, rough and ready in speech and manners, and with a liberal sprinkling of open sinners among them—Jesus allows His sweet Self to be, so to say, captured by them and led, with a well-meaning, gentle violence, into their city. And He remained three days in their midst; and they were all subdued and captivated by His meekness and loving compassion and by His divine teaching, the fruits of which appeared soon after the Descent of the Holy Spirit upon the Apostles, Peter and John being sent into Samaria to receive the first disciples from among them. (Acts 8) Verily the *Fields were white for the harvest*" (John 4:35). But how these simple-hearted people must have been delighted at meeting Our Lord! And how surprised they would have been, had they been told that they were actually practicing divine contemplation. For, so indeed it was.

See then, in the inhabitants of these two cities an apt image of the contemplative and of the non-contemplative. These last will not have speech with Our Lord, except just to let Him know, in so many words, that they do not want His company. Oh! they are polite about it. *Ce sont des gens comme il faut!* but they have quite made up their mind to do without Him. The reason? Simply because if Jesus stayed with them, their herds of swine—their filthy lusts—would have to go. On the other hand there are those in all conditions of life, especially in the humblest, who, touched by the grace of God, crowd affectionately around the Blessed Saviour, ready to break with a sinful past, and to forgo worldly advantages, in order to enjoy His sweet presence.

Truly, whether we enjoy God, whether we seek and find our delight in God, or whether we center our life in things created, is purely a question of self-determination with or against the grace of God; it is a question of the will, of the free choice of man—a question of love.

As I have devoted a small treatise wholly to this subject of the enjoyment of God by the fervent Christian—my first published work, *On the Mystical Knowledge of God*—I may perhaps be permitted to refer to it anyone who may desire to go a little deeper into this subject.

CHAPTER IX

DIVISION OF CHRISTIAN CONTEMPLATION DIGNITY OF BODILY WORSHIP

NOW that we have elucidated in the preceding chapter—as far as we were able—the right notion of Christian Contemplation, we may proceed to its proper division.

The first and obvious division of Christian Contemplation, taken in its broadest acceptation, is into (1) Bodily Worship, and (2) Mental Prayer.

Bodily Worship is a dealing with God, or a kind of prayer, in which certain set attitudes, or even motions of the body, and the use of the organs of speech by vocal allocution or recitation or song, hold a large place—not, however, without due application of the mind.

Mental Prayer is that in which, ordinarily, the body being at rest or in gentle motion, or the hands being busy with some easy mechanical work, the mind alone seems to be concerned in the enterprise of divine contemplation and praise, thus coming nearer, in its dealings with God, to the ways of pure spirits. In the present chapter we are concerned with Bodily Worship only.

It is not one of the least mistakes of writers on the subject of prayer, during the last three centuries, that they conspicuously fail to appreciate bodily worship at its full value, or to understand the mind of the Church about it. They seem not to have even so much as suspected the efficacy of bodily worship as a means of closely uniting us to God, a means which at times opens the way to the sublimest flights of pure mental prayer. Even the venerable Father Baker, otherwise so admirable in his *Holy Wisdom*, seems not to have sufficiently seized this truth. Thanks mostly to the labors of the illustrious Dom Guéranger, a serious movement of reaction in the right direction has now set in. It is my most ardent wish to promote it according to the grace that may be imparted to me.

Bodily worship holds a considerable place in the corporate life of the Church as well as in the spiritual life of each one of its members individually. It is a mode of prayer divinely ordered, befitting the complex nature of man. It is the prayer of the whole of him, and not of a part only. Being compounded of flesh and spirit, man is bound in strict justice to approach God with his whole being, and to worship the Divine Majesty at once with his body of flesh and with his spiritual soul. Nay, he is compelled thereto by the very laws of his nature, since he can perform no single act of the mind without some participation of his bodily organs.

I submit the following considerations as calculated to help us to realize how grand and noble a thing bodily worship is in itself, and how profitable to us it is intended to be.

The first act of Our Lord as God made man, at the very moment of his Incarnation, was, according to the testimony of the Psalmist (Ps. 39:7-9) and of St. Paul (Heb. 10:5-10), a most solemn act of bodily worship. For, "*when he cometh into the world he saith: Sacrifice and oblation thou wouldst not, but a body thou hast fitted to me; holocausts for sin did not please thee: then said I: Behold I come.* In the head of the book it is written of me that I should do thy will, O God." Upon which St. Paul comments in this wise: "*In saying before, Sacrifices and oblations and holocausts for sin thou wouldst not, neither are they pleasing to thee, which are according to the law. Then said I Behold I come to do thy will, O God: he taketh away the first that he may establish that which follows. In the which will we are sanctified by the oblation of the body of Jesus Christ, once.*" An act of bodily worship—as we see by the last words—so wide and so mighty in its scope that it takes in all who are ever to be members of His Church and His Mystical Body; an oblation which, though made once for all, we can take it for granted Our Lord renewed thousands of times during his life on earth.

To say nothing of the rest of his life, the whole sacred Passion of Our Lord from beginning to end, from his agony in the garden to his last cry on the rack of the Cross, is a bodily prayer.

Holy Mass, on the part of Our Lord, is a bodily prayer: for it is the oblation, even as on the Cross, of His Flesh and Blood; and of course, on the part of Holy Church it is the supreme act of Corporate, Congregational and Bodily Worship, wherein, with voice and gesture and attitude, together with whole heart and soul, priest and people unite themselves to the Divine Victim.

Holy Communion, in particular, is an act of Bodily Worship, both on the part of Our Lord and of the communicant: Jesus giving His Flesh to be eaten by fallen man, in order that he may rise again and begin to live to God; and each one of the communicants receiving this Heavenly Bread in his open mouth, in his body, in the folds of his flesh, thus being made for the time being, during a few precious moments, the living tabernacle of the Incarnate God, even as was the Blessed Virgin Mary during the nine months of her miraculous pregnancy.

We have just named the Blessed Virgin Mary. Her reply to the angel of the Annunciation: *Behold the handmaid of the Lord, be it done unto me according to thy word*—what was that but a most sublime act of Bodily Worship? Was it not the solemnly spoken surrender of her whole sweet self, body and soul, into the hands of the Holy Spirit, for the performance of God's holy will?

In the mystery of her Visitation to St. Elizabeth, in the first words of her canticle, Mary furnishes us with the best description of what every act of vocal or bodily prayer ought to be: namely, a sound of the lips, a vibration of the whole body, and at the same time a song of the mind, a jubilee of the soul. *My soul doth magnify the Lord, and my spirit hath rejoiced in God my Saviour.* (Luke 1:46, 47.)

Again, what was it but bodily worship on the part of the Blessed Virgin, when she stood on Calvary, facing the Cross, her whole motherly frame pulsating with unspeakable sorrow and compassion for her dying Jesus?

The consummation of their sacrifice in the midst of the most cruel torments, in union with our Lord Crucified, was, on the part of the holy Martyrs of all succeeding ages, a most glorious act of bodily worship.

The personal prayer of intercession of Our Lord in heaven as the *Christus assistens pontifex futurorum bonorum*—"*an high priest of the good things to come*" (Heb. 9:11), and as "*a Lamb standing as it were slain*" (Apoc. 5:6): what is it but a bodily prayer, a showing forth of His Wounds which He received for us, a repeating with utmost insistence to His Divine Father?—"*With these I was wounded in the house of them that love me*" (Zach. 13:6).

It were grievous error to imagine that our contemplation would be more excellent, were it, like that of the angels, performed without participation of our bodily organs. No doubt the contemplation of God by the Saints in Paradise, as they now enjoy it, is more perfect than it was during their bodily lives on earth, because then they walked by faith, they saw then as in a glass dimly, whilst now they see God face to face: nevertheless their present contemplation is not more perfect than it will be "*in the rebirth*" *(in regeneratione)* (Matt. 19:28), after the general resurrection, when their souls will have been reunited to their risen, glorified, spiritualized bodies: nay, it is decidedly less so. Man is man, not an angel. He cannot be raised higher than his true self by the temporary loss of a portion of his natural being, but only by the elevation and transformation and spiritualizing of that portion of his nature. Only when he can meet God in the bliss of heaven, in the integrity and fullness of his nature made whole and transformed in Christ, will man be able to render to his Maker the full meed of praise and accidental glory that God has a right to expect of him.

By overlooking the great and dignified part which bodily worship holds in Christian life, and by giving so much prominence to mental prayer considered as a thing by itself, to be attended to mostly in private, the theorizers about Divine Contemplation have unwittingly wrought twofold harm: (1) they have in a way, and to a greater extent than can easily be realized, robbed solemn public worship of what is its very life, the spirit of internal prayer; and (2) they have deprived mental prayer of its natural auxiliary, the body of the worshiper, and turned it into an enemy. For we cannot get away from this fact, that if our body is not given its due share in acts of Divine Worship, then it will at that very time, seek its own satisfaction elsewhere, thus creating a diversion and thwarting the efforts of the mind that seeks union with God.

Every act of bodily worship ought, as a matter of course, to be made a real, hearty, *felt* act of communing with God: nothing less. Every liturgical prayer sung or recited by the priest in the celebration of the Divine Mysteries; every Psalm sung by the choir-monk in his stall; every *Pater* and *Ave* told on their beads by lay-brothers or lay-folk, in church or out of church, in Latin or in the vernacular; every sign of the cross and genuflection, every ejaculatory prayer; *a fortiori* every attendance at Holy Mass, or any of the other sacred functions, ought to be on the part of the Christian, a deliberate, intentional and eager communing with God. Only such bodily worship does justice to God Who exacts it, to Holy Church who orders it, and to the Christian who performs it.

CHAPTER X

FURTHER OBSERVATIONS ON THE GREAT WORTH OF BODILY WORSHIP

COMMUNING with God may be attempted, and occasionally practiced, apart from the Divine Office, under the most varied and apparently the most unlikely conditions—in the midst of strenuous manual labor, amid bustle and jostle and the loud talk of others; in the street, on country roads, in railway carriages. The last time I was in London, as I walked out of the British Museum, I saw a business man pass through the crowd, a portfolio of documents under his left arm and a small rosary in his right hand. He moved swiftly and quite unconcernedly, and as absorbed in his prayer as though he were in a wilderness. Is there, indeed, for the soul a greater wilderness than a crowd? There, one may feel quite alone with God. One knows full well that, as far as men are concerned, one is of no account: why not, then, turn the mind towards God and pray to Him? Unless it be done in an ostentatious manner (and who would do that but a Pharisee?) nobody will take the least notice: people are too engrossed in their own concerns.

Still, it remains true that, if there be a place where, and a time when, Divine Contemplation ought to be particularly practiced, it is in the place and at the time specially set aside for Divine Worship—that is to say, in the Church, at the time of office. So true is this, that the practice of communing with God in the privacy of one's own chamber, or anywhere else, ought to be, really, a corollary to, or prolongation of, what has been begun in the Church.

It was with a live coal of fire, taken by the Seraph from off the altar in the Temple, that the lips of Isaiah were purified in order to render him capable of entering upon his prophetic mission. In like manner, it is with this live coal of fire, taken by the priest from off our altars—the sacred Body of Christ in the Blessed Sacrament—that the lips of the Christian ought to be purified, and his heart set all aglow with the love of God, before he starts out upon his weekly or daily mission of edification among his fellow men. After a fervent communion, a man ought to be able to retire to the privacy of his apartment, or go to the public resorts of men, and still find a way of keeping united to God. It was after Sunday Mass and Holy Communion, it was with such a provision of spiritual viaticum, that our forefathers, in the lowliest walks of life, used to take up with fresh courage their task of earning in the sweat of their brow, bread for their growing family.

Too much praise cannot be given to Bodily Worship. It is only through its acts that one is enabled to carry out to the letter the injunction given by our Lord *ever to pray and never to faint* (Luke 18:1), because it is so much easier to sustain, in some form or other, than is purely mental prayer. Besides, it is by acts of bodily worship that man takes his proper place and discharges his solemn office as priest and pontiff of this material universe, making it what it ought to be—a temple to the glory of its Divine Maker. By means of the Sacred Liturgy, the Christian, instructed by Our Holy Mother the Church, lays hold of the succession of the hours by day and night, and of the succeeding seasons of the changing year, and gives a tongue to the material elements of the world, making them yield due praise to the Lord of all.

In this connection it ought to be to English Catholics a subject of deep gratification that Westminster Cathedral is, by competent authorities, pronounced to be by far the finest modern church in England, perhaps in the world; a building really and naturally religious, a cathedral—according to the dream of Cardinal Vaughan—not only to worship God *in*, but to worship God *with*; a building so impressive in its unfinished state, that some would prefer to see it remain so, fearing (wrongly, as I think) that its due vesture of ornamental stone and designs may detract somewhat from its severe beauty.

In his book on the Cathedrals of Northern France, Mr. T. J. Bumpus gives this account of a ceremony in the cathedral of

Rheims at which he happened to be present (this was, of course, before German Kultur exercised its influence on the noble edifice):

"It was Rogation Sunday, when most of the young people go to their first communion, and a large confirmation by the archbishop took place. The latter was one of the most impressive ceremonies I have ever witnessed in a Continental church. The magnificent cathedral was completely filled with a dense crowd (always to my mind in itself an affecting spectacle), and every step or column or grille was occupied by eager crowds, clustered like bees. From noon till five the mitred Cardinal archbishop continued to circle from the high altar down to the west doors of that long building, administering the rite to successive lines of candidates. Twelve attendant priests assisted him in his arduous task, two monsignori, in purple, holding open his cope. The archbishop's robes were the most splendid I ever saw worn by an ecclesiastic, and his throne, which an emperor might covet (crimson, velvet and gold, with large white plumes), occupied the spot where a long line of Kings had sat at their coronation. The female candidates were all in white muslin, with long veils; the youths wore each a white silk maniple on the left arm, edged with a broad fringe of gold. All the while the great organ in the north transept beautifully played (with a pause now and then when a litany was chanted and joined in very generally by the young people) continuing to pour forth its notes, now seeming to die away amidst the vaulting and anon making the fabric vibrate with its thunders.

"The concluding tableau was most imposing. The archbishop, divested of his mitre, came down from his throne to a footstool in front of the altar, with all his suite posed round him; the canons left their stalls, the six priests who officiated at the altar knelt around it in their golden copes, with other lesser officials many in number. The altar itself, gorgeous with rich candelabra, the gifts of successive monarchs, became a blaze of light. I had noticed a great flickering of candles behind the grilles round the *arrière chœur*, and at this moment fifty of the most meritorious candidates filed in, each bearing a long lighted taper, and added themselves to the kneeling crowd. The two marvellous windows at the west end began to blaze with emeralds and rubies as the sun declined and tinged the clouds of incense that rose up when the glittering monstrance was elevated. The great bell of Rheims, heard above the jubilant notes of the organ, added its voice, with a few, deep, solemn thrilling tolls, and the ceremony was over."

I hope it will not be considered as an anticlimax if from this gorgeous description I invite the attention of my readers to an account which appeared in the *Tablet* of January 18th, 1919, over the signature of E. Rambert. It is entitled "Vespers in the Alps."

"I was staying at Hanghaumalp, in the Catholic canton of Uri, and, after supper, the first evening I was there, a *boûbo*, or shepherd-lad, planted himself before the chalet door, and began to sing with his whole soul, as if he wanted to be heard far off. We paid no particular attention to him, thinking of him as just some happy boy giving vent to the joy of his heart. It rained next evening, but the *boûbo* came out again, and, just as he had done the night before, sang loud and long, not pausing for full a quarter of an hour. As I listened more attentively I caught some of the words he sang; they were in a foreign tongue, and I inquired what they were and was told they were the words of a "Vespers." Further questioning brought me the information that, there being no chapel on the mountains, and consequently no evening offices, the *boûbos* did their best to replace them.

"What," I asked, "is the same thing done at other chalets?"

"Yes, it is the custom of the country," was the reply.

When the little lad had finished his Vesper song, I asked him to tell me what the words were, and with great simplicity he recited the first five verses of St. John's Gospel and some prayers and invocations of the saints. I asked him to write it all out for me, which he said he would do if I could wait till next day. And next day, accordingly, he brought me a well-written, faultlessly spelt copy of his beautiful Vesper prayers, the writing a formed hand.

"That evening his Vespers touched me as they had not done before. Other shepherds had I seen at devotion, but not like this child's prayers. When the wind favored, he told me, he could hear the shepherd at the Oberalp, but, on those evenings, the shepherd there could not hear him.

"And, this evening," I asked, "was it you that heard him, or he you?"

"Ah!" he answered, "neither heard the other: the streams are too full."

"But those clear, penetrating notes, the head notes of the shepherd calling in the mountains, still rose, whether response returned or not, floating in that childish voice, up above the noise of the torrent, like the echoes of bells in the hills forming an orchestra, placed at irregular distances, and melting and continuing each other's sound as an accompaniment to the voices rising up to the place where wells the Eternal Word, speaking to the hearts of those who dwell on the heights, above the winds and waters that are below."

CHAPTER XI

BODILY WORSHIP OF LITTLE CHILDREN AND DISTRACTED PERSONS

WE have to offer a last remark on Bodily Worship, considered in its general aspect. There will be, a little further on in this volume, a whole chapter on the important question of "Distractions at Prayer;" but we must anticipate it here, to the extent of showing how, when we are so vexed by distractions as to be absolutely unable to give ourselves up to mental prayer, it is bodily worship—in particular, vocal prayer—which saves the situation for us.

Take the case of a priest who happens to be a prey to involuntary distractions during the whole of his Mass and Divine Office (not an imaginary case, as we know but too well): provided his conscience render him this testimony, that he has gone through it all, to the best of his ability *digne, attente ac devote*, as the Prayer before the Office puts it, he may remain perfectly assured that he has discharged his obligation and that God is pleased with him.

Digne—that is to say, without levity of manner or unseemly precipitation; *attente*—doing his best to prevent his imagination and senses from ranging far and wide, and carrying him away from the present occupation of meeting God and praising Him; *devote*—with an actual stirring of love, as much as he is capable of, according to the grace of God that is given him. Provided a priest performs his sacred office under these conditions, all is well, even though he may not find actual consolation in the performance.

The primary object of divine worship, whether by bodily prayer or pure mental orison, is not our own gratification and enjoyment, but the praise of the Divine Majesty. In heaven perfect bliss and full enjoyment are necessarily inseparable from the act of praising God. It cannot be so for us whilst we are still on earth, and in our present state of infirmity. But what of that? Provided God indeed be praised, provided He be pleased, we ought to feel satisfied. *Dicite justo quoniam bene!* O man of good will, remain assured *that all is well and that thou shalt yet reap the fruit of thy faithful labors.* (Is. 3:10.)

St. Angela of Foligno, in her book of *Revelations,* makes this interesting confession in regard to her own self: "Bodily worship supposes the concourse of voice and of the limbs: one speaks, one articulates sounds, one makes signs of the cross and genuflections. This form of prayer I never abandon. There was a time when I wished to suppress it altogether for the sake of mental prayer; but then, sleepiness and sloth would intervene, and I was losing the spirit of prayer." (*Revelations*, ch. 62.)

Has the choir-nun who understands Latin a great advantage in the recitation of her Office over one who does not? St. Teresa thanked God that she did not understand a word of the Office she had daily to recite. Doubtless, the possession of the Latin tongue is some advantage to her, but it is not so very great after all. It is true that, in theory, she can follow the meaning of all she reads in the Psalms and Lessons; but as a matter of fact, how does she stand in practice? Do not distractions, for nine-tenths of the time, rob her of actual attention to the meaning of what she is saying or singing in choir? In reality, as far as actual devotion is concerned, there is very little difference between her and her Sister who knows no Latin.

In his *Theologia Mystica Practica,* Gerson observes that, in the performance of the divine psalmody, there is sometimes more devotion where there is less knowledge, and that love is allowed to come in where knowledge is bidden to stop at the door. Wherefore he would have all those who engage in the performance of the Divine Office imitate persons who, though but little skilled in music, take great delight in hearing the sound of the instruments. This is as much as telling us that, in this as in so many other things, we should be as little children. For who is less skilled in music than they?—yet it may be doubted whether the greatest artist in the world derives so keen an enjoyment from it as they do. Thus should we take delight in the mere act of devout vocal prayer and singing of the Psalms, even though we cannot always keep our mind fixed on their literal meaning.

Whilst speaking of little children and their devotions, I feel impelled to say something more in regard to them; for their vocal prayers and reverent demeanor in Church, as well as those of ignorant and simple folk, are genuine acts of divine contemplation. The whole process has God for its direct object, and who shall dare to contend that it does not attain Him? These lowly ones of the flock of Christ raise their minds and hearts to God as well as they can, and give Him praise as well as they know how; and the loving God testifies to His being pleased with their simple worship by granting them spiritual comfort and diverse graces. Clever people who, perhaps, plume themselves upon the fine speeches they are wont to make to God in their mental prayers, may happen to be very far indeed from being so closely united to Him in the bonds of love as are these little ones, whose somewhat crude performance they eye with a slight cast of disdain. More than one illustrious servant of God, now raised to our altars, made it his practice, whilst on earth, to beg of God certain favors through the prayers of little children, and was wont to obtain thus what might not have been granted him otherwise.

Last year, on a week-day, shortly after Christmas, an incident occurred in our village of Buckfast, which entertained and edified us. The little Catholic children of our school had evidently been telling their non-Catholic playmates of the Board School, about the wonders of the Christmas Crib in our Church. All at once—like a flight of birdlings that circle in the air, and then, all together, make for a certain tree and settle on it, and there chirp to their hearts' content—these children, Catholic and Protestant together, about thirty strong, bore down upon the Church, burst into it tumultuously and yet reverently enough: the Catholics making the sign of the cross and the genuflection before the High Altar, the non-Catholics awkwardly trying to imitate them. They crowded around the miniature grotto, to the grievous annoyance of an old lady whom they disturbed in her devotions. They said some prayers aloud; then those who knew some verses to the Infant Jesus recited them; then there was a hush as the Brother sacristan, coming upon the scene, took in the situation, and turned the electric light full upon the grotto, to the infinite delight of the little ones. Then they made their comments.

This was really divine contemplation: collective, cumulative, divine contemplation: What of it if the ox (they called it a cow), and the donkey, and the black king, and the little angels with wings, came in for a good deal of their attention? Baby Jesus was the center and the hero of it all; to Baby Jesus they said their prayers, and recited their verses, and sang their carols. For they sang. Oh! how these dear children did sing! Their piping voices rose high and penetrated the stillness of the cloister and attracted several old monks, who thought that some function was going on in the Church. And so there was indeed: King Jesus was holding a levee of His young courtiers.

Finally, when they had feasted their eyes and their little hungry souls on the marvellous Crib, and sung to their hearts' content, with one accord they rushed out of the Church and scattered through the village, shouting as they went: "We have been in the Church! We have been in the Church!" Doubtless this surprise visit of theirs to Our Lord had been to them quite an event, and there is no telling how Jesus spoke secretly to their innocent hearts, nor how deep the impression has been, nor what it may lead to in after life.

Who would not admire the knowledge of human nature which the Catholic Church, guided by the Holy Spirit, displays when she speaks to the ignorant in signs and beautiful images which they can understand? "In a picture," says St. Gregory the Great, "they who know no letter may yet read."

A Protestant lady who, as a nurse, had wide experience of the ways of children, remarked once that they are all born Catholics, and take quite naturally to pictures and medals and rosaries, and she sadly added: "It has to be taken out of them." Alas! good lady, the pity that you should think so! "But we are forbidden to worship images." So we are: but listen again to the same St. Gregory the Great: "It is one thing to adore images, and another thing to learn from them what we must adore." *(Greg. Magn. Ep.* ix). Does not Our Heavenly Father know what is good for His children? See what a picture-book He gives them to look at! This gorgeous world of sunlight by day and starlight by night, of sea and land, of snow-capped mountains, and hills and vales and rivers, of forest and meadow, with shrubs and trees and flowers and all forms of animated life. Pictures, all these, which rightly used will lead us to God and not away from Him; and so also are meant the pictures in our pious books, and on the portals of our cathedrals, and in the interiors of all our churches; at once for the delight and edification of God's children, big and small, learned and ignorant; but more especially of the little ones and of the simple-hearted.

Man will have pictures: if not sacred ones, to speak to him of God and of the Saviour and of the Saints, then profane ones. Your thoroughgoing Protestant's house is full of pictures—pictures of his horses and of his dogs, of famous jockeys and prize-fighters and actresses, and (the irony of it) of the false, impure gods of antiquity! His growing boys and girls may make their meditations before Venus and Adonis.

In touching on this question of the use of pictures, we have not strayed away from the subject in hand—Bodily Worship considered as one of the parts of Divine Contemplation.

CHAPTER XII

DIVISION OF BODILY WORSHIP

THE acts of bodily worship fall naturally enough into three distinct groups: (1) All the sacred rites and ceremonies of the Church; (2) Certain public, or semi-public, or private devotions, which are not imposed by the Church; (3) Austerities of the flesh, either imposed by the Church, or self-imposed, or inflicted by Divine Providence, making our bodies a living sacrifice with Our Lord Crucified. In the first group of acts the most salient character is their being of divine or ecclesiastical institution; the second bears upon it the stamp of popular inspiration; whilst in the third, the strictly personal element is more in evidence.

First and foremost, then, among the acts of bodily worship, come all the sacred rites and ceremonies of public divine worship as ordained by our Holy Mother the Church. Such are the Holy Sacrifice of the Mass, the Canonical Hours of the day and night, the celebration or collation of the Sacraments, solemn blessings and solemn processions and the like functions, ordered to be made at certain times of the year or on certain feast-days, such as Candlemas, the Rogations, Palm Sunday, Corpus Christi, or the solemn supplication of the Forty Hours.

These public acts of divine worship usually take place in buildings of more or less vast proportions, reared, and set apart and consecrated for distinctly and exclusively religious use. They are conducted with proper display of special ornaments, in the midst of the concourse of the faithful, to the accompaniment of both vocal and instrumental music, as was customary in the Temple at Jerusalem under the Old Dispensation. It is even held by some authorities on the subject, that the Gregorian melodies which have been handed down to us from remotest Christian antiquity, were originally adapted from the melodies of the Synagogue, in use at the time of Christ and His Apostles. Be this as it may, there is now in all our Churches great and small, an adjunct to divine worship which could not without difficulty be dispensed with, I mean the organ, a whole orchestra in itself.

At the same time as this picturesque and aesthetical form of collective or congregational prayer charms the senses and captivates the wandering imagination, it has the advantage of laying under contribution the whole material universe and employing its elements in the worship of God. Stone, wood, iron, brass, silver, gold, precious pearls, diamonds; all sorts of linen and silken fabrics; the arts of embroidery, ornamental writing, stained-glass, painting in all its branches, sculpture, architecture: all are pressed into service and contribute to the splendor of divine worship. The very steeples are made tuneful with the melody of the bells, sending out on the four winds of heaven their summons and message to hundreds and thousands of Christians scattered in cities, villages and hamlets, causing their loving hearts to beat with joy, or sorrow, or alarm, in supplication or in thanksgiving, for the living, for the dying, for the dead: thus bringing home to everyone the pulsations of the life of the whole Church, and at the same time feelingly illustrating the great dogma of the Communion of Saints.

Eloquence, sometimes of the highest order, more often homely and popular, adds its charm to the grand display. The humblest parish priest is a father to his flock, and finds in his love for the souls committed to his care, and in the sublimity of the divine Gospel, an inexhaustible fund of simple eloquence. At the altar, or in the pulpit, the priest is the leader in the grand act of collective, cumulative, divine contemplation, when all join at the same time in the same mystery of faith and open their hearts to the same impressions of divine love.

About these acts of collective and cumulative divine contemplation, Dionysius the Areopagite says *(De Hierarchia Coelesti*, cap. 1), "It is by means of such material emblems that our unfledged minds are rendered capable of contemplating and representing the heavenly hierarchy. The visible ceremonies of divine worship tell us of splendors which are invisible; the perfumes pleasing to the senses represent the sweetness of spiritual consolations; the shining lamps are the symbols of mystical illumination; the feeding of the mind has its emblem in the doctrinal exposition of the gospel; the divine, peaceful harmony of the heavenly choirs is figured by the various orders of the faithful; and our union with Christ, by the reception of the Holy Eucharist."

A second group of acts of bodily worship is made up of a large variety of other public, or semi-public, or private devotions, which the Church does not, as a rule, prescribe to her children, but of which she greatly approves.

Such are pilgrimages or devout visits to the Holy Places where some mystery of our religion took place, in Palestine, in Rome, at the Martyrs' tombs, or wherever effects of the mercy of God have been manifested, as, for instance, at Lourdes. These pilgrimages may be performed singly by individual persons, or collectively by more or less large crowds of people.

Such, again, are pious exercises like the Way of the Cross, the more or less dramatic recitation of the Rosary, the May and October devotions; solemn novenas preparatory to certain feasts; vocal prayers accompanied with genuflections, prostrations, devout kissing of holy relics or pious pictures, the wearing about one's person of medals and devout emblems, pious songs in the vernacular, ejaculatory prayers, etc.

We must also refer to this group, as real and distinct helps to popular devotion, and therefore to divine contemplation, the mystery plays and miracle-plays which delighted our forefathers in the Middle Ages; and, in our own days, the celebrated Passion-play of Oberammergau, which, before the war, periodically attracted from all parts of the world, hundreds of thousands of spectators, a large proportion of whom were non-Catholics, and made such a deep religious impression upon them all.

The humble way-side shrines, and the more or less elaborate calvaries still to be seen in many Catholic provinces on the Continent; the statues or pictures of the Madonna, with a lamp in front of them, in the streets of Italian cities; the pious forms of salutation in use in Spain, Ireland, Tyrol, the Catholic Swiss Cantons and some other thoroughly Catholic countries; all these help materially to create a religious atmosphere, and to keep men of good will in touch with the supernatural.

The third group of acts of bodily worship is made up of austerities of the flesh, whether spontaneously self-inflicted, or humbly received at the hands of God through the workings of natural agencies, or, finally, prescribed by Holy Church: inasmuch as they contribute to make our bodies, in the words of St. Paul, *a living oblation, holy, pleasing to God* (Rom. 12:1).

Note the special aspect under which these penitential acts are viewed here: namely, that of a homage to God, a veritable act of divine worship; at the same time as they are acts of necessary repression or castigation of our sensuality, as we shall see later on (in a subsequent volume), when we treat of Saintly Action.

Such are the observance of the fasts and abstinences and vigils ordained by the Church; the voluntary wearing (with due permission of the spiritual director) of the hair-shirt, the cincture or bracelet with steel points inside, scourging oneself with disciplines made of whip-cord, or iron chains, or nettles; all bodily pains coming to one through illness, accident, old age, the severities of the seasons, the privations of poverty, the hardships of necessary labor, the malice and cruelty of wicked men.

All these bodily pains, whether self-inflicted or not, if accepted with resignation and borne with meekness and patience, in a spirit of sacrifice, in union with our dear Crucified Saviour, will indeed make our bodies a *living oblation, holy, pleasing to God*, even though, at the time, under the strain of bodily pain or of anguish of mind, we cannot pray much mentally. We are then in a state of prayer: thus, to suffer is to pray.

To this group belong also the act of religious profession, that is to say the taking of the vows of poverty, chastity and obedience, in a religious order approved by the Church, together with the consequent life of self-renunciation which it entails; the solemn vow of chastity of clerics in Holy Orders, and the many acts of self-renunciation imposed on them, but more especially on priests, by their sacred calling; those private vows, occasionally taken, with due permission, by persons in the world, as well as the strict observance of the laws of Christian continence, temperance and modesty, corresponding to each one's special state of life; and, in general, such a noble and modest composing of all our attitudes and motions of the body as befits persons who know that they are ever in the presence of the Divine Majesty—nay, that they are themselves its living, breathing temples.

It will not be out of place to say here a few words about the purpose of religious life, and its place in the great scheme of divine praise instituted by the Church.

From the very beginnings of the history of Christianity we see that the Holy Spirit inspired some of the more fervent brethren with the wish to withdraw from the world and dedicate themselves exclusively to the work of divine contemplation. When this movement had spread and regularized itself, introducing among the faithful a permanent *special* form of life, the Holy Spirit inspired the Church to lay hold of it, and to sanction it with the seal of her supreme authority. The communities of holy men and pious virgins thus formed the Church took under her special guidance and protection, and she officially entrusted to them the duty of praising God, solemnly and perpetually in the Divine Office, day and night, in the name of the whole congregation of the faithful.

It is true that the secular clergy, sub-deacons, deacons and priests, are also entrusted by the Church with this work of the daily praise of God, in the name of all Christian people, by the recitation of the Breviary: but priests as a rule are isolated, each one being compelled to say the Office where and when he can, as convenience and the call of other and often heavy duties permit. On the other hand, choir religious, whether monks or cloistered nuns, have their various occupations so disposed that nothing is allowed to interfere with the Divine Office, which is solemnly discharged at set hours of the day and night, and at which they attend in a body, in the Church, with due pomp and ceremony; thus emulating by the fervor of their worship of God at the altar, the burning love and loud hosannahs of the angels and saints around the throne of the Lamb in the glory of Paradise.

Thus the life of an ideal community of Benedictine monks, of Carthusians, of Carmelite nuns, of ever so many other contemplative fraternities, is fully occupied with the work of divine praise discharged as a corporate obligation, perpetual, and practically uninterrupted, all their other occupations being subordinated to this great end. Can anything on earth be thought of more sweet, more beautiful? The very austerity, which is a necessary accompaniment of such a life, brings into still higher relief its heavenly beauty and supernatural sweetness.

The strict enclosure of most religious communities, and the grilles of their parlors, have given rise to no end of misunderstanding and silly or malevolent talk on the part of heretics. There is this to be said: When the Church places her contemplatives behind the bars of their cloisters, it is not with a view to take away from them the power to return to the world, but simply to protect them against the world's invasion of their sacred precincts. The locks and grilles are not for keeping them in but for keeping the world out: so that there may still be a few small bright spots on earth where consecrated virgins, assembled together in the name of their heavenly Spouse, and with Him in their midst, can enjoy the liberty of true children of God.

To sum up these considerations on bodily worship: is not the fact that the Church entrusts her contemplatives with the solemn performance of the Divine Office, the best proof of what a high and large place bodily worship holds in her estimation? In reality, the sacred Liturgy, as instituted and ordered by the Church, is the most admirable blending of the two forms of divine contemplation, bodily worship and mental prayer. May we not hope that the time is coming when, not only religious but all classes of Christian people, each in its degree, will understand this more perfectly, and will begin to live again the liturgical life in all its richness and abundance?

CHAPTER XIII

OF MENTAL PRAYER IN GENERAL

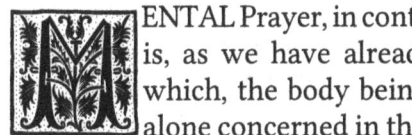

MENTAL Prayer, in contradistinction to Bodily Worship, is, as we have already seen (Ch. ix), the prayer in which, the body being at rest, the mind seems to be alone concerned in the work of divine contemplation.

In extolling bodily worship as much as we have done in the preceding chapters, it has been far from our intention to belittle mental prayer.

Great as is the dignity and worth of bodily worship, much greater still is the dignity and worth of mental prayer. It must be so, considering that mental prayer is the very life and soul of bodily worship, even as our soul is the very life of our body, and that just as the capacity of our soul surpasses the range of its life in the body, so also does mental prayer reach out far beyond the conditions and limitations of bodily worship.

Mental prayer is essentially the adoration of God in spirit; that is to say, the act of a created spirit going forth to meet the Uncreated Spirit; for, says our Lord: *God is a Spirit and they that adore Him must adore Him in spirit and truth* (John 4:24), that is to say, must perform this act of meeting God in as intensely spiritual a manner as is possible in present conditions. Thus, by mental prayer, we come as near as possible to the mode of action of the pure spirits.

It will, therefore, be no surprise to us to be told that mental prayer is the Alpha and Omega of Christian life: its very beginning, its progress, its climax or consummation; that mental prayer is the heart, the soul, the blood, the very breath, one might almost say the all-in-all of true Christian life; so that where there is no mental prayer, there is no real Christian life, but only, at best, an appearance. Where there is little mental prayer, there is little Christian life; where there is much mental prayer, there is an abundance of Christian life.

Whosoever, therefore, wishes to begin really to love God with his whole heart and soul can do so only by the use of mental prayer; and whosoever wishes to make progress in the love of God, must continue to use mental prayer. Stop mental prayer and you stop love! Deprive yourself of mental prayer and very soon you will cease loving God, even though you should say no end of vocal prayers and sing no end of psalms in choir. If the spirit of mental prayer does not breathe through all your acts of bodily worship, God will say of you as he did of the Israelites of old: *This people honors me with their lips, but their heart is far from me.* (Matt. 15:8.)

It is by mental prayer more than by any other means that we are made Godlike, that we transform ourselves supernaturally into God's likeness. It is the act by which we are allowed to look into the shining mirror of the Godhead: dimly, at present, it is true, *as though through a glass darkly* (1 Cor. 13:12), and yet very truly. We stand, so to say, the mirror of our soul facing the mirror of the Divine Essence: "Mirror against mirror," says Ruysbroeck, so that we may catch the reflection of its rays. Of course, for this purpose, the mirror of the soul requires to be kept very bright. No film of secret self-seeking must be spread over it; no layer of dust or of anything that can tarnish or soil it, such as unruly passions or inordinate attachment to creatures, must be allowed to settle upon it. Then will the shining of God into the soul really take place. It will be effected suddenly, in an instant, in the twinkling of an eye, in an *immediate* manner, straight from the heart of God into the soul of man; and the vivid light will carry with it an intense heat to vivify the recipient as much as the light illumines him.

St. John, speaking of the glory which awaits us in Paradise, says: *Dearly beloved, we are now the sons of God, and it hath not yet appeared what we shall be. We know that when he shall appear, we shall be like to him, because we shall see him also as he is.* (1 John 3:2.) We shall be made like unto God supernaturally, by contemplating Him face to face; we shall be invested and wholly permeated with the splendor of the Godhead shining full upon us: without let or hindrance we shall be filled with the influx of His divine life in sanctity and bliss ineffable: we shall, in a word, be changed into divine beings. The beginning of this process of our active transformation into God's supernatural likeness has to take place during our lifetime, while we are here on earth: this is inaugurated by the reception of the Sacraments, and it is furthered by the help of mental prayer.

The object of our contemplation in mental prayer is twofold: first, the Divine Essence of the Most Holy Trinity, and, secondly, the Sacred Humanity of our Lord Jesus Christ. Of this twofold object did the psalmist speak when he said: I *have lifted up my eyes to the mountains.* (Ps. 120:1.) These two sacred objects of our contemplation are, so to say, the Mont Blanc and the Himalaya range of mountains of the spiritual world; and the mystics are the true mountain climbers, fearless and undaunted, eager by dint of mental prayer to scale the heights and explore the immaculate fastnesses.

We may also compare this twofold object of our loving contemplation to two wonderful bunches of grapes, more marvellous than those of the Promised Land, to which we have access and on which we are allowed to feast. The more we eat of them by means of mental prayer the more insatiable we become. Or again, let us liken them to two marvellous honeycombs eternally dripping with infinite delights in the eager mouths of those who apply themselves to divine contemplation. *Open thy mouth wide*, says God, through the Prophet, *and I will fill it.* (Ps. 80:11.)

In reading what mystical writers have to say about divine contemplation we must be very careful to bear in mind the distinction between *the acts* of contemplation and *the states* thereof.

When God is the object of one's loving attention only for a few passing moments, there is an act, and only an act, of divine contemplation. Even beginners are, by the grace of God, capable of performing such separate, occasional acts, recurring more or less frequently. But when a fervent Christian, by the help of the Holy Spirit, sustains his loving attention to God during a somewhat protracted period—say, some hours or days at a stretch—there is, at least for the time being, *a state* of contemplation. As a rule this is vouchsafed only to such as are already advanced in the spiritual life. And, again, it may be but a transitory state, recurring at very long intervals, or it may be a kind of solidly confirmed habit or gift. In this last way it is found with the perfect only.

We may safely say, therefore, that all mystics, all Christians of goodwill, upon whatever rung of the ladder of perfection they stand, are capable of performing acts of divine contemplation; whilst only the more advanced can sustain it for any length of time, and this, in proportion to their progress in the spiritual life.

This explains the caution given by spiritual writers, and especially by Gerson, not to try and go beyond one's actual gift of grace, not to attempt to fly higher than one's wings will warrant. In the same strain St. Benedict gives this direction: "In community let (mental) prayer be brief and pure, unless it happens perhaps to be prolonged by the influx of the inspiration of divine grace." (Reg. c. 20)

It is well, when reading books on contemplation, to keep constantly before one's mind this important distinction between acts and states; otherwise, one may be bewildered by apparently contradictory statements, when, in reality, one author is simply speaking of the passing acts of contemplation, and another is alluding to the habit or state of contemplation, and yet a third may be treating only of some very special states of it. One may even be speaking of contemplation in its sublimest sense—that is to say, of the obscure meeting of the soul with God in perfect nudity of spirit (as we shall see later)—and yet not be careful enough to avoid confusing this, in the mind of the reader, with humbler yet genuine degrees of divine contemplation.

CHAPTER XIV

DIVISIONS OF MENTAL PRAYER

THE present chapter is an important one. It may happen that some persons will consider it revolutionary, because it unceremoniously sweeps out of the way a good many conventional divisions; yet I hope that the greater number of readers will see it rather as of a conservative or justly reactionary character, inasmuch as it aims at bringing us back to the bedrock foundations of human nature as God made it and the common workings of divine grace.

Strictly speaking, there are but three species of mental prayer. Discursive Prayer, Affective Prayer, and the Prayer of Quiet. All varieties of mental prayer, whatever their names, can be and ought to be, reduced to one or the other of these three species.

Discursive Prayer is the mental prayer in which the Holy Spirit moves the mind of a fervent Christian to many considerations concerning the Divine Essence of the Blessed Trinity, or the mysteries of our Blessed Lord.

Affective Prayer takes place when the Holy Spirit puts a stop to the arguments of the mind, and acts directly on the sensitive faculties and on the will, drawing the soul towards God, with great sweetness and vehemence.

The Prayer of Quiet is when the Holy Spirit stays even the multiplicity of the affective movements of the soul, and reduces it to silence, but a silence pregnant with unutterable love, in presence of the Divine Majesty.

In its turn the Prayer of Quiet has to be subdivided into two species according as it is wholly passive or only partly so. The Passive Prayer of Quiet is that in which the loving God seems to take upon Himself to do all there is to be done, so that it is not in the power of the contemplative to inaugurate the process of prayer at will; nor can he interrupt it, were he so minded; nor, of himself bring it to a close: all he can do is to acquiesce in it and sweetly to co-operate, as long as God is pleased to favor him with it. When, on the other hand, a man has the power of inaugurating the Prayer of Quiet, and yet retains throughout the free use of his faculties, then it is the Semi-Passive Prayer of Quiet.

The first kind, the absolutely Passive Prayer of Quiet, is the kind of contemplation which St. Teresa, with many other writers, calls by the somewhat disconcerting name of "supernatural"; as though every grade, even the very humblest, of Christian contemplation were not supernatural. (We shall have more to say, later on, about this equivocal term "supernatural" used in this connection.)

Finally, the Passive Prayer of Quiet is, at times, accompanied with miraculous phenomena, such as levitation of the body, suspension of some of the functions of the sensitive life, interior or exterior stigmata of the Sacred Passion, distinct visions or locutions, either imaginative or wholly spiritual, etc. Then we have properly *Miraculous Contemplation.* To this kind only would I reserve the appellation of "Extraordinary" which has been lavishly and indiscriminately applied, in recent works on mysticism, to any prayer or contemplation above the average.

In order that a state of Prayer be legitimately called extraordinary, it has to be ascribed to an exceptional intervention of God, suspending even the laws of nature. The gifts of Wisdom and Understanding, which all Christians alike receive in the Sacrament of Confirmation, are sufficient to account for the sublimest varieties of the Passive Prayer of Quiet when unaccompanied with miraculous phenomena; therefore, such Prayer of Quiet is ordinary, is indeed due to the common workings of the grace of God, such as is given, or at any rate, offered, to all Christians. Much as the Passive Prayer of Quiet can be called the borderland of the miraculous, the line is crossed only when some of the above phenomena take place. All that is this side of the line is ordinary. Hence I draw this conclusion: all Christians have a right to wish for, and to aim at, and to prepare themselves for, the Passive Prayer of Quiet. This species of prayer, by right, and in the plan of God, is the crowning glory and consummation of common or ordinary Christian life on earth.

Thus, then, finally, we obtain as full nomenclature of the different species of Mental Prayer, the following:

1. Discursive Prayer.
2. Affective Prayer.
3. Semi-passive Prayer of Quiet.
4. Passive Prayer of Quiet, and
5. Miraculous Contemplation.

We shall do well to keep resolutely to this simple and natural division. It covers the whole field of Divine Contemplation and will be found to answer all practical purposes. It will enable us to discern, in others as in ourselves, the operations of the Holy Spirit, and also to understand what competent mystical writers have to say on the subject.

There is no such thing as "acquired contemplation" in contradistinction to "infused contemplation." This division introduced by some modern writers cannot be upheld. If it be a question of Christian contemplation it is infused. Divine Contemplation in the sense of mental prayer is all infused, all supernatural, all a pure gift of God; always, in all its degrees, in all circumstances, whether as separate act or acts, or as a state, it is infused direct from God into the soul. *No one can say: The Lord Jesus, but by the Holy Spirit.* Much less could anyone, without the Holy Spirit, gaze lovingly upon Him *on Whom the angels desire to look.* (1 Pet. 1:12.)

What is—or at any rate may be—acquired, is the habit of preparedness to divine contemplation.

We must not forget that divine contemplation is the finest product of our joint life with God. The Holy Spirit Himself operates it in us. It is His action, His own doing, with our co-operation. First, we have to be made proximately capable of receiving such a divine operation: this is done by the efficacy of the Sacraments, which infuse into us the virtues of Religion, of Faith, of Hope, of Charity, and the Gifts of the Holy Spirit.

Thereafter it devolves upon us to prepare ourselves. This we do by purity of life, interior recollection, willingness to allow God to have His own way with us, and actual and persevering responsiveness to His secret inspirations and motions. This is our part in the joint venture of Divine Contemplation.

We must also carefully distinguish between contemplation itself and what are only its preliminaries, such as spiritual reading, methodical application of our faculties, using certain industries, placing ourselves under favorable circumstances, taking certain attitudes of body and mind. Now all these things depend on our own initiative and are a part of Saintly Action (as we shall see in another volume). Wherefore, these preliminaries, though conducive to contemplation, must not be confused with it. These acts certainly may pass into a habit, an acquired habit, and thus favor the action of God in infusing Divine Contemplation; but they are not the thing itself, and there is no such thing as *acquired* divine contemplation.

The question may be asked: does it or does it not lie with us to procure Divine Contemplation? Now, after what we have just said, it is not difficult to perceive that this is merely a question of words, for it must be answered in the affirmative or in the negative according to the special aspect considered.

Inasmuch as divine contemplation is a pure gift of God, and cannot be acquired by any efforts of ours, it is clear that we must answer this question in the negative; but, inasmuch as it lies with us to prepare ourselves for this gift of God, to accept it and to make the most of it, then it is to be answered in the affirmative.

To make this still clearer, let us have recourse to some homely illustrations. We may compare the soul to the fireplace in a house. It lies with the tenant of the house to keep the flue free of accumulated soot, to remove ashes, and to lay dry sticks and other kindling materials in the grate, so that at the touch of a match the whole will burn up. It is God's part thus to light our fire, and He is sure to do it as soon as we have done our part: God waits upon our good pleasure.

Again we may liken the soul to a lamp which the Christian can clean out, provide with a wick, and fill with oil; so that when a match is applied it will catch fire and illumine the room or the path one has to tread. It certainly depends on the interested party either to dress the lamp properly, or to let it be uncared for as did the foolish virgins of the parable in the Gospel. So it lies with us to keep our soul clean by banishing from it all frivolous or sinful affections, and to provide the wick of an attentive mind and the oil of good will; but it lies with God alone, Who is the master of His gifts, to touch the soul with the flame of His Holy Spirit, and thus set the lamp burning with the light of divine contemplation. This God never fails to do whenever He finds a lamp well trimmed.

To use yet another simile: it is for us, as it was for Abraham (Gen. 15), to take the victims which the Lord has asked for, to slay and divide them, and to drive away the birds of heaven that seek to prey upon the flesh of our holocaust. It is for us to present, on the one hand our mind, on the other our will, and to drive away resolutely all importunate distractions, until such time as it please the Lord to cast upon us the mystical sleep of divine contemplation, and to pass between the divisions of our offering and consume it with fire, at the same time consoling us with mysterious words and assurances of the beatific vision which awaits us in the Promised Land of Paradise.

CHAPTER XV

ON THE THRESHOLD OF DISCURSIVE MENTAL PRAYER

ON the threshold of a treatise on Mental Prayer written in our days, there must present itself inevitably the question of method; although not a trace of method appears previous to the sixteenth century.

It is in itself a very small question when we take a proper view of mental prayer and divine contemplation in their fullness. At best it concerns beginners, and not even all beginners, this question of how to start on the quest of the divine encounter; how to handle one's refractory teams of faculties, when they have not yet been thoroughly broken in; how to employ to one's own satisfaction and advantage the set half-hour told off for meditation in our modern programmes of piety.

I do not say it in a carping spirit; but prompted by deep conviction, born of life-long observations, I feel bound to assert that too much importance has been assigned to method in the preoccupations of modern piety. It has been made by some writers the all-in-all of the adoration of God. It has been made an end in itself, whilst it is but a means, and even then an artificial one. It has been used, no doubt unconsciously, by some directors, as a means of spiritual domination, to chain down and keep under their hands, and hold back on the threshold, souls whom the Holy Spirit urged to go forward, urged to run, urged to soar to the very heights of Divine Contemplation.

By all means, let one who feels the need of a method make use of one; and let him use it as long as he finds it helpful; but let him discard it as soon as he can possibly do without it. One who has been lame for a time is not told to go on using a crutch after it has ceased to be necessary. In his search after God, in his dealings with Him, let the fervent Christian take, as soon as he can, to the unceremonious way of the little child. See with what an artless, unpremeditated, spontaneous start, or burst, it throws itself towards the object of its love. The great trouble with most methods is that they tend to render one self-conscious, spiritually speaking: one never loses sight of oneself.

In his *Souvenirs et Causeries* the Marquis De Ségur introduces a poor woman, eighty-five years of age, Colette by name, who delivers herself of this charming piece of information: "I am very stupid, I know. At home, when I was little, we were eleven children and had to be put to work very early. I never could learn to read and write. Occasionally I grievously feel the want of this, but I must say, it never interfered with my prayers: rather the reverse. I talk aloud or under my breath with the good God; I tell Him all that comes into my head, just as it comes. Books, I fancy, would be in my way for this. They would overmaster me. Now I want to be free in my prayers. I have always spoken my mind to my gossips, friends and neighbors, in fact to everyone: why should not I do exactly the same with the good God?"

Very remarkable this outburst of brave, old, ignorant Colette! St. Teresa herself does not speak otherwise. To be free in one's prayer, to be oneself, to speak one's mind, to pour out to God one's heart, unchecked and unfettered by any convention: is not this the ideal of genuine mental prayer?

Let us lay stress on the fact that, as we understand it, and as we treat of it in this volume, mental prayer, whether discursive or otherwise, is not an artificial contrivance, nor is it confined to a set time, be it a quarter of an hour, or half an hour, or a full hour, or several hours. It is a living process embracing and pervading the whole life of a fervent Christian; a living process which we may liken to the growth of a tree and its putting forth, in due season, periodically or even perennially, of flowers, leaves and fruit.

Naturally a tree must be planted in congenial soil, must be duly protected against destructive agencies, must be fed with dew and sunshine and air from above, and with what nourishment it can draw up by its roots from the earth. In such conditions the vital process of the growing of the tree goes on uninterruptedly, though secretly and silently. In very much the same way does the process of mental prayer and divine contemplation go on in the soul of good will. It is not a matter of half-hours at set times, it is a matter of the whole life, down to its humblest details: a *state* of mental prayer is established, and divine contemplation becomes the very substance of one's life.

Indeed, separate acts of mental prayer are either signs, or fruits, of a state of contemplation already firmly established in the soul; or, they are ordered, and naturally tend, towards the establishing of such a state; otherwise, I do not see why they should be performed at all. It is non-apprehension of the necessary connection between isolated acts of mental prayer and the state they are meant to establish, that has so lamentably narrowed the outlook of modern piety and made it such a poverty-stricken, cramped, abortive thing.

In very truth we may liken the relation between the contemplative soul and God, to that which necessarily exists between the tree and the whole mighty process of nature. We live in the sunshine of the felt and loved presence of God, rooted in the Sacred Humanity of our Lord Jesus Christ *(radicati et superædificati in ipso*, Col. 2:7). Now, just as the vital process of the growth of the tree is associated with the whole work of nature at large, and depends on it, and is a part of it, so does the process of mental prayer link each soul which applies itself to it with the mighty scheme of divine grace in the Church at large, and associate it with the very life of the glorified Saviour and of the Blessed Trinity Itself. Here is mysticism, indeed, if ever mysticism be!

We come to the root of the matter when we observe the importance of holy reading and meditation (apart from any method) with a view to divine contemplation, and especially with a view to Discursive Prayer. St. Thomas (II IIæ *quæst* 180) considers these two acts of holy reading and meditation as necessary parts of the vital process of which we have been speaking. We may call these functions "the feeding of the tree by its roots."

The Church makes her contemplatives read a great deal, and of course expects them to assimilate, by thoughtful consideration, what they read. The Priest with his daily breviary; the Religious with his or her choir-office; the fervent Christian, who follows in detail the development of the sacred liturgy throughout the year—what readers they are obliged to be! Into what rich soil they plunge the roots of their attention and affections! What essential juices they constantly imbibe and assimilate! Then there are the books of God—Nature, the Holy Scriptures, the Holy Crucifix, and the human heart—to be diligently conned by them. And they may add the books written by the servants of God to elucidate these books of God. What a vast field for holy reading and thoughtful consideration is opened before us!

On the other hand, the world, too, imposes a mighty deal of reading on its votaries: Periodicals without number—filled with deliberate lies, or suppressions of the truth, to suit the needs of political parties; with unwholesome, poisonous, vitriolic, hellish *faits divers;* faked history; with garbage literature of infinite variety, pandering to all the morbid appetites of an effete society;—and books of demi-science, with trumpery articles on all the branches of human speculation, creating the impression that man, puny man, has solved all the riddles of the universe, fathomed all the great deeps above his head and under his feet, and weighed God in the balance and found Him wanting!—man, that thing of yesterday, whose body, to-morrow, rots in the grave, while his soul goes to its judgment!

From such mental seed what harvest can be expected but utter bewilderment, anarchy of thought, desperate materialism with its attendant evils? A plentiful crop of these evils we see ripening under our eyes, promising a terrible reaping in the near future. The horrible world war we have just gone through; the present labor unrest with its arrogant, unreasonable demands; Bolshevism rampant everywhere: what are these but the fruits of that precious so-called liberty of the Press? This is not liberty, but most unbridled license—license to utter, declaim, print, read, disseminate broadcast, without check or restraint, monstrous, immoral, blasphemous, subversive doctrines. A stronger social order than ours would soon suffer disintegration under such powerful dissolvents. As for the effect on the individual—it is simply frightful.

Do most people in our midst, now-a-days, know whether there is a God? or whether they have an immortal soul? or whether there is such a thing as moral responsibility? They are no longer quite sure of anything. They hold that it would be wrong for anyone to rob *them* or kill *them:* but it is not so clear to them that, for instance, adultery is a crime. One thing only looms big before their mental vision: they must have what they call "a good time"; they want to amuse themselves—and following out this simple programme, they proceed to make a hash of their lives. And under all their dissipation, there is a sadness bordering upon despair.

If a Christian dabbles in this sort of literature, he unfits himself for divine contemplation. If he must touch it, through no choice of his own, and under pressure of circumstances, he must surround himself with every sanitary precaution that prudence can suggest, otherwise he runs a mortal risk: he is like a man who would rashly handle poisonous gases, or powerful acids, without putting on a mask to protect his face, or gloves to save his hands.

There are those among the educated and wealthy who think that they cannot possibly find a place in the order of their day for holy reading. Let me tell them bluntly: You do not want to; you have no relish for it. That is the plain truth.

No time for holy reading! If those same unworthy Christians would write down an enumeration of all the items of newspapers, novels, and other frivolous reading they contrive to get into a week, they would be amazed at the quantity. Now it is simply a case of, *Ceci tuera cela*: this will kill that. Either holy reading or pernicious reading: it is clear that the two cannot thrive together: either holy reading and as its fruit, divine contemplation; or no holy reading at all, and, as a fatal consequence, no divine contemplation at all.

CHAPTER XVI

ON THE PRACTICE OF DISCURSIVE PRAYER

DISCURSIVE Prayer is the mode of mental prayer familiar to the greatest number of Christians during the greater part of their lives. It may not be amiss, therefore, to give some suggestions as to how to begin this sort of prayer, and how to proceed in it.

What is it you want to do? You wish to have speech with the good and loving God even as though He were here? Is He not here? Even as though He heard and took notice of all you are going to tell Him? Is not this the case? Even as though He wished you to speak to Him and liked you to do so? Can we doubt that this is so? You want, also, to listen to God speaking within you, as though He really had something to tell you. And has He not? As though you had set your heart upon not missing one of His interior monitions. And as though you highly appreciated the honor of this communing secretly with God and made it your delight?

Now, what will you say to God?

Say anything you like—anything that is to the purpose, or even things which are apparently not to the purpose. Let us go again for our instruction to the children, these great masters and models in the art of dealing with God with simplicity.

I have just heard this charming story.

Some children had been told to speak to Our Lord simply, in their own way. In the afternoon a small boy was very late in returning from school, and after half an hour his mother set out anxiously to seek him. She found him coming out of the church, and when she asked him what he had been doing, he replied: "Oh! I went right up to the front bench and told Our Lord a robber story!"

This brings to my remembrance a story, long buried in the catacombs of my mind. Some thirty years ago I was a missionary among the wild Indians of North America. In the Osage tribe, at a place called Pawhuska, I had a flourishing school kept by Franciscan Sisters, who were very zealous in teaching my dusky neophytes, young and old, the rudiments of Catholic Faith and practice. One day, as I was passing through the Sisters' garden I was surprised to find, all by herself, a little girl of six or seven, gravely walking up and down. "Coaina, my child," I said to her rather severely, "why are you not with the other children?" "Oh!" she answered, in a confidential whisper, "I am talking to the Great Spirit." "Indeed; and may I know what you are telling Him?" "I tell Him I would like to see Him and kiss Him!"[7]

That is just the way. You want to talk to God? Do it, simply do it, talk! talk with the simplicity of a child. In this connection I know nothing sweeter, more suggestive, more helpful than the example set by the Carmelite nun of Lisieux, Sister Thérèse de Jesus, "The Little Flower." Her life related by herself should be read and re-read by all who wish to learn the precious art of sweetly and simply conversing with God.

Conversing with God is an art. It must be acquired; it ought to be cultivated, for it may be brought to a high degree of excellency and effectiveness; as also, if not practiced but neglected, it may be lost; one may lose the cunning of it. "We ought always to pray and not to faint." (Luke 18:1.) Prayer, like fire, ought never to be allowed to go quite out, or we may experience trouble in kindling it again.

Do not forget, as I am afraid too many people do, that the very idea of conversation calls for at least two people. In the work of mental prayer the two are, first the loving God, and then yourself, God being given precedence as He is the more dignified. But He is so good, so gentle, so homely and familiar, that you are allowed to open the conversation whenever you

---

[7] It would not be surprising if these two stories brought upon me an avalanche of others quite as charming. In this case they will be very welcome. I shall select the very best, and try to induce my publishers to let me make of them an Appendix to this work in its next edition, if there be one. The stories should be short, well told, and to the point: i.e., illustrating the directness and simplicity of children's communings with God.

wish, whenever it suits your convenience. He is always there, always ready, always willing to listen to you.

Now then, open the conversation: give Him a word of recognition and greeting, and at once profess your readiness to hearken to Him, and do listen. "I *will hear what the Lord God speaks unto me."* (Ps. 84:9.) God may just be pleased to speak to His servant, to make Himself heard in the secret of your heart. He may want to infuse into you feelings of spiritual joy or sorrow, to impress you with some vivid light: for such is the way of speaking of a pure spirit. If God does so speak to you, oh! then, what happiness! Blessed are you, indeed! Then listen: listen in silence. Do not break in upon God's discourse to you. Let Him have all His say. And even after He has done speaking, still listen; wait for more; beg for more. When you see that no more is forthcoming, turn in your mind what has been said or impressed in you by the loving God. Taste its sweetness, soak yourself in it. Finally, do not fail to express your sense of gratitude, as also your sense of your own unworthiness.

And then, in your turn, when the interior spirit moves you (I mean the Holy Spirit Who is in you as long as you are in the state of grace), do you also, in all lowliness of spirit, speak lovingly to the Lord God. Pour out your heart to Him in burning words. No need of books for that: you want, like old Colette (cf. supra C. xv) to say what is in your mind, what is in your heart, not what someone else has thought out and written.

You have plenty to say to the loving God, if only you knew it. Talk to Him of yourself, of your neighbor, of Himself. Here is an inexhaustible fund of conversation.

You will please God whenever you talk to Him about yourself. He loves that. Tell Him, even as though He did not know them, your troubles, your joys, your fears, your defects and your successes; your wants and wishes; your plans for the future.

We often make the great mistake of pouring into the ears of others what concerns ourselves. They do not like it. They are not interested. They have but little sympathy with us—or none at all. Our most confidential outpourings leave them cold, indifferent; there may even lurk in their very smile a touch of contempt.

Never so with the loving God.

He will be still more pleased, if, forgetting yourself, and bearing in your mind and heart the many necessities of others, you make it your business to recommend them to God. Each one of us may bring a large heart and an apostolic spirit to his communings with God; so that without going abroad, or stepping out of our humble employment, we may obtain no end of conversions of sinners and precious favors from Our Lord for the whole Church. Many a humble lay-brother, many a poor old woman or pious youth has done so. Oh! how beautiful is such prayer of intercession on the part of the confidential friends (as we may call them) of the good God!

Still, you will please God most, and obtain most for yourself and the whole world, when, moved thereto by the Holy Spirit, you will lose sight of yourself and the whole world of creatures, and speak to God of His Own Divine Self, in the pure prayer of adoration: applying your mind and your heart solely to Him.

Then is the time to play melodiously the harp of your heart and to dance in measure before the Ark like King David. Then is the time to emulate the highest choirs of Angels in heaven, and to sound out of your whole being the loud song: Holy, Holy, Holy, the Lord God!

And perhaps the moment will arrive when a divine silence will be cast upon you, and you will be seized with an overwhelming sense of the presence of God, of His absolute loveliness, of His infinite sanctity! Lie there, before Him, motionless, O Christian soul, as though annihilated; know that although you seem to be doing naught, great things are being done in you: there is being wrought a union of your whole being with God, an infusion of Him into you, a transformation of your whole self into His likeness, beyond word or thought, and thereby a praising of God, a glorifying of the Divine Majesty incomparably greater than could be rendered by any other work of your own!

But are we not here anticipating somewhat? Yes: we have been carried away by the logical sequence of things over ground which must be retraced and explored more slowly.

CHAPTER XVII

THE PLAGUE OF DISTRACTIONS

THIS Chapter is written for the consolation of souls of good will.

The difficulty of distractions at prayers is to be met with in all the degrees of the spiritual life, even in the very highest, as is shown by the lives of the Saints.

It is a very serious trial to souls of good will. They find it hard to bear when from end to end of their prayers, do what they will, they are vexed by these importunate distractions as by so many flies.

To souls who are not very generous, to the weak and ignorant, this trial may become a sort of scandal and an occasion to relax their endeavor. They will say: "What is the use of my trying to pray? What is the good?" They had set out to find God and taste His sweetness, but He did not come to meet them, nor did He give them anything. They cannot understand it.

First of all, we might ask those weaklings: Is it not your own fault if you encounter so many difficulties in the act of praying? If you come to it with a frivolous mind; if you lead a life of dissipation; if you bring to God an unmortified interior, can you hope that He will be pleased to pour into you His heavenly consolations? The milk and honey and wine and delicate fruits of the spiritual life require an empty vessel, and a clean one.

There are also those people who, when the world does not want them any longer, or when they can no longer enjoy its pleasures because of advancing age, turn to piety after a kind, and seem to say: "Now, my God, your turn! Let me see what enjoyments you can give. I have heard so much of the consolations of piety, I want to have my share of them:"—forgetting that in order to taste and see how the Lord is sweet, there is preparation of soul to be made.

Finally, there are also those, mostly ignorant people, who are not even aware that they have distractions at their prayers, though they are simply eaten alive with them as with a plague of locusts. There is a story to the point. The great St. Bernard was riding through a forest, and a peasant trudged at his side to guide him. The Saint spoke, as was his wont, of the things of God, and lamented bitterly his inability to pray without distractions. The peasant, much surprised, asserted that as for himself, he never had any. "You are a wonderful man," said St. Bernard, "but let me see if you are not mistaken. If you recite the *Our Father* without distraction, I will make you a present of this horse." To win such a prize was to the poor man the chance of a lifetime. He eagerly closed the bargain, made a great sign of the Cross, and began. He had not gone half way through the prayer before he stopped short with—"I say, Father, you will give me the saddle with the horse, won't you?"

Without stopping any longer to argue the case of the tepid souls, we must acknowledge that distractions at prayer and meditation happen to the most faithful servants of God, and are to them a heavy cross. What have we to say about this? That it is indeed a very profitable thing for them. When a man happens to be full of distractions from beginning to end of his holy exercises; when, do what he will, he does not succeed in fastening for a single instant the gaze of his mind upon God, or in drawing out of his heart a single effusion of love, can he be said to have performed an act of divine contemplation? Decidedly so.

If he has not consented to those importunate distractions, if they have displeased him, if he has fought them as well as he could, he has done the work of a true contemplative. He wished to meet God, he set out on this errand, and strained every nerve to accomplish it; therefore God was the immediate object of his attention: and that is the very essence of Divine Contemplation. He went to the trysting place of God, and although Our Lord did not see fit to show His blessed countenance, yet there is no doubt but that He was there, well pleased with the anxious quest of Himself, by His faithful servant.

Whether God should show you His sweet face, and make you hear His loved voice, and fill you with consolation, is for Him to decide. When He treats you with apparent harshness, leaving you to your own weakness, in the dark, a prey to distractions, utterly desolate, quite crushed down in the dust, He is treating you as fully grown in spiritual life. He is secretly feeding you with the marrow of lions, with the bread and wine of the strong. He is, in spite of appearances, adorning your soul and enriching it with countless merit.

Never say that a half hour, wholly spent in the unwelcome task of struggling against sleepiness, or of chasing away distractions, is lost time. Nay, it is as profitable a half hour as it has been a laborious one. You proved your loyalty, and you gave glory to God, by continuing to seek for Him and to call after Him—at least to desire Him with your whole heart and soul—in the midst of distressing circumstances. When does a soldier most please his king? When, spick and span and trim and happy, with drums beating and banners floating, he goes on parade? Or when, black with smoke, stained with earth, covered with blood, his own or that of the enemy, he is fighting for king and country?

What matters it that during the whole time of some pious exercise your imagination danced the wildest whirligig? That could not destroy the fact that you came there for the sake of God, that you were in quest of Him, that He was then truly the sole and immediate object of your occupation. What happened in the way of distraction was outside the essence of your human act: it was purely accidental, wholly involuntary; it passed no deeper than the surface of the soul, if I may so speak, and it did not detract in anything from what you intended to do: you were really seeking God, and God was really, though invisibly, meeting you.

The soul of good will, occupied wholly, during a holy exercise, with the effort of chasing away distractions, resembles Abraham, when, as related in Genesis (Ch. xv.) he had prepared a sacrifice to the Lord, and was kept till evening busy driving away birds of prey which endeavored to snatch at the flesh of the victims. God at last appeared to him, and told him how pleased He was with him: then the fire of heaven came down upon his sacrifice and consumed it.

When a good soul, passing through certain of the more distressing phases of this trial of distractions, comes to us and tells us: If I only was sure it was not my fault! If only God was not offended by this! I am so afraid it is on account of my sins!—you may rely upon it that all is well with that soul. God is only refining it as gold in the furnace. It is with her as with the Blessed Virgin Mary and St. Joseph, when in great trouble and confusion, blaming themselves as though guilty of unpardonable negligence, they were seeking the Divine Child among their friends and acquaintances, and not finding Him!

What! can this possibly be one of the forms of passive purification of which mystical writers speak? Yes, even so, especially when, do what one may, one does not succeed in giving comfort and peace to the poor sufferer—and yet he remains of good will and perfectly obedient to his spiritual director. He suffers, and is willing to suffer, and God, for a wise purpose, does not permit him to see the perfection of his dispositions.

In the ordinary train of Christian life, the plague of distractions at prayers comes in spells, like bad weather. When it rains, we do not say: Oh! there will never be an end of it! We know very well that the sun will shine again: so we wait with what patience we can until the clouds roll away. Rain does a great deal of good: it is one of the chief providential agencies for bringing forth the fruits of the earth. So also is it with the plague of distractions when it settles on the soul of good will. What a holiday when the sun shines again! What joy for the soul when the clouds roll away! Mary Magdalen at the empty tomb of her beloved Lord will not be comforted even by the Angels in bright garments: she turns away weeping and addresses, as she thinks, the gardener. "If you have taken Him away ..." Jesus utters just one word: "Mary!" It is enough! Then, what a change from tears of sorrow to joy inexpressible! Thus is it at last with the soul, who, through darkness and desolation, perseveres in prayer.

Many years ago I came across what purported to be one of the unedited letters of St. Teresa, written towards the end of her life. She was giving to Father Alphonso Alvarez, her spiritual director, an account of her mental prayer. She related how, that same morning, on going to the Chapel for Mass and Holy Communion, she was vexed by the untidy appearance of the cloister, due to the fact that masons were engaged upon some repairs in the convent. On crossing the chapel entrance, she signed herself with holy water and tried to compose her thoughts and apply them to her Saviour present on the Altar: unfortunately her sharp eyes caught sight of some stains of plaster on the floor: all her irritation came back. Then also she began to speculate upon the length of time the masons were taking over repairs that could have been done much more promptly. Meanwhile Mass had begun and was well under way. As the Sanctus bell rang she tried again to collect her thoughts: all to no purpose. Even when she was bending low at the moment of consecration to adore her beloved Lord, she caught herself ejaculating almost aloud: "Oh! those masons! And the price they charge for doing nothing!" In great confusion when the moment of Communion arrived, she went up to the altar-rail and tried to make amends to Our Lord for the vagaries of her mind, and then she came back to her place and endeavored to make her thanksgiving: but she found herself deeply interested in the worn sandals of the Sister who was kneeling in front of her. To escape this new distraction she closed her eyes, burying her head in her hands: the thought of the masons returned more besettingly than ever. In sheer despair, she opened a book so as to fix her eyes upon some holy picture. She lighted on one of the ugliest that she had ever seen, and said to herself: "What a sin to give the dear saint such hideous features! Whoever saw a saint with squinting eyes, a long nose, and such thick lips?" and then, turning fiercely upon herself: "Who ever made such a thanksgiving after Holy Communion?" And she concluded her account by saying playfully: "You see, my Reverend Father, how your spiritual daughter is progressing in the ways of mental prayer."

Reader, if this is not a genuine letter of Saint Teresa, it deserves to be. At any rate it has done me good service and encouraged and comforted many a soul of good will.

CHAPTER XVIII

THE LITERATURE OF GOD

IF I had to sketch out the plan of an ideal course of holy reading with a view to divine contemplation, upon lines so large and generous that it might serve for a lifetime, I would proceed in this wise:

First of all, I would have such a course of holy reading to revolve around the Holy Scriptures, rearranged to suit the convenience of the contemplative soul.

The Bible is the book of God; nay, it is a whole library; a whole literature in itself, quite apart from all others, and covering a period of time not less than two thousand years, possibly much more, and going to the very root of all things; a literature of which God Himself is the author, whilst the human writers whose names are inscribed on each of the books as they succeed one another, are but the scribes to whom their contents, as well as those of the Divine Traditions, were dictated by God Himself: *Spiritu Sancto dictante*, says the Council of Trent, *cum utriusque unus Deus sit auctor.* (Sess. IV.) The contemplative is in search of God: where can he hope better to find Him than in God's own books? There God Himself speaks of Himself, and of all His doings with the much-loved but wayward human race, and with each soul individually.

This literature of God consists, according to the *canon* or official catalogue, definitely settled by the Council of Trent (Sess. IV.), of forty-six Books in the Old Testament, and of six Books and twenty-one Epistles in the New: the Historical Books being in the main placed in their order of production, and the Moral or Sapiential ones, as they are called, which belong exclusively to the Old Testament, being set together in one group.

I give here the order in which I would suggest that the various parts of Holy Writ might be rearranged for the use of the mystic in his striving after Divine Contemplation.

I would put the New Testament before the Old. As the Old

Dispensation is abolished and we now live under the New, the Scriptures of the Old Testament, which at the time of their writing, were prophetic as well as historical, are now of most use in our spiritual lives as allegories of the Church of Christ and of Heaven: but this full and proper mystical meaning of theirs can only be got at in the perfect light of the Divine Gospel, as the Fathers of the Church—particularly, St. John Chrysostom, St. Gregory Nazianzen, St. Augustine and St. Gregory the Great—have eloquently demonstrated. In regard to the contemplation of Our Lord, it must be owned that in the splendor of His Divine Personality as we see It in the Gospel page, it is rather the New Testament which reveals to us the Old, than *vice versa.* By the light of the New we discover in the Old, meanings which would otherwise have remained unsuspected, and which decidedly add to our knowledge of the Divine Saviour, inciting us to love Him still more. I may be allowed to refer the reader to what I have already said on this subject in Chapter X of *Mysticism—true and false;* also in Chapter X of *The Mystical Life.* Something further will have to be added in my next volume on *The Loving Contemplation of Our Lord.*

Now, the books of the New Testament I would propose to the contemplative in the following order:

1. The Gospel according to St. John: because there, from the first, is presented to us the Divine Teacher of the art of mental prayer, in His true and full Personality of the Only Begotten Son of God, the Word made Flesh.

2. St. Luke's Gospel: because it has sprung from the lips, nay, from the very heart, of the blessed Virgin Mother of our Lord, and is redolent of the sweet perfume of this Mystical Rose.

3. Then St. Matthew and St. Mark, who give us more, perhaps, the Sacred Humanity of our Blessed Lord, without, however, allowing us for a moment to lose sight of his Godhead.

4. Then the Apocalypse, which is the Gospel of Jesus risen from the dead and seated in glory, and from His high throne presiding over the providential government of His Church on earth.

5. Then the Acts of the Apostles, where we see the Gospel

teaching of Our Lord illustrated by the doings of his mystical Bride the Primitive Church.

6. Then the Catholic Epistles of SS. James, Peter, John and Jude, giving voice to the *Ecclesia docens* at this early date, under the direct inspiration of the Holy Spirit.

7. Finally, as a grand and magisterial summing up and interpretation of the spirit and of the mystical doctrine of the whole New Testament, St. Paul's wonderful Epistles.

As regards the Old Testament, let us repeat that for the purposes of Divine Contemplation, it comes not before, but after the New. To be read usefully, to be rightly understood in its bearings upon our individual piety, it must be viewed in the full light of the Holy Gospel, in the splendor of the Word made flesh, since He it is who gives the Scriptures their unity and fullness of meaning. *"I am the Alpha and Omega, the* (first) *beginning and the* (last) *end"* he declares. (Apoc. 1:8.) *"It is written of me at the head of the book"* he says in Psalm 29:8. And the Apocalypse again shows Him to us as the Lamb who breaks the seven seals of the mysterious book on the altar of heaven (Apoc. v, 8), of which book both Testaments are but a faint foreshadowing.

This being so, we may group the books of the Old Testament thus:

The larger Historical ones, namely: The Pentateuch of Moses (i.e. the five first books of the Bible), Josue, The Judges, the four books of Kings, the two Paralipomena and the two of Esdras. These books, in their mystical meaning, so dear to the Fathers of the Church and some medieval Doctors, symbolize the episodes of the Christian's journey through the wilderness of this life to the Promised Land of heaven. Leaning on this oracle of St. Paul: (1 Cor. 10:6, 11) *"Now these things were done in a figure of us"*, *"Now all these things happened to them in figure: and they are written for our correction,"*—leaning, I say, on these words, the contemplative finds marvellous food for his piety in the history of the People of God, not only in its beginnings, but also throughout its checkered career. For this view of the Sacred Books I would specially recommend the works of Richard of St. Victor (Migne: *Patrologia Latina. Tom.* 196); one of which, the

Benjamin Minor can be obtained in an English translation (Edmund Gardner, New Medieval Library, London, 1910).

The smaller historical books: Ruth, Judith, Esther, Tobias, Job—all so rich in mystical meaning. Ruth is the loving Christian soul, Booz the Divine Goodness; Holophernes is the devil, Assuerus is the King of glory. As for the books of Job and Tobias I would at first be satisfied to have them studied from the point of view of their purely literal meaning: for even thus, these holy personages, Job and the two Tobias, do represent to us in a vivid manner the life of the mystic on earth in the midst of the world, in the holy state of matrimony, passing through the most trying vicissitudes. Only as an after treatment or *retractatio* of the subject would I recommend the mystical interpretation of Job in the *Moralia* of St. Gregory the Great: it will then prove very acceptable indeed.

And here comes the very paradise or garden of delights of the true contemplative. It is made up of these books: The Canticle of Canticles (interpreted in part by St. Bernard); The Psalms (interpreted by St. Bruno, the founder of that great school of sanctity, the Carthusian Order); Isaiah, that anticipated Gospel; Proverbs; Wisdom; Ecclesiasticus.

For the further purification and illumination of the soul, I would recommend Ecclesiastes, Jeremiah, Baruch and the twelve Minor Prophets.

(5) Ezechiel, Daniel, and the two books of the Machabees I consider as forming, historically, a kind of immediate preface or introduction of the New Testament; and, therefore, I would have the contemplative soul look upon them as pointing spiritually to the second advent of our Lord, when He shall come to judge the living and the dead, and to inaugurate the feast of His Eternal Nuptials with His Bride, the New Jerusalem of the Blessed. The wars of the Machabees serve as a fine illustration of the heroic courage which, at the end of the world, will be required from the small band of the faithful, in their resistance to Antichrist: a contingency which may not be very far off.

Such would be our Bible of the Contemplative.

To priests and to those of the laity who read their Bible in the

Latin text, I would recommend, in preference to all others, the edition of the Vulgate of the Abbé Fillion of St. Sulpice (Paris: Letouzey et Ané), because, though retaining, for the sake of reference, the old division into chapters and verses, it contrives nevertheless to put into evidence the natural divisions and subdivisions of the matter, and the difference between historical prose and the rhythmic effusions of the prophetic spirit. Thus set clearly before us, the inspired word of God takes quite a new and clearer aspect. I look upon it as an inspiration of genius on the part of the learned Sulpician, to have given such a text of the Bible. Had he done nothing more in the field of Biblical studies (which is far from being the case), he would have richly deserved the gratitude of all lovers of the Word of God. It is my humble opinion that this work, now in its sixth or seventh edition, deserves to be known and spread all over the world, and should be in the hands of every priest and every ecclesiastical student.

As for the spirit in which this reading should be carried out, it need hardly be said that we ought to work in the field of the Scriptures with a view solely to discover in them, and bring out, and publish to all the world, the message of divine love they contain. Whosoever loses sight of this end is a great fool. O my good Lord, how many such fools have been, in our days, busy with thy Holy Writ!—learned men, of great talent and research, glib of tongue and of pen, and yet fools!

It must be observed that the fervent Christian is a whole God's breadth apart from the Modernist. The former takes up his Bible-reading in no mood of hypercriticism. Of course, at the hours when he is attending to the sacred page for learning's sake and when studying for the purpose of teaching others, he is as exacting and severe and conscientious a critic as any man; but when he reads for his own edification, to comfort his soul and render his union with God still greater—in a word, when he reads for the express purpose of Divine Contemplation—he finds it is enough for him to know that the canon of the inspired books has been definitely settled by the Council of Trent, and that the same unimpeachable authority has decided that the Vulgate, such as we possess it, is the official text, and all sufficient for every practical purpose. Nor does he fall into the mistake of those who make the herculean task entered upon by the Biblical Commission an excuse for laying aside the Holy Scriptures, crying (as I have heard it with my own ears): "Oh! I shall wait till the difficulties have all been cleared away. What is the use of troubling about it before this has been done?"

One might as well say: "Oh! before I practice my religion I shall wait till all the difficulties raised about it by true or false science have been answered." There will never be any end of difficulties being raised; meanwhile a man has to live and to die, that is to say, work out his eternal destiny. In the same way we may take it for granted that there will never be an end to the labors of the Biblical Commission. It will continue to issue, from time to time, its learned decisions, long after we shall have gone to our reward: therefore we cannot afford to wait. Let us take our Bible—the Book of God—as it is, as it is handed to us by Holy Church, and be satisfied to use it thus, for to it do the words of St. Paul apply: *All scripture inspired of God is profitable to teach, to reprove, to correct,* to instruct in justice; that the man of God may be perfect, furnished to every good work. (2 Tim. 3:16, 17.)

The Modernist does not find God in the Holy Scriptures which he handles so rashly and irreverently, though God has written Himself in them and wishes to be sought in them—and found. The truth is that the Modernist does not seek Him or wish to meet Him: what he seeks is purely and simply self—his own conceited little self, his Lilliputian self, which he idolizes and would fain propose to the worship of the whole world, instead of God. But to him that seeks God with simplicity and love, in the Sacred Writings God reveals Himself.

The revelation contained in the Holy Scriptures and the Divine Traditions forms a fathomless luminous abyss, into which man's spiritual eye penetrates but to a very limited depth. This suffices, however. We feel therein the divine presence, hidden and yet resplendent. Our Blessed Lord Jesus Christ and the Most Holy Trinity are presented to us in the manner in which we can best bear to contemplate them, in our present condition. In holy reading and devout consideration we obtain a glimpse of the fringe of the garment of our God and take hold of it, and kiss it rapturously: then we sigh after the blessed hour when all the shackles being broken, all the veils rent, all the mists dissipated, we shall at last see Him, Whom we love, face to face, in the full radiance of His infinite Sanctity and Goodness. O God! Beloved! when will this be?

CHAPTER XIX

THE LITURGICAL BOOKS OF HOLY CHURCH

OUR Holy Mother the Church has a twofold mission in the world: first that of attending officially to the solemn worship of God; then that of administering to the faithful the good things of God, namely His divine Revelation and His Sacraments.

In the discharge of this twofold duty the Church has, under the special guidance of the Holy Spirit, composed or compiled, for the use of her ministers, her liturgical books, six in number, namely: the MISSAL, the BREVIARY, the MARTYROLOGY, the RITUAL, the PONTIFICAL and the Ceremonial of Bishops.

It has been said: "Lex orandi, lex credendi": that is to say, the prayers of the Church show forth the whole content of her faith. Indeed she has contrived to press into her liturgy all the dogmatic teaching which came to her either by the written word or by divine tradition, and to give it a popular, poetical, spectacular and highly dramatic expression.

Unfortunately, since the dawn of modern times, heralded by Protestantism, the liturgical sense has been gradually waning among Christians. The Church has not the same facility as of yore to develop the pomps of her solemnities and to penetrate into the very life of the people. It must be frankly admitted that the general state of society, in our days, is a formidable obstacle in the way of a thorough revival of the liturgical spirit. In spite of the powerful movement of reaction which was inaugurated by Dom Guéranger, which has been gathering momentum during the last three quarters of a century, the liturgical spirit is still too much in abeyance. The collection of the liturgical books as an object of pious and intelligent study is almost wholly a *terra incognita,* a buried and hidden treasure to the generality of educated Christians—even sometimes to those who should know best its wonderful value, because constantly called upon to make use of one or other of these books. It is one thing somehow to use an instrument and quite another thing to employ it to the highest advantage.

Therefore, in our ideal course of reading with a view to Divine Contemplation, immediately after the inspired word of God as it is in the Bible, I would place the liturgical books. In this chapter I aim at showing briefly what an inexhaustible fount of inspiration in prayer and of spiritual enjoyment lies at hand in these books.

The first three, the Missal, the Breviary, and the Martyrology, are closely connected, as they concur together to the one purpose of ordering the official prayer of the Church around its proper center, which is the Holy Sacrifice of the Mass. From the real presence of Our Lord in the Blessed Sacrament and His mystic Sacrifice on our altars, as from the sun in the high firmament of nature, comes to the Church light, vitality, beauty and fruitfulness. Year after year, from the first Sunday in Advent to the Saturday of the last week after Pentecost, this sun seems to run its course through the divine Zodiac of the Mysteries of His Advent, Life, Death, Resurrection and glorious State in heaven, until He shall come again, to judge the living and the dead: in reality it is the Church herself, who like a humble and obedient and loving satellite, dutifully circles around the mighty orb, the Lord Jesus Christ, to Whom be glory for ever!

To help us to penetrate below the surface of the liturgical books we should read in connection with them such works as *Les Institutions Liturgiques* of Dom Guéranger; his well known and deservedly popular *Liturgical Year*, and *Le Livre de la Prière Antique* of Dom Cabrol.

The Missal and the Breviary have been translated into more or less felicitous English, so that their incomparable collection of prayers are at hand for those who care to use them in their private devotions. In no other way will one be enabled to understand the mind of God and of Holy Church in regard to all the vital issues of either time or eternity. What an education in the highest spirituality it is in our power to give ourselves by such a study! It should suffice to render us great contemplatives and mystics of the first order.

It is a matter of regret that the Martyrology is very little known outside Religious houses. It is a glorious book. To a devout listener it seems to diffuse at the same time an inebriating perfume and a triumphant music. Day after day, from its crisp notices of mysteries and martyrs and all other species of saints, there is so to say, shaken out, a mingled perfume as of warm bread fresh from the oven, of ripe apples long garnered in a closed room, of generous wine poured out in torrents with the blood of the martyrs, of incense burnt over the glowing coals, of sheaves of lilies and of all paradisaic flowers of sanctity which have bloomed awhile upon this earth of ours and been gathered by the blessed Angels. There is also triumphant melody in these short lines: melody to which the Christian worthy of the name can hardly listen without feeling himself raised far above earthly things. Oh! I would the Martyrology were sung, not read, in every Monastery and Convent, irrespective of whether the rest of the office be solemnized or not: beautifully, feelingly, sweetly sung out; not by any one, but by the very best cantor, instead of being, as is but too often the case, tamely and badly read or rather stammered out by some unripe tyro of a Novice, who murders almost every word of the text. The dear Saints deserve better treatment than this. It is martyrdom twice over. The worst of it is that thereby the glorious page loses much of its fascinating beauty, and a great deal of its stirring appeal is wasted upon disgusted, often indignant listeners.

Messrs. Burns and Oates have issued a beautiful *Layfolks' Ritual* with Latin text and English translation. It would be a mistake to think that the Ritual is a book for priests only, it is as useful to know it, for those who receive the sacraments as for those who administer them. If there is a lesson which ought to be impressed upon us by such a perusal, it is that the very act of receiving a sacrament is first of all and before anything else an act of adoration of the Divine Majesty. It is the act of one who draws near to God, for God's sake, irrespective of any view to self interest. Even in the imperfect contrition of a poor sinner who wishes to receive holy absolution, there must be, of necessity, an initial love of God for God's sake. Besides, in the very act of drawing nigh to God by the worthy reception of any of the Sacraments, we make a confession of His sovereign goodness: we proclaim Him to be the absolute good, the fountainhead from which all good, whether natural or supernatural, perpetually flows: *The Father of lights from whom every best gift and every perfect gift, comes down.* (James 1:17.)

Take only one instance. Do not the Christian man and woman, by the reception of the sacrament of Holy Matrimony, proclaim in the face of the whole world that they wish to abide with God and God to abide with them, in the most secret and intimate and emotional part of their lives? He issued forth at the beginning this command upon the first couple: *Grow and multiply and fill the land.* (Gen. 1:28.) They mean to carry out this command, under His divine blessing: from His hands they desire to receive the natural joys of their mutual love, the fruitfulness *of the womb and of the paps* (Gen. 49:23), the virtuous increase of their family, and all the graces necessary for them to carry with alacrity such a heavy burden.

Now if that is not first and foremost an homage of adoration to the loving God, then what will ever be one? And if it be thus with this sacrament, the lowliest of the seven, since it comes right down into the animal portion of the life of man and woman, how much more clearly can this homage of adoration be predicated of all the other sacraments? Every one of them is for the explicit, emphatic purpose of bringing God into our lives. By a positive act of our free and deliberate will, we open to God the doors of our own being and invite Him to come in and take possession, from the inside, of what is already His by every right, though He has placed it in the hands of our own counsel. Clearly the immediate result is a great personal advantage to us and a distinct gain for our own spiritual benefit. Many discern but this aspect of the transaction: but it is not doing justice either to the intention of Our Lord or to the mind of the Church in the institution and the administration of the sacraments. The act of receiving a sacrament remains, by right, essentially an act of worship of God. Faith, Hope, Charity and often Contrition largely enter into it; therefore it has God in view; it glorifies Him and it stands as our own practical translation of this petition of the Our Father: *Thy kingdom come.* Therefore it is essentially an act of Divine Contemplation.

The Ritual, no less than the Missal and the Breviary, sets in a marvellous light the doctrine I am trying to inculcate, that the mystical life or the union of love with God is for all men, absolutely and indiscriminately, whatever be their age, profession, position in society and accomplishments. Baptism is for all, and Baptism makes us by right *adorers of God in spirit and truth.* (John 4:23.) If the baptized adult should fail to become such, it is because he will have put obstacles in the way of the action of the Holy Spirit in him. Confirmation is for all. Now Confirmation arms and strengthens the Christian so that he is enabled to render to God this homage of adoration in spirit and truth, even in the midst of enemies, visible and invisible, and of the conflicts of the world. As for Holy Orders, they make the Christian who received them a captain, a leader among those who thus adore God in spirit and truth and an official teacher of Divine Contemplation.

The Pontifical is the Bishop's book or the ritual of Episcopal functions. Besides the rite of Confirmation and Ordinations, it contains such impressive ceremonies as the blessing of abbots, abbesses, nuns, the coronation of kings, the laying of foundation-stones, the consecration of churches, altars, chalices, and the blessing of bells.

Not to every one is it given to witness even once in a lifetime the consecration of a Church. Many persons are debarred from witnessing even those functions which are fairly frequently performed, such as the blessing of an altar, ordinations, religious professions, the blessing of the Holy Oils and Balm by the Bishop on Maundy Thursday ... Therefore, if they wish not to remain in total ignorance of this part of the spiritual treasury of the Church, there is nothing left for them but to read for themselves and picture as best they can with their imagination these gorgeous services. They will be more than repaid for their pains, by a deeper insight into the life of the Church, that grand mystical drama of the Bride and the Heavenly Bridegroom; not in the dead past as a matter of ancient history, but in the living present. By the grace of the Holy Spirit they will be enabled to discern their own personal part or concern in the reciprocal love of our Lord Jesus and His Church, whose children we are; *Come*, says the angel to St. John in the Apocalypse, Come and I will show you the Wife of the Lamb.

Most Catholic publishing firms have issued in penny-pamphlet form, in the Latin text with English translation, the rite of the Blessing of the Oils on Maundy Thursday, that of the Blessing of Bells, that of the consecration of a Church and other sacred functions.

Some short liturgical formulae, when closely scanned with the eyes of a loving soul are a never-ending source of delight. I will point out a few.

DOMINUS VOBISCUM: THE LORD BE WITH YOU. This is the greeting, from the altar, of the Priest to the People; it recurs also in the Divine Office and in the administration of the sacraments. It expresses the most unequivocal and outspoken wish for the realization of the purest, highest mystical life, in those to whom it is addressed. Now, to whom is it directed? To a few only? No, but to all absolutely and without exception. All are greeted with the same sublime wish and each one is expected so truly to take it to heart that he is made to retort in the same vein to the priest: ET CUM SPIRITU TUO: THE LORD BE WITH THY SPIRIT. What an exchange of heavenly courtesies is this! But also what a lesson in the doctrine of the mystical life for all!

PER OMNIA SAECULA SAECULORUM: THROUGH ALL THE AGES OF AGES. The Priest and the Christian people deal in eternity. They hardly seem concerned with the paltry years of the present time, except in so far as they have a bearing upon the eternal years which are coming. The mind of the contemplative is raised above the miserable contingencies of the present life: he lives already with God and is given a foretaste of the fullness of enjoyment of an interminable life of glory.

SANCTUS! SANCTUS! SANCTUS! HOLY, HOLY, HOLY! In this simple word thus three times repeated, what an intensity of admiration, adoration and love can be concentrated! Also in such other formulae as this one, culled out of the GLORIA IN EXCELSIS: GRATIAS AGIMUS TIBI PROPTER MAGNAM GLORIAM TUAM: O GOD WE GIVE THEE THANKS FOR THE GREATNESS OF THY GLORY. What pure, fragrant, disinterested love of God is here breathed out! It is just such a love that God is worthy of receiving from all His reasonable creatures.

Mark yet another and perhaps the most admirable of all: PER DOMINUM NOSTRUM JESUM CHRISTUM: THROUGH OUR LORD JESUS CHRIST. All the prayers and supplications of the Church end with these words, thereby proclaiming that He is the great and only Mediator of Worship and Salvation and that all good comes to us through Him alone.

Each particular OREMUS is a study in spirituality; each is worthy of special attention for its own sake; and if duly pressed would yield great store of divine information and edification.

Now I say that a Christian saturated with the grand thoughts these liturgical formulae suggest, cannot but be genuinely spiritual. There will be no nonsense in his piety, no twist in his mind, no narrow corner in his heart; the Holy Spirit will find him a fit organ of divine praise and adoration and will not fail to use him, whilst still on earth, for this exalted purpose.

It is therefore evident that a loving and consistent study of the liturgical books both at Church and at home, must be a marvellous help in the work of mental prayer and divine contemplation. No other books will set before us such a dramatic presentment of the dealings of God either with His Church or with each soul individually. The sacred liturgy sets before our eyes the whole order of religion in the past, the present and endless ages of eternity, in a never ending, ever living, ever fresh and new and entrancing panorama, of which the pageant of the years with their recurring seasons and the reposeful alternations of day and night are but a faint image.

CHAPTER XX

THE WORKS OF THE SAINTS

THE Holy Scriptures having been laid down (in Chapter XVIII) as the sure foundation of all our holy reading and meditating with a view to Divine Contemplation—as the center around which it will revolve and to which it will be referred and indissolubly connected—as the framework within which it all will find place and be orderly disposed—our Contemplative should, in addition to the Liturgical Books, lay up a store of the best works written by the Saints and other pious personages, on their own account, but not without the evident help of the grace of God, on the subject of our intercourse with Him.

In regard to these latter I would again enforce the golden rule already given as to the methods of mental prayer. I would say: use the books that help you; use them as long as they do help you and not a minute longer. As soon as a book, be it ever so good, has ceased to impress you, to command or retain your attention, to stir up your will, it ought to be laid aside, at least for a time. Later, perhaps, you will feel inclined to turn to it again, and then you will do so with greater relish and deeper insight of its meaning. Books are good-natured, unselfish friends: they never resent being put on the shelf for a time or for good; they are ever ready, after years of neglect on our part, to pour out their treasures in our lap, the moment we have recourse to them again.

Another application of the golden rule is this: as soon as you feel drawn, by the spirit of prayer, away from what you are actually reading, lay the book aside and follow where the Holy Spirit is leading, and as long as He deigns thus to make Himself your guide. For, says Our Lord: *The Spirit breathes where He will; and thou hearest His voice, but thou knowest not whence He cometh and whither He goeth.* (John 3:8.) It would never do for us to tell the Holy Spirit to wait till we have read our allotted page, or give Him an appointment for another time. It is for the servant to follow at once the inspirations and movements of the Divine Guest and Master.

Now, then, as an almost necessary accompaniment to our Bible of the Contemplative, sketched out in Chapter XVIII, I venture to submit a small list of the books of saintly men, which seem to me best calculated to give help in any attempt at discursive and affective prayer. Where I give a Latin or French title it is that I am unaware of the existence of an English translation of the work; and where I refer to such a collection as "Migne" or the "Opera Omnia" of an author, it is that I am not aware of the special book in question having been published separately. This rule will hold good throughout all my works.

Besides such books of the Saints as I have already mentioned in the preceding chapter, which have for their direct object the interpretation of Holy Scriptures, and which would suffice to form an immense library, I would recommend a selection of books which present a concise and connected and suggestive view of Catholic Doctrine. Such are:

The Catechism of the Council of Trent.

Denzinger's ENCHIRIDION SYMBOLORUM (the latest edition with its invaluable Index Systematicus).

Moehler's Symbolism.

THE CATECHESES OF ST. CYRIL OF JERUSALEM.

The EPITOME INSTITUTIONUM DIVINARUM of Lactantius.

St. Augustine's Enchiridion de Fide, Spe et Charitate.

The OPUSCULUM II ET IV of St. Thomas Aquinas.

The BREVILOQUIUM of St. Bonaventure.

St. Francis of Sales' Treatise on the Love of God.

Bossuet's Discourse on Universal History.

Sir Bertram C. A. Windle's Key to Civilization.

The MEDULLA ANIMAE seu INSTITUTIONES DIVINAE of John Tauler.

Then would follow a selection of such other books as give a concrete example of discursive or affective mental prayer, and therefore may be considered as a kind of practical introduction into the art itself of communing with God.

Such are, among a host of others:

The CONFESSIONS, MEDITATIONS, and SOLILOQUIES of St. Augustine.

THE FOLLOWING OF CHRIST, especially the 3rd and 4th books.

THE BOOK OF EXERCISES OF THE SPIRITUAL LIFE of Abbot Cisneros.

John Gerson: De Mendicitate Spirituali.

St. Ignatius Loyola's Book of the Spiritual Exercises.

Father Vincent Carafa's Elevations to God.

Cardinal Bona's Via Compendii ad Deum.

A book of SPIRITUAL INSTRUCTION—and other works of L. Blosius.

THE PARADISE OF THE SOUL, by Mello Horstius.

St. Teresa's Seven Meditations on the Lord's Prayer.

Only after these would I place the special treatises on Mental Prayer, because I consider that the art is not learnt at first by rules and lessons but by practice and experience. Only after a beginning has been made and some progress achieved in Divine Contemplation, will it be possible to derive any considerable advantage from special treatises such as, for example:

St. John Climacus: Scala Coeli.

The MYSTICAL THEOLOGY of the Pseudo-Areopagite.

St. Bernard: De Consideratione.

The BENJAMIN MINOR of Richard of St. Victor.

St. Bonaventure: Itinerarium mentis ad Deum.

St. Alphonsus Liguori: Practice of the Love of Jesus.

St. Peter of Alcantara: On the Art of Meditation.

John Ruysbroeck: The Kingdom of the Lovers of God.

Father Nieremberg: ADORATION OF GOD IN SPIRIT AND TRUTH.

Bossuet: ON THE Knowledge of Oneself and of God.

Veil. De Ponte: The Practice of Mental Prayer.

Lessius: DE SUMMO BONO, Liber Quartus.

LA DOCTRINE SPIRITUELLE du Père Lallemant.

Bishop Waffelaert: LA MYSTIQUE ET LA PERFECTION CHRÉTIENNE (Bruges 1911).

PRAYER AND CONTEMPLATION, by the late Bishop Hedley (London, Catholic Truth Society).

Each one of these books, small in bulk, great in meaning, is a perfect gem in its way; each can be used for its own intrinsic worth, to lead one deeper into the secret nature of Divine Contemplation, and also as a means to help one to think of God, to realize His nearness to us, to begin lovingly and familiarly to converse with Him.

Then there are certain collections of readymade prayers of extraordinary virtue to set one's heart all aglow with the love of God.

Besides the official Prayers of the Church to be found in the liturgical books, especially the Missal and the Breviary—to which we have already drawn attention, and which are the very best that could ever be used—I would recommend the following:

The Raccolta, or official collection of the indulgenced prayers of the Church.

The Prayers of St. Gertrude.

J. Gerson: De MENDICITATE SPIRITUALI. Pars Secunda.

St. Alphonsus Liguori's Visits to the Blessed Sacrament.

DE LAUDIBUS SUPERLAUDABILIS DEI of Dionysius the Carthusian. (Op. Minora, tom. II.)

De LAUDIBUS SANCTISSIMAE TRINITATIS, of the same (ibid. tom. III.)

D. Michael of Coutance's Carthusian Spiritual Exercises.

IGNIARIUM DIVINI AMORIS of Blosius.

Father Augustine Baker's DEVOUT EXERCISES (at the end of Holy Wisdom).

Various Anthologies of religious poems.

LES POÉSIES de Soeur Thérèse de l'Enfant Jésus (the Little Flower) in appendix to her Life.

The LIFE and LETTERS of Marie Eustelle Harpain (surnamed

the Angel of the Blessed Sacrament.)

These are only a few out of the many most excellent spiritual books which might be recommended: but we must limit ourselves. Besides, I intend to make it a point, henceforth, as we proceed, whenever occasion offers, of giving a sufficient indication of the useful literature on the precise subject under consideration. I say the useful literature, not the so-called bibliography of the subject, because I have found, to my intense disgust, how misleading are those indiscriminate lists of books and essays of all the authors great and small, competent or incompetent, good, bad or indifferent who happen to have touched on the subject. We shall have none of this here; we are bent upon spreading light, not darkness and confusion. The books I shall recommend I know to be good and to the point. Most of them I have read more than once and pen in hand, the better to rip them open and tear the heart out of them, for my own benefit and the instruction of souls confided to my care.

Let no one be frightened at the large programme of holy reading here submitted and in prospect. No one is expected to read all this all at once, or within any given time. It is a programme to select from. Besides, a lifetime is a long time, and it is well to foresee years of drought and famine and to lay up a goodly store of provisions against them. After the seven years of great plenty of the dream of Pharao, came the seven years of great scarcity. In the same way, after the ease and consolation of the beginnings of a fervent life, there may set in a season of aridity and helplessness, when it will seem impossible to produce any fruits of discursive or affective prayer, and when even the loving God will appear to have withdrawn Himself from the desolate soul. Then the humble and laborious employment of holy reading and thoughtful consideration will have to be taken up again, and the more a contemplative man is familiar with the Holy Scriptures, the books of the Church, and the works of the Saints, the better will he be able to cope with his own difficulties.

Even the Christian who knows no letters can read a good deal or make an equivalent to it. In what way? First, by hearing others read for him or discourse to him upon the divine mysteries. Then he has under his eyes (if he will but pay attention to it) the wonderful book of nature; and in his hands, this other wonderful abridgment of all God's works, the Holy Crucifix. Some persons are indeed none the worse, in regard to the spiritual life, for not knowing letters: I have had proofs of this many a time. I will relate here one particular instance which came under my direct observation some years ago.

I was doing duty as chaplain for a time in a community of French nuns. In confession I imposed on one of them, as a penance, the recitation of the Litanies of the Holy Name of Jesus. To my surprise, the good nun a lay-Sister, begged to be given another penance as she did not know the litanies by heart and could not read, and did not know much more than the Our Father and Hail Mary. Notwithstanding this, she proved to be one of the most experienced persons in the ways of mental prayer I have ever met. Her case interested me; so I put her through a sort of examination and took note of her answers while they were yet fresh in my memory. I found that she was really accustomed to spend the whole day in simple and familiar intercourse with God. Whilst taking care of the cattle, digging in the garden, going to and fro in the service of the household, she was at the same time busy talking to God or hearkening to Him. I asked her what she said. She answered: "I am never tired of repeating: Lord, my God, lo, I am thy handmaid! O Jesu, I am thy bride, thy little bride, thy little spouse. My God, be ever with me! Be ever all in all to me! My God, cleanse me thoroughly and fill me wholly with thy very Self. When I go up some stairs: My God, make me to climb all the degrees of perfection according to thy holy will!—Down stairs: My God, see to it that I do not go down into sin and then into the abyss of eternal damnation.—When I meet one of the workmen: My God, see to it that he does not lose his soul and become one of the reprobates. Then I say as many Our Fathers and Hail Marys as I can, as fervently as I know how, and many ejaculatory prayers. The day is too short for all I should like to say, but I wake up also during the night and begin again forthwith; I find this very sweet."

This good lay-Sister did not seem to suspect that God was doing great things in her soul. I found also that, by a marvellous instinct of humility, she was, in her intercourse with other people, as reserved and reticent about these graces as she had been simple and straightforward in giving an account of them to me as her spiritual Director.

Let us close this chapter with a last advice about holy reading. The spiritual man has to be on his guard against the subtle temptation of making reading an end in itself, for thus it would become an obstacle instead of a help to Divine Contemplation. The danger is not an imaginary one. Who has not met, at some time or other, the voracious reader with whom gulping down book after book has become a passion, a mania, a necessity, a sort of morbid craving? No sooner has he begun a book than he must go through with it; no sooner has he finished it than he must take up another; and thus, on and on, without pause, and without ever any end. He simply reads for reading's sake: no profit is aimed at and of course none is attained. The man has become a reading-machine. He may eventually become very erudite: he certainly will never be a contemplative.

CHAPTER XXI

OF AFFECTIVE PRAYER AND THE GIFT OF THE PRESENCE OF GOD

AFFECTIVE Prayer, as we have already seen, takes place when the Holy Spirit stays the discourses of the mind and draws to Himself, sweetly and strongly, the affective powers of the Christian soul. Now when this has become a confirmed habit or a state, its distinguishing feature is the gift of the Presence of God.

In order the better to understand this wonderful grace, it will be useful for us to take a rapid survey of the whole workings of the spirit of Prayer in the Christian soul who offers no resistance to the Holy Spirit.

We read in the Book of Proverbs: "*Wisdom hath built herself a house. ... She hath sent her maids to invite to the tower. ... Whosoever is a little one, let him come to me. ... Come, eat my bread ... forsake childishness, and live, and walk by the ways of prudence.*" (Prov. 9:1-6.)

Men on earth are the little children of the Father who is in heaven; very little children indeed, when compared with the Blessed Angels and the full-grown Saints of paradise; very little children, and at times very unwise, naughty and disobedient. They play at all sorts of dangerous games: at Kaiserism of one kind or another, at Kultur and Frightfulness and Socialism and Bolshevism; dancing on powder-magazines, making love without marriage, marriage without offspring, driving madly about, diving in the deep and flying in the air. They make a noise for a time until all of a sudden they are tripped up by death and are seen no more. Meanwhile they forget the errand upon which they had been sent by God in the present world, that of making their way to the House which Wisdom has built to Herself, to the Tower of Divine Contemplation, pending the time when they would have been admitted to the vision of God face to face.

Alone the fervent Christian (we call him a mystic) is mindful of his condition of a child of God, and of the purpose for which his Heavenly Father has sent him into this world. Though but a little child, he knows that he has divine powers, that is to say supernatural faculties, added to his natural ones, in order to enable him to make his way to the Tower of Divine Contemplation. Added to his natural faculties of Intellect and Free Will, which are as the two feet upon which he can stand erect and walk wherever he will, he has received in Baptism and Confirmation six wings with which to raise himself from the ground and accelerate his pace, three on one side and three on the other, thus: the three infused theological virtues of Faith, Hope and Charity, and the three most excellent Gifts of the Holy Spirit: Filial Fear of the Lord, Understanding and Wisdom.

Ordinarily the first manifestation of the spirit of prayer in a Christian who has just emerged from a slothful, negligent state of life, is that of Discursive Prayer. It is easy to understand why. The first need of such a one is that his mind should be enlightened as to the perfect loveliness of God: accordingly the Holy Spirit begins by flooding his mind with vivid lights, which, as it were, automatically start the process of discursive prayer. This has to take place before the fervid acts of affective prayer can be expected.

At this first stage of the journey, the exercise of the presence of God costs an effort or rather a long series of painful efforts. The little child making his first experiments in the art of walking is a very good illustration of what happens to the beginner in his efforts to realize the presence of God and to start forth upon his journey of the mystical life, with Divine Contemplation in its highest degree as its goal.

Look at the little child crawling on all fours. Soon, however, he grows ambitious and wants to stand upright and walk as he sees grown-up people doing all around him. So, he makes a brave attempt and, of course, falls to the ground. After crawling again on all fours a little while, he tries again to raise himself upright and to balance himself on his unsteady short legs and to take a step or two, when he tumbles over again. Nothing daunted he scrambles to his feet yet another time and yet another time tumbles over. And so the whole day long. Next day he will begin again, and so day after day for many months. Finally a time comes when his efforts are crowned with success; nature helping him, and as he has grown stronger every day and more skilled in the use of his limbs, he has at last acquired proper control of all his movements. There he stands firmly planted on his feet, erect and noble, looking like a little god, moving freely about as the very lord of creation which he is indeed.

Thus it is also with us in the beginning of our conversion, with regard to the habitual practice of the presence of God. Success is the reward of our persevering efforts, coupled of course with the help of divine grace. We have first to drill ourselves into practice. We have to bring under control not only the attention of our mind and our will, but also and primarily our inferior powers: memory, imagination, the exterior senses, the whole nervous system itself. A fine and wholesome discipline, and one which is by and by rewarded with the infused gift of Divine Contemplation.

At first this gift will show itself by the rapid moving of the Christian upon his journey towards the Tower of which we spoke a while ago, built by Divine Wisdom and where She invites all the children of men to come and feast upon the good things she has prepared: the Tower of the Prayer of Quiet, if we must give it its proper name.

At this new stage of the journey it would be wrong to insist upon speaking of discursive and of affective prayer as though they were two separate, widely distant, almost contrary species of intercourse with God. Rather they should be considered as very slightly different manifestations of the same spirit. They are simply *different moods,* and nothing is more natural than the passing from one of these moods into the other. In a soul which goes to God with great liberty and allows the Holy Spirit to have His own way with her, the acts of one mood constantly alternate with those of the other. Quite simply and almost unconsciously, under the impulse of the Holy Spirit, the contemplative man produces some act or acts of discursive prayer and then forthwith acts of the most tender or burning affections; as at other times he will on the contrary be moved, at first, to pour out fervid acts of love, and then, as he cannot remain a long time at that white heat, because poor human nature, in its present condition, could not stand it, he lapses again quite naturally, into the discursive mood. Thus it is with him, till the time comes when the Holy Spirit sees fit to raise His faithful servant to the Prayer of Quiet.

Therefore, it seems to me that we are justified in likening the discursive and affective moods of Mental Prayer to the two sides of an avenue leading up to the Tower of the Prayer of Quiet, away from the wretched, sordid world of sinful creatures.

As he walks or rather flies over the very broken ground along the avenue, now leaning more on the side of Discursive Prayer now more on that of Affective Prayer, and getting nearer and nearer to the coveted goal of his journey, the fervent Christian becomes aware of a greater ease and sweetness in the practice of the Presence of God. At last the mood of Affective Prayer becomes decidedly predominant and the feeling of the Presence of God has become a gift. The practice costs him no effort. He has not to force himself into an attitude, or do violence to his mind; to be repeating to himself: I am in the Divine Presence. He feels himself there and the feeling is infused from God. He holds himself in the divine presence, simply, sweetly and joyfully. He disports himself in the divine presence with the abandon of a child say of five or six years, in the presence of his mother. Does the little fellow work his brain fearfully and violently to maintain his attention to her presence? He need not do that, because it comes quite natural to him.

See him for instance, with his mother on the sea-shore. He may be very busy looking out for shells, digging holes in the sand and picking up curious sea-weeds. Then, perhaps, he wants to pull off his shoes and stockings and paddle in the surf. He is quite engrossed with all this, and yet, does he forget his mother? does he not turn to her for approval of all he does; and quite naturally, without having to force himself into an attitude? He only, from time to time, looks up to her and shouts a few joyful words, and returns to his childish play. But he is all along, even when not actually engaged with her, conscious of her presence. He will not go far away from her, or stay long out of her sight. Now and then he comes back and nestles close to her, wistfully looking up in her eyes, and gives her a hearty kiss and receives a shower of loving caresses.

The contemplative about to enter into the castle of Prayer of Quiet has become a little child again, and God is to him a true mother full of the tenderest love. He holds himself in the divine presence sweetly, joyfully and lovingly. Love does it all. Give me a man who really loves God and he will soon arrive at this point. Love does it all: see there the predominance at last of the affective mood. The little child loves his mother: that is his secret, his talisman: that is why he experiences no difficulty in basking in the sunshine of her presence. To lose sight of her and do without her would be the real difficulty with him, the real hardship. And so also with the advanced contemplative, with regard to the presence of God. On the other hand it need hardly be said that this holding himself perpetually in the presence of God is done by him without ostentation or singularity. He hides his secret as much as he possibly can, though it will betray itself in spite of all his efforts.

We may well understand that when the gift of the presence of God is granted to the Christian, the mood of affective prayer should prevail. *God is love!* Then also, think how with a human lover the presence of the object of his love is wont to throw him into raptures!

But what do these two lovers, God and the fervent Christian, say to one another?

They say but one word, this namely: "Love!" but oh! the accent with which they say it, and the meaning they can impart to it!

They say it, not with any articulate speech, nor with any sound of voice, but with an all-consuming contact of one another.

If I were to translate it in our halting, coarse, human language, I should express it thus:

God is the first to speak. He says:

"Fear not, dear child of my heart: it is I. I am He Whom you seek. Peace be with thee!" and in saying this God establishes that soul in great peace.

He speaks again: "Dear child of my heart, take heed, understand: I am love! I am love in three divine Persons! I, the Father, am love abysmal; I, the Son, am love resplendent and made man; I, the Holy Spirit, am love diffusive, and I abide in thee!"

A third time, God says with infinite tenderness:

"I love thee, little one! I want thee. Give me thy heart; I shall first make it very pure, very holy, and then I shall fill it with what it can hold of my own happiness, I shall fill it with my very self. Let me be thy All in all. You to Me, and I to thee: the one to the One!"

Wounded to the heart, pierced through and through, the contemplative can only sigh and sob out:

"My God! my dear God! my Love! my All! I believe in Thee, Love! I hope in Thee, Love! I love Thee who loved me so! I love Thy love!"

The repetition of this one word LOVE A million times, is not monotonous. It has always A new charm to him.

Let us state the case boldly. If Jesus is Love made man, the mystic who is arrived at this stage of Divine Contemplation is man made love. He is one who from a clod of earth and a sinner, has been by the touch of the grace of God turned into a burning seraph. Seraph means flame, devouring fire. The highest angels are all ablaze with divine love; and so is also the fervent Christian on earth, when he is brought up by the Holy Spirit, in front of the House and Tower of perfect Divine Contemplation which Wisdom Herself built and which is no other than the Mental Prayer of Quiet.

Let this stand as some poor description of the state of Affective Prayer.

And now it seems to me as though I heard the loving Lord telling his poor servant *who is but dust and ashes* (Gen. 18:27): *Gird up thy loins like a man.* (Job 38:3.) *Thou hast yet a great way to go* (3 Kings 19:7). On with the work. Tell souls of good will something of the wonders of my love. *He that hath ears to hear, let him hear.* (Matt. 11:15.)

CHAPTER XXII

ON THE THRESHOLD OF THE UNITIVE WAY

AT the end of the Illuminative Way in the spiritual life of a fervent soul, there is already, as we have noticed in the foregoing chapter, the gift of the Presence of God and a marked prevalence of the affective mood of prayer. The entrance into the House of Prayer of Quiet marks the beginning of the Unitive Way.

In Psalm 26:4, we read: *One thing I have asked of the Lord, this will I seek after, that I may dwell in the house of the Lord all the days of my life, that I may see the delight of the Lord and may visit his temple.*

Dwelling in the house of the Lord all the days of one's life is nothing else than the attaining to and the persevering in the Prayer of Quiet. To see the delight of the Lord is to feed one's soul upon the delightful mysteries of the Sacred Humanity of Our Lord. *O taste and see that the Lord is sweet,* says the Prophet. (Ps. 33:9.) Visiting the temple of the Lord here means to be raised occasionally to the ecstatic contemplation of the Divine Essence of the Blessed Trinity.

It has been the most ardent desire of our pious pilgrim to reach this noble House of the Prayer of Quiet, as the goal on earth of his spiritual journey. That he might the more freely come to it, he has left everything behind, divesting himself of all created attachment. He has strenuously sought after it by an intense and unremitting exercise of his faith, hope and charity, and of the three gifts of the Fear of the Lord, Understanding and Wisdom in discursive and affective prayer. Bearing in mind the instruction of Our Lord: *Ask and it shall he given you; seek and you shall find; knock and it shall he opened to you* (Matt. 7:7), he has persevered petitioning for this favor and pressing onward in his quest; and now at last, he sights from afar the noble, majestic mansion.

Usually, this stage, the Unitive Way, is reached only late in life; but it is to be aimed at from the very beginning by every one, the more so that no one can promise himself a long life. To him who is destined to die early, Our Lord will not fail to give exceptional graces, if he will only receive them, so that it may come true of him also as has been said: *Being made perfect in a short space, he fulfilled a long time.* (Wisd. 4:13.) Such has been the case with, for instance, St. Agnes, Blessed Joan of Arc, St. Stanislaus Kostka, the "Little Flower of Jesus," Gemma Galgani: those lovely youthful patterns of Christian perfection.

The Unitive Way should be reached at least by all Christians who pass the meridian of life. The experience they have gained of the vanity of all things here below, the habit of prayer they must have developed, the cumulative effects of the Sacraments, as well of those which are received but once, as of those which may be received hundreds and thousands of times; the providential snapping of the bonds of human friendship and love, by the deaths of their dear ones, as they proceed onwards on their pilgrimage, and finally the flagging of their own energies for active life: all these things ought to concur at last to fit them for the Unitive Way. If they are stripped bare, figuratively speaking, it is in order that they might go naked to God and adhere to Him, giving themselves up entirely to a life of prayer. Such is really the case with the old people in intensely Catholic countries, as Brittany, Ireland, Spain, etc.

It is not my intention to follow our contemporary writers on Prayer, in their scientific analysis of the diverse states or degrees of contemplation: nothing seems to me more useless or misleading; but I aim at giving such a summary description of these as will kindle in the soul of good will a desire to know them by personal experience.

On account of the strangeness of the divine happenings we are attempting to describe, we are in the necessity of making a liberal use of parables, metaphors and images vivid and varied. The Holy Scriptures stand as our model and our justification in this. See the lavish use our Blessed Lord makes of parables in His Gospel of love, and to what good purpose. See the mixed metaphors he accumulates in that celebrated page in Matt. 13:24-

52, where He gives us a forecast of the history of His Church. He calls it a Kingdom: *The Kingdom of Heaven* on earth, and compares that Kingdom *to a sower whose seed fell partly by the wayside, partly upon stony ground, partly among thorns and the rest on good ground;—to a field in which the husbandman sowed good seed and the enemy, by stealth, overnight, sowed cockle;—to a grain of mustard-seed which is very small, but grows up and becomes a mighty tree; to leaven which a woman hid in three measures of meal until the whole was leavened; to a treasure hidden in a field; to a merchant in search of precious pearls; to a net cast into the sea and gathering in all kinds of fishes.*

We have another strong example of mixed metaphors from our Blessed Lord, when He informs us that *we are His sheep and that He is the Good Shepherd, and at the same time the Fold, the Door of the Fold and the very Pasture.* (John 10.) What in the mouth of a mere mortal man would be an abuse of human language verging on extravagance is here the expression of an absolute truth and the only way of conveying somehow fully, if piecemeal, the mystery of all that Jesus is to us.

It is Our Lord also, prophetically, Who with the pen of Solomon, describes in the Canticle of Canticles the reciprocal love that exists between Himself and His Church, and again between Himself and every individual Christian soul.

What shall we say of the wonderful imagery of the Prophets Ezechiel and Daniel, or of the spiritual or symbolical meanings which the Fathers of the Church discover all over the Old Testament? It is true that these mystical interpretations hardly appeal to our modern mentality; but it must be owned also that modern mentality is not the measure of all things—least of all, of the divine mysteries.

In his treatise, "De Divinis Nominibus," and in his epistle to Titus, the Pseudo-Areopagite speaks of the Scripture-metaphors as of so many fictions which are at the same time bold and reverential, palpably representative of things hidden from the senses, divisible symbols of things without parts; such, in one word, that if a man will but penetrate into their hidden beauty, he will find them overflowing with mysterious, divine, theological light. He goes on to say that "the veil is lifted only in favor of the true lovers of holy things, because they are sure not to interpret in a puerile way these pious symbols. Thanks to the purity of their mind and the power of penetration of their contemplative faculty they are enabled to discern the truth in its intimate simplicity under its supernatural depth, which so excellently transcends any coarse material image." (Dionysius, Ep. 9, 1.)

Before we venture inside the House of Quiet, there is one thing for us to do.

When Moses was feeding the sheep of the priest of Madian, one day he drove his flock to the inner part of the desert, and came to the mountain of God, Horeb. The Lord appeared to him in a flame of fire out of the midst of a bush, and he saw that the bush was on fire and was not burnt; and Moses said, "*I* will go and see that great sight. When the Lord saw that he went forward to see, he called to him out of the midst of the bush and said: Come not nigh hither; put off the shoes from thy feet, for the *place whereon thou standest is holy ground.* (Exod. 3:5) O my reader, the ground on which we now venture is so holy that even angels might well tremble to tread it: let us then, put off our shoes from our feet; I mean, let us agree that before we take one more step forward in this matter of the Prayer of Quiet, we do here and now divest ourselves of all purely human curiosity: the better to understand these things of God which now lie before us, we put off all inordinate affections to created things. We want to gaze upon all that will be shown us in the House of the Lord, with the clean and bright eyes of the soul; we want to understand all that is going to be related to us, in a purely spiritual, not carnal, sense.

CHAPTER XXIII

INSIDE THE HOUSE OF QUIET

HE that has come so far in his spiritual life as to catch a distant and yet distinct view of the House or Citadel which Wisdom built herself, is already a Knight. Whether man or woman (for spiritual life knows not the distinction of sexes), he has won his spurs. In many a hard-fought battle against the world and the devil and still more against self, he has distinguished himself in the sight of God and his blessed Angels. He has no sooner caught sight of the severe and imposing structure in the distance, than he quickens his pace and stretches forward and will give himself no rest until he has come up quite closely to it.

But here a sore disappointment awaits his eager soul. Where there should be a door there is no door, only two marvelously sculptured figures of heroic size half set in the wall, at a height of three feet from the ground: the one on the right representing the Blessed Virgin Mary, that on the left, the Key-bearer of heaven, St. Peter. He then makes a tour all round the huge building, scanning the walls to discover some aperture; there is none; no door, no window.

Twice he made this journey, only to become absolutely sure there was no entrance of any kind anywhere. What was he to do? Clearly it was out of his power altogether to effect his entrance into the so much coveted place. He could not even knock at the door, since there was none. And yet Our Lord has said: *Ask and you shall receive, seek and you, shall find, knock and it shall he opened unto you.* (Matt. 8:7.) All he could do was to knock by his loud prayer, and he did pray, if not with a loud voice, for the solemn silence of the place impressed him, at least with a loud clamor of his whole soul. At last, wearied as well as exhausted by the previous fatigue of the journey he fell asleep, there at the feet of the Virgin: a deep, refreshing sleep, and he had a vision as Jacob on his way to Haran, of the golden ladder that goes up from earth to heaven, on which angels go continually up and down and at the top there is God, the loving God, looking down with a benign face, and saying words of blessing and encouragement.

When he awoke, what was his surprise to find himself inside the House. It took him some time to realize this. He could hardly believe his own eyes, for he found himself at one end of an immense hall; at the foot of a huge cross, with a monumental fountain of many-colored marble in front of it, and on turning his head towards the wall against which the huge cross was reared, he discovered a great fresco painting which at once riveted his attention. On the left side of the cross was represented a strange flock of lions, tigers, panthers and other fierce animals, who yet allowed themselves to be driven with menacing gesture and clamor by a chubby little boy, seemingly towards the pool of water in the lowest basin of the fountain. It appeared as if the waters had the virtue of bringing about a wonderful transformation, for on the right side of the cross he saw the same chubby little boy, looking very sweet now, clapping his little hands in childish glee, his flock of cruel, wild beasts all turned into so many lambs innocently frisking around him, whilst doves fluttered over his head and shoulders.

At this our Knight could not contain his joy; he ran up to the wall and kissed the child saying, "Thou art Jesus, art Thou not? I have known Thee all my life. Oh! how I love Thee!" And Jesus seemed glad of the caress and without sound of words He spoke to the heart of His friend, telling him to go and refresh himself at the fountain, to drink of the seven basins and then look well at the place He had prepared for him, and return and recount his impression.

Here then, at last, was the House of the Prayer of Quiet, and this is how it appeared to him. At first he was simply dazed by the splendor of it: it struck him with speechless amazement. All he could do was to roam in it aimlessly, and pause and gaze at the walls from end to end and from top to bottom, and at the marvellous mosaic pavement, and at the open sky overhead, for there was no ceiling: but this last feature was hardly noticed by him at first: he had too many other things at which to wonder.

When he came back after his first ramble, he kissed the child again and said: "Jesus, I love Thy House, *our house* I should say: but I do not understand it yet. All I can make out thus far is that I am to be here the happy prisoner of Thy love, as long as I live or as long as I like. Then it will be as long as I live: *This is my rest for ever and for ever; here will I dwell for I have chosen it.* (Ps. 131:14). *This is no other but the house of God and the gate of heaven.* (Gen. 28:17.) *It is good for us to he here.* (Matt. 17:4.)"

"But, my dear," says the child, secretly into our Knight's heart; "look at yourself, how thinly clad you are: you will have to abide here day and night and in all seasons, without any protection; besides, you will have no companions; only Me; and I shall not always speak into your heart, at least audibly; and you will have to undergo here some terrible, mysterious trials, I will not say what nor how long."

"You speak darkly, Jesus, my Brother and my Lover, answered the Knight: but whatever may betide me in this Thy House, never on any consideration shall I want to leave it, if only I am permitted to love Thee. O my dearest, O my darling God! Thou sayest I shall have no other companion than Thy sweet Self! All the better, for another companion would take away some of my attention from Thee and perhaps a part of my affections.

"As for my appearance, I had not noticed any change in me thus far: but I see now there is. I am almost naked. I suppose this is the way in which St. John the Baptist was clad in the desert; or perhaps the way Adam and Eve were clad by Our-Heavenly Father with the hide of beasts before He drove them out of the earthly Paradise. It is very light and does not interfere with my freedom of movement, and I like it!"

We must now attempt a description of the inside of the House of Quiet. Represent to yourself an immense lofty hall, the lines of which are so harmonious that you do not at first realize the vastness of its proportions: something in the style of a Roman basilica, St. Paul outside the walls for instance, but without pillars, altars or furniture of any kind, and without windows or chandeliers or contrivance of any kind for the purpose of giving light. All the light streams, not from the open sky, but from the great crucifix at the east end of the hall, and the contemplative understands now that even the light of the sun by day and that of the stars by night is borrowed from the dying figure of the Saviour of the world. He said: *I am the Light of the world.* (John 8:12.) Indeed He is, and in more senses than the obviously supernatural one, if only men could be made to see it. Even for all the gifts of nature we are beholden to Jesus Crucified.

To the beholder who stands at the west end of the great hall, with his back turned to the wall, the vista that stretches out before him is at once simple and rich in the extreme. The walls on the right and on the left are covered at their base with a course of lofty, dark oak panels elaborately sculptured and surmounted by a course of magnificent embroidered tapestry. Above this again there is an expanse of brightly colored fresco-paintings; and crowning the whole, at a dizzy height, a gallery of three hundred and sixty statues of Saints, which must be of extraordinary size, for they appear, even at that lofty position, as though they were life-size and ready to move or to speak; the same is true of all the personages in the paintings or tapestries or wood panels; at whatever height they be, they appear life-size and alive, and they speak into the very heart of the beholder.

Most marvellous of all are the scenes embroidered on the tapestries. These are all taken from the mysteries of the life and death and resurrection and glory of Our Blessed Lord. Those on the south wall, from its west end till it reaches the great crucifix, represent the earthly life of Our Lord till his death on the Cross; those on the north wall beginning near the great crucifix and returning to the west wall are the glorious mysteries. There are twenty-five scenes on the south wall and as many on the northern one: a glorious, uninterrupted series of all the mysteries of Jesus in their proper order, from His Incarnation till His last coming to judge the living and the dead, and His Nuptials with His Heavenly Bride, the Church of all the Blessed. There is no mistaking the purpose of these scenes nor escaping their effect:

the aim kept in view is to draw out one Person, just one, to impress His figure in the mind, in the heart, in the imagination, in the sensibility of the beholder! Turn where you will, there you meet Him, oh! so lovely! so beautiful! so majestic! so sweet! Not only is He the central figure in each scene, but all the other personages are so well subordinated to Him that they seem to borrow all they have from Him alone and completely to melt into His radiance, the result being a still more forcible impression of Him made on the contemplative mind and heart.

Over every one of these scenes from the life and mysteries of Our Lord, is a corresponding scene from the life of His Church (we might even say, of His life in the Church) on earth, in the fresco-paintings: whilst below, sculptured in the black wood panel is also a corresponding scene of the spiritual life of the individual soul. For instance, above the Last Supper embroidered on the tapestry is a fresco-painting of the Holy Sacrifice of the Mass being offered up in the Catacombs, in a Gothic cathedral, in a virgin forest of South America, in an African village, in far away China by a mandarin-priest, in the trenches at the battle front by a soldier-priest. Below the same picture of the Last Supper, in the wood paneling the sculptor has had the skill to represent a great crowd pressing around the Holy Table to receive Communion. There you see little children of six and seven, bright adolescents of both sexes making their solemn Communion in what used to be the apparel of First Communicants, young people of all ranks and professions, newly married couples in their bridal dress, soldiers, sailors, officers of the army and navy, men wearing the badge of the air-force, fathers and mothers of families, old people feeble and decrepit, and in a corner a dying Christian on his pallet, transfigured in the joy of receiving Holy Viaticum from the hands of a youthful priest.

Thus, if you look at the pictures as they are superimposed one over the other, you find that the central one (which is a scene of our Lord's life) gives its significance to the one above it and to the one below it. Thus also, if instead of considering these as they are disposed one over the other, you look at their succession along the walls, you perceive that you have in the fresco-paintings the whole history of the Church past, present and future, viewed in the light of the mysteries of Our Lord; and also parallel with these two upper series of paintings, but under them, you have in the sculptured oak panels the whole history of the spiritual life of a fervent Christian, equally interpreted in the light of the mysteries of Our Lord; and it is to be noted that as the history of the Christian proceeds, his resemblance to his divine model becomes more marked in the painting as it is also in real life.

Superimposed columns, half emerging from the wall, gradually diminishing in size, divide off the twenty-five sections or sets of pictures on each side, and with the ornamental transverse courses of sculptured stone running in three parallel lines all along the walls, form a suitable framing to each scene.

They serve at the same time the purpose of breaking the monotony of such immense walls. The capitals of these half columns support a running corbel which forms a sort of dais or canopy over the heads of the Saints of the gallery, by groups of seven, one for each day of the week.

Besides these columns half emerging from the thickness of the wall, and of common white stone, there stands in each corner of the building and half way along the north and south wall six huge monoliths of most rare marble, and a seventh one dividing off the west wall into halves. In the right-hand half are depicted in a vivid manner the horrible torments of the damned in Hell; and in the other the sufferings of the poor souls in Purgatory.

These monoliths are the seven columns hewn out by Divine Wisdom, each bearing the name of one of the gifts of the Holy Spirit. The central column of the west wall is called THE FEAR OF THE LORD. The two in each corner of the same wall are PIETY and SCIENCE, the two at the other end of the hall are COUNSEL and FORTITUDE, and the two half way up the hall are WISDOM and UNDERSTANDING. The four columns in the corners, corresponding to the gifts which are devoted to heroic saintly action, namely PIETY and SCIENCE, COUNSEL and FORTITUDE, support at each end of the hall a large Roman arch of a magnificent amplitude, with the sweep of a rainbow in the sky. The other three, Fear of the Lord, Wisdom and Understanding, as they are for pure Contemplation have no superincumbent weight. Over their capital there is a sphere, and on the sphere is perched an emblematic bird: on the Fear of the Lord a cock flapping its wings as though in the act of crowing; an eagle with outstretched wings on Understanding; and a brooding dove on Wisdom.

It is time our attention was directed to the marvellous mosaic pavement. It spreads out under the feet of our Knight like a carpet of green grass enameled with all sorts of flowers and insects and birds and beasts, to show us the childlike delight with which a true contemplative looks upon the lovely face of nature, and watches all its moods—the more so that it helps him to raise his mind and heart to the loving God. The immense majority of men, shut up in their wretched towns, or stupidly inattentive, miss a good deal of the purest joy of life through the want of this childlike simplicity; *Theirs is the kingdom, of heaven* says Our Lord, of the little ones and of those who resemble them; and not only the kingdom of heaven, but in addition, also the kingdom of nature. By a last stroke of genius the maker of this pavement has contrived to give by small instalments, cleverly distributed here and there among the flowers, the whole miraculous history of the Old Testament, so rich in dogmatic or spiritual or symbolical lessons, from the Six Days of Creation to the apparition of the Angel to Zacharias the father of the Precursor, whilst he was offering the evening sacrifice in the Temple.

At the foot of the large cross and at some distance below the body of the Crucified Saviour, the marble fountain sends out its crystal waters from under the raised foot of a lamb. These waters do not rise up in the air to descend with a splash: they only bubble forth and run over the margin, falling from basin into basin seven times with a murmurous sound as of a thousand softly-whispered prayers, and swiftly disappear in underground channels to carry refreshment and fecundity to the ends of the world. This refreshing movement of the waters is the only sound heard in this hall, except when, from time to time, flights of invisible angels seem to sweep through the hall: for then, snatches of heavenly music are audible as of thousands and hundreds of thousands of voices softened by infinite distance.

A princely row of eleven majestic Apostles, St. Peter being in the middle, is seen above the top of the Cross, and as this east wall is finished in a semi-circle spanned by a Roman arch, a most gorgeous mosaic fills this space with the figures of God the Father and God the Son side by side on the high throne of heaven, in flowing robes sweeping far down over the seven steps of the throne. The two are lovingly facing each other and the Holy Spirit is between them as a dove with out-stretched wings, so that one wing touches the breast of the Father and the other the wound in the side of the Son. At the right hand of Jesus stands, in sweetly majestic attitude, the lovely Queen of Paradise, invested with the glory that radiates from her divine Son. All sorts of precious stones are set in her diadem and over her mantle. Again on the right of Mary stands St. Joseph, then St. John the Baptist. On the left of the eternal Father stand the three archangels, Michael, Gabriel and Raphael. Flights of lesser angels and innumerable winged-headed Cherubs all around in a receding vista in the back-ground create an impression as though there were millions of them.

Such then, symbolically, is our House of the Lord, the House of the Prayer of Quiet. Least of all is it a house of Quietism: for everything in it is calculated to provoke and stimulate both the mind and the heart of the dweller therein, to very intense, though very quiet action. Except at those precious moments, rare and rapidly passing away, when God himself takes the Contemplative in hand, here in the midst of this marvellous display on walls and pavements, it is simply impossible to do otherwise than think and love and pray and adore. The faculty of discursive and affective prayer is not lost nor torpid: it is silenced only in the actual moments of passive or semi-passive contemplation, which, according to the testimony of St. Teresa, hardly ever lasts so much as a half hour at a time.

Jesus is All in All in this house; He is everywhere; He is everything: He and He alone. Is, then, the contemplative who has arrived at the Prayer of Quiet, alienated from his brethren, separated from the rest of the Church? Far from it. He is even more united with them, more devoted to the Church, more useful in every way than he ever was before. How is that? It is through Jesus Christ and in Jesus Christ. Our Lord in becoming his All in All has made Himself the bond of union of this Christian with his brethren, even as He is the bond of union of this same Christian with His Heavenly Father. So it has always been with all the Saints, even with those who buried themselves alive in the depth of the deserts.

Do you now ask who has been the architect, who the painter of the House? Who conceived the idea of this hall and reared it and adorned it? It is the very same who introduced our Knight into it: Love, Love eternal, Love essential and supersubstantial, Love Triune: God, God Himself and alone, the loving God.

And do you say with impetuous enthusiasm: Oh! I also want to come to this House of the Lord and live in it till the end of my days on earth? Well said, my brother! well said! this is the way to speak. But mind, you must not try to come in but through the avenue and with the wings we have described in Chapter XXI, you must pay the price in utter self-surrender; further you must be ready to undergo in that very House of the Lord the most severe trials. Love reigns supreme here, but Love is a terribly exacting Master to us poor mortals; in fact he is a tyrant. He wants to change the clay and base metals of our present composition into the gold and precious stones that will make us fit for the Heavenly Jerusalem. The process of such a transformation implies some violence. Of this we shall speak presently.

CHAPTER XXIV

THE PASSIVE NON-MIRACULOUS STATES OF PRAYER

IN crossing the threshold of the Unitive Life, we have reached such communings with God as are properly those of the Perfect.

The divers species of divine contemplation which precede this stage are no doubt very wonderful effects of the grace of God, and very sweet in themselves, but they cannot be compared with the Prayer of Quiet. They are of an inferior quality; they bear to it the relation of means to end, designed to bring the soul up gradually to the Prayer of Quiet, and yet incapable of introducing her into it. That must be God's doing exclusively, and it is the most perfect contemplation that can be vouchsafed to man here below.

By being introduced into the House of Quiet, has the soul come to the end of her labors? Is she going to do no more than simply sit down and enjoy God and herself in God? Far from this being the case, it seems as though it is now only that she begins really to work, and dare, and do wonders, to labor and spend and be spent and consume herself, never resting, never ceasing, never saying "It is enough." All that the Christian has done hitherto looks like child's play compared with what is in store for him.

Here human language conspicuously fails us. Whoever tries to express these higher realities is betrayed into using the words Quiet, Quietude, Passive states, Passive Contemplation and the like, when really he speaks of a stage of the spiritual life of the most intense and consuming activity, because, forsooth, there is not found in it that outward show and bustle and noise which men call activity. Let us be content then, to use these words, being careful, however, not to allow ourselves to be deceived as to their real import.

The Contemplation of the Perfect is distinguished from that

of the Beginner and the Pilgrim by the following characteristics: (1) Simplification of the Soul; (2) Continuousness of her Prayer; (3) Passive Purifications; (4) Passive Illuminations; (5) Passive Unions; (6) Divine Fruitfulness.

First, then, we must note the utter simplification of the soul's outlook on the world and on all things. She does not desire to look at anything but God, and she sees Him by one simple gaze. She tastes the mysteries of Jesus as a marvellous draught, which a man should drink without stopping to analyze the divers elements of its sweetness. Her neighbor she sees only in God. To her, every man, woman and child, is Jesus, either in reality or in potentiality: Jesus by proxy. Little children are so many replicas of the Child Jesus. It is not So-and-So, a sympathetic person, or the reverse: it is Jesus living in His mystical member. If the man be an enemy to Jesus, then the mystic sees but this fact, and any other feature vanishes from before his eyes. He will oppose the man in as much as he is an enemy to Jesus; he will sorrow about such a horrible and dangerous state of affairs, he will pray for him, and do all he can to wrench him from the grip of the devil and win him over to Jesus. As for his own self, he sees it also in God: and there he values himself highly: but how he does hate his own sinfulness and imperfections, past and present, seen in the white and scorching light of His infinite sanctity! In a word God is for him all in all. God limits his entire horizon and fills the sphere of the universe wholly with His divine splendor, giving to every object its proper subordinate place, its meaning, its color, and superseding or transcending everything infinitely.

Mental prayer is now a state, a gift, a permanent endowment. It is practically uninterrupted; it comes as naturally to the soul as breathing to the body, and it is almost as little noticed by her. Spontaneously and constantly, the soul breaks into acts of Faith, Hope and Charity; whilst the Holy Spirit gives her still a higher impulse by means of the gifts which regulate man's immediate dealings with God—the Fear of the Lord, Understanding and Wisdom. It is the gift of the Fear of the Lord which comes prominently into play in the Passive Purifications of which we shall speak presently; whilst the gift of Understanding presides over the Passive illuminations, and the gift of Wisdom over the passive states of ecstatic Union.

Passive Purifications.—Up to now the fervent Christian has taken himself in hand, strenuously working at his own correction from sins and imperfections; now, it is God Himself who takes him in hand and will do for him what he himself never could achieve: silence his faculties one by one, strip away his natural activities, divest him of the subtle and elusive forms of self-love, reach down to the very center of his being, to the division of the soul and the spirit, to the very marrow (so to say) of his faculties, in order to eradicate the most secret roots of former sin. This done, God plunges the mystic into the abyss of his own native nothingness and impotence, rolls him over and over in it, makes him go through periods of doubts, scruples, darkness, aridity, temptations of the flesh, of blasphemy, of despair. Sometimes the persecutions of men or excruciating infirmities of the body or both at the same time are added over and above measure. This is really terrible. This soul who loves God so vehemently sees herself on the very brink of hell. She is in a black hole; she is stifled and cannot so much as cry out for help. It seems that heaven is deaf to her prayers, and that God has abandoned her. The darkness that settles round her is so thick that she cannot see her Crucified Saviour, or any of His mysteries, or any work of His goodness in the world of nature. She comes to persuade herself that she is no longer in the House of the Prayer of Quiet. She blames herself for having, as she thinks, deserved to be expelled from it: and yet, though she cannot perceive this, she is praying as she never did before, and her prayer is vastly more meritorious than when she was enjoying all the beauties of the place, and the consolations of sensible devotion. She holds on to God by the apex of her will, and Our Lord is invisibly, most tenderly, most firmly, supporting her.

The Blessed Joan of Arc in her donjon, St. Francis of Sales in his youth at Bologna, St. Alphonsus de' Liguori in his old age, Cardinal Vaughan towards the end of his life, are examples of these passive purifications of a perfect soul. There are also great historical examples in the Old Testament, such as those of Tobias the Elder, David when he composed his sublime penitential Psalms, and holy Job, as we see by his soul-stirring lamentations on the miseries of man, and on his own terrible afflictions.

To their amazement, persons who have the privilege closely to observe her will discover that a generous soul thus in treatment at the hands of the loving God is at bottom perfectly indifferent to either consolations or pain. She has but one wish: to do God's holy will. She may in the greatness of her sufferings utter a cry of pain, but never the least complaint, never so much as a secret wish to see her severe trial come to an end. O how thoroughly has Our Lord killed self-love in His servant! To Him the glory!

On the other hand, when the darkness has passed, and the servant of God finds himself in the midst of consolation; when the Holy Spirit makes him yearn with unutterable tenderness *to die and be with Christ*, even then—if you press the question whether he would not consent to abide here below—you find that even in this regard of going to heaven, he has no will of his own; he is content to stay where he is as long as it may be the pleasure of his Lord, his only love. He has in very deed learnt the lesson of self-abnegation perfectly: there is in him not a shadow of secret self-seeking in the things of God.

This stage of the spiritual life is marked by passive illumination of the soul through the vision of God in the Dark Cloud. Until now the Christian has been working with might and main at his own enlightenment, by reading the word of God, by hearing it preached, and by making his own reflections upon it, thus building up for himself the edifice of his knowledge of the supernatural as well as of the natural truths. This is a very gratifying exercise of his natural faculties upon the subject-matter of divine revelation. But at this stage it happens that God reduces the natural faculties of the contemplative to silence and blindness. God introduces the naked soul into a region without language, without image, without a glimmer of created light. He seems to take away also all the soul's previous knowledge, reducing her to a marvellous ignorance: the whole world of creatures, past or present, and all her experiences of them, past or present, seem to fall away from her as a worn garment. God is emptying the vessel of the soul, and wiping it perfectly dry, and mysteriously pouring Himself into it by a new kind of presence, to be thus the sole object of her contemplation, in His own divine essence, in absolute simplicity.

But the light of God in Himself is too intense to be received by the bat-like eyes of a soul still a wayfarer: it dazzles her by its very radiance: all she perceives is a dark, luminous cloud. But she knows it to be the very object of her love: in contemplating it rapturously she receives greater illuminations than she ever did from the volume of Nature, from the pages of Holy Writ, from the paintings on the walls of the House of Prayer; only she cannot put her new knowledge into words, nor can she long sustain gazing upon this luminous dark cloud. But, oh! during these brief ecstatic moments, how profound is the impression that she receives!

When the trance is over, the faithful lover of God has perforce to fall back upon his former, less sublime way of dealing with the divine mysteries. He must resort again to discursive prayer, meditation and holy reading. Such a recoil, though a relief to weak human nature, is extremely painful to the soul. It costs her an effort to adjust herself again to this comparatively lower plane of life. She cannot help behaving as does the little infant whom its mother takes away from the breast, and who, by tears and cries, protests vehemently that there, in that lovely maternal bosom, is all he desires.

I take it that nothing can give a better approximate idea of the nature of the sufferings of the holy souls in Purgatory, and of their absolute surrender and loving patience under the heavy hand of God, as also of their contemplation and gradual enlightenment, than the passive purification and passive illumination of the Christian at this stage of the spiritual life.

Further, the way of the Perfect is marked by a species of passive union with God to which nothing else she had hitherto experienced can be likened. Up to this point the Christian has worked at procuring his own union with God. He has effected it by the worthy reception of the Sacraments and by producing, with the help of grace, fervid acts of Faith, Hope and Charity. All this was good in so far as it went, only it did not reach the point of effectiveness willed for him by the loving God. So it is left to God Himself to take this soul into His own hands, so to say, and perform the act of uniting her still more closely to His own Divine Goodness. It will be God's own doing. All that is required of the soul is that she should lie passive and unresisting; gently, lovingly, acquiescing in all that God does with her and in her; co-operating as best she may in this—God's—action.

There is then effected such a union of the soul with God, such an absorption of her in Him, that, for the time being, she seems irretrievably lost to the world of sense and the company of created things. It is as though she had temporarily lost her identity, and become one with God. Represent to yourself a shepherd's cabin, abandoned, wide open, on a river bank, and overtaken by a mighty flood. As the cabin does not adhere to the ground because it is on wheels, and offers no resistance, it is soon lifted from its place and carried away by the rushing waters. It becomes, so to say, the prey of the mighty flood, wholly passive in its embrace, absolutely at its mercy, one with it. So it is with the soul of the Perfect, in the overwhelming embrace of the Divine Essence, at certain ecstatic moments of passive union. But whilst the adventure of the shepherd's cabin will soon end in total wreckage and annihilation, the Christian soul comes out of this divine adventure amazingly strengthened in all her faculties. It is as though from being previously compounded of base metals, it found itself suddenly turned into gold.

When the Pseudo-Areopagite tells us that his master the holy man Hierotheus, experienced in himself divine phenomena—*divina patiebatur*—he means that these spells of passive purification, passive illumination and passive union were manifestly taking place in him.

CHAPTER XXV

MARVELLOUS FRUITFULNESS OF THE PERFECT SOUL

IN the depth of her quietude, the soul of the dweller in the House of Prayer is intensely active and extraordinary fruitful. In this she shows herself the true child of the Heavenly Father.

What is there so supremely and transcendently quiet as the Divine Essence, and what is there whose operation is (to speak in a human way) so protracted, so intense in itself, so wonderful in its results? Within Himself, the intensity of the life of God produces the Eternal Generation of the Divine Word and the Eternal Procession of the Holy Spirit. Outside of Himself God sends forth His Divine Word and His Holy Spirit, and the universe of things visible and invisible is created out of nothing, held in continued existence, and governed with infinite wisdom; angelic natures are proved, sifted, and assigned each to his proper place and treatment according to his desert; man is created, and at first established in a state of supernatural innocence and happiness foreshadowing the state of glory promised him as the reward of his remaining faithful. When the sin of Adam and Eve would have encompassed the ruin of the whole race, God promises, and in due time sends, His Divine Son to become man and achieve the salvation of the world. Then follow in wonderful sequence the mysteries of the Incarnation, the Redemption, the Church of Christ, the making of the Saints, the gathering of the elect in heaven, until the day of General Resurrection and the Last Judgment. In very deed God is intensely active and most wonderfully fruitful in the midst of His supremely transcending quietude.

As regards the true contemplative, a first harvest of fruits is made up of prayers, attendance at Mass, Holy Communion and all his other acts of religion, to which must be added the merits of all the simple, common, human acts of his life—even the most lowly in character, such as manual labor, recreation, taking of meals, retiring to rest. Thanks to the wonderful purity of intention and the supernatural fervor of love with which he performs all these actions, they are every one of them good works of prime quality. Like ripe, well-flavored, perfectly wholesome fruit, they are free from the canker of secret self-seeking, which often spoils the value of the good works of tepid souls—free, also, from the exterior blemishes usually found upon fruits of inferior grade.

On this score alone the Christian, who is in the Unitive Way, gives to God great glory, at the same time as he wins for himself an unimaginable store of merits for heaven. Yet this is but the beginning of his gains.

Over and above this fruit harvest, there comes another made up of acts of perfect charity, either springing up straight from the positive acts of religion, and especially from the reception of the Sacraments, or having no apparent connection with these. An act of perfect charity is one which is performed with all the intensity of love of which the soul is capable, purely and simply for the sake of God, without any regard to self. Such an act is but rarely and with difficulty performed by Beginners or Pilgrims, because of its intrinsic difficulty; that is to say, in plain language, because of the obstacles they find to its accomplishment in their unmortified or imperfectly mortified selves.

Any single act of perfect charity has for its first effect the cleansing of the soul from all former sins and the cancelling of all her debts to the Divine Justice. It makes her as pure as the freshly baptized babe and as fit as he for the immediate possession of God in the Beatific Vision, should death intervene at that moment. Moreover, it has the virtue of enlarging the capacity of the loving soul so that she receives a larger infusion of the Holy Spirit. Finally, it increases in the soul the inclination and ability for the further performance of similar acts of perfect charity. Thus, whilst the Beginner and Pilgrim plod slowly and painfully along the path of virtue, the Perfect climbs with giant strides the lofty heights of sanctity; and far from finding weariness and exhaustion in this exercise, the higher he rises the more fit and eager he finds himself to mount still higher. St. Thomas, treating of Charity, assures us that no other virtue possesses so great an inclination to perform its proper acts, or finds in them so much relish. (II IIæ *quæst.* 23.2.)

In multiplying his precious acts of perfect charity the lover of God is not bent upon piling up for himself treasures of merits in heaven: were he so, it might somewhat lower the standard of his charity; he is bent purely and wholly upon loving his Lord, and that is the very secret of the perfection of his act. All the same, he does obtain this secondary result of producing spiritual wealth beyond all reckoning; and when he adverts to the fact, he is filled with humble joy and gratitude. But so natural to him has become the divine atmosphere of sanctity, in which he moves and has his being, that he achieves many of these acts of perfect charity quite unconsciously, without taking any more notice of them than of his breathing.

We must notice that the commandment of perfect charity is given to all men, whereas it is really fulfilled only by the dwellers of the House of Quiet. Is not this a fresh proof and a very strong one, that all men are called to the fullness of mystical life and to Divine Contemplation at its highest, though but few attain it?

To every one, to me, to you, dear reader, is this absolute and peremptory command given: *Thou shalt love the Lord thy God, with thy whole heart, and with thy whole soul, and with thy whole mind, and with thy whole strength.* (Mark 12:30.) Now it is evident that the Christian who is in the third stage of the spiritual life—that is to say, the Unitive Way—is the only man who carries out this command to the letter and in its fullness. Devout Christians of an inferior degree make attempts at compliance which are only partly successful. They honestly try to accomplish the law of love in its entirety; they fall short of it because of their defects, more or less numerous and taking time to remove. Their will is good and is turned in the right direction, and though it does not at present reach far enough, God is satisfied with them for the time being, in consideration of the fact that at some future period, known to Him, they will reach to the perfection of the law of charity—if not during their life, certainly immediately after death.

As for the acts of perfect love of God in the service of one's neighbor, there again the Christian who is in the Unitive Way surpasses all his brethren. His burning prayer of intercession vivifies the whole Church of God. In addition to this it makes him the father of innumerable souls, who will owe to him their triumph over temptation at some critical moment of their life, or perhaps their vocation to the holy priesthood or to the religious life, or their final perseverance and salvation. At his entrance into Paradise he will be shown all this spiritual posterity. Then he will exclaim in glad surprise: "Whence come to me all these children whom I did not even know? The Lord has done great things to me: holy is His name!"

Besides all this, when, being moved thereto by the Holy Spirit, our perfect Contemplative and lover of God turns to works of mercy, spiritual or corporal, he brings into them the spirit and the power of his Divine Master, our Lord. How can he fail to bear much fruit there also? Thus are explained the wonderful achievements of a St. Benedict, a St. Dominic, a St. Francis of Assisi, a St. Ignatius Loyola, a St. Teresa, a St. Vincent of Paul, and all the other founders of religious Orders. Thus, also, is accounted for the wonderful harvest of souls secured by apostolic men, in the pulpit, in the confessional, by their books, by their correspondence, by their private conversation. How these men of God do indeed edify, enlighten, comfort and save souls!

Taking all this into consideration, it is no wonder that spiritual writers should assure us that one such Christian alone does more good in the world—and, in consequence, is dearer to God—than hundreds of others less fervent; just as one grown-up man will do, single-handed, more profitable work than hundreds of little children put together.

EPILOGUE

We have now reached the end of our task.

In this volume I set out to disentangle the true notion of Divine Contemplation, and it seems to me I have, by the grace of God, somehow accomplished it. It is now for you, dear reader, to turn it to your own advantage.

It will be noticed that in this volume the word "Contemplation" has been used in three different acceptations. First, in its widest meaning—in contradistinction to Saintly Action—Contemplation includes any species of direct intercourse of the fervent Christian with the beloved God. Then, it is taken in the more limited sense of mental prayer of whatsoever kind. Finally, it is used in its strictest meaning, namely, that of a loving but speechless gazing upon the person of our Blessed Lord, or upon the Divine Essence of the Most Holy Trinity. In each case the context will have sufficiently shown the peculiar shade of meaning we then attached to the word.

It is through no choice of his own that the writer thus makes use of one and the same word to express different meanings; but it should be noted, for his justification, that in no other field of intellectual speculation so much as in this, is man made to feel the galling inadequateness of language as an instrument for the expression of truth.

A prospective pilot of a flying machine has first of all to take his machine to pieces and put it together again. It appears that when he has succeeded in this, more than half the technical part of his task of learning how to fly is accomplished: the rest is only a matter of daring and experiment. He may trust himself to fly who has the will and a good machine, and knows its working; who, moreover, is wide awake to all contingencies that he is liable to encounter when once he has climbed into the sky.

It is very much the same with the Christian who is desirous to take his flight into the lofty realm of Divine Contemplation. Let him but have the will and a thorough knowledge of the workings of Divine Grace in his soul, and let him act with all his faculties on the alert, and he will succeed.

No set of rules will ever supersede actual practice and personal experience. This is the reason why I have directed all my energies to spreading out before my reader's eyes the intricacies of the genuine notion of Divine Contemplation. When he has mastered this exposition, he can fly.

A priori rules have a tendency to make a man too self-conscious, and thereby take away his freedom of action. A reminiscence of my early childhood may serve to illustrate the point. When I was seven or eight years of age in "la douce France," my native country, it was the custom for our teachers at the end of the year to make us write a letter of good wishes, "un compliment de bonne année," to our dear parents. This proved a laborious task, and more than once our page was adorned with ink-stains and smudges—not the page only but our fingers, and even our face. This letter was to be read with great solemnity on the morning of New Year's Day, before the whole family assembled, previous to our receiving the New Year's presents.

Looking back upon it now I must say it strikes me that it was a very absurd performance, stiff and unnatural for us little ones. We hardly understood the high-flown language of what we had written; certainly we did not mean it. But the bright moment for parents and children came, when, tossing away the silly paper, we threw ourselves into the arms lovingly outstretched to us, and kissed, and were kissed, to our heart's content. *Ah! that was the real thing!* Then came the toys and boxes of sweets, and on our part a fresh outburst of embraces and laughter and babbling talk. This second part of the performance was undoubtedly the greatest success.

The true contemplative is like those little children: he brings to his intercourse with God a filial spirit of freedom and tenderness, not one of compulsion and formalism. He loves, and knows himself to be loved; he is incessantly playing the divine game of love. Do the same, dear reader: and may God speed you, till we meet again, if you will, in my next book on "The Loving Contemplation of Our Lord Jesus Christ!"

www.ingramcontent.com/pod-product-compliance
Ingram Content Group UK Ltd.
Pitfield, Milton Keynes, MK11 3LW, UK
UKHW051323090425
5374UKWH00057B/577

9 781957 066226